THE LAND THAT BECAME ISRAEL
STUDIES IN HISTORICAL GEOGRAPHY

Translated from the Hebrew by
Michael Gordon

THE LAND THAT BECAME ISRAEL
STUDIES IN HISTORICAL GEOGRAPHY

Edited by

RUTH KARK

YALE UNIVERSITY PRESS, NEW HAVEN AND LONDON
THE MAGNES PRESS, THE HEBREW UNIVERSITY, JERUSALEM

This Publication was made possible by a generous grant from
the James Amzalak Fund for Research in Historical Geography

Published in the United States and
the United Kingdom 1990
by Yale University Press

ISBN 0-300-04718-5

Library of Congress no: 89-51752

Printed in Israel
by 'Graph-Chen' Press Ltd., Jerusalem

CONTENTS

PREFACE

Over a period of one hundred and fifty years, from 1800 onwards, Eretz-Israel (the Land of Israel, Palestine) was transformed from a neglected backwater of the Ottoman Empire to a focal point of world attention.

During this period, the Holy Land was rediscovered by the European powers and intense interest was rekindled in the Judeo-Christian world, after centuries of remoteness. The area underwent sweeping changes in population, rural and urban settlement, economy and culture. This century and a half, under the rule of first the Ottoman Empire and subsequently the British Mandatory Government, marked one of the most eventful eras in the history of the land. It is this process of change that has attracted, in ever-increasing numbers, the attention of Israeli geographers and historians, who have attempted to describe and interpret the spatial phenomena within the framework of the ongoing and altering forces of the times.

To acquire some understanding of the processes taking place in the land that became the State of Israel, historical geographers in Israel have necessarily researched the background and the determinants of change prevailing in earlier times. Without a consideration of the historical framework, both locally and abroad, a comprehension of the present is unlikely. Indeed, the history of an area is embedded in its geography. While the late eighteenth and early nineteenth century became a natural starting point for investigation of recent times, earlier historical periods provide an arena for further study. As elsewhere, historical geography in Israel is concerned with the interaction over the course of time between social, cultural, economic and political factors and the environment.

This volume provides a forum for historical-geographic research undertaken in Israel during the 1980's. It is being published in advance of the International Conference of Historical Geographers, scheduled for July 1989 in Jerusalem. The collection reflects the considerable activity and rapid development of local researchers in this domain, which has evolved from its infancy to early adulthood in a time span parallel to human ontogenetic development.

The roots of Israeli historical geography can be traced to the 1950's and 1960's, when geography was coming into its own as an academic discipline in Israel. During this period, emphasis was placed on the regional paradigm. Scholars such as David Amiran, Yehuda Karmon and Dov Nir engaged in regional case studies of a descriptive nature, concentrating on the twentieth century. Presentation of the general historical background of the areas studied relied largely on secondary and tertiary sources.

In the 1970's, stimulated by the enthusiastic endeavors of Yehoshua Ben-Arieh, the field of historical geography greatly developed in Israel. It focused on Eretz-Israel from 1800 onward. A dynamic group of young geographers promoted an exchange of ideas with historians, and integrated the use of field work with historical, archaeological and other primary sources from the period under study. These sources were located in libraries and in government, public or private archives in Israel, Great Britain, France, Germany, Switzerland, Australia and the United States. Most researchers adopted an inductive approach, attempting to draw generalizations and comparisons only after an in-depth examination of particular phenomena and processes. As in North America, the philosophical underpinnings of the discipline tended to lag behind the empirical advancements made in the field. Herein lies a focus for future thought and investigation. Many of the major themes occupying historical geographers in Israel are comparable to those elsewhere, including that of significant transformation induced by European immigration to frontier areas throughout the world.

Four central fields dealt with by Israeli historical geographers in the past two decades are:

1) the local scene: changing demographic and spatial features of the population; patterns of land ownership in the Middle East and Eretz-Israel and their implications for settlement; the Arab village; Arab entrepreneurship in land investment, building and commerce; penetration of modern technology into Palestine; material culture of Arab and Bedouin inhabitants;

2) cities: the extent to which they fit into the patterns and generalizations prevalent in the academic literature on the traditional and developing Middle Eastern city; their ethnic heterogeneity; urbanization; monographs on selected sites, such as Jerusalem, Hebron, Jaffa, Acre, Tel Aviv and Haifa, and studies of urban neighborhoods and quarters, including by-laws and regulations (numerous English-language publications have made these urban studies more accessible to a wider readership);

3) Western-Christian civilizations and the Holy Land: rediscovery of Eretz Israel; perceptions of the Holy Land; pilgrims and travelers; activity on the part of the Western powers and their consulates; involvement by the Catholic, Protestant, Greek Orthodox and other churches; missionary activities by Europeans and Americans; settlement plans and attempts by German, British and American Christians; the impact of all the above on land acquisition and construction, architecture, society and culture;

4) pioneering Jewish settlement from 1882 onward: plans and attempts to set up new rural communities; growth and nature of new settlement types: moshava, kibbutz, moshav; ideology, perceptions and nature of the settlement institutions; social and cultural characteristics of the settlers, and their outlook; entrepreneurial groups; the role of private and public capital in the process; development of agricultural frameworks; comparisons with parallel settlements and processes elsewhere in the world.

Also notable were studies on the historical geography of ancient times and the Middle Ages, as well as on the history of cartography.

The twenty articles presented herewith provide a selection of current studies on Eretz-Israel, composed by Israeli historical geographers at universities throughout the country. It was my intent to provide a platform not only for senior investigators, but for young researchers as well, who are in the final stages of the Masters or Doctoral dissertations. Preference was given to a broad, rather than limited, range of topics and time span. The papers reflect original research. A unifying thread between the essays is their concern with a defined territory and the emphasis on the processes of transformation, innovation and modernization, and their determinants.

The division of the volume into four parts follows both chronological and topical order. The first section provides a general background with an overview of the demarcation of Palestine over the millenia, and its changing boundaries as reflections of historical events. It traces the scope of recent studies of Eretz-Israel in ancient periods undertaken by geographers, historians and archaeologists, and emphasizes European and American perceptions and imagery of the Holy Land in past centuries, which influenced the events that were to follow.

The essays in the second part, on the nineteenth century, attempt to offer insights into the determinants and agents of the modernization. These served as a turning point in the settlement process. Here the role of transportation, agricultural innovation, new settlement patterns and the influence of local entrepreneurship are addressed. Cultural phenomena, such as Christian missionary activity, German Templer colonization, establishment of a Bahai world center, and pre-Zionist Jewish settlement initiated or accompanied these developments.

Sections three and four present selected elements of the transformation in the twentieth century. These resulted in the establishment of unique basic settlement types which were to form the rural backbone of Israel. The influence of modernization on changing patterns of traditional Arab rural settlements, and on the trend away from nomadism to permanent agricultural settlement among the Negev Bedouin tribes are stressed. The final articles, incorporating a comparative approach, consider institutional and governmental activities in the settlement process, including urban social planning. The collection concludes with a view of the effects of land partition and population transfers on the settlement map of the State of Israel.

Terms of Hebrew origin which are included in Webster's International Dictionary, e.g. kibbutz, moshava, moshav ovdim, moshav shitufi, are not printed in italics. The spelling of local place names is largely according to List of Settlements, Antiquity Sites and Road Distances, published by the Survey of Israel, Tel Aviv. The conversion factor with regard to measurement of area is: 1 dunam = 1,000 square meters or 0.247 acre. The Plates, printed on chrome paper, are located at the end of the book.

This publication was made possible thanks to the generous support of Mr. James Amzalak, grandson of the British vice-consul in Jaffa and founder of the James Amzalak Fund for research in historical geography. Finally, I would like to express thanks to Yehoshua Ben-Arieh for his assistance and comments, Michael Gordon, who faithfully translated the papers from Hebrew, Robert Amoils, who edited the text, the cartographers Tamar Sopher and Michal Kidron, and the managers of the Magnes Press.

Ruth Kark
Jerusalem, June 1989

PART I:

HISTORICAL GEOGRAPHY OF
ERETZ-ISRAEL IN PAST TIMES

THE NAMES AND BOUNDARIES OF ERETZ-ISRAEL (PALESTINE) AS REFLECTIONS OF STAGES IN ITS HISTORY

GIDEON BIGER

INTRODUCTION

Classical historical geography focuses on research of the boundaries of the various states, along with the historical development of these boundaries over time. Edward Freeman, in his book written in 1881 and entitled *The Historical Geography of Europe*, defines the nature of historical-geographical research as follows: "The work which we have now before us is to trace out the extent of territory which the different states and nations have held at different times in the world's history, to mark the different boundaries which the same country has had and the different meanings in which the same name has been used." The author further claims that "it is of great importance carefully to make these distinctions, because great mistakes as to the facts of history are often caused through men thinking and speaking as if the names of different countries have always meant exactly the same extent of territory."[1] Although this approach — which regards research on boundaries as the essence of historical geography — is not accepted at present, the claim that it is necessary to define the extent of territory over history is as valid today as ever. It is impossible to discuss the development of any geographical area having political and territorial significance without knowing and understanding its physical extent.

Of no less significance for such research are the names attached to any particular expanse. The naming of a place is the first step in defining it politically and historically. Many localities have been given a wide variety of names, by different nations. The inhabitants of a certain region may assign various names to the land over time, while the residents of neighboring areas affix others to it. The political upheavals that an area undergoes over the generations, and the various nationalistic attitudes toward it, are reflected in the variety of its appellation over the course of history.

---

1   E. Freeman, *The Historical Geography of Europe*, I, London 1881, pp. 1–3.

1

The present study deals with the geographical expanse of Eretz-Israel, and the array of names which have been given to this land. Because Eretz-Israel has undergone countless changes and upheavals for 5,000 years — the period in which historiographers have been familiar with this area — it serves as an ideal test case for the hypothesis presented above. The uniqueness of Eretz-Israel derives from the fact that large portions of humanity are linked to it historically and culturally. This land is not merely a small territorial segment of the globe, but a cultural entity exerting a profound cultural influence over various parts of the world. It holds special significance for Judaism, Christianity and Islam, and has played a singular role in the development of human thought and belief. In diverse historical periods people throughout the world have had free ties with this stretch of land, and have given it various names reflecting whatever attitude they have held toward it. These ties often took the form of active control over the area, control which altered its territorial expanse. By tracing the geopolitical extent of Eretz-Israel throughout the ages, one can demonstrate the connection between its name and borders on the one hand, and the religious-cultural perception of its rulers on the other hand. This phenomenon has become more pronounced with time, and today, as in the past, there are different attitudes toward the name and spatial dimensions of Eretz-Israel.

THE ESSENCE OF ERETZ-ISRAEL

"Eretz-Israel" is more a geohistorical concept rooted in historical consciousness than a defined and measured stretch of land lying within clear geographical boundaries or stable political borders. With the exception of the Mediterranean Sea, there are no geographic limits based on prominent topographical features which separate Eretz-Israel from the larger region in which it is situated, and for this reason it has always served as a passageway. Topographical features have played only a minor role in determining its political and historical boundaries.

In most periods the borders hinged upon the outcome of a struggle between world powers for control over the entire region; in some cases political and cultural frontiers divided the country internally, while on other occasions the land in its entirety became a part of a much larger political unit. Only for brief periods was the area under the uniform control of its residents. However, despite the perpetual instability and vicissitudes with regard to its ethnic, cultural and political status, "Eretz-Israel" did exist as a concrete geohistorical unit with unique qualities of its own. This singularity derived mainly from the historical consciousness of the Jewish people, as well as the influence of this consciousness over other nations and faiths.

Because of the political and cultural changes that Eretz-Israel underwent, its boundaries and its status in the area constantly fluctuated, and its name was often altered. The first reference to "Eretz-Israel" per se appears during the reign of Saul (I Samuel 13:19), and the name gained currency at the time of the first *aliyot* (waves of Jewish immigration) in the latter part of the nineteenth century, and during the British Mandate period, when the country was officially titled "Palestine," with the addition of the Hebrew acronym for Eretz-Israel.

Before this, Eretz-Israel had been called many different names and sobriquets that reflected the way the Jewish people and other nations regarded the status and qualities of the land — both the reality and the ideal: Judea, the Land of the Hebrews, Zion, the Holy Land, the Sacred Land, Palestine, the Promised Land, and the Land of the Deer.

Thus a survey of the boundaries of Eretz-Israel has two divergent starting points: the definition of the physiographic limits on the one hand, and the political borders in different periods on the other hand. In dealing with the latter, one should distinguish between periods in which Eretz-Israel was divided internally, thereby losing its political uniformity, and times when the land formed a single sovereign unit or a district belonging to a larger political entity. In terms of Jewish history, one must draw a distinction between the ideal borders as dictated by a religious-biblical perception, and the borders of sovereign Israel. Similarly, one must differentiate between the boundaries of Jewish settlement on the one hand, and the presence of ethnic, cultural and political enclaves on the other hand. The political borders of Eretz-Israel were dictated by various geostrategic and political considerations, along with the international status of the land and the regime in power during one period or another.

PHYSIOGRAPHIC DEMARCATION

"Physical demarcation" is the marking off of boundaries through a clear and unequivocal delineation of a certain territory, which sets it off from the neighboring territories and creates a separate geographic unit. The commonly used phrase "natural boundaries" implies something similar, but because its connotations go beyond the sphere of physical demarcation, the latter term is preferable. Eretz-Israel comprises a part of an expansive geographic region that stretches from the Mediterranean Sea to the Red Sea and the Persian Gulf. In its entirety, this region is called the Fertile Crescent. It consists mainly of plains and lowlands, and is bounded in the north and the east by the Taurus (in Turkey) and Zagros (in Iran) mountain chains. On the south it is open toward the Arabian Desert, part of which, the Syrian Desert, penetrates deep into its center. The Fertile Crescent averages around 600 km. in length and 90 km. in width (from the sea to the desert). Its southwestern section is separated from the rest of the area by the deep Syrian-African rift that in Eretz-Israel forms the Jordan Rift Valley, the Arava plain and the Gulf of Elat. This rift on one side, and the Mediterranean Sea on the other, have constituted the country's boundaries in the twentieth century, and the stretch of land between them comprises Eretz-Israel in the limited sense of the term.

Eretz-Israel can be defined geographically as a land on the outskirts of Syria, integrally related to the latter.[2] The Syrian Desert separates Eretz-Israel from the biblical Aram-Naharaim, or Mesopotamia (modern Iraq), while the Sinai Desert separates it from Egypt. This location has had a decisive influence on the history of this land as a passageway and as a frontier district. Neither the Syrian Desert nor the Sinai Desert constituted an impassable natural barrier, and the eastern and southern borders changed over the generations in accordance with the vicissitudes of the ongoing struggle between settlement and desolation, and between various world powers. For extensive periods the desert was the boundary of Eretz-Israel, but the exact nature of this delimitation was determined by the prevailing political circumstances and the state of settlement in the east and south of the land.

The territory east of the Jordan River for the most part tended to have political and ethnic ties with western Eretz-Israel, despite the topographic obstacle posed by the Jordan Rift, which often served as a political border. When there was a stable, permanent settlement east of the Jordan, the Syrian Desert served as the boundary of Eretz-Israel, while in periods without such settlement, when most of the population consisted of nomadic tribes, the Jordan Rift and the Dead Sea formed the eastern limit. As a political border, this line was tenuous, since the Jordan Rift does not constitute a substantial natural barrier, and to the east of it, in Edom, Moab, Gilead and the Bashan, there are fertile settlement areas.

Similarly in the south, the Sinai Desert is a buffer zone serving as a passageway between Egypt and Eretz-Israel. Although this desert is desolate, with only a few oases and sparse settlement sites located around quarries, topographic difficulties preventing passage from Egypt to Eretz-Israel are nonexistent. Because most of the oases and settlement sites are located on the western margins of the Sinai Desert, they have been tied to Egypt, while only a few small oases, situated in the northeastern part of Sinai, have been tied to Eretz-Israel. From a geographic perspective, the Sinai Desert has not usually been considered a part of Eretz-Israel, even when Israelite settlements have existed there. The boundary between Eretz-Israel and the Sinai Desert has been shifted several times in accordance

2   Y. Karmon, *Eretz-Israel*, Tel Aviv 1978, pp. 11–12 (Hebrew).

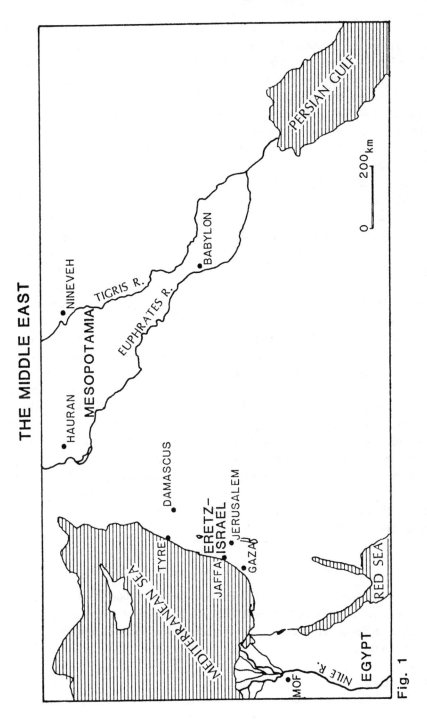

Fig. 1

with the settlement and political reality, and there were times when they were not contiguous at any point. The most blatant geographic demarcation between Eretz-Israel and this desert is Wadi el Arish, which reaches the Mediterranean Sea 45 km. southwest of Rafah. Most of the ancient sources refer to this wadi as *Nahal Musaru*, the Assyrian term for "the Egyptian water course." The Hebrew equivalent — *Nahal Mitzrayim* — appears in the Bible, but usually in a context that does not pinpoint its locality. However, in one instance the easternmost tributary of the Nile — "Shihor" (I Chronicles 13:5) — is referred to as "Nahal Mitzrayim."

The northern border from the geographic standpoint is the Lebanese mountain range, and the lofty Mount Hermon. The Phoenician coast and Lebanon Rift constitute a direct extension of the northern part of Eretz-Israel. Therefore Syria and Eretz-Israel have been regarded by foreigners as a single geographic unit ever since the Sumerian Empire. Nevertheless, there are a number of salient geographic features and locations within Eretz-Israel — the Hauran, the Bashan, the Damascus Rift, the Litani River and the sources of the Jordan — all of which have been the object of political and settlement struggles between the various sovereign entities that have controlled the area.

Since all the land's boundaries have changed so frequently, it would be arduous and arbitrary to fix exact borders based on geographic lines. The perception of Eretz-Israel's physical boundaries — or natural boundaries, as they are sometimes called — changes with the viewer's vantage point. Forces outside the region regarded Eretz-Israel as an intermediate land between the sea and the desert, and a single unit with Syria. By contrast, the perspective of the kingdoms that have arisen within Eretz-Israel and Syria has been greatly influenced by the geographic lines of the land, as well as the settlement configuration and prevailing political and military circumstances. While outside observers viewed Eretz-Israel as an important passageway on the edge of the desert, the inhabitants of the land regarded it as the heart and soul of the entire geographic region.

THE NAMES OF THE LAND OVER HISTORY

Two names have been attached to the land for over 2,000 years. The Jewish-Hebrew world has used the term "Eretz-Israel," while others have called it "Palestine," or different derivatives thereof. Nevertheless, various other names preceded these.

In the Ancient World
The Sumerian Empire, which laid the foundations for civilization in the Fertile

Crescent in the third millennium B.C.E., named Eretz-Israel — together with all of the remaining land west of the Euphrates — *Maat Amurru,* "the Land of the Emorites" or "the western land." According to Mari documents from the end of the eighteenth century B.C.E., Amurru is a defined political unit south of a small city, while in the New Egyptian Dynasty the kingdom of Amurru was centered in Lebanon.

Ancient Egyptian sources apply the name *Haryosha* ("the Land of Sand-Dwellers") to the desert and the sandy coast of Eretz-Israel, but during the Middle Dynasty Eretz-Israel and Syria were called *Retenu,* which evidently means "the Land of Rulers." Eretz-Israel itself was dubbed *Upper Retenu,* designating its position relative to Egypt. The Sinuhe Scroll from the New Dynasty period used the appellation *Tshahi,* while the name *Huru* — "the Land of the Hurrians," referring to a people originating in the Mitanni kingdom — stems from this same period.

Another contemporary name that gained wide acceptance was *Canaan.* The name *Canaana* first appears in the fifteenth century B.C.E. El Amarna Letters, where it refers to an Egyptian province. Initially the term Canaan was applied only to the Phoenician coast (Joshua 5:1), but afterwards it came to include the northern Jordan Rift (Numbers 13:29), and the whole of Eretz-Israel and Syria. In the Bible the earliest mention of this appellation is in the stories of the Patriarchs (Genesis 11:31), in reference to western Eretz-Israel. It was in this period that the Land of Canaan became a unified political entity under Egyptian hegemony. It extended up to the Hittite border, and its capital was the city of Gaza. The borders of this political unit, which are delineated in Numbers 34:1–12, evidently comprised the boundaries of "The Patriarch's Land," or "The Promised Land."

According to this source, the boundary of Canaan begins in the southern part of the Dead Sea, and turns southward until Ma'ale Akrabim, whence it curves southwestward up to Kadesh Barnea, El Qusaime (Atzmon) and Wadi El Arish (the Egyptian water course). In the east the border passes from Lebo-hamath — evidently the village of Labweh on the Orontes (Asi) River — in the north of Lebanon, up to the desert northeast of Damascus. From there it winds south to the Sea of Galilee and along the Jordan River to the Dead Sea. In the north the boundary passes from Mount Hor, whose location has yet to be decisively determined, to Lebo-hamath, while to the west the border is the Mediterranean Sea. These borders do not coincide with the area settled by the Tribes of Israel, and apparently demarcate the Egyptian province. Scholars are divided as to the exact position and the furthest north–south extension of these frontiers.[3]

3   N. Tokchinski, *The Boundaries of the Land,* Jerusalem 1970 (Hebrew).

"THE PROMISED LAND"

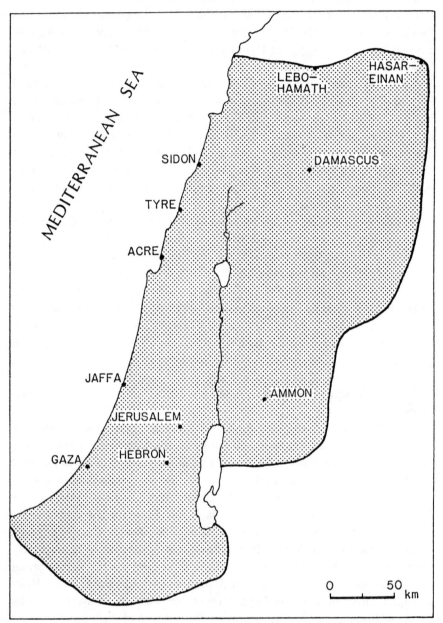

Fig. 2

The name "Eretz-Israel" emerged at the outset of the settlement in the land by the Tribes of Israel, and it defined only the area in which the Israelites settled (Joshua 11:22: "Land of the Children of Israel"). The land was divided among the various nations residing in it, and the southern coastal strip up to the Carmel, which was inhabited by the Philistines, was called *Glilot Pleshet*, or simply *Pleshet*. From this was derived the name "Palaestina," although this later version did not appear until after the Bar Kochva revolt. The name was rendered as "Filistin" in Arabic and Turkish — and this same label was applied to the British Mandate.

Along with these "ideal" boundaries specified in the Bible, also mentioned in the Scriptures are borders coinciding with the areas in which the Tribes of Israel settled, whether initially or at a later stage. Tradition renders these as "the Borders of Those Who Left Egypt," or "the Borders of Moses and Joshua" (Deuteronomy 34:1–4). From the time of the kingdom of David, the actual borders nearly coincided with the "Promised Borders," despite the fact that they encompassed enclaves of other nations (II Samuel 24:5–7; I Kings 5:7).

The expression "from Dan to Beersheba" was coined in this period as a description of the central area settled by the Israelites. This demarcation later became the accepted description of Eretz-Israel (I Samuel 24:2; I Kings 5:5), and it largely influenced the location of the country's northern border during the British Mandate.

At the outset of David's kingdom in 1,000 B.C.E., "Judah and Israel" emerged as a term defining the entire kingdom, and subsequent to its division "Judah" denoted the area ruled by the House of David, while "Israel" signified the kingdom of Israel.

After the Return to Zion in the days of the Persian Empire, the area occupied by the Jews returning from Babylonia was called *Yahad*, and generations later the name "Land of Judah" was accepted as denoting all of Eretz-Israel. In the Bible the name "Eretz-Israel" signifies the kingdom of Israel only (II Kings 5:2).

The combined borders of the kingdom of Israel and the kingdom of Judah changed in accordance with the military and political dictates of the time. The annexation of Aram Damascus up to Lebo-hamath by Jeroboam II marked the height of territorial aggrandizement (II Kings 14:24–28).

Shortly thereafter, in the years 732–734 B.C.E., the Assyrian king, Tiglath-Pileser III, conquered Gilead, the Galilee and the coastal plain, and the kingdom of Israel dwindled to the vicinity of Mount Ephraim. With the final Assyrian conquest of Samaria, the area was transformed into an Assyrian province called *Shomreinu*. Uzziah, king of Judah, later captured the coastal plain and Edom, and the interim period between the fall of Assyria and the rise of Babylonia allowed Josiah, king of Judah (609–634), to expand the borders of his realm to

Gideon Biger

KING DAVID'S KINGDOM

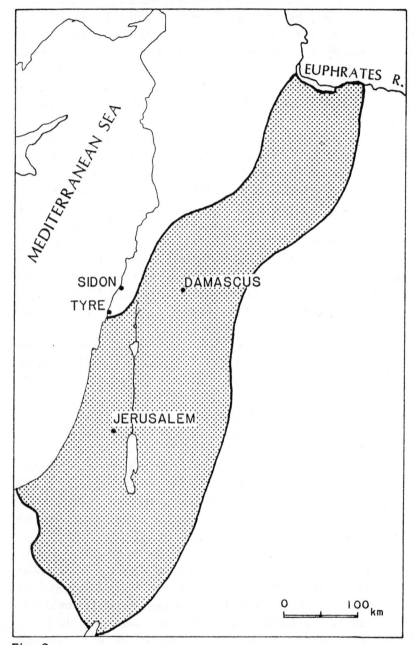

Fig. 3

THE KINGDOMS OF ISRAEL AND JUDAH
EIGHTH CENTURY B.C.E.

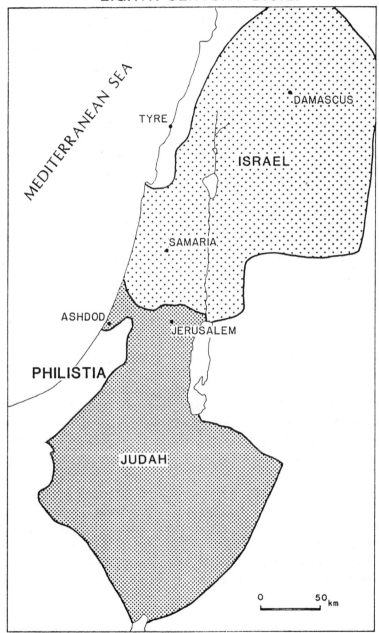

Fig. 4

include "the cities of Manasseh and Ephraim, and Simeon, even unto Naftali...throughout all the land of Israel" (II Chronicles 34:6–7). This occurred after the Assyrian conquest led by Sennacherib had reduced the size of Judah. The ascendancy of Babylonia gave rise to repeated truncations of Eretz-Israel, accompanied by exiles that diminished the Jewish population. The southern part of the Judean Hills up to the vicinity of Bet Tzur was inhabited by Edomites and now called *Edom*, while the Jewish population was concentrated in Benjamin and the Negev, and along the Pleshet border.

Eretz-Israel in the Second Temple Period
The Babylonians, like the Sumerians before them, viewed Eretz-Israel and Syria as one unit, which they called *Ever Nahari*, meaning "the land beyond the river," with reference to the Euphrates. The Persian Empire, which supplanted the Babylonian Empire, adopted the Aramaic version of the name — *Ever Nahara* — and applied it to the province (*strepia*) that encompassed Syria, Phoenicia and Eretz-Israel (Ezra 4:10). *Yahad*, one district (*pahva*) within this province, encompassed the area between Jerusalem and Hebron, the Judean Desert and the coastal plain — a total of around 1,600 sq. km. The division of this territory did not change with the conquest of Alexander the Great and the Hellenistic hegemony soon to follow. The Ptolemaic dynasty, and later the Seleucid dynasty, re-divided the land into districts, one of which was *Iuda*, which was later changed to *Iudea*.

The Hasmonean House steadfastly endeavored to expand the borders of the independent Jewish regime in Eretz-Israel. From the days of Judah Maccabee and his brother Simeon until the death of Alexander Yanai in 76 B.C.E., the Hasmonean kingdom had come to encompass the coastal plain from Mount Carmel to El Arish (*Rinocorura*), excluding Ashqelon, which remained independent. The Galilee and Judean Hills, the land around the Dead Sea, the northern Negev and sections east of the Jordan were also included in the Hasmonean kingdom.[4]

Although various sources refer to this area as "the territory of those who returned from Babylonia," the borders were actually established by the Hasmoneans. These boundaries hold great importance for the Halacha, as they determine *inter alia* the lands to which the *mitzvot hatluyot ba'aretz* ("commandments dependent upon the land") apply. Apparently these borders have come to be accepted over the generations as demarcating the domain of

---

4   M. Avi-Yona, *Carta's Atlas of the Period of the Second Temple*, Jerusalem 1960, p. 44, map no. 66 (Hebrew).

THE HASMONEAN KINGDOM

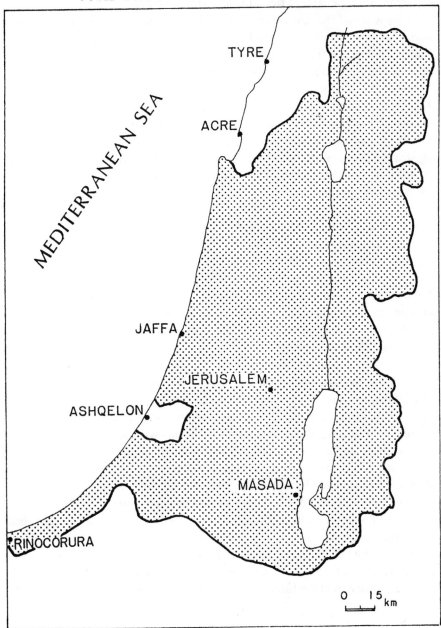

Fig. 5

Eretz-Israel, and up to the beginning of the twentieth century they have come to signify for the Jews and at times for non-Jews the boundaries of Eretz-Israel.

In the wake of the Roman conquest, Eretz-Israel was again reduced to the area of Judah, including eastern Edom from Adoraim to En Gedi. The Jezreel Valley was severed from the Galilee, which remained Jewish. During Herod's reign *Iudea* once more expanded, as Augustus annexed Jaffa, Jericho, and Yavne to Herod's kingdom, as well as Geva Susita and Gader to the east of the Jordan. Later the areas of the Bashan, Golan and Hauran were also annexed, along with Pamias (Banias) and the Hula. Following Herod's death the kingdom was divided among his three sons and his sister Shlomit. The great Jewish revolt against the Romans broke out in these areas, after the activities of Jesus caused the territorial image of Eretz-Israel at the time to be embedded for generations in the minds of the Christian world.

The Roman-Byzantine Period: 70–638 C.E.
After the revolt against the Romans was crushed, Iudea became a province of the Roman Empire. Called *Provincia Iudea*, it encompassed most of the coastal cities and the Decapolis cities in the north of the land and east of the Jordan. Following the death of Agrippa II, most of his kingdom in the north was also annexed to the Roman province. In the year 106 C.E. *Provincia Arabia* was established; it encompassed the Negev, and later Rabat Ammon (Amman), Gesher and Dibon.[5]

In the wake of the Bar Kochva revolt and its suppression, the old name Pleshet (*Palasta* in Roman usage) gained wide currency. The emperor Hadrian endeavored to quash Jewish nationalism and thereby extirpate the roots of the revolt. Jerusalem was rebuilt as a pagan city, and called Aelia Capitolina, while the name *Palaestina* or *Provincia Syria Palaestina* was used for Eretz-Israel, in an attempt to eradicate any trace of Judaism in the land.

The Roman province of Palaestina was a part of Syria. During the later Roman period and the Byzantine period its borders were altered as neighboring tracts of land were added to it. The emperor Diocletian annexed the province of Arabia to Palaestina, but in 385 C.E. this territory was separated and called *Palaestina Salutaris*.

In the year 425 C.E. the remaining territory was divided into two additional provinces: *Palaestina Prima*, which included the coastal towns, the Judean Hills and the Jewish part of the Jordan Rift; and *Palaestina Secunda*, which comprised

5   Z. Baras et al., *Eretz-Israel: From the Destruction of the Second Temple to the Muslim Conquest*, Jerusalem 1982, p. 11 (Hebrew).

ROMAN PALAESTINA

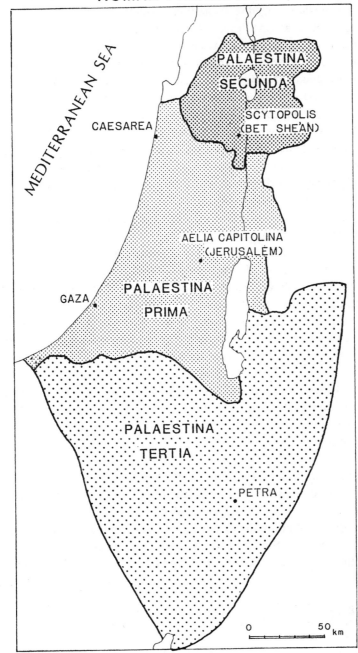

Fig. 6

the Jezreel Valley, Upper and Lower Galilee and the Golan. The name of the third province was changed to Palaestina Tertia.[6]

The capital of Palaestina Prima was Caesaria, and that of Palaestina Secunda was Bet She'an (*Scytopolis*). After the Arab conquest in 638 C.E. the administrative division was maintained, but the names of the geographic units were changed and their capitals relocated. Palaestina Prima was renamed *Jund* (military district) *Filistin*, and was administered from Lod, and later from Ramla, a city that had been built by the Arabs.

Palaestina Secunda was renamed *Jund Urdun* after the Jordan River, and Tiberias was made its capital. Although the border between the districts was occasionally shifted, it generally preserved the Roman-Byzantine framework — dividing Eretz-Israel horizontally, unlike the modern border demarcation, which runs from north to south.

Both of these districts lay between the Mediterranean Sea on the west and the desert on the east. Palaestina Tertia had ceased to exist as an independent unit, and most of it was absorbed into what Arab historians referred to as *Tiha Bani Israil* — the area of the wandering of the Children of Israel — or *Tiha* for short. This area included the Negev and most of the Sinai, and at times was combined administratively with Jund Filistin. Both districts, Filistin and Urdun, were incorporated into the large geographic unit of Syria, or *Ash Shams* in Arabic. This name was widely used, and the territory became a separate geographic entity alongside Egypt, Iraq, Arabia and Yemen. These districts, although not at all similar to the modern countries bearing the same names, were usually perceived as social, cultural and at times even economic-political entities with distinct and contiguous territory. Ash Shams stretched southward from the southern Taurus Mountains, while the districts of Filistin and Urdun consituted its southern border.[7]

Eretz-Israel under Crusader Dominion: 1099–1291

The Crusader conquest in 1099 led to the reunification of Eretz-Israel. "The Latin Kingdom of Jerusalem" — its official title — came into existence as a small territorial unit, and gradually expanded until it engulfed the entire area from north of Beirut to the Sinai Desert, as well as Mount Se'ir south of Elat, and many sections east of the Jordan and south of the Yarmuk.[8] The boundaries of

---

6   *Ibid.*, pp. 352–380.
7   J. Prawer, *The History of Jerusalem — The Early Islamic Period (638–1099)*, Jerusalem 1987, pp. 9–30 (Hebrew).
8   J. Prawer, *A History of the Latin Kingdom of Jerusalem*, I, Jerusalem 1971, pp. 151–220 (Hebrew).

THE LATIN KINGDOM
OF JERUSALEM

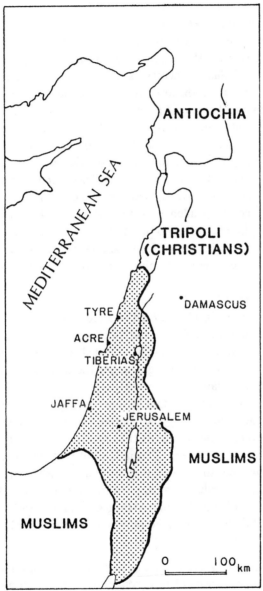

ANTIOCHIA

MEDITERRANEAN SEA

**TRIPOLI
(CHRISTIANS)**

•DAMASCUS

TYRE

ACRE

TIBERIAS

JAFFA

JERUSALEM

MUSLIMS

MUSLIMS

0   100 km

Fig. 7

this kingdom constantly fluctuated up to its destruction in 1291, but the Crusader period instilled in the Gentile world the historical consciousness of Eretz-Israel as a single geographic unit, and heightened the religious associations with the land.

The Mameluke Period: 1291–1517

The renewed conquest of Eretz-Israel by the Muslims did not lead to a resumption of the earlier Muslim administration or the adoption of the names Filistin and Urdun. Saladin's successors, and to a greater extent the Mamelukes following them, who ruled the area from the middle of the thirteenth century, redivided the land, and created a growing number of subdivisions, each one of which was named after its principal city. There was no attempt to devise an overall, unifying name. During most of the Mameluke period the land on both sides of the Jordan was divided into six subdistricts whose centers were Gaza, Lod, Qaqun, Jerusalem, Hebron and Nablus. These subdistricts comprised part of the Ash Shams province, whose center was Damascus. At times Gaza, Lod and Qaqun enjoyed independence. At the end of the Mameluke period Eretz-Israel was divided into two *niyabets* (military districts), Gaza and Safed, with the latter encompassing the districts of Tibnin and Tsur (Tyre) in southern Lebanon. These military districts were under the control of the viceroy in Damascus.[9]

Ottoman Eretz-Israel: 1516–1918

The Ottoman conquest in 1516–17 led to a redivision of Eretz-Israel into the *sanjaks* of Gaza, Jerusalem, Nablus and Safed west of the Jordan — and Ajlun east of it.[10] Later the district of Lajun was formed, also west of the Jordan. As in the past, these districts were brought under the jurisdiction of the *bilarbay* (governor general) of Damascus.

These districts underwent constant changes during the 400 years of Ottoman rule in Eretz-Israel, dictated by the varying relations in the Ottoman state between the central regime and the district governors, and between the former and the other European powers. Through all of the internal vicissitudes, the name "Filistin" was conspicuously absent; it had vanished since the Crusader conquest. The name "Urdun" was applied to the river only. Throughout this entire period the Jewish world employed the name "Eretz-Israel," while "Filistin" was initially used by the Muslims to refer to a subdistrict only and eventually

9   Y. Friedman, "Eretz-Israel and Jerusalem on the Eve of the Ottoman Period," A. Cohen (ed.), *Jerusalem in the Early Ottoman Period*, Jerusalem 1979, pp. 1–38 (Hebrew).

10   M. Gichon, *Carta's Atlas of Eretz-Israel from Bether to Tel-Hai (Military History)*, Jerusalem 1969, p. 75, map no. 131 (Hebrew).

disappeared. On the other hand, the name "Palestine" was preserved by the Christian world, although in the Middle Ages the Christians usually called the land the "Holy Land" or "Judea."

The Renaissance and the renewed interest in the classical world imparted new significance to the Roman name "Palaestina,' which was incorporated and commonly used in most European languages. This European usage was carried to the Orient by Christian Arabs who were subject to a Western Christian influence. The second Arabic newpaper to appear in Eretz-Israel, edited by a member of the Greek Orthodox Church and printed in 1911, was called *Filistin*.

It was only toward the end of the Ottoman period — first in 1856 and again in 1873 — that the southern portion of Eretz-Israel was detached from the spacious districts above it, from the Yarkon-Wadi Auja line in the north to the Dead Sea–Rafah line in the south. Following its severance, this territory was converted into an independent *sanjak* — or *mutessarif* — under the direct control of the capital of the Empire, Istanbul. It was demarcated by administrative boundaries appearing on a map, but not existing on the land itself, and was called "Mutessarif El Kuds," referring to Jerusalem. Now too, the name "Filistin" was not mentioned officially. North of this unit the area was a part of the *iyalet* (province) of Beirut, divided into the *sanjaks* of Nablus, Acre and Beirut (including the subdistricts of Sidon, Tyre and Marj Ayun). The territory east of the Jordan was part of the *iyalet* of Sham Sharit, or Damascus. The area south of the Dead Sea–Rafah line belonged to the Hejaz district which in the nineteenth century extended into the Sinai Peninsula, and east of the Arava. In 1906 an administrative boundary was drawn between Sinai and the remaining part of the Ottoman Empire along the Rafah–Taba line, while in 1908 the territory between this line and the Arava (the Negev Triangle) passed under the control of the governor of Damascus. The Hejaz railroad track laid in the early part of the twentieth century formed a sort of demarcation between the land east of the Jordan and the desert, a boundary that was frequently identified with the eastern border of Eretz-Israel.

The lack of clarity regarding the borders of Eretz-Israel found expression in dozens of assorted publications written on the eve of World War I, each of which cited a different boundary. These publications, however, unanimously included certain territory: Upper and Lower Galilee, the Judean Hills up to the Dead Sea–Rafah line, and the area east of the Jordan from the Hermon to the Arnon River, which debouches into the Dead Sea. These contours were not at all reflected in the modern demarcation of Eretz-Israel following World War I.[11]

11   G. Biger, "Where Was Palestine? Pre-World War I Perception," *Area*, XIII, no. 2 (1981), pp. 153–160.

The British Mandate over Eretz-Israel: 1918–1948
With the entry of the British into the area, Eretz-Israel was separated from the
rest of the Ottoman Empire, and was reestablished as an autonomous
administrative unit. During the British military administration, from 1917 to
1920, the land was called "Occupied Enemy Territory (South)," and its borders
were: in the north, a line from Rosh haNiqra to the Hula; in the east, along the
Jordan; and in the west, the sea. Although it is not certain where the southern
border was, it apparently passed along the Arava to the top of the Gulf of Elat.

It was the Mandatory government that recreated Eretz-Israel as an integral
territorial unit, and that, for the first time in the modern era, demarcated clear
boundaries for it on maps, and in certain sections on the ground as well. The
process of demarcation was part of the reorganization of the Middle East.[12]
Eretz-Israel's northern border was established after long and tiresome
negotiations between the French, who controlled Syria and Lebanon, and the
British, who ruled Eretz- Israel. A variety of factors — historical formulations,
the Zionist movement's plans for future development, the actual state of Jewish
settlement, and physical elements such as watershed lines — combined together
in the delineation of Eretz-Israel's northern border. This boundary, which was
finally determined in the spring of 1923, has remained until today the border
between the State of Israel and Lebanon.[13] In 1922 it was agreed to draw a line
along the Jordan River and the Arava, in order to separate Eretz-Israel from
Trans-Jordan. In 1928 it was decided that the border would pass along the
course of the Jordan.

The southern border had been determined earlier, as it was less problematic.
The British adopted the 1906 line as the boundary between Eretz-Israel and
Egypt, even though this decision was never officially publicized. Along with the
border demarcation, the British simultaneously revived the territory's old name.
Faithful to European Christian tradition, they opted for the name "Palestine,"
while adding two Hebrew letters standing for "Eretz-Israel."

In the course of the Mandate various plans were proposed for a territorial and
political divison of Eretz-Israel between its Jewish and Arab inhabitants. The
United Nations resolution of November 1947 called for a partition into two
independent political states, but the war of 1948 and the armistice agreements
that followed it engendered a new political and geographic delimitation, in the
center of which was a national entity with a new-old name: the State of Israel.

---

12   G. Biger, *Crown Colony or National Homeland*, Jerusalem 1983, pp. 12–41 (Hebrew).
13   G. Biger, "Geographical and Political Issues in the Process of the Creation of the Northern
     Boundary of Eretz-Israel during the Mandatory Period," A. Shmueli et al. (eds.), *The Lands of
     Galilee*, Haifa 1983, pp. 427–442 (Hebrew).

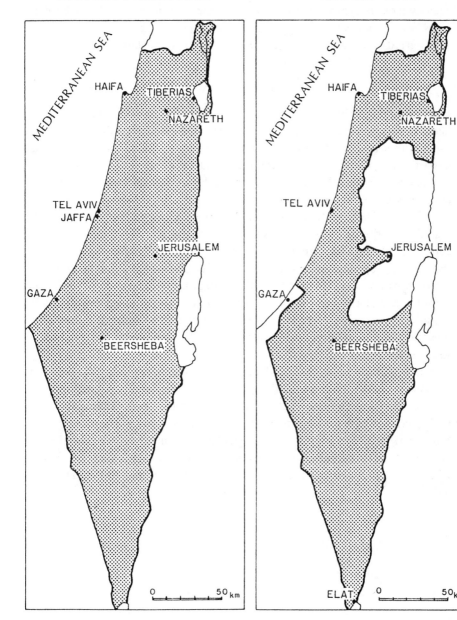

BRITISH PALESTINE   ISRAEL 1949

Fig. 8   Fig. 9

This division held sway until the Six-Day War, and since June 1967 the land has been undergoing a process of continual change in terms of its political borders. In 1979 a peace treaty was signed between Israel and Egypt, in which the two sides agreed to recognize the 1906 line as the international border between them.

CONCLUSION

Historical-geographical research relating to the names and boundaries of Eretz-Israel in various periods focuses both on this land as a geographic unit, and on the fact that it is an integral part of a larger region. These dualistic qualities impart a singular character to the land, and create a sense of geohistorical uniqueness. On the other hand, the external borders of the area have been in a constant state of flux over the generations. Several areas have repeatedly been included in Eretz-Israel in the course of these changes, and these may be regarded as the heart of Eretz-Israel. It appears that of all the geographic definitions of Eretz-Israel that have been formulated throughout its long history, the most appropriate one was "from Dan to Beersheba," i.e. from the sources of the Jordan in the north to the edge of the contiguous settlement in the south, and from the Mediterranean Sea to the Jordan River. In various periods the area considered part of Eretz-Israel was either expanded or diminished, but in the mind of the nations emotionally attached to Eretz-Israel, it has essentially signified the area in this "heart."

A survey of the names and borders of Eretz-Israel over history thus makes it possible to better understand the changes that the land has undergone — changes deriving from the activities of man in this area. Hence the great variations that have occurred in the border demarcations and the names form a framework in which geographic changes have taken place in each and every period. These variations also underscore the need for such a survey — a need which was noted over a hundred years ago, and which remains equally valid today.

HISTORICAL GEOGRAPHY OF ERETZ-ISRAEL: SURVEY OF THE ANCIENT PERIOD

REHAV RUBIN

INTRODUCTION

Eretz-Israel, with its long, variegated and eventful history, poses a challenge to studies in the fields of history, archaeology and historical geography. Although the present volume deals with the modern period and its achievements, research on the historical geography of the ancient period began long ago, and is sufficiently distinct to warrant being classified as a sub-category of the general historical, archaeological and geographical investigation of Eretz-Israel. The following is a survey of the annals of this sub-category. We shall analyze the trends that have dominated this specific realm, and attempt to discern its most striking features, especially those of greatest importance to a geographical approach in historical-geographical research.[1]

THE EARLY FOUNDATIONS

Biblical geography, i.e. the attempt to identify the names of places mentioned in the Bible with various locations throughout Eretz-Israel, dates back to the end of the ancient period. At the start of the fourth century, Eusebius, Bishop of Caesaria, composed a book entitled *Onomastikon*, in which he lists biblical sites, recording beside each one, to the best of his knowledge, its location in the Eretz-Israel of his time. Around a hundred years later this work was translated into Latin by St. Jerome, and it was widely used for hundreds of years thereafter as a basic text for the study of biblical geography.[2]

Interest in biblical geography as "Sacred Geography" (*Geographia Sacra*) continued through the Middle Ages, and it remained an accepted field of

---

1 The treatment of various studies mentioned throughout this article makes no pretense of being a complete bibliographical survey, but rather a sampling of characteristic approaches. Although the author does not mention numerous studies which employ the different approaches to be discussed, this should by no means be construed as a slighting of their importance.

2 Eusebius, *Das Onomastikon der Biblischen Orstnamen*, E. Klosterman (ed.), Leipzig 1904.

research among Christians, Jews, and even scholarly Muslims. This inquiry engendered numerous traditions regarding holy places, the graves of historical figures, and other sites, which were recorded in the writings of travelers, pilgrims and others.[3]

With the onset of the modern period and the advance of the sciences in Europe, historical geography also underwent a process of development, and opened itself to scholarship and criticism. During the sixteenth to eighteenth centuries, numerous treatises were written — some of them wide-ranging and of major significance — on the geography of Eretz-Israel, its landscape and its past. In most of these works a historical-biblical approach is evident; with regard to each settlement, they cite whatever information can be gleaned from the Bible and other historical sources.[4]

Biblical geography also played a prominent role in the cartographic endeavors of this same period. Many of the maps of Eretz-Israel produced at the time contain a division of the land into the territories held by the Tribes of Israel. These maps were drawn by the foremost cartographers, and were incorporated not only into treatises on Eretz-Israel but also into many general atlases.[5]

Beginning of Modern Research—Travelers and Investigators in the Nineteenth Century

Modern geographical research on Eretz-Israel, which has been based on critical studies and precise scientific cartography, had its beginnings in the nineteenth century.[6] This process was accompanied by a concomitant development of historical geography, centering around biblical geography. One of the founders of this discipline was the American Edward Robinson, whose comprehensive books on the land and its history were based on two expeditions to Palestine, carried out in 1838-1839 and 1852.[7] Many researchers followed in Robinson's

---

3   M. Ish-Shalom, *Christian Travels in the Holy Land*, Tel Aviv 1979 (Hebrew); R. Röhricht, *Bibliotheca Geographica Palaestinae*, Berlin 1889 (1963).

4   Only a few examples shall be cited, particularly the comprehensive studies composed by scholars, rather than accounts written by travelers:
    A. Relandus, *Palestina ex Monumentis Veteribus Illustrated*, Trajecti Batavorum 1714.
    O. Dapper, *Beschryving von Gantsch Syrie en Palestyn of Heilige Landt*, Amsterdam 1677.
    T. Fuller, *A Pisgah-Sight of Palestine*, London 1650.

5   K. Nebenzhal, *Maps of the Holy Land*, N.Y. 1986; E. Laor, *Maps of the Holy Land*, Amsterdam-N.Y. 1986.

6   Y. Ben-Arieh, *The Rediscovery of the Holy Land in the Nineteenth Century*, Jerusalem 1979.

7   E. Robinson & E. Smith, *Biblical Researches in Palestine*, London 1841; E. Robinson, *Later Biblical Researches in Palestine*, Boston 1857.

footsteps, and shortly after his works appeared another scholar, George A. Smith, published his own book entitled *Historical Geography of the Holy Land*.[8]

In these studies, like many others, biblical geography played a central role. The identification of places mentioned in the Bible greatly occupied Robinson and those who followed him, and he devoted much of his writing to an analysis of the Arabic names attached to various sites, as well as the ancient names preserved in the Arabic appellations. Robinson provided the basis for a field that has been central to historical geography up to the present day: "historical toponymy," the study of the names and identification of places.

The development of this research gave rise to heightened scientific and critical trends, which were most apparent in three areas:

a. A more profound discussion on the landscape of Palestine, and the nature and geographic features of the land; and a presentation of the research as a study of the geography lying behind the history — i.e. how the landscape of Palestine and the quality of the land influenced the flow of history.[9]

b. Broadening of the historical canvas to encompass the Hellenistic, Roman and Byzantine periods as well.

c. Expansion of the discussion on historical sources and securing a critical basis for it. Father Abel's work entitled *Géographie de la Palestine*, evidently the crowning achievement of this development, marked the end of the formative period and the start of modern critical research. The first part of this book was devoted to a survey of the geography of Palestine, and later sections to a historical-geographical description of its districts and regions, as well as various historical periods.[10]

PRESENT-DAY HISTORICAL-GEOGRAPHICAL RESEARCH
ON THE ANCIENT PERIOD

From the basic elements of historical geography, as described above, there developed the main trends accepted today in research on the ancient period in Eretz-Israel. As it is impossible to review all of the studies in this field, we shall examine only the main approaches, and present alongside each a few selected examples. Many of the researchers cited are not geographers, and some of them

---

8   G.A. Smith, *Historical Geography of the Holy Land*, London, 1894.

9   Several researchers who were inclined toward this approach arrived at an extreme deterministic-environmentalistic position. The most blatant of these is: E. Huntington, *Palestine and Its Transformation*, Boston 1911.

10   F.M. Abel, *Géographie de la Palestine*, Paris 1938.

do not regard the works they produced as geographical in nature. Nonetheless, the gamut of approaches and topics covered in these studies calls for an examination from a geographical perspective in general, and from a historical-geographical standpoint in particular.

Historical Geography of the Defined Periods
The foundations of historical-geographical research were laid by investigators who were largely continuing the approach that had been practiced earlier. Their work combined biblical, historical, archaeological, and geographical studies into an integrated picture depicting the appearance of Eretz-Israel at a given period. Thus Michael Avi-Yonah traced the borders of the land, administrative districts, settlement locations and the network of roads in the period from the conquests of Alexander the Great (333 B.C.E.) to the Arab conquest (640 C.E.). In similar fashion Yohanan Aharoni and others confronted the biblical period.

This trend gave rise to numerous treatises, among them several volumes entitled *Historical Geography*.[11] Its achievements are also expressed in numerous maps and in biblical and historical atlases printed in Hebrew, English and other languages.[12]

However, alongside its myriad achievements, several weaknesses of this type of static investigation can be discerned in these same books and, especially, atlases. While it focused on a toponymical identification of names, and a reconstruction of the geographical conditions that prevailed, via a cross-section of defined time periods, it failed almost entirely to deal with the dynamic, developmental dimension that characterizes studies in the diverse areas of human geography, and which constitutes an essential component of historical-geographical research in general.

A different approach to biblical geography was pioneered by Menashe Harel. He too integrated geography, the Bible and archaeology in his studies, but laid even greater emphasis on the natural conditions of Eretz-Israel: climate, topography, and water, wildlife and plant sources — so that his research gained a slight deterministic tinge. Often the time and space units with which he dealt were limited in scope. He focused on a geographic analysis of specific biblical

---

11   M. Avi-Yonah, *The Holy Land from the Persian to the Arab Conquests (536 B.C. to 640 A.D.). A Historical Geography*, Michigan 1966; Y. Aharoni, *The Land of the Bible*, London, 1979; Z. Kallai, *Historical Geography of the Bible*, Jerusalem-Leiden 1987; J. Simons, *The Geographical and Topographical Texts of the Old Testament*, Leiden 1959.

12   D.H.K. Amiran et al. (eds.), *Atlas of Israel*, Sect. IX, Tel Aviv-Amsterdam 1970; Y. Aharoni & M. Avi-Yohah, *The Macmillan Bible Atlas* (prepared by Carta, Jerusalem), N.Y.-London 1968.

incidents, and sometimes broader topics such as the journeys of the Tribes of Israel through Sinai or the economy of Eretz-Israel in biblical times. Harel asserted that "historical geography is a study of the struggle between man and nature, which forms the cultural landscape over generations."[13] In my opinion, the use of the term "struggle" and the stress on the relationship between man and nature serve to limit the fields of investigation, place the inquiry on a deterministic basis, and downgrade the settlement and cultural aspects, which are not necessarily dependent on the natural geographic conditions.

Onomastics

The large number of historical settlements in Eretz-Israel through the ages and the numerous sources in which they are mentioned made it necessary to create research tools in which the voluminous information on these settlements could be concentrated. Thus a type of literature-research evolved that, in the form of comprehensive articles, encompassed the names of the settlements, each one accompanied by the sources providing historical information or noting events that took place there. Notable among the earliest of these publications are: *The Settlement Book (Sefer Hayishuv)* — whose editor, Shmuel Klein, was the first professor of historical geography at the Hebrew University;[14] and the treatise by the German Peter Thomsen.[15] Other works of this kind were also published at around the same time.[16]

The "Gazeteer of Roman Palestine", published in the 1970's, has become an essential work adorning the desks of modern scholars.[17] Two wide-ranging onomastic research projects are currently being carried out at the Archaeology Institute of the Hebrew University: one by Israel L. Levine on the settlements whose names appear in Hebrew and Aramaic sources from the time of the conquests of Alexander the Great until the Muslim conquest (333 B.C.E. to 638 C.E.), and the other by Yoram Tsafrir on the settlements mentioned in Greek and Latin sources during the very same period.[18] These studies surpass all

---

13 M. Harel, *The Sinai Journeys*, San Diego 1983; M. Harel, *Journeys and Campaigns in Ancient Times*, Tel Aviv 1980 (Hebrew); M. Harel, address to M.A. seminar in historical geography at the Hebrew University, Jerusalem, September 11, 1987.

14 S. Klein (ed.), *The Settlement Book*, I, Jerusalem 1939 (Hebrew); S. Asaf & L.A. Meir, *The Settlement Book*, II, Jerusalem 1944 (Hebrew).

15 P. Thomsen, *Loca Sancta*, Halle 1907.

16 J.S. Horowitz, *Palestine and the Adjacent Countries (A Geographical and Historical Encyclopedia of Palestine, Syria and the Sinai Peninsula)*, Vienna 1923 (Hebrew).

17 M. Avi-Yonah, "Gazeteer of Roman Palestine," *Qedem*, V (1976).

18 I am grateful to Prof. Israel Levine and Prof. Yoram Tsafrir, who described their studies to me and allowed me to use this information here.

previous ones in terms of scope and number of sources examined. When completed, the critical discussion will relate to the identification of each and every entry and the significance of its having been mentioned in the various sources. The latter project breaks new ground by including the Greek and Latin sources both in the original and in translation. Both are likely to become inclusive collections of historical sources, advancing the historical study of the settlements in Eretz-Israel in the said periods — and essential tools for those engaged in this field.

Environmental, Regional and Spatial Historical Geography
Out of the historical-geographical research described above there evolved an approach integrating archaeological, historical and geographical studies in a wider inquiry based on a regional framework. A comprehensive investigation of a geographical region is carried out, involving archaeological excavations in certain sites, and parallel archaeological surveys throughout the region. The findings are integrated as part of a comprehensive study, with a twofold aim: firstly, to describe the development of the settlement pattern, with all of its components, over an entire region during consecutive historical periods; and secondly, to analyze the interrelationships between a variety of factors — geographical, cultural, economic and social — that have influenced this development. The discussion of an entire region stresses the reciprocal relations between diverse elements of the settlement pattern: urban and rural settlements, large and small ones, and the links between several of the major settlements.

It seems that the origins of this approach can be traced to the studies of Yohanan Aharoni and his colleagues in the Beersheba plain, where the goal of investigating numerous sites in the framework of a defined geographic region was first proposed. This trend later became a central one, followed by numerous Israeli archaeologists.

The approach proceeds along two main paths. One utilizes information gathered from archaeological excavations and surveys, and geographical tools deriving from the analysis of distribution and spatial patterns and the creation of mathematical models, in order to analyze the settlement distribution pattern and the relationship between major settlements and the smaller ones on their periphery.[19] The other places greater emphasis on the reciprocal relationship

---

19   A. Ben-Tor et al., "A Regional Study of Tel Yoqneam and Its Vicinity," *Qadmoniot*, XX, Nos. 1–2 (1987), pp. 2–17 (Hebrew); Y. Portugali, "A Field Methodology for Regional Archaeology (The Jezreel Survey 1981)," *Tel Aviv*, IX (1982), pp. 170–188; idem, "The Settlement Pattern in the Western Jezreel Valley from the 6th Century B.C.E. to the Arab Conquest," in A. Kasher, A. Oppenheimer & U. Rappaport (eds.), *Man and Land in Eretz-Israel in Antiquity*, Jerusalem 1986, pp. 7–19 (Hebrew).

between man, society and culture on the one hand, and the conditions of the environment on the other hand. This approach finds expression, for example, in the introduction to a book on the archaeology of Eretz-Israel during the period of settlement by the Tribes of Israel, and the period of the Judges. According to its author, Israel Finkelstein, "the settlement process is organically connected to the nature of the land — its landscape, climate and economy." Despite the fact that the term "geography" is not mentioned, the research can in fact be defined as "the study of the history of settlement."[20]

A similar trend surfaced in the study of later periods of Eretz-Israel's history — the Hellenistic, Roman and Byzantine periods (from the fourth century B.C.E. to the seventh century C.E.). Two doctoral dissertations may be cited as examples: one by Shimon Dar and the other by myself. Dar's thesis relates to western Samaria and analyzes the rural village, the agricultural system, various structures related to farmlands, the size of the farm unit, types of produce, and other topics, as they existed in the region from the Hellenistic period to the end of the Byzantine period.[21]

The second work deals with agricultural and urban settlement in the Negev during the Byzantine period. Under examination are the society, institutions, agricultural methods, produce and nature of different settlement types then existing. Diverse aspects — economic, social, and agricultural-ecological — are explored.[22] The regional approach, and the broadening of the canvas both spatially and temporally, highlight the dynamic nature of historical-geographic research, and the tendency to explore the interrelationship between various settlements in the region, as well as their development over time.

Topical Historical Geography
Like geography in general, historical geography pertains to numerous areas that are investigated by various disciplines. Consequently, studies are at times conducted in spheres of geography, such as urbanization and urban planning, water sources and water systems, etc., by investigators who do not regard themselves as geographers but as historians, archaeologists, and so forth. Nevertheless, it seems that the centrality of these fields of research to geography

20   I. Finkelstein, *The Archaeology of the Period of Settlement and Judges*, Tel Aviv 1986 (Hebrew).

21   S. Dar, *Settlement Distribution of Western Samaria in the Second Temple, Mishnaic, Talmudic and Byzantine Periods*, Tel Aviv 1982 (Hebrew).

22   R. Rubin, "Settlement Pattern and the Agricultural Base in the Rehovot-Ba-Negev Region during the Byzantine Period," Doctoral dissertation submitted to the Hebrew University, Jerusalem 1986 (Hebrew).

and the contents of these studies require geographers to take into account all of the following:

1. Given the climatic conditions of Eretz-Israel, water constitutes a vital and limiting factor in the development of a settlement. The ability to locate water sources, dig wells and create aqueducts and other apparatus for carrying and storing water, as well as reservoirs for both public and emergency use, is of extreme importance in this process. Hence the investigation of water installations comprises a substantial part of the research on settlements and their development.[23]

2. The history of agriculture and farming in Eretz-Israel, even when detached from rural settlement and inspected on its own, is very significant in analyzing the rural landscape of Eretz-Israel in the past, as well as the economy and settlements of the land.[24] As rural settlement was so prominent in Eretz-Israel of ancient times, it is essential to arrive at a thorough understanding of this domain.

3. Demographic-historical research, attempting to reconstruct the size and distribution of the population of Eretz-Israel in various periods, is based on an analysis of the size and distribution of archaeological sites and the population density in built-up areas.[25]

4. The integration of demography, water resources and agriculture is expressed in an analysis of the "bearing capacity" of the land and its demographic significance in different historical periods.[26] This topic has thus far been examined only partially, and a comprehensive treatment of it must take into account not only the natural bearing capacity of the land but also the significance

23 S.M. Paul & W.G. Dever (eds.), *Biblical Archaeology*, Jerusalem 1973, pp. 127–143; Y. Shiloh, "Underground Water Systems in the Iron Age," *Archaeology and Biblical Interpretation, Colin Rose Memorial Volume*, Philips University (in press); Y. Hirschfeld, D. Amit & J. Patrich (eds.), *Book of Water Systems*, Yad Ben-Zvi (in press, Hebrew).

24 Y. Felix, *Agriculture in Palestine in the Period of the Mishna and Talmud*, Jerusalem 1963 (Hebrew); A. Kasher, O. Oppenheimer & U. Rappaport (eds.), *Man and Land in Eretz-Israel in Antiquity*, Jerusalem 1986 (Hebrew); R. Frankel, "The History of the Processing of Wine and Oil in Galilee in the Period of the Bible, the Mishna and the Talmud," Doctoral dissertation submitted to Tel Aviv University, 1984 (Hebrew).

25 Y. Shiloh, "The Population of Iron-Age Palestine in the Light of Urban Plans, Areas and Population Density," *Eretz-Israel*, XV (1981), pp. 274–282 (Hebrew); M. Broshi, "La population de l'ancienne Jérusalem," *Revue Biblique*, LXXXII (1975), pp. 5–15; idem, "The Population of Western Palestine in the Roman-Byzantine Period," *Bulletin of the American School of Oriental Research*, 236 (1979), pp. 1–10.

26 M. Broshi, "Demographic Changes in Ancient Eretz-Israel: Methodology and Estimates," A. Kasher et al. (note 24, supra), pp. 49–56.

of imports, exports, pilgrimage to the Holy Land, and other factors in each and every period.

5. Research on architecture and planning traces the development and functions of the home and yard, and the rural and urban settlement patterns. Some of these studies are devoted to description and documentation of the architecture on all of its levels, while others deal with its changing functions over time, and the significance of this evolvement.[27] Inquiry in the field of architecture gives rise to a study of the urban pattern of large and developed cities, including their development, appearance and the sources of influence on their design and planning.[28]

6. Research on cities leads us from the architectonic aspect to the social structure and cultural fabric of urban life in ancient Eretz-Israel. Notable investigations have been carried out on cities such as Caesarea and Bet Shean, entailing an analysis of their social history against a background of the convergence of Greek and Roman history with eastern and Jewish cultures,[29] as well as a thorough study relating to the city in Eretz-Israel as a general social phenomenon.[30]

7. Research on the social and cultural aspects of cities ties in with broader aspects — and not only urban ones — concerning the relations between society, culture and cultural conflict on the one hand, and populations and settlements on the other hand. Answers are sought to the following questions: How do social mechanisms and phenomena affect population and settlement? What are the relations between the penetration of a new culture into a particular settlement type and changes in the settlement distribution? How have cultural and social factors shaped the settlement pattern, economy, agriculture, etc.?

An excellent example of a wide-ranging discussion on these questions is M. Avi-Yonah's book, which surveys the history of the Jewish population under Roman and Byzantine rule, against a background of the cultural conflict between

27 Y. Hirschfeld, *Dwelling Houses in Roman and Byzantine Palestine*, Jerusalem 1987 (Hebrew); H. Kazenstein et al. (eds.), *The Architecture of Ancient Israel*, Jerusalem 1987 (Hebrew).

28 A. Segal, "Roman Cities in the Province of Arabia," *Journal of Society of Architectural Historians*, XL (1981), pp. 108–121; A. Segal, "The Byzantine City of Shivta (Esbeita), The Negev Desert, Israel," *British Archaeological Reports*, 179 (1983); J. Shershevski, "Urban Settlements in the Negev in the Byzantine Period," Doctoral dissertation submitted to the Hebrew University, Jerusalem 1986 (Hebrew).

29 L.I. Levine, *Caesarea under Roman Rule*, Leiden 1975; L.I. Levine, "Roman Caesarea, an Archaeological-Topographical Study," *Qedem*, II (1975); G. Fuks, *Scythopolis — A Greek City in Eretz-Israel*, Jerusalem 1983 (Hebrew).

30 Y. Dan, *The City in Eretz-Israel during the Late Roman and Byzantine Periods*, Jerusalem 1984 (Hebrew).

Judaism on the one hand and the pagan Roman regime, and later the Christian
Byzantine regime, on the other hand.[31] Another example is my article dealing
with the ancient monasteries in the Judean Desert as a settlement type whose
founding, development and continued existence were forged in the cultural-
religious framework of Christian monasticism. Despite its religious uniqueness
the monastery possesses many characteristics of a settlement: location, water
sources, livelihood sources, a network of ties with other settlements, etc. All of
these components must be examined as they would be in the case of settlements
of a different nature, with tools from the realm of settlement geography.[32]

8. One of the fundamental approaches in historical geography is the investigation
of relics from the past that stand out in the landscape. At first these are studied as
phenomena in their own right, and only after information is assimilated at this
stage can they be linked to particular periods or defined activities that led to their
creation. Since there are abundant relics throughout Eretz-Israel, some of which
are not integrally related to remains of settlements from any specific period,
investigation of such relics came to play an important role in historical-
geographical research. We shall note three of the studies that employed this
approach:

a. Studies on ancient agricultural fields in the Negev, which focused on their
dispersion, characteristics of the construction and operation of field systems,
and the relationship between rain, runoff and plant life — all without first
relating to the question of when these agricultural systems were set up, and by
whom.[33]

b. Studies of the "bell-shaped caves" in the Judean Coastal Plain, especially in
the vicinity of Bet Guvrin. Under investigation were the man-made caves in the
chalk rocks, their nature and distribution, and how and for what purpose they
were quarried — from which information were gleaned the time of the original
quarrying and the main reason underlying it, and even parallels in other
countries.[34]

c. Study of agriculture as practiced in the Judean Hills and Samaria, which
began as an investigation of the agricultural systems based on irrigation using

---

31   M. Avi-Yonah, *The Jews under Roman and Byzantine Rule*, Jerusalem 1984.

32   R. Rubin, "The 'Laura' Monasteries in Judean Desert during the Byzantine Period," *Cathedra*,
      23 (1982), pp. 25–46 (Hebrew).

33   Y. Kedar, *The Ancient Agriculture in the Negev Mountains*, Jerusalem 1967 (Hebrew).

34   Y. Ben-Arieh, "Pits and Caves in the Shephelah of Israel Compared with Similar Pits in East
      Anglia," *Geography*, LIV (1969), pp. 186–192.

water from underground springs, and later developed into comprehensive research on the hilly terraced landscape.[35]

What is common to all of these studies is their starting point: the relics extant in the landscape, their investigation as phenomena and the appraisal of their function and significance; only at a later stage are historical questions touched upon and historical sources employed — provided they exist. From a methodological standpoint this type of research is characterized by the central position accorded to the relics themselves.

CHARACTERISTICS OF HISTORICAL-GEOGRAPHICAL RESEARCH ON THE ANCIENT PERIOD

As noted in the introduction, and as this very anthology makes clear, most of the studies in historical geography conducted by Israeli geographers relate to the modern settlement of Eretz-Israel and the processes of change which the landscape and settlements have undergone over the past two centuries. In contrast, research on the ancient period possesses a number of distinguishing features.

The Bond between Historical Geography and Archaeology

Research on ancient settlements, settlement patterns, roads, administrative districts and their borders, agriculture and various installations demands a close tie with archaeological findings, even when geographical tools and approaches are employed. As mentioned above, many of the studies bearing the title "historical geography," or possessing a historical-geographical nature, have been conducted by archaeologists and at times by historians. However, even when the approach is geographical, one of the important sources of information is archaeological evidence, and hence the researcher is obliged to rely upon data arising from archaeological excavations and surveys. Unfortunately, often such data are either totally lacking or are insufficient, in which case the researcher must perform the archaeological tasks himself, i.e. he must have archaeological training. The field work, one of the fundamental elements of historical-geographical research in every period, demands specific skills and the ability to conduct surveys, excavations and analyses of archaeological finds.

---

35   Z. Ron, "Agricultural Terraces in the Judean Mountains," *IEJ* 16 (1966), pp. 33–122; Z.Y.D. Ron, *Stone Huts as an Expression of Terrace Agriculture in the Judean and Samarian Hills*, Tel Aviv 1977 (Hebrew).

The Nature of the Historical Sources

In Israel, as is the case with historical-geographical research the world over, an approach has evolved which incorporates a thorough examination of the primary sources. However, in the study of the ancient period, only rarely do previously unknown early records come to light, and for the most part historians have already scrutinized the primary sources that are available. Among these are the Bible, Jewish rabbinic literature, and the writings of Josephus Flavius, the founding fathers of the Church, Greek, Roman, Byzantine and Arab historians, and others. Since these sources have already been examined, the role of the historical geographer is not to discover new facts, but to analyze the documents anew, from a viewpoint unfamiliar to, or at times unaccepted by, historical research. Often this entails reading "between the lines" and searching for clues among the familiar texts, from which can be extracted geographical information attesting to the nature of the settlement and the settlement pattern, the size and composition of the population, the economy of Eretz-Israel in each region, etc.

Epigraphical Finds

At the point where archaeological evidence and historical sources converge, one encounters the epigraphical finds, i.e. ancient inscriptions, papyrus scrolls, ostrakons, and other written documents. Although such finds are investigated by archaeologists and historians, they hold enormous importance for historical geography because they frequently offer direct testimony from the period in question about the daily life of the settlement under investigation. An outstanding example of this is the papyrus archive discovered in Nitzana (ancient Nessana) by the Colt delegation in the 1930's.[36] It includes personal, legal and economic documents belonging to the residents of Nitzana, a Negev city, from the sixth to seventh centuries B.C.E. Some of the records provide information that would otherwise have been unobtainable — such as the crop yield, the amount of tax paid by the residents of the city, and the kinds of merchandise paid as taxes.

Lack of Quantitative Information

One of the drawbacks of the available historical sources is the almost total absence of quantitative data. We have no census to go by, nor reliable data on the size of the settlements, the cultivated fields, or the crop yield. Even in the rare instances when such data do appear in these sources, they are of dubious

---

36   D.H. Colt (ed.), *Excavations at Nessana*, I–III, especially III; C.J. Kramer, *Non-Literary Papyri*, Princeton 1958.

credibility and should be approached cautiously. This imposes a qualitative nature on the research, and limits the possibility of conducting a quantitative analysis of the sort that is considered desirable in historical-geographical studies of the modern period, especially with regard to the economic and demographic aspects.

Constant Alteration of the Landscape

Although one of the substantive components of historical-geographical research is field work, the study of the ancient period in Eretz-Israel is encumbered by the fact that constant, rapid changes have occurred in the landscape there. The process of modern settlement precipitates such alterations and the disappearance of assorted relics that are important for an understanding and reconstruction of the ancient landscape. Consequently, secondary evidence on the condition of the landscape decades ago, such as old aerial photographs and maps, and nineteenth-century travel literature — all of which were produced before the changes caused by modernization took place — can often aid the investigator, even when he is interested not in the period in which these documents were composed, but in the testimony which they provide about the landscape in an earlier period. Thus a strong bond is created between historical geographers researching the modern period, and those who are investigating the ancient period.

Comparison and Analogy between the Recent and Distant Past

An additional link between historical geography of the modern period and that of the ancient period is the similarity and affinity that exist between life-style and settlement in the remote past and in the traditional Arab society of Palestine on the eve of the mid-nineteenth century modernization. In the initial stages of the research a romantic trend was dominant, especially among investigators of the nineteenth century. It tended to view the life-styles of the ancient and the traditional Arab societies in Eretz-Israel as similar and analogous to each other, and drew conclusions about the former from information gathered about the latter. This tendency is apparent in scientific literature and accounts by travelers, and is even reflected in artistic depictions by painters of the period. From out of this tendency there arose a parallel trend that was more stringent and scientific, as it meticulously documented the life-style, home and settlement structure, agricultural and industrial activity, and trades of traditional Arab society at the turn of the century.[37]

---

37 G. Dalman, *Arbeit und Sitte im Palästina*, I–VII, Gütersloh 1928–1942.

It appears that the question of similarity and analogy between traditional and ancient societies remains unanswered, and insufficiently examined. It has not been established that traditional Arab society resembled its predecessors in Eretz-Israel. Even if it did, it is unclear whether the likeness was greater to the biblical, Second Temple, or Roman-Byzantine period. Furthermore, was the similarity of a general nature, or did it extend to particulars? These questions deserve extensive investigation, and their answers can reinforce the link between historical-geographical research of the ancient period and that of the modern one.

Comparison and Analogy between Eretz-Israel and Neighboring Countries

A second kind of comparative research seeks similarities between Eretz-Israel and its neighbors. Historical geography must take into account the broad geographical and cultural setting of the land during each and every period. Comparative studies on the biblical period must look for similarities between Eretz-Israel and Egypt, Syria and Mesopotamia, while in a later period the cultural and political influence stemmed from Greece, Rome and Byzantium. In my view, such research is the key to numerous questions relating to the history and distribution of settlement in Eretz-Israel, changes in the material culture, and the penetration of various technologies and artistic and architectonic styles.

Moreover, comparative research allows historical geography to break out of the accepted inductive framework and examine to what extent similar settlement processes took place in different areas during a given period or even in different periods, and whether we can formulate rules and draw an analogy between a historical event involving settlement in one place and other events of a similar general nature elsewhere.

CONCLUSION

Research on the historical geography of Eretz-Israel in the ancient period is perforce interdisciplinary, integrating work in history, archaeology, Bible studies and geography. Hence it is complex, and carried out by diverse investigators, with different backgrounds and approaches. At times the geographical approach is deliberate and distinct, while at other times it emerges between the lines, without any conscious or deliberate effort by the investigator himself. This survey has presented only a few examples of the various trends existing in this field. Nevertheless, it should hopefully serve as a basis for a methodological discussion on the importance of historical geography of the ancient period and the trends that are desirable as guidelines for future studies.

PERCEPTIONS AND IMAGES OF THE HOLY LAND

YEHOSHUA BEN-ARIEH

INTRODUCTION

Six different perceptions of the Holy Land were prominent in the Western world of the nineteenth century. These views, which all appear in the travel literature of the time, lend themselves to comparison and contrast. In some cases they are complementary, in other cases mutually exclusive.

A LAND OF DIVINE HOLINESS

For hundreds of years Palestine has been perceived by the Western world as a holy, ethereal, timeless land — both geographically and cartographically. The divine presence is thought to dwell in this land, and the periods when the Jewish and Christian faiths came into being and crystallized are considered to be the most decisive eras in its history.[1]

A religious-mystical perception of the area and its holy sites — especially Jerusalem — was entertained by the great majority of nineteenth-century writers of travel literature. These itinerant travelers had absorbed a Western-European culture imbued with a wide variety of beliefs, views and opinions regarding the Holy Land. In all of these outlooks, the concept of "the Holy Land" was laden with emotional and sentimental associations. In this land God Himself established laws and commandments, dispatched angels as emissaries, and conducted conversations with people. This is the land where, according to the belief of these Europeans, God was revealed to man. It is here that the son of God descended in the form of man, it is here that he treaded — and from this land he returned to the heavens. The holiness of the region in Christianity derives first and foremost from Jesus' central role in that faith. The New Testament doctrine of holiness calls for worship of the divine spirit and sanctification of the land where the divine revelation transpired.[2]

1   I. Schattner, *The Map of Eretz-Israel and Its History*, Jerusalem 1951 (Hebrew).
2   G. L. Robinson, *The Biblical Doctrine of Holiness*, Chicago 1903, p. 34; M. Grindea (ed.), *ADAM, International Review, A Literary Quarterly in English and French* (1968), pp. 205–209.

Over the years the view that Jesus' presence sanctified his physical environment, and that one could draw near to God by coming to know and sense this environment, gained currency in Christianity. This idea constituted one of the motivations behind the Crusades, and it led the Church to regard the Crusader ideal as an integral part of its creed. For Christianity, the sites related to the life of Jesus — his travels, meetings and tribulations — are of far greater importance than the earlier holy sites that had already been regarded as sacred in Jesus' own lifetime. Christian dogma stressed the role of the holy places as they attest to everything that the Christian messiah underwent.[3]

Many nineteenth-century Europeans found it difficult to make the transition from a transcendental, incorporeal perception of the "Holy Land" to a realistic, physical one. This was true not only for those who had only heard or read about the land without ever having set foot there, but also for the many people who had begun visiting it and who had come to know it first hand. Thus images and perceptions of Palestine as a divine, sanctified land can be found in the most modern European literature of the nineteenth century.

The very use of the term "the Holy Land," which spread steadily during the nineteenth century, is an indication of how deeply the transcendental perception had taken root. This term served to demarcate a particular geographical entity, despite the fact that in many periods of history the land had no distinctive political status.[4] One of the Christian theological encyclopedias offered the following explanation for the term "Holy Land": "Name commonly given to Palestine on account of the many places sanctified by the presence of Jesus and identified on the grounds of scriptural documents, history or legend."[5]

Only with the inception of the British Mandate period was modern Palestine given concrete borders — and it appears that this development would not have transpired were it not for the perception of the land as a distinctive entity, a unique "Holy Land," the residence of history's sacred figures. It was here that both the First and the Second Temples were located (Judaism), the human divinity was born (Christianity), and the Prophet ascended heavenward (Islam). From a historical perspective the uniqueness of the land bestowed upon it a unique status: the center of the world. The idea of the Holy Land occupying the

---

3   W.D. Davies, *The Gospel and the Land*, California 1974; F.H. Epp, *Whose Land Is Palestine?*, Grand Rapids, Mich. 1974, p. 87; L.I. Vogel, *Zion as Place and Past: An American Myth, Ottoman Palestine in the American Mind Perceived through Protestant Consciousness and Experience*, University Microfilms International, Ann Arbor-London 1984, pp. 24–26.

4   For more on this, see the article by G. Biger in this volume.

5   G.A. Barrois, *Twentieth Century Encyclopedia of Religious Knowledge*, Grand Rapids, Mich. 1955, p. 523.

central geographical position on earth derived from the fact that it was perceived as having witnessed the revelation of the divine presence and having become a focal point for various faiths. This notion of the Holy Land's centrality originated in Jewish biblical and rabbinical literature, whence it found its way into Christian literature.[6]

The Holy Land's distinctness from other lands, including its important neighbors Egypt and Mesopotamia, inspired numerous attempts in the nineteenth century to discover unique geographical features there. Many writers stressed the fact that the land's nourishment depended upon "heavenly rainfall," unlike Mesopotamia and Egypt, where agriculture based on river irrigation was practiced. Other writers saw its topographical location, i.e. the fact that it formed a bridge between two continents and a passageway between Egypt and the Fertile Crescent, as the most significant geographical datum. Still others noted the extraordinary topographical diversity. Finally, there were those who called attention to the desert-like quality of much of the area — the desolateness and secretiveness of the Judean Desert, and the Sinai Desert, scene of the unique revelation of the divine presence.

As a result of the land's many singular qualities, Western literature on Palestine commonly contained the notion that the geography of the region played an important role in the land's holiness. The land was thus conducive to the emergence of spiritual ideas, which explains its being the cradle of abstract monotheistic thought. By contrast, the religions that sprouted in the area ascribed to the land a qualitative and eternal holiness.[7]

LAND OF THE BIBLE AND THE HOLY PLACES

A second perception of Palestine was as the land of the Bible and the holy places. This view largely resembled the one just described, regarding the area as a land of divine holiness. The two approaches differed, however, in that one was theological and based on faith, while the other was historical and factual.

The idea spread in the nineteenth century that the uniqueness of Palestine derived from its being the land of the Bible. It was through the Bible that European thinkers were introduced to the concept of the area as a physical entity. Translations of the Bible into the various European languages during the

---

6   M. Eliade, *The Sacred and the Profane*, N.Y. 1959, p. 199; Vogel (note 3, supra), pp. 21, 23.
7   See for example: G.A. Burton, *Archeology and the Bible*, Philadelphia 1976, p. 94; A.P. Stanley, *Sinai and Palestine in Connection with Their History*, London 1856; G.A. Smith, *Historical Geography of the Holy Land*, Edinburgh 1894, Preface.

previous centuries, along with the invention of printing, made possible its widespread distribution, turning it into a central component of Western Christian culture in the early modern period. The Christian child was taught from his early years not only to read the Bible, but also to hear it being recited in his family, in Sunday school, as part of holiday texts, and during the prayer service read both in churches and in private homes. The Holy Land was the land of the Bible, the land that had become familiar through the old tales, whether based on faith or merely on cultural heritage.[8]

As the number of visitors and tourists to the Holy Land swelled, these people began to search for the sites and scenes with which they had become vicariously familiar since childhood. Whether these nineteenth-century visitors were researchers, writers, artists or simply tourists, the vast majority of them had studied the Bible. They sought not only the holy atmosphere of the Holy Land, but also the locations about which they had heard and read at great length. Because of the almost universal popularity of Bible reading, these people were intimately acquainted with biblical events, figures and sites. Their visits served to reinforce their attachment to the Bible, and upon their return to their home countries they tended to re-read the portions of the Scriptures dealing with the places they had visited.

Among the travelers to the Holy Land were scholars who strove to locate and identify biblical sites and events, and to inscribe them on maps. The nineteenth century was a time of flourishing Bible study. Biblical dictionaries, books and articles — both popular and scientific — as well as biblical atlases and maps, were printed with great frequency and distributed throughout Europe and the entire Western world.

The scientific spirit led to the development of an empirical approach in the study of the Holy Land, and an attempt to treat the biblical events as actual, palpable happenings. The great majority of writers, being Christian, regarded their scholarly endeavors and the works they produced as a search for the origin and roots of the Christian religion.[9]

The same was true for art. Well-known Western artists began visiting the area, with the goal of sketching and drawing the holy places and the biblical landscapes, and making them available to Europeans. The extent to which these drawings became fashionable is demonstrated by the practice current among

8   See for example: E. Robinson & E. Smith, *Biblical Researches in Palestine...*, London 1841, p. 46.

9   Vogel (note 3, supra), pp. 40–45. See also the sources referred to in this volume. C. Kopp, *The Holy Places of the Gospels*, Freiburg-London 1963.

travelers in that century to supplement the written impressions of their trips to the Holy Land with pictorial sketches that, upon their return, were submitted to professional artists for full-size renderings. Among the travel books of the period are works in which the drawings of landscapes from the Holy Land became the primary part of the work, while the written text merely provided accompaniment. Similarly, illustrated editions of the Bible began to appear, containing drawings of not only events and landmarks but also landscapes, maps, ethnic types and architectural designs.[10] The Pre-Raphaelite movement in art, whose foremost representative was William Holman Hunt, got under way. It maintained that in order to accurately draw the biblical sites, one had to visit the Holy Land and witness first hand the places and types of people mentioned in the Bible, as a means of portraying them as truthfully as possible, with maximum attention to detail and precision.[11]

It was generally believed at the time that the people, dress, and customs of the Middle East had, miraculously, remained unchanged over the centuries, and for artists they therefore constituted an important link to the biblical past. The Arab sheikh in picturesque garb resembled, the artists felt, the Jewish patriarchs. The Bedouin caravans crossing the desert reminded them of the Israelites carrying the Holy Ark over the same desert. Arab women drawing water from a well recalled the image of Rebecca serving water to Abraham's servant Eliezer, etc.[12] The geographical identification of places bearing Arab names with biblical sites — a popular endeavor at the time — further instilled in the Western world the notion that Arab society and life-style reflected those of the biblical period.[13]

Another factor leading people to think of the land in biblical terms was the rapidly spreading influence of Bible criticism, which reached a peak in the nineteenth century. During the Middle Ages the biblical exegesis limited itself to literal, moral and allegoric interpretation, in accordance with the inclinations and needs of the critics and their audience. As a result of the Reformation, this type of exegesis gained nearly universal and unchallenged acceptance. However,

10   J. Parkes, *A History of Palestine from 135 A.D. to Modern Times*, London 1949, pp. 215–216; T.H. Horne, *Landscape Illustrations of the Bible*, London 1836; Y. Ben-Arieh, *The Rediscovery of the Holy Land in the Nineteenth Century*, Jerusalem 1979, pp. 15–16.

11   W.H. Hunt, *Pre-Raphaelitism and the Pre-Raphaelite Brotherhood*, London 1905; A. Rose, *The Pre-Raphaelites*, Oxford 1984; M. Bennet, *Catalogue of Exhibition, Willam Holman Hunt*, Liverpool-London 1969.

12   M. Werner, "The Question of Faith: Orientalism, Christianity and Islam," *The Orientalists: Delacroix to Matisse, European Painters in North-Africa and the Near-East*, Royal Academy of Arts, London 1984, pp. 32–39.

13   Parkes (note 10, supra), pp. 232–233.

the nineteenth century ushered in a trend of skepticism as to the unassailable accuracy and credibility of the Bible. This approach precipitated the scientific materialism that came to characterize the century, as expressed by Charles Lyell in *Principles of Geology* (1830), and in the anti-creation theories advanced by Charles Darwin in *Origin of Species* (1859). Western thought of the time came to regard the analytical and textual criticism of the Bible as a major challenge. Thinking believers began to seek new paths in their faith.[14]

On the other hand, these same phenomena led to increased scientific interest in the land of the Bible, and to a heightened desire among devout biblical scholars to visit the area. They hoped to be convinced of the existence of the sites, landscapes and stories mentioned in the Bible by familiarizing themselves with the actual background and environment of the biblical events.[15]

However, the biblical concept of "the Holy Land" also presented them with a certain difficulty. For instance, they grappled with the question of how the region depicted in the Bible as "a land of milk and honey" could have degenerated into such a desolate state. Earlier believers had responded that this development was an incontestable divine curse. However, the scientifically-bent biblical critics of the nineteenth century attributed the gap between the scriptural description and the reality to inaccuracy on the part of the Bible. The Scriptures, they claimed, had simply exaggerated the fertility of the land.

In seeking a scientific explanation, some of the nineteenth-century believers ascribed the woeful transformation of the land to climatic change. Others, however, claimed that explanations based on the altered physical conditions of the land were superfluous, as the drastically different social conditions and agricultural methods that had become prevalent provided sufficient insight into the land's decline. The forests that had once covered the hillsides had been destroyed, as had the terraces that formerly preserved the soil and allowed for its cultivation. This neglect was compounded by fundamental changes in the population and culture. Advocates of this latter theory (which has been accepted up to the present) concluded that there was no contradiction between the biblical rendition of the land's natural geographical conditions, and the reality that had been disclosed in the nineteenth century. Furthermore, they believed that the appearance and the landscapes of the Holy Land in their lifetime served to verify the contents of the Holy Scriptures.[16]

14   Werner (note 12, supra), pp. 32–39.
15   Vogel (note 3, supra), pp. 40–46. See the sources referred to in the text.
16   I. Schattner, "Ideas on the Physical Geography of Palestine in the Early 19th Century," *Eretz-Israel*, II, Israel Exploration Society, Jerusalem 1953, pp. 41–49 (Hebrew); Ben-Arieh (note 10, supra), pp. 100–105, 137–140.

LAND OF ANCIENT HISTORY

Palestine was perceived by the cultured Western world not only as the Holy Land and the land of the Bible, but also as part of the ancient world, whether classical-Mediterranean (Hellenistic-Roman) or ancient Middle Eastern. Already in early times the people of Europe evinced respect and esteem for the ancient lands in the annals of mankind. However, these lands lay at a great distance, and in fact were unknown to most Westerners. From the eleventh century, the Europeans were familiar not only with the Bible, but with the sagas of Alexander the Great and of other prominent Hellenist figures. In the later Middle Ages interest in these areas increased steadily, and the number of Western visitors to the Mediterranean region and to the Orient rose accordingly — at first to the classical, Hellenistic-Roman world, and afterwards to the centers of even earlier civilizations.[17]

In the seventeenth and eighteenth centuries it became fashionable in Europe — especially in England — for young members of the wealthy class to participate in what was known as Grand Tours, geared to imparting knowledge of neighboring countries, refinement and prestige. As the Napoleonic wars wreaked havoc in Europe, these tours began reaching more distant lands, and consequently the number of Europeans attracted to the classical world and the ancient Middle East grew. Whether as individuals or as members of societies and associations, intellectuals, archaeologists, philologists, antiquaries, adventurers, the infirm seeking the sun, voyagers wishing to expand their horizons — all set out on journeys to Italy, Greece, Spain, North Africa and Egypt, Turkey and the Levant. For the most parts these trips were made in comfort, with ample, even superfluous supplies. Occasionally the travelers donned eastern outfits, carried light supplies and penetrated into remote and uncharted areas, thus encountering numerous difficulties and grave dangers.[18]

These journeys were attended by the practice of amassing antiquities and transferring them to the travelers' country of origin. Often these items were handed over to prominent museums in these countries — the British Museum in London, the Louvre in Paris, the German museums in Berlin, etc. — but they found their way to private homes and gardens as well. No feelings of guilt accompanied the act of uprooting these antiquities from their natural milieu. Good relations with the "Sublime Porte" — the Turkish authorities — facilitated this plunder of precious artifacts, and their being spirited away to safe quarters

---

17   M.E. de Meester, *Oriental Influences in English Literature of the Nineteenth Century,* Heidelberg 1915, Preface.

18   *Travellers Beyond the Grand Tour, Catalogue,* The Fine Art Society, London 1980.

in Europe. Thus, for example, a well-known obelisk from Luxor found its way to the Place de la Concorde in Paris. Another obelisk, "Cleopatra's Needle," was moved to the banks of the Thames in London. A third was transferred to New York's Central Park.[19]

The antiquities of the Holy Land were also pillaged. De Saulcy, who conducted the first archaeological excavation in the Tomb of the Kings in Jerusalem, moved sarcophaguses he had found there to the Louvre. The famous Mesha stone, discovered in Moab, was also housed in the French museum. The Shiloah inscription was shipped to a museum in Istanbul. And these are only a few of the examples.

The situation in Iraq-Mesopotamia (Assyria-Babylonia) was no better than that in the surrounding countries. The antiquities located to this very day in the British Museum, the Louvre, the museums in Berlin and elsewhere attest to the dimensions of the plunder.

On the other hand, the lively interest of the nineteenth century in the ancient lands brought on not only damage, but also scientific research on the ancient world. Important discoveries in Egypt and Mesopotamia led to the intensive study of ancient languages and cultures of the Near East. Many of the travelers and researchers were attracted to these field of study. The Egyptian pyramids, the deciphering of the Rosetta stone hieroglyphics (1822) by Jean-François Champollion, the Layard excavations in Nineveh (the 1840's), and other developments transformed archaeology from a hunt for antiquities into a basic science for the study of many and varied languages and cultures. Egypt and Mesopotamia, which until the Napoleonic era had been nearly unknown lands from a scientific standpoint, became central subjects of investigation for researchers and other interested parties throughout the world. Similarly, the ancient history of the Mediterranean region, including the classical and the Middle East countries, became focal points for scholars throughout the West.[20]

Interestingly, the discoveries in Egypt, Mesopotamia, Asia Minor and Syria aroused great emotion in Europe, primarily because of the affinity of these finds to the Bible, and the light they shed on this work. Numerous Europeans still regarded the entire Middle East as the land of the Bible. The heart of archaeological study in the first half of the nineteenth century was Bible research. Archaeologists adopted this field as their own — with one of their aims being fund-raising. In the course of time, however, the study of the great civilizations

---

19   S. Searight, *The British in the Middle East*, London 1979, pp. 231–151.
20   R. Irwin, "The Orient and the West from Bonaparte to T.E. Lawrence," *The Orientalists* (note 12, supra), pp. 24–26.

of the past came into its own as an independent field, eclipsing Bible study. It could be seen from the history of the ancient empires, which was meticulously being pieced together, that Palestine and the Bible played only a very minor role in the development of these civilizations. Only rarely were places and concepts related to the Holy Land and the Bible mentioned in the Assyrian, Babylonian and Egyptian documents that were discovered.[21]

Hence it can be concluded that Palestine was viewed by Western travelers not only as a divine, ethereal holy land and the land of the Bible, but also as an ancient historical land, a part of the ancient Middle East.

AN UNKNOWN, DESOLATE AND DEVASTATED LAND

In addition to the three perceptions outlined above, all of which were based on the importance of the area's unique historical past, there can also be found in Western literature, especially that of the nineteenth century, an outlook that stressed the state of the land at the time of the writing: backward, undeveloped, devastated, desolate and sparsely populated — all this in contrast to its glorious past, and to the West-European countries from whence came most of those who visited Palestine and wrote about it.

Following an excursion to the region in the middle of the century, Henry Baker Tristram, among the foremost nineteenth-century researchers of the area, noted that he had been shocked to see the extent to which the Holy Land, the land of the Bible with such singular historical significance, had become devastated and desolate, and unfamiliar to the Western world. No scientific study of Palestine had ever been conducted, and in the wake of his visit he determined to dedicate himself to precisely this sort of study.[22] Scientific research of the area in the nineteenth century, and the findings it produced, are in many respects similar to parallel endeavors in many other unexplored countries. For example, until the beginning of that century there were no maps with accurate measurements of either the area as a whole or of its important cities. The location and altitude of the sites and settlements were completely unknown. Numerous historical sites could not be identified, and the flora and fauna were "terra incognita," an untouched field. Many regions of the Holy Land had not been visited by West Europeans for hundreds of years.[23]

---

21 For details on the founding of the Egyptological Society of London and the beginning of Egyptology, see, for example: P.A. Clayton, *The Rediscovery of Ancient Egypt, Artists and Travellers in the 19th Century*, London 1982.

22 Ben-Arieh (note 10, supra), pp. 161–163; H.B. Tristram, *The Land of Israel, a Journal of Travels in Palestine*, London 1865.

23 Ben-Arieh (note 10, supra), pp. 14–16.

Scientific study of the area got under way in the early part of the nineteenth century. Ulrich Jasper Seetzen and Johann Ludwig Burckhardt, pioneers of the scientific research of the region, originally traveled to the east with the goal of reaching central Africa and discovering the sources of the Nile. Their expeditions and study in Palestine constituted at the outset merely a preparatory stage in this master plan. Burckhardt, in fact, was sent on his mission by the British Association for Promoting the Discovery of Interior Africa. He reached the Levant in the footsteps of his predecessor, Seetzen. Aleppo was his first stop, and from there he proceeded to Syria and Palestine.

It was Burckhardt who revealed to Western Europe the exact location of Petra — a disclosure that attracted to the city a host of researchers and other notable figures. In the course of their excursions, Seetzen and Burckhardt were forced to disguise themselves as Muslims, and even went so far as to accept this faith. Seetzen became known in the east as Sheikh Musa, and Burckhardt as Sheikh Ibrahim. Although they were not acquainted with each other, their *modus operandi* was quite similar. They were both students of a renowned scholar from Göttingen, Professor Johann Friedrich Blumenbach, who had inspired them and trained them in the identical scientific approach. The two men also met an identical end. They died in the east while on excursions, and while preparing for the implementation of their master plan, which was never realized — penetration into interior Africa.[24]

Other examples of pioneering research into the Holy Land were the attempts to investigate the Sea of Galilee, the Jordan River and the Dead Sea. One such project was carried out by a group of Americans headed by Lieutenant Lynch. In the national atlas of the United States Lynch's contingent has been designated as the second American scientific expedition to perform a mission anywhere in the world. This group's work had been preceded by that of individuals who sought to explore the depth and character of the Sea of Galilee, the course of the Jordan River, and the depth and features of the unique sea into which the river flowed — the Dead Sea. Lynch's expedition, conducted in 1848, was beset with countless dangers, including disease and attacks by Bedouin tribesmen. The delegation itself suffered losses, as the group's artist, Lieutenant Dale, was stricken by a fatal disease, and others also fell seriously ill.[25]

The study of the Holy Land also demands a continuous focus on topics related

---

24   Y. Ben-Arieh, "Pioneering Scientific Exploration in the Holy Land at the Beginning of the Nineteenth Century," *Terrae Incognitae, The Annals of the Society for History of Discoveries*, IV (1972), pp. 95–100.

25   Y. Ben-Arieh, "Lynch's Expedition to the Dead Sea (1847/8)," *Prologue, The Journal of the National Archives*, V, Washington, D.C. 1973, pp. 14–21.

to the land itself. It was with an emphasis on this aspect that Edward Robinson, one of the most important researchers of the region in the nineteenth century, lay the foundations for biblical, historical-geographical, and archaeological research of the area. He was the first to discover the location of Massada, a quest that numerous earlier investigators attempted in vain. In Jerusalem he discerned the well-known arch on the western side of the Temple Mount wall, which has ever since been referred to as "Robinson's Arch." He explored the Shiloah tunnel and uncovered remnants of the city's third wall, from the Second Temple period. Robinson was also the researcher who correctly pinpointed the location of Beersheba, Israel's fourth largest city — an identification that had been lost to Western Europe, which since the period of the Crusades had tended to identify the city with Bet-Guvrin.[26]

Dozens of other researchers and scholars arrived in Palestine, and laid the foundations for the scientific study of the land. This research embraced not only the biblical period, and was not merely historical-archaeological, but comprehensive, spanning diverse aspects and fields. It soon became apparent that significant exploration of the area demanded the work of teams rather than individuals, whatever their stature might be. Thus the Palestine Exploration Fund was established in London, and similar societies were founded in America, Germany and Russia. French investigators as well, such as Clermont-Ganneau, played an important role in the activity of these societies.

During the nineteenth century the European powers deepened their involvement in the political aspects of the region. Geographical details about Palestine, as well as the neighboring lands, became important from various perspectives, including a military one. Precise facts, data and descriptions, as opposed to romantic-imaginative versions of the Orient, grew increasingly significant. The Palestine Exploration Fund provided much of the necessary information. After two of its investigators, Charles Wilson and Charles Warren, produced the first precise map of Jerusalem and laid the foundations for archaeological research of the city, especially the area of the Temple Mount, other members of the society drew the first accurate maps of the entire western part of the region, spanning the area from Dan to Beersheba on twenty-six sheets accompanied by three volumes of memoirs. Afterwards the Arava, Sinai, and parts of Transjordan and the Negev were charted.[27]

The desire to gain an accurate picture of the land also found expression in nineteenth-century paintings and photographs. Many of the artists who painted

26   Ben-Arieh (note 10, supra), pp. 68–77.
27   *Ibid.*, pp. 177–215.

the land specialized in topographic portrayals. Others were architects whose profession led them to sketch maps, panoramas and models of sites, cities, and landscapes in the area. A detailed and accurate model of Jerusalem from the early 1870's has recently been discovered — a result of the interest that has constantly been growing with regard to nineteenth-century research on the region. Created by the Austrian Catholic priest Stephan Illes, the model is currently displayed in "David's Tower" in Jerusalem.[28] This model, and the entire phenomenon of sketching "Cosmorama" scenes and creating models of Jerusalem and the sites within it (the Temple Mount, the Church of the Holy Sepulcher, etc.) should be seen as part of a general trend to produce creations of this kind in the nineteenth century. It was then customary to display paintings and models of cities and landscapes as part of exhibitions that, accompanied by explanations, traveled from city to city and from place to place, at times in tents set up for this purpose.

The nineteenth-century scientific discoveries covering diverse aspects of the Holy Land, the scholarship, the detailed investigation of its cities and sites, and the spread of this knowledge throughout Western Europe bore a similarity to processes taking place simultaneously with regard to other remote and unexplored parts of the world. However, the lack of information about the area was particularly striking in light of the familiarity with its past.

Some Western researchers, struck by the sheer lack of empirical facts about the Holy Land, went so far as to compare the local Arab populace to the native inhabitants of the lands that had just recently been discovered by Europeans. The itinerant researcher John MacGregor, who had been captured by Bedouin tribesmen in the Hula region while rowing down the Jordan River, painted his captors as American Indians. The renowned investigator Claude Renier Conder noted that the Muslims who were natives of the area were generally considered to be on a parallel level with the American Indians and the Australian aborigines.[29]

---

28   R. Rubin, "The Search for Stephan Illes," *Eretz Magazine* (Autumn 1985), pp. 45–48; R. Rubin & M. Yair, "The Maps of Stephan Illes — A Cartographer of Jerusalem in the Nineteenth Century," *Cathedra*, 36 (1985), pp. 63–72 (Hebrew).

29   J. de Haas, *The History of Palestine: The Last Two Thousand Years*, London 1938, p. 411; the book quotes page 386 of Conder's work. J. MacGregor, *Rob Roy on the Jordan*, London 1870. A detailed work that stresses the degeneration and desolation of Eretz-Israel and quotes at length from the travel literature of the nineteenth century is S.S. Fridman, *Land of Dust: Palestine at the Turn of the Century*, 1982. On this same topic, also see: D.S. Landes, "Palestine Before the Zionists," *Commentary* (February 1976), pp. 47–56.

An Exotic, Oriental Land

One very different perception of Palestine envisioned an Oriental land, a part of the surrounding Muslim-Arab world. As far back as the eighteenth century Orientalism began to occupy a central niche in European thought and culture.[30] Evidently the West's growing acquaintance with the East during the nineteenth century was largely inspired by several key figures and literary pieces that appeared at the beginning of the century, and that influenced and guided the following generations toward a more scientific approach to the East.[31] Foremost among these works was *A Thousand and One Arabian Nights*, which by the eighteenth century had been translated into French and English. This anthology won nearly unprecedented popularity. Nearly all educated Europeans read these tales in their youth, and remembered them vividly. The stories enriched the Western languages with expressions and images, and imprinted many pictures of the Oriental life-style on Western minds. They served as a marvelous introduction to the lands of the East, and deepened the perception of these areas as totally and thoroughly Oriental and exotic.[32]

In addition to the *Arabian Nights*, many other Arabic stories were translated into the European languages, thereby heightening the influence of the East over the Western cultural world. This influence found expression among a good number of European figures, and it seems as if not a single Western writer of the nineteenth century failed to demonstrate, in one fashion or another, that he was well versed in this translated literature. It also appears that hardly a Western traveler to the East failed to relate or record in some form his impressions of the particular populace, culture and environment he encountered.[33]

Still, each of these travelers viewed the Orient differently. In fact, certain of the perceptions were diametrically opposed; some brimmed with acclaim while others were filled with repulsion.

The items of special interest to the Western visitors included, on the one hand, castles and fortresses of governors, along with the garb worn and customs

---

30   Much has been written lately about the term "Orientalism." What this author means by this term is simply interest in and a study of the Islamic lands of the Middle East in the nineteenth century. The term had different applications. Abbery coined it for researchers of the languages and literature of the Eastern lands, and Said used it to attack Westerners who, he felt, offered incorrect explanations of the East. See A.J. Abbery, *British Orientalists*, London 1930; E.W. Said, *Orientalism*, London 1978.

31   De Meester (note 17, supra); M.P. Conat, *The Oriental Tale in England in the Eighteenth Century*, N.Y. 1908.

32   De Meester (note 17, supra).

33   *Ibid.*

practiced in these places, and on the other hand the simple pastoral atmosphere of the Bedouin tribes. The enthusiasm for the East was so great that some of the travelers viewed it as a place of refuge from European civilization. For these people, the penetration of the West and the enormous influence it exerted on the East seemed a potential disaster and a blemish on the pristine and noble beauty of the Orient.[34] Sharing in this romantic and imaginative approach were political and scholarly circles that, in the framework of the West's aspirations to investigate and penetrate into the area, strove to impart respectability to the topic of the Muslim lands.

The Orient fascinated Western painters as well. They were attracted by more than just the landscapes and the sites of biblical or historical relevance. For them the Orient was a veritable gold mine. As of the seventeenth century, Constantinople and the splendor the Ottoman sultans captured the interest of French, Italian, Flemish and German artists. France was largely responsible for the *turqueries* fashion of the eighteenth century, and mainly French artists painted and described the dress, ceremonies and grandeur of the Ottoman court. At the end of the eighteenth century English artists also visited Constantinople, and paintings of scenes from daily life in Turkey, Egypt, Syria, Palestine and the remainder of the Ottoman Empire became quite fashionable.[35]

During the nineteenth century an additional element was incorporated into paintings of the Orient — the influence of realism, which led to greater exactness, detailing and objectivity in the portrayals of the Eastern populace and landscapes. Simultaneously, a new approach in painting known as ethnography began to gain ground, as a result of a growing interest on the part of the European realist painters in assorted populations and societies, and in the precise, minute differences between them. The realist painters working in the East went so far as to distinguish between the physiognomies of the different Eastern types: Turks, Egyptians, etc. Similarly, they noted the differences in the architecture and the decorative features of various groups — Mamelukes, Ottomans, etc. The paintings of the Orient generated great enthusiam, and were widely distributed and displayed at international and ethnic exhibitions, the London Royal Academy of Art, and Parisian salons.[36]

With the introduction of the camera, photographs of the Orient came to fulfill

---

34 The best-known example in this regard is that of Lady Hester Stanhope, who built her home on Mount Lebanon, and resided there. Much literature about her exists.

35 See note 18, supra, p. 27.

36 C. Bugler, "Innocents Abroad: Nineteenth Century Artists and Travellers in North-Africa and the Near-East," *The Orientalists* (note 12, supra), pp. 27–31.

most of the functions that the paintings had performed. The approach to the East, however, remained unchanged.[37]

Palestine was viewed as a part — but only a very marginal part — of the Middle East, the exotic Orient. Some of the travelers, researchers and painters interested in the East failed to write much, or anything, about the area, even if they visited the Middle East. The land was swallowed up in the vast expanses around it. The major centers of the exotic Orient lay elsewhere: Turkey, Egypt, Baghdad, Damascus, North Africa and Arabia.[38]

A LAND OF NEW BEGINNINGS

The final perception of Palestine that we shall survey from among those appearing in the nineteenth-century travel literature is that of "a land of new beginnings." This view evolved out of three main factors.

First come the actual developments, events and changes that occurred throughout the entire Ottoman Empire in the nineteenth century, but that made the deepest mark in Palestine. These ranged from modernization and constitutional reforms to heightened involvement in the region on the part of the European powers and increased Jewish immigration. At times these developments were not in fact so far-reaching as they appeared to observers, but they generated a sensation of new beginnings in the Holy Land.

Secondly, greater involvement by the Christian Church whetted the longing of the various denominations for the Holy Land, and this in turn precipitated an increase in the number of Christian pilgrims, and accelerated church activity in the area. This awakening was most pronounced among Protestants. The evangelical revival that characterized the first half of the nineteenth century also ushered in various forms of millenarianism, and induced diverse groups of Americans, Germans and Swedes to settle in the region. These groups hoped to witness the Second Coming. This outlook also encouraged the return of the Jewish nation to its land, as millenarians regarded the ingathering of the exiles as the first stage in the process, to be followed by the Jews' acceptance of Jesus as their messiah, and, consequently, Jesus' second revelation on earth.[39] People

---

37 Y. Nir, *The Bible and the Image, The History of Photography in the Holy Land 1833–1899*, Philadelphia 1985; Y. Ben-Arieh, "Nineteenth Century Western Travel Literature on Eretz-Israel: A Historical Source and a Cultural Phenomenon," *Cathedra*, 40 (1986), pp. 159–188 (Hebrew).

38 Regarding three well-known orientalists who did not write about Palestine, see: T.J. Assad, *Three Victorian Travellers, Burton, Blunt, Doughty*, London 1964.

39 R. Kark, "Millenarism and Agricultural Settlement in the Holy Land in the Nineteenth Century," *Journal of Historical Geography*, 9 (1983), pp. 47–62.

like Lord Shaftsbury, Colonel Charles Henry Churchill, George Gawler and his son John, Lawrence Oliphant and many others gave their enthusiastic support to the new beginnings in the Holy Land. These beginnings were to introduce changes in the depressing and humiliating situation of the land under Ottoman rule, and to restore it and the ancient nation residing in it to their former glory.[40]

The third factor portending momentous change was the enormous growth during the nineteenth century of what had for hundreds of years been a very small Jewish community in Palestine. This development was accompanied by ferment in the Jewish world as a whole, heralding Zionist ideology. The first Jewish neighborhoods in Jerusalem built outside the walls of the Old City, the support the community received from Jewish philanthropists such as Moses Montefiore, the Rothschild family and others, the aid tendered by Jewish communities and organizations throughout the world, the pioneering farming communities of the earliest Zionists and their followers — all of these developments reinforced and justified the feeling that a new beginning was in the offing.

CONCLUSION

The six nineteenth-century perceptions of Palestine presented above can all be found in the Western European literature of the time. Two of them pertained exclusively to Palestine, viewing it *a priori* as a divine, holy land, and as the land of the Bible and the biblical sites. Two other perceptions regarded the land as an integral part of the broader expanse in which it was located, whether the ancient Middle East or the Middle East of the nineteenth century. Palestine did not figure prominently in either of these two outlooks. The land occupied only a small and unimportant corner of the ancient Middle East, relative to Egypt, Mesopotamia, and other civilizations in the region. Similarly, in the Middle East of the nineteenth century the area played a minor role vis-à-vis Constantinople, Cairo, Baghdad, Damascus and other centers.

As opposed to the latter two perceptions, the two remaining ones — like the first two — sought the distinctness and uniqueness of the land. True, other Middle East lands were also utterly desolate, and new developments could be discerned in these places, but the perception of Palestine as a land of new beginnings stemmed from the land's unique background and ancient history; the depressing condition of the Holy Land was juxtaposed with its former grandeur.

---

40   B. Tuchman, *Bible and Sword, England and Palestine from the Bronze Age to Balfour*, London 1956, Chs. X–XII.

Similarly, the new beginnings bore special significance because they sprang directly from the land's singular history. Thus these last two perceptions resemble the first two in that they stressed the uniqueness of the area. Most nineteenth-century writers had no desire to detach themselves from the ancient history of the land, and they viewed the fact that Palestine was organically part of a much larger region as a temporary phenomenon. They considered Palestine to be different from the rest of the Ottoman Empire. It was the Holy Land, the land of the Old and the New Testaments. Its decline had been brought on by divine decree. They anticipated a new beginning.

PART II:

BEGINNING OF THE MODERN ERA — INFRASTRUCTURE, ENTREPRENEURSHIP AND SETTLEMENT IN THE NINETEENTH CENTURY

TRANSPORTATION IN NINETEENTH-CENTURY PALESTINE: REINTRODUCTION OF THE WHEEL

RUTH KARK

INTRODUCTION

After hundreds of years of neglect and decay, a marked resurgence and development of transport occurred in Palestine in the second half of the nineteenth and the beginning of the twentieth century. We shall examine this process, while stressing the motivations and initiatives that set it in motion. Our findings shall be compared with research in this field relating to Turkey in the decades preceding World War I, and with the model of transport development in underdeveloped countries in general.

DEVELOPMENT OF THE NETWORK AND MEANS OF TRANSPORT

Roads

In the first half of the nineteenth century, there were almost no roads in Palestine. By then wheeled vehicles, which first appeared in the region in the days of the Hyksos (seventeenth century B.C.E.), had long been forgotten, and the fine network of roads of the Roman and Byzantine periods had fallen into decay.[1] All goods were transported by camel, mule, donkey and horse. Travelers usually moved in caravans along the ancient trails.[2]

The situation before 1860 was effectively summed up by Abraham Moshe Luncz, the nineteenth-century Jewish historian of Eretz-Israel:

> ...there were no paved roads at all in the country and, of course, there were no carriages or carts, and travel between towns was by donkey, mule or on horseback, and the fellaheen also rode camels. The donkey ride from Jaffa to Jerusalem took a whole day and those who came from abroad rode mules on which all their effects were loaded.... To Hebron it took eight

---

1   S. Avitzur, "From Saddle to Wheel," *Adam Va'amalo*, 7 (1968), p. 3 (Hebrew).
2   Y. Karmon, "Communications," D. Amiran et al. (eds.), *Atlas of Israel*, Amsterdam 1970, Section XIV.

hours by donkey, and to Safed and Tiberias one only rode mules (for it was impossible to ride a donkey for such a long distance) three to four days, but to the other towns of the Holy Land no man dared go without being accompanied by an armed escort.[3]

The British Consul in Jerusalem, James Finn, wrote in 1856 that "there were no wheeled carriages or carts of any description in all Palestine from one end to the other."[4] Finn's wife mentions the remarkable feat of Ferdinand de Lesseps, who came to Jerusalem in 1861 by traveling the short desert route from Egypt to El-Arish in a four-wheeled cart hitched to camels — the first time this was done for hundreds of years.[5]

The situation changed toward the end of the 1860's as a result of initiatives by German and American settlers in Jaffa and Haifa who reintroduced carts — mainly for the transport of passengers.[6] The Ottoman administration cooperated by financing and paving the first carriage road in Palestine — the Jaffa–Jerusaelm road which was opened for use at the end of 1868.[7]

The three tables below show the development of various means of transport in Palestine up to World War I. They indicate the gap between planning and implementation, and focus on the motivations and initiatives behind the development of transport, as reflected in the human forces at work, the financing and the execution. The categorization of the motivating factors is based on two different articles — one by Taaffe, Morrill & Gould,[8] and the other by Kolars & Malin[9] — so that a comparison between them is possible.

The tables distinguish between six categories of motivating factors: I. administrative, political and military control (within regions); II. external political control on contacts (over regions); III. agricultural exploitation of the hinterland; IV. exploitation of mineral resources of the hinterland; V.

3   A. M. Luncz, *Palestine Calendar for the Year 1910*, 15 (1909), pp. 17–18 (Hebrew).

4   J. Finn, *Stirring Times*, II, London 1878, p. 142.

5   E.A. Finn, *Reminiscences of Mrs. Finn*, London 1929, pp. 226–227.

6   A. Carmel, *German Settlement in Eretz-Israel at the End of the Ottoman Period*, Jerusalem 1973, pp. 24–29 (Hebrew); letter from L.M. Johnson, the American Acting Consul in Jerusalem, to W.H. Seward, Secretary of State, Washington, September 30, 1868, The National Archives of the United States (hereafter: USNA), T471.

7   *Ibid.* M. Johnson reports that an American citizen started a carriage service on the road and comments about "some of his passengers never having having seen a wheeled vehicle, an artificial road or the ocean."

8   E. J. Taaffe, R. L. Morrill & P. R. Gould, "Transport Expansion in Underdeveloped Countries: A Comparative Analysis," *The Geographical Review*, 53 (1963), pp. 503–529.

9   J. Kolars & H.J. Malin, "Population and Accessibility: An Analysis of Turkish Railroads," *The Geographical Review*, 60 (1970), pp. 229–246.

development of potential markets or economic branches, such as those related to pilgrimages; and VI. religious ideology.

The entrepreneurs, initiators, financiers and executors are divided into five categories: a) the Ottoman administration (mostly via taxation or forced labor); b) foreign powers; c) public philanthropic or religious bodies; d) local individuals or private companies; e) foreign individuals or companies. Wherever possible, the nationality of the agent with the initiative or motivation is also indicated: A — Austrian; B — British; E — Egyptian; F — French; G — German; L — Lebanese; O — Ottoman; and R — Russian.

Two main phases can be identified in the development of the carriage-road network, as Table I demonstrates. During the first phase, from the end of the 1860's to the end of the 1880's, the network of roads grew slowly, mainly connecting the coastal towns with those of the interior. The initiative, taken by both local and foreign philanthropic and religious bodies, stemmed from either foreign political or religious factors.

The second phase was planned in the early 1880's and executed with considerable momentum from the end of that decade. During that time the initiative came mainly from the Ottoman government, which implemented the projects until the end of the period to be discussed. Besides the roads connecting the chief coastal towns to the interior, and extending beyond, to the adjacent regions eastward, roads were also constructed between one interior town and another, as well as between the towns on the coast (see Fig. 1). Economically-motivated initiatives for the development and operation of municipal omnibus services, and plans for motorized interurban transport, were advanced by foreign and local entrepreneurs and commercial companies.[10]

Railroads

Although the first railway in Palestine was constructed only at the end of the nineteenth century, proposals for a railway between Jaffa and Jerusalem had already been mooted at the end of the 1830's.[11] The date of the planning is surprisingly early, considering that the first regular public railway line, between Liverpool and Manchester, had only begun operating in 1830, and that trains started running in the Middle East only in 1855 in Egypt, and in 1860 in Turkey.

Apparently inspired by grand-scale plans of the kind that resulted in the construction of the Suez Canal, proposals were made in the 1860's and 1870's for

10   Letter from Z. D. Levontin, Jaffa, to the Eretz-Israel Research Committee, March 17, 1905, Central Zionist Archives, Jerusalem (hereafter: CZA), L1/4; *Falastin*, October 19, 1911.

11   L. Loewe (ed.), *Diaries of Sir Moses and Lady Montefiore*, I, pp. 58–61, and II, p. 193, London 1890.

Ruth Kark

Table I
The Development of Carriage Roads in Palestine 1868–1914

Source	Link	Planned	Executed	Motivation	Entre-preneurs
1	Jaffa–Jerusalem	1859	1868	II, VI	a
2	Haifa–Acre	1870	1870	V	e
3	Haifa–Nazareth	1874	1875	V, VI	c, d
4	Acre–Nazareth	1874	—		
5	Jerusalem–Nablus	1880	(1881)	I	a
6	Jerusalem–Beth-lehem–Hebron	1880	1889	I	a
7	Jaffa–Nablus	1880	1902	I	a
8	Nazareth–Jenin	1887	1912*	I	a
9	Acre–Safed–Tiberias	1887	1912*	I	a
10	Jerusalem–Jericho	1889	1892	I, VI	a
11	Jericho–Jordan River	1889	1900	I	a
12	Hebron–Gaza	1889	—	I	a
13	Haifa–Jaffa	1898	1900	I	a
14	Nazareth–Tiberias	?	1900	I	a
15	Motor transport				
	Jaffa–Jerusalem	1905	—	V	d, e
	Jerusalem–Nablus	1905	—	V	d, e
	Jerusalem–Hebron	1905	—	V	d, e
16	Nablus–Jenin	1912	—	I	a
17	Jenin–Haifa	?	1912*	?	?
18	Tiberias–Samakh	?	1912*	?	?
19	Omnibus service around cities		1911	V	d

* Date of completion unknown, reported in use in 1912.[20]

1 John Gorham, the American Consul in Jerusalem, to L. Cass, Secretary of State, Washington, January 19, 1859, USNA, T471; Johnson to Seward (see footnote 6).
2 Carmel (see footnote 6).
3 *Ibid.*
4 *Ibid.*
5 *Jewish Chronicle*, September 17, 1880, p. 11; the private diary of Johannes Frutiger, 1881.
6 *Jewish Chronicle, loc. cit.*, and *Die Warte des Tempels*, March 5, 1883, p. 2.
7 *Jewish Chronicle, loc. cit.*; A.M. Luncz, *Palestine Calendar for the Year 1903*, 8 (1902), p. 108 (Hebrew).
8 *Palestine Exploration Fund Quarterly Statement* (hereafter: *PEFQSt*), 19 (1887), p. 30.
9 *Ibid.*
10 *Ibid.*, 21 (1889), pp. 8–9.

Sources (to Table I)

11 *Ibid.*

12 A.M. Luncz, *Jerusalem*, 3 (1889), p. 202 (Hebrew).

13 A.M. Luncz, *Palestine Calendar for the Year 1899*, 4 (1888), p. 157 (Hebrew).

14 A.M. Luncz in Y. Schwartz, *Book of the Country's Crops*, Jerusalem 1900, p. 492 (Hebrew).

15 Levontin (see footnote 10).

16 K. Baedeker (see footnote 21).

17 *Ibid.*

18 *Ibid.*

19 *Falastin*, October 19, 1911 (Arabic).

20 Baedeker (see footnote 21).

a modern deep-water port at Jaffa and for the laying of a ramified rail network in Palestine and the adjacent regions to the east, north and south — and even to remote areas further to the east.[12]

In this same context of grandiose designs should also be viewed the various plans put forth for digging a system of canals from Haifa through the Jezreel Valley to the Jordan Rift Valley, and from the Dead Sea through the Arava to Aqaba, in order to afford direct passage between the Mediterranean and the Red Sea.[13]

As can be seen from Table II, the motivation for these plans originated mainly with the foreign powers (chiefly Britain, France and Austria), which strove to gain control and political hegemony, and to develop new markets. Religious factors also played a role. The entrepreneurs were mostly nationals of these powers — individuals as well as corporations. The American Consul in Jerusalem, Selah Merrill, quoting from a book by T.F. Henley, notes in an official letter the advantages of a typical plan for connecting the seas:

> ...it would be the best and cheapest route for shipping proceeding to or from the East...it would open new and valuable countries and people, to the benefit of commerce and civilization...it would assure a profitable, and permanent investment for capital...it would afford unusual facilities for visiting the Holy Land.[14]

12 C. F. Zimpel, *Neue oestliche topographische Beleuchtung des Heiligen Weltstadt Jerusalem*, Stuttgart 1853; F. Zimpel, *Strassen Verbindung des Mittellandischen mit dem Todten Meer und Damascus, ueber Jerusalem*, Frankfurt 1865.

13 S. Merrill, the American Consul in Jerusalem, to J. Davis, Assistant Secretary of State, Washington, July 31, 1883, USNA, T471.

14 *Ibid.* The quotation is from T. F. Henley, *Memorandum on the Jordan Valley Canal*, London 1882.

Table II:

Development of Railroads, Canals and Trams in Palestine, 1838–1914

#	Source Link	Planned	Executed	Motivation	Entrepreneurs	Cost in francs	Ottoman Concession
1	Jaffa–Jerusalem	1838	—	VIB	c		+
2	Mediterranean––Red Sea Canal	1855	—	IIB	b		
3	Jaffa–Jerusalem	1856	—	IIB+A, V, VI	b, c, e		+
4	Jaffa–Jerusalem	1857	—	IIF, V	b, d		
5	Jaffa–Jerusalem	1862	—	IIB, V, VI	b, c, d		+
6	Jaffa–Jerusalem–Bethlehem–South; Jerusalem–Jordan Valley–Nablus–Nazareth; Jordan Valley–Der'a–Damascus; Jordan Valley–						
7	Hula Valley–Saida	1864	—	II	e		
8	Jaffa–Jerusalem	1872	—	IIF, V	e	18,000,000	+
9	Jaffa–Suez Canal	1879	—	IIF	e		
10	Jaffa–Jerusalem	1880	—	IIB	e		
11	Acre–Haifa–Jezreel Valley–Hauran–Damascus	1882	—	IIIL+B	d, e		
	Mediterranean–Red Sea Canal	1882	—	IIB, III, V	e		+
12	Jaffa–Jerusalem	1888	1892	IIF, V, VI	b, c, d, e	10,000,000	+
	Jaffa–Nablus	1888	—	IIF, V, VI	b, c, d, e		+
	Jaffa–Gaza	1888	—	IIF, V, VI	b, c, d, e		+

Source Link		Planned	Executed	Motivation	Entrepreneurs	Cost in francs	Ottoman Concession
13	Acre–Haifa–Damascus	1890	—	IIB, IV, V	b, e		+
14	Haifa–Der'a	1904	1905	I, III	a		
15	Jaffa–Port Said	1909	—				
16	Tramway: Jaffa–Jerusalem, Jaffa–Petah Tiqwa, Jaffa–Rishon LeTziyyon	1909		V	e		
17	In Jerusalem, Jaffa and Gaza	1910	—				
18	Jaffa–Petah Tiqwa	1912		IF, V	e		
19	Afula–Nablus Nablus–Jenin–Jerusalem	1912	1913	I	a		
	Jerusalem	1912	—	I			
20	Haifa–Acre	1912	1914	I	a		
21	Rayak–Safed–Jericho–Jerusalem–Hebron–Beersheba; Jericho–Kerak	1913	—	IIF	e		
22	Jaffa–Tyre–Saida–Beirut	1914		II	e		

Sources (to Table II)

1   Loewe (see footnote 11).

2   W. Allen, *The Dead Sea, a New Route to India*, I, London 1855, pp. 338–361.

3   Grunwald (see footnote 16).

4   James Finn, the British Consul in Jerusalem, to Lord Clarendon, London, June 6, 1857, PRO, FO 78/1294.

Sources (to Table II)

5   Grunwald (see footnote 16).

6   Zimpel (see footnote 12).

7   N. Verney & G. Dambmann, *Les Puissances Etrangères dans le Levant, en Syrie et en Palestine*, Paris 1900, p. 355; *Jewish Chronicle*, July 25, 1873, p. 282; Baedeker (see footnote 21), p. 132.

8   *Hatzfira*, 6, No. 42 (1879), p. 333 (Hebrew).

9   Grunwald (see footnote 16), p. 261.

10 Oliphant (see footnote 15).

11 Henley (see footnote 14).

12 Dickson to Earl of Roseberry (see footnote 16).

13 *Die Warte des Tempels*, March 22, 1883, pp. 5–6 and December 9, 1883, pp. 3–6; V. Cuinet, *Syrie, Liban et Palestine — Géographie Administrative, Statistique, Descriptive et Raisonnée*, Paris 1896, p. 361.

14 *PEFQSt*, 36 (1904), pp. 188–189; A. M. Luncz, *Palestine Calendar for the Year 1909*, 14 (1908), p. 189 (Hebrew).

15 Ruppin (see footnote 21), pp. 75–78.

16 Smilansky and McGregor (see footnote 17).

17 *Ibid.*

18 *Moria*, 3, No. 12 (1912), pp. 2–3 (Hebrew).

19 Ruppin (see footnote 21).

20 *Ibid.*

21 *Ha'or*, 32, No. 2 (1913), p. 8 (Hebrew).

22 *Moria*, February 5, 1914 (Hebrew).

Merrill adds that in view of his reservations regarding this project, it would be advisable to survey the region south of the Dead Sea, where he believed salt, bitumen, sulfur, liquid petroleum and other mineral resources could be found.

Plans somewhat more modest were put forward in the 1880's and 1890's. These were motivated by economic considerations and aspirations regarding the agricultural exploitation of the Palestine hinterland — in particular the rich cereal grain crops of the Hauran and the Jezreel Valley. Among the entrepreneurs were to be found local businessmen such as Sursock, who wished to build a railroad from Acre and Haifa via the Jezreel Valley to the Hauran region and on to Damascus,[15] and Yosef Navon, who was behind the first actual railway construction in the country and who succeeded in bringing it to completion after a twenty-year delay— albeit with recourse to foreign backing and financing.[16]

15   L. Oliphant, *Haifa or Life in Modern Palestine*, London 1887, p. 60.

16   J. M. Dickson, the British Consul in Jerusalem, to the Earl of Roseberry, November 4, 1892, Public Record Office (hereafter: PRO), FO 4432, No. 2244; K. Grunwald, "Origins of the Jaffa–Jerusalem Railway," M. Friedman, B. Yehoshua & Y. Tubi (eds.), *Chapters in the History of the Jewish Settlement in Jerusalem*, II, Jerusalem 1976, pp. 255–265 (Hebrew). For

Most of the projects mooted in the first and second stages entailed the laying down of penetration lines from the coast to the interior of the country, with no regard to the longitudinal connections along the coast or the central mountain ridge. The development of railroads in the country gained substantial momentum in the early years of the twentieth century with the completion of the Hejaz railway in Transjordan in 1901–1904. Most of the initiatives during this period came from the Ottoman government, which was motivated by administrative, political, military and economic considerations. However, the Porte frequently required assistance and financing from foreign business corporations and firms. Such was the case with the completion of the Dera'a-to-Haifa line in 1905 (partly to counterbalance the port of Beirut and French influence in Lebanon), the construction of the Haifa–Acre line, and the completion of the Afula–Nablus line in 1914 as part of the network connecting Jerusalem and Jaffa to the Hejaz railway, to Haifa, and to the rail network in Transjordan and Syria.

During these years, proposals were also made by foreign companies for the construction of a railway along the coast between Jaffa and Beirut, and a line in the interior between Rayak and Safed–Jericho, with one branch line to Jerusalem–Hebron and Beersheba, and another to Kerak. It is noteworthy that, as the table makes apparent, the Ottoman administration showed interest in developing railroads in Palestine from the 1850's, granting concessions on the basis of plans submitted by both local and foreign companies.

The geographic development pattern of the rail network thus conformed to that of the carriage roads, with penetration lines from the coast to the interior in the first stage, and eventual connections on north–south axes along the coast or the central mountain ridge.

During the first decade of the twentieth century, plans were proposed (apparently following the example of Damascus, Beirut and Tripoli) for developing electric tramway lines between Jaffa and Jerusalem, between Jaffa and the Jewish colonies of Petah Tiqwa and Rishon leTziyyon, as well as within Jaffa, Jerusalem and Gaza (between the town and the port). For some of these projects, tenders were issued by the municipalities, and foreign and local firms showed interest in them. The outbreak of World War I postponed these schemes indefinitely.[17]

details on Navon, see J. Glass's article in this volume; for more on the Sursock family, see: L.T. Fawaz, *Merchants and Migrants in Nineteenth-Century Beirut*, Cambridge, Mass. 1983, pp. 91–94.

17 Letters from Eretz-Israel, May 2, 1910, Jaffa-Tel Aviv Archives, David Smilansky Archive; Peter James McGregor, the British Consul in Jerusalem, to Gerald Augustus Lowther, the British Ambassador in Constantinople, March 31, 1911, Israel State Archives (hereafter: ISA), 123–1/11.

MODERN TRANSPORT IN PALESTINE AND SYRIA

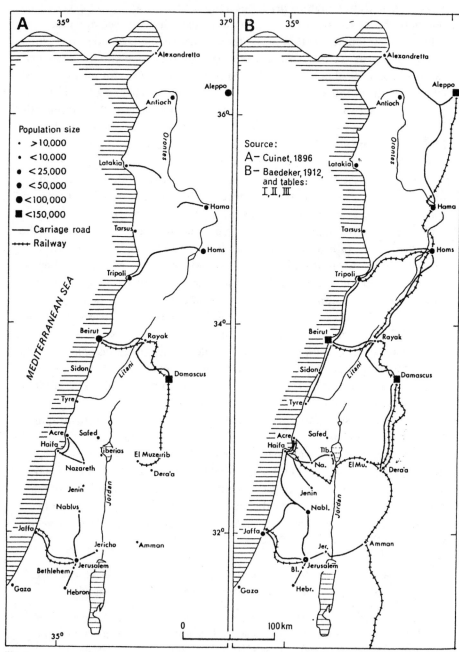

Fig. 1

Ports

At the beginning of the nineteenth century, the ports of Palestine were small in area, as well as in population and the amount of trade passing through them. In 1825–1826, the total exports via Acre amounted to £15,870, and via Jaffa to £11,295.[18] In those days Gaza was a relatively large town, but the activities of its port were virtually nil. The situation was similar in Haifa, where the population barely exceeded one thousand souls.[19]

Maritime trade was characterized by low-tonnage sailing vessels which could utilize the small, natural anchorages along the Palestine coast. From the 1830's the use of steamships grew, and with the increased safety of voyages and the reduction of traveling time, the ports of the eastern Mediterranean — especially Beirut, Haifa, Acre, Jaffa and Gaza — were included in the main Mediterranean shipping itineraries. This trend was strengthened by the completion of the Suez Canal in 1869.[20]

From the end of the 1850's, a regular service was gradually established by French, Austrian, British, Russian, North German, Italian, Egyptian and other shipping companies. Some of them ran several lines and kept to a more or less dependable schedule, carrying passengers as well as freight.[21]

Up to the 1880's trade in the port towns of Palestine increased considerably, amounting to £905,584 in Acre, £454,616 in Jaffa, and £84,377 in Haifa. In Gaza too there was growth — if we are to judge by the figures for the 1890's.[22] In 1912 there was a marked decline in the foreign trade of Acre, with a shift of business to Haifa — even before the construction of the railway to Dera'a, and of course, thereafter. The amount of trade through Haifa port reached £875,700 in 1912, through Jaffa £2,058,108 (in 1913), and through Gaza £269,350 (also in 1913).[23]

The number of ships calling at Haifa in 1913 was 1,597 (1,111 sailing vessels and 486 steamships), at Jaffa 1,341 (676 sail and 665 steam), at Acre 727 (691 sail and 36 steam), while at Gaza there were only four. According to these figures,

18   G. Douin, "La Mission Du Barron De Boislecomte, l'Égypte et la Syrie en 1833," De l'Institut Français d'Archéologie Orientale du Caire pour la Société Royale de Géographie d'Égypte (MDCCCCXXVII), p. 269.

19   R. Kark, "The Decline and Rise of the Coastal Towns in Palestine, 1800–1914," G. Gilbur (ed.), *Ottoman Palestine 1800–1914: Studies in Economic and Social History* (in press).

20   S. Avitzur, *The Rise and Decline of the Port of Jaffa*, Tel Aviv 1972, pp. 28–30 (Hebrew).

21   W.H. Bartlet, *Jerusalem Revisited*, London 1855, pp. 5–7; K. Baedecker (ed.), *Palestine and Syria, Handbook for Travellers*, Leipzig 1876, pp. xvii–xix; A. Ruppin, *Syria: An Economic Survey*, New York 1918, p. 77; *A Handbook of Syria (including Palestine)*, British Admiralty, Geographical Section of the Naval Intelligence Division, London 1920, p. 294.

22   Kark (note 19, supra), Table III.

23   *Ibid.*

Table III

The Develpment of Ports in Palestine, 1832–1914

Source	Port	Name of Planner	Planned	Executed	Motivation	Entre-preneurs	Cost in Franks	Ottoman Concession	Type
1	Jaffa	Ibrahim Pasha	1832–1834	–	IE, III, V		b		Deep-water
2	jaffa	Lynch	1848	–	V		500 thous.		Deep-water
3	Jaffa	Zimpel	1864	–	IIG, V, VI	b, c, e	20 mil.		Deep-water
4	Jaffa	Forbes	1872	–	IIF, V	e		+	Deep-water
5	Jaffa	Hasan Fahmy	1880	–	I	a	4 mil.		Deep-water
6	Jaffa	Bumex	1882	–	IIA, V	b, e	4.851 mil.		Deep-water
7	Jaffa	Falanga	1893	–	VI				Deep-water
8	Jaffa		1900	–		e			Deep-water
9	Jaffa		1906	–					Deep-water
10	Jaffa	Jaffa Committee	1910	–	I	a	2 mil.		Deep-water
11	Jaffa	Jylio	1912	–	IIF, V	e			Deep-water
12	Jaffa	Porte	1912	–	IO+F, III, V	a, b, e	24 mil.		Deep-water
13	Haifa	Russian		1857	IIR, VI	b	3 thous. (Turk. pds.)		Jetty
14	Haifa	Templers		1872	VG	d			Jetty
15	Haifa	Porte	1901	–	I, III	a			
16	Haifa	Porte	1909	–	III, V	d			
17	Haifa	Porte	1911	–	I, III	a	15–20 mil.		
18	Acre	French	1911	–	IIF	e			
19	Gaza	Porte	1905	1905	I	a			Jetty

Sources

1   S. Avitzur, "First Plans of an Improved Port in Jaffa," *Ha'aretz Museum Yearbook.* 7 (1965), pp. 23–32 (Hebre..).

2   W.F. Lynch, *Narrative of the U.S. Expedition to the River Jordan and the Dead Sea*, Philadelphia 1849, p. 440.

Sources (to Table III)

3   Zimpel (see footnote 12); Avitzur (source 1, supra).

4   *Ibid.*

5   *Ibid.*

6   H. Loehnis, *Beiträge zur Kenntnis der Levante*, Leipzig 1882, pp. 44–48.

7   Beit Halevi, *Letters from Eretz-Israel*, 4 (1893), p. 39 (Hebrew).

8   Avitzur (see footnote 20).

9   *Ibid.*

10   *Ha'or*, 1, No. 24 (1910), p. 2 (Hebrew).

11   *Falastin*, September 8, 1912 (Arabic).

12   *Ibid.*, February 29, 1912.

13   M.E. Rogers, *Domestic Life in Palestine*, London 1863, pp. 391–392.

14   Carmel (see footnote 6).

15   Y. Wacshitz, *The Arabs in Eretz-Israel*, Merhavia 1947, p. 148 (Hebrew).

16   *Hazvi*, 25, No. 13 (1909), p. 2 (Hebrew); *Ha'or*, 4 (31), No. 84 (1912), p. 3 (Hebrew).

17   *Ha'or*, 2 (27), No. 325 (1911), p. 3 (Hebrew).

18   A. M. Luncz, *Palestine Calendar for the Year 1906*, 11 (1905), p. 222 (Hebrew).

activities at Jaffa and Haifa increased measurably while Acre and Gaza maintained more limited services — usually during the harvest seasons.[24]

In view of the growing scope of commercial activity and shipping movements to and from Palestine, many plans were advanced for the development of a modern, deep-water port to answer the needs of the expanding network of land transport. Most of these plans concentrated on the Jaffa region, and only toward the end of this period on Haifa.

The initiative for most of the development schemes for ports came from foreign interests who were ready to provide the entrepreneurs and the funds. The Ottoman administration did not ordinarily grant concessions or allow any improvements — notwithstanding the income from customs. For this reason, apparently, none of the plans were ever implemented, the only good modern port on the Syrian–Palestine coast in the first decade of the twentieth century being the one built in Beirut by a French company.[25] Only on the eve of World War I did the Turkish authorities show concrete interest in turning Haifa harbor into a modern, Turkish-Islamic port to counterbalance Beirut, and in constructing a deep-water port at Jaffa.

Since in the meantime almost nothing was done to enhance the infrastructure of the ports, ships were obliged to anchor at some distance from the shore, thus necessitating the use of barges and boats for loading and unloading passengers

---

24   D. Ben-Gurion & I. Ben-Zvi, *Eretz-yisrael in Forgangenheit und Gegenwahrt*, New York 1918, p. 168; Kark (note 19, supra), Table IV.

25   Ruppin (note 21, supra), p. 73.

and freight. In stormy weather the ships had to anchor in open sea. Despite the immense increase in port activity, the totally inadequate infrastructure of Jaffa port bore no relation to the needs, providing only a lighthouse, crowded customs house, small pier and a few storage sheds — so that most of the goods had to be stored in the open. The absurdity of the situation was patent in that the terminal of the railway from Jerusalem to Jaffa lay some distance from the port. In Haifa, too, the port installations consisted only of a small jetty, while the shallow harbor of Acre progressively silted up. A small jetty was built in Gaza at the beginning of the twentieth century, but by 1914 it had already become half ruined.[26]

The conditions of the ports in Palestine were succinctly summed up in the report by E. Weakley, published in 1911.

> *Harbours* — with the exception of the port constructed at Beirut, which is protected by a breakwater, and the natural harbour at Alexandretta, the coast at no point offers any safe shelter to shipping. Vessels have to lie far out at the road-stead of Lattakia, Tripoly, Akka (Acre), Haiffa [*sic*], Jaffa, and Gazza, and the operations of taking and discharging cargo and passengers are generally attended with difficulties and some risk, and become quite impossible during bad weather. The construction of a breakwater and port at Haiffa is to be undertaken by the Hedjaz Railway Administration, but the matter has not yet taken definite shape, as the necessary financial arrangements have still to be made.... Schemes have from time to time been mooted for building a protected port at Jaffa, but in view of the projected harbour at Haiffa and the construction of a line branching off from the Haiffa–Dara'a section of the Hedjaz Railway to Jerusalem...it is likely that all idea of improving the Jaffa road-stead will, if not abandoned, be set aside for the present.[27]

PREVIOUS STUDIES AND MODELS, AND THEIR APPLICABILITY

Taaffe, Morrill and Gould aimed at presenting a general growth model of transport networks in underdeveloped countries, according to comparative research in tropical Africa and other regions of the world. Their point of departure was:

26   R. Kark, *Jaffa — A City in Evolution, 1799–1917*, Jerusalem 1984, pp. 204–211 (Hebrew; English edition in press); *Military Handbook on Palestine (secret)*, British Government, Cairo 1917, pp. 32, 52; *Handbook on Northern Palestine and Southern Syria*, British Government, Cairo 1918, pp. 9, 13, 74.

27   E. Weakley, "Report upon the Conditions and Prospects of British Trade in Syria" (London 1911), C. Issawi (ed.), *The Economic History of the Middle East 1800–1914*, Chicago 1966, p. 277.

> In the economic growth of underdeveloped countries a critical factor has
> been the improvement of internal accessibility through the expansion of a
> transportation network. This expansion is from its beginning at once a
> continuous process of spatial diffusion and an irregular or sporadic process
> influenced by many specific economic, social or political forces.[28]

They distinguished six phases in the development of transport in modern
times,[29] which can be summarized as follows:

Phase A — a scattering of small ports and trading posts along the seacoast;

Phase B — the emergence of penetration lines, reduction of hinterland
transportation for certain ports, market expansion at port and interior center,
and the beginning of port concentration;

Phase C — development of feeder routes for the major ports and interior
centers;

Phase D — the feeder routes give rise to a sort of hinterland piracy that permits
the major port to enlarge its hinterland at the expense of adjacent smaller ports;
small nodes begin to develop along the main lines of penetration;

Phase E — some of the feeder lines begin to interconnect;

Phase F — emergence of high-priority "Main Streets."

According to these researchers, the most important phase in the development
of transport in underdeveloped countries is Phase B, when the first penetration
lines are established. The other phases come into being around these. The
following objectives are suggested for establishing penetration lines:

I — connecting an administrative center on the seacoast with an interior area for
political and military control;

II — reaching areas with mineral deposits;

III — reaching areas with potential for agricultural export.

To what extent does the evolution of transport in Palestine during the latter
part of Ottoman rule conform to this model? At the beginning of the nineteenth
century, Palestine was in the stage corresponding to Phase A in tropical Africa,
with a network of ancient trails used by pack animals and men in the interior,
with several small coastal towns serving the coastal trade of the region, and a
limited hinterland in the interior of the country. From mid-century onwards,
there began a development of penetration lines from the coast inland, with the
addition of hinterlands at the head of these lines, a growth of markets in the
coastal towns and conditions of port concentration. All of these phenomena fit
Phase B of the model.

---

28   Taaffe et al. (note 8, supra), p. 503.
29   *Ibid.*, pp. 503–515.

In the following stage, there occurred a combination of phases C, D, and E —
with certain variations, such as cases of hinterland piracy as between Haifa and
Acre, and the growth of Haifa and Jaffa at the expense of the other ports. The
small towns of the interior which existed before the penetration — Nablus,
Hebron, Ramle, Lydda, Tiberias, Safed — began to connect longitudinally to
the network, although this did not necessarily contribute to their development.

Further development of these stages, and of the last stage (F) took place after
the close of the Ottoman period (see Fig. 2).

Research on the development of railways in Turkey, conducted by Kolars and
Malin, confirmed the conclusions of Taaffe et al. regarding the three primary
motivating factors — especially the first two — behind the growth of the Turkish
railways. However, these two researchers emphasized that since one was not
dealing with a closed system, an additional important motivation, stemming
from exogenous political origins, should be considered.[30] This additional factor
also applied to Palestine, where in the first stages of development the network
apparently fitted the model, but where the motivations were in part different and
more varied. At this point we must consider the gap between planning and
execution, the diversity in the development of the different means of transport,
and the existence of two separate systems operating at different levels — the
Ottoman Empire and the Western powers.

The chief motivation behind the planning of port development, railways and
navigation canals in Palestine stemmed from political and economic factors,
exogenous to the Ottoman Empire. The network in Palestine was considered
part of a regional and international network connecting it with Transjordan,
Lebanon, Syria and Egypt, and likely to serve as a link between Europe and
Asia. Mineral exploitation was not a major motivation, since it was not
considered important enough at the time. In actual practice, two railways into
the hinterland were constructed, and most of the plans were never carried out.

The construction of carriage-roads, and also of railways, was more the result
of various administrative, political and military motivations of the Ottoman
government in its efforts to enforce law and order and to establish effective
control — although at times external pressures and considerations of prestige
played a role as well.[31] An additional rationale was the desire to develop certain

30   Kolars & Malin (note 9, supra), p. 239.
31   An example is the intensive development of roads by the government in preparation for the
      visit of the German Kaiser, Wilhelm II. See: C. Schick, "Preparations Made by the Turkish
      Authorities for the Visit of the German Emperor and Empress to the Holy Land in the Autumn
      of 1898," *PEFQSt*, 31 (1899), pp. 116–118.

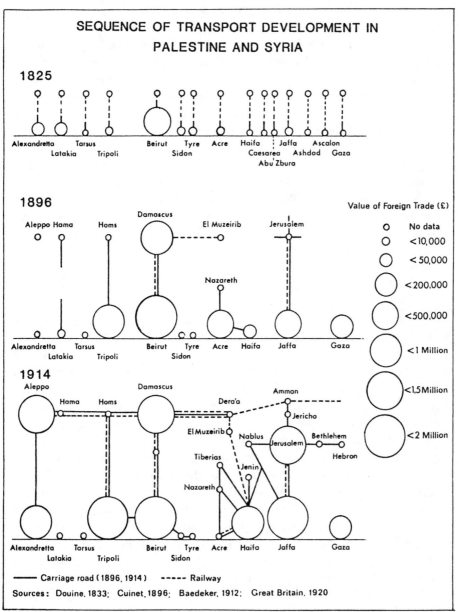

Fig. 2

economic branches and markets (such as those related to pilgrimages), and to gain access to regions of high agricultural potential, such as the Hauran.

The discrepancy between planning and execution resulted from a deliberate policy on the part of the Ottoman government to restrain the development of the ports. The regime feared that modernized harbors would enhance the influence of the European powers, and therefore it retained the policy of the Mameluke rulers of the late Middle Ages, who had purposefully checked the growth of the coastal towns. As an alternative, the Porte made efforts to develop latitudinal and longitudinal carriage-roads, which, being internal, presented less of a threat. This gave rise to an absurd situation whereby even after a network of carriage-roads and railways from the coast into the interior had been constructed, there was conscious neglect and delay in the development of ports by the government. The main gateway to the country, which emerged on the coast despite this policy, was Jaffa — until the Turkish government decided to develop Haifa at the close of its rule over the area.

There are discrepancies between the findings of the present survey and previously published research on the development of transport in Palestine in this period. Perhaps this is because transportation in the nineteenth century was not always studied ontogenetically, and the conclusions were based solely on the situation as of 1918. This research method was susceptible to distortions because it overlooked the fact that during World War I there had been a great flurry of road and railway construction. Had the research been conducted on the period ending four years earlier, it would have determined the weight of military considerations, relative to economic ones, to be much smaller. Hence it is difficult to accept fully the position of Karmon that the roads and railways of the country developed not out of local, economic needs, but out of military considerations and the desire to cater to the Christian pilgrimage industry.[32]

Reichman, who has carried out studies on the Mandate period, stated that the growth sequence suggested by Taaffe et al. did not apply to Palestine because of historical reasons.[33] Detailed reconstruction of the growth sequence at the end of the Ottoman period shows that the evolution of a modern transport network closely followed the model — excepting only the motivations and the fact that Palestine did not constitute a closed system, which increased the importance of contacts with the neighboring countries.

Perhaps the development of modern transport in Palestine, at least in its

32   Karmon (note 2, supra); see also: C. Issawi, *An Economic History of the Middle East and North Africa*, U.S.A. 1982, pp. 44–61.

33   S. Reichman, "The Evolution of Transportation in Palestine, 1920–1947," *Jerusalem Studies in Geography*, 2 (1971), pp. 87–90.

initial phases, should be viewed in the context of the Levant as a whole. As demonstrated in Fig. 2, there is a marked similarity between the process in Palestine and that in Lebanon and Syria, which also fits the initial phases of the model.

CONCLUSION

We have seen that during the nineteenth century modern technologies were introduced (or reintroduced) into Palestine — including steamships, animal-drawn wheeled vehicles and trains. In the years immediately preceding World War I, a few motorcars had also made their appearance, and plans were afoot to develop motor and electrically powered transport. The network of roads and railways was extended, and the level of service improved. This entailed sizable financial investments which, however, cannot be estimated with any precision. Charles Issawi has already indicated that of the capital investments in Syria and Palestine at the end of the Ottoman period, the greatest share went into transport.[34]

These developments resulted in shortened travel time. For example, the trip between Jaffa and Jerusalem was reduced from a whole day at the beginning of the nineteenth century to seven hours by carriage, and further shortened to three-and-a-half hours by train. Moreover, the journey was made in greater comfort and for cheaper fares.[35] The reduction in fares stemmed from the competition between horse-drawn carriages and the railway over parallel routes, and between both the railway and carriages on the one hand and the camel on the other, for the latter had the advantage of direct access to private homes, and from the port to the shop. The camel, which could carry loads of up to three hundred kilograms, performed the function of the modern truck, especially in areas not reached by the railway or by the improved roads. The railways and roads proved, after a trial period, to be quite profitable enterprises, and provided employment not only to those directly connected with them but also to many others who offered ancillary and technical services.[36]

---

34 Issawi (note 27, supra) p. 210.
35 According to Baedeker (note 21, supra), the cost in 1876 per passenger of a one-way carriage trip was 10 francs in season and 6 francs off season. According to a 1912 edition of Baedeker's book, the carriage price was 10–15 francs in season as compared with 5.3 francs to 15 francs by train, depending on the class.
36 The Jaffa–Jerusalem Railway operated initially, according to Ruppin (note 21, supra, pp. 75–78), without profit. In 1895 the gross profits reached 51,949 francs (£2,078) and by 1911 — 1,388,755 francs (£55,550). The total freight for 1913 was 47,500 tons and the number of travelers totaled 182,700.

Many students of transport have emphasized the reciprocal influences between the development of transport networks on the one hand and the growth of settlements and the economy on the other hand. It has been argued that the more developed the transport network was, the higher the cultural and material level of the population.[37] Taaffe et al. have pointed to the connection between the development sequence that they had traced and W.W. Rostow's stages of economic development.[38]

In Palestine too, there seems to be a connection between the growth in transport on the one hand and urbanization and economic progress on the other hand. It is thus hard to accept the view that transport in Palestine in Ottoman times lagged drastically behind social and economic change.[39] Ostensibly the development of both proceeded concurrently, with transport leading at times, and at other times social and economic growth outpacing it. The question, however, warrants deeper investigation.

37   S. Reichman, "Trends in the Development of Land Transportation in Eretz-Israel," *Im Eshkakheh* (1968), p. 179 (Hebrew).

38   Taaffe et al. (note 8, supra), p. 505. According to them, Phase A might be evidence of the isolation of Rostow's traditional society; Phase B is a sort of spatial "take off," and Phase C might be a symptom of the internal diffusion of technology.

39   Karmon (note 2, supra).

THE BIOGRAPHY IN HISTORICAL-GEOGRAPHICAL RESEARCH: JOSEPH NAVON BEY — A CASE STUDY

JOSEPH GLASS

INTRODUCTION

A biography in the historical-geographical sense is a wholistic portrayal of the subject with an emphasis on the interplay between him and his surroundings. This homocentric approach to research, derived from what is termed "the History behind the Geography,"[1] regards man as the harbinger of change within his environment, while taking into account the limitations that existed or that man perceived as existing. Man's contributions are evaluated as a series of actions, each one understood in terms of his expectations, which, in their turn, had been based upon the acceptance of a theory. The basic model for this rational explanation for actions consists of two parts: first and foremost, the ascertaining of the intention of the agent with regard to the action performed, and secondly the understanding of the theoretical ideas that had been employed by him in his diagnosis of the situation.[2] Thus a biography, which may be an end in itself, provides raw material for the reconstruction of the rational thought behind action.

The criterion for an individual's membership in a specific group is the similarity of his actions and rational thought process to those that characterize the group by definition. At the same time, this focus on the decision-making unit rather than on the aggregate will eventually lead to a greater understanding and a clearer definition of the group as a whole. As T. Hagerstrand commented, "nothing truly general can be said about aggregate regularities until it is made clear how they remain invariant for organizational differences on the micro-level."[3] Alan Baker states further:

1   Y. Ben-Arieh, "Historical Geography in Israel — Retrospect and Prospect," A.R.H. Baker & M. Billinge (eds.), *Period and Place: Research Methods in Historical Geography*, Cambridge 1982, pp. 3–9.
2   L. Guelke, "An Idealist Alternative in Human Geography," *Annals of the Association of American Geographers*, LXIV, No. 2 (June 1974), pp. 193–197.
3   T. Hagerstrand, *What about People in Regional Science?*, Copenhagen 1969, p. 2; A.R.H.

The possibilities, then, of analysing the decision making process in historic time should not be underestimated. Focusing attention on the decision making unit rather than on aggregate geographical patterns will involve examining more closely than hitherto the records of individual events, such as families, farms, and firms. It will involve looking fresh at the historical sources irrationally used by geographers, as well as investigation of new sources.[4]

In the following pages the development of the local entrepreneur class in the Middle East during the nineteenth century will be described. Then the case study of Joseph Navon Bey (1858–1934) will be discussed, through a brief biographical sketch that calls attention to certain rational thought processes.

THE DEVELOPMENT OF THE LOCAL ENTREPRENEUR CLASS

The nineteenth century saw the slow but steady development of Palestine. This change was precipitated by both external and internal factors, the latter stemming from the improvement of institutional, political and security conditions.[5] Two distinct groups were involved in this process, namely newcomers from abroad and the local entrepreneur class — defined as those who organize and direct business undertakings, while assuming risk for the sake of profit.[6] Through their economic activities they contributed to the introduction of changes in the landscape and the local economy.

Historiography has emphasized the role of the first group, which included foreign consuls, philanthropists, and European and Jewish settlers. The second group, which has been largely neglected, appears to have contributed greatly to the region's development. It consisted mainly of Christians — Greek Orthodox and Armenian — as well as Sephardi Jews.

The origins of the local entrepreneur class in the Middle East can be traced to the turn of the nineteenth century, a time when the economy — based on agriculture for local consumption, and small crafts and trade on regional and

Baker, "Rethinking Historical Geography," A.R.H. Baker (ed.), *Progress in Historical Geography*, London 1972, pp. 24–28.

4 Baker (note 3, supra), p. 26.

5 N. Gross, "Economic Changes in Eretz-Israel at the End of the Ottoman Period," *Cathedra*, 2 (November 1976), p. 124 (Hebrew); A. Schölch, "European Penetration and the Economic Development of Palestine 1856–1882," R. Owen (ed.), *Studies in the Economic and Social History of Palestine in the Nineteenth and Twentieth Centuries*, Oxford 1982, p. 28.

6 J.L. McKechnie (ed.), *Webster's New Twentieth Century Dictionary of the English Language*, I, New York 1969, p. 608.

international levels — was almost stagnant. The Ottoman Empire served as a market for European-manufactured goods as well as a source of raw materials and foodstuffs for industrialized Europe. The Empire also acted as a middleman for trade; merchandise from India and Persia was forwarded via Aleppo, from Africa via Alexandria, and from the Caucasus via Constantinople. A small merchant class existed, but with little liquid capital and little reason to invest in the area.[7]

Europe perceived the Ottoman Empire as an untapped market, ready to be exploited. The number of European commercial agencies established in Middle Eastern ports increased rapidly during the mid-nineteenth century, mainly as a result of the economic treaties of 1838 which protected Europe's economic interests as never before during Ottoman rule. The privileged position of these firms gave them an economic advantage over local merchants and guaranteed them a large share of the profits.[8] The quantity of exports to the Ottoman Empire grew rapidly. England's exports increased almost sixteenfold between 1814 and 1850, while France's nearly tripled between 1816 and 1850. Trade with other countries — Russia, Belgium, Holland, the United States, Italy and Austria — also expanded.[9]

During this period of commercial growth, difficulties arose in dealing with the interior of the land. There developed a group of local intermediaries who served as middlemen between European merchants located in the coastal towns, and the inland areas. They provided the Europeans with services indispensable for the conduct of business. Slowly the local population took on the functions of the foreign merchants, partially replacing them in Constantinople, Izmir, Alexandretta, Beirut, Alexandria and Jaffa. Both the intermediaries and the local merchants came from minority populations: Catholic, Greek Orthodox and Armenian Christians, and Sephardi Jews. They had an advantage over the Muslim population in that they were under the protection of foreign consuls. They also possessed the knowledge of both European and local languages, which facilitated their position as middlemen.[10]

Under the patronage of the foreign consuls, they became eligible for the same judicial, financial and economic privileges as had been granted to the Europeans.

7   C. Issawi, "The Entrepreneur Class," S.N. Fisher (ed.), *Social Forces in the Middle East*, New York 1953, pp. 117–119.

8   O. Okyar, "The Role of the State in the Economic Life of the Nineteenth Century Ottoman Empire," *Asian and African Studies*, 14 (1980), pp. 143–153; L.T. Fawaz, *Merchants and Migrants in Nineteenth Century Beirut*, Cambridge, Mass. 1983, p. 74.

9   E.R.J. Owen, *The Middle East in the World Economy*, London 1981, pp. 72–75.

10   Schölch (note 5, supra), p. 31; Fawaz (note 8, supra), p. 85; Owen (note 9, supra), pp. 72–81.

Many of these local entrepreneurs offered their services, sometimes free-of-charge, to the consuls in order to ensure the protection offered by these officials, as well as the attendant advantages.[11] They took on various roles: as intermediaries between European wholesalers and local retailers, and between European merchants and cultivators of crops; as partners with Europeans in land ownership during the period of restrictions; as lenders of money to cultivators, usually at exorbitant interest rates; and as middlemen for manufacturers.

These activities resulted in the accumulation of capital, as well as the development of close connections with European financial institutions. The prevailing trend was reinvestment in other sectors, which are divisible into five distinct categories: 1) land; 2) industry; 3) natural resources; 4) banking; and 5) public works.

From the mid-nineteenth century the acquisition of land was seen as an investment; prices were rising rapidly and agricultural development promised high profitability. According to Claude R. Conder, the coastal plain around Jaffa was bought up by Jewish, Maronite and Greek Orthodox capitalists.[12] Beirut businessmen — Habib, Butros, Niquala, Sursuq, Tuwaini and Farah — purchased the lands of seventeen villages in Marj Ibn 'Amir (the Jezreel Valley) in 1869.[13]

Industry evolved as another new sphere in which the local entrepreneurs could increase their wealth. In Lebanon the silk industry came to be considered a desirable target for investment. Between 1862 and 1880 the number of silk factories rose from 33 to 100, with no increase in the number of those owned by foreigners.[14]

Local entrepreneurs exploited areas rich in natural resources, such as Anatolia. Banks sprouted up throughout the Empire, some of them small and family-owned, having connections with larger European banks, and others commercial institutions organized through joint stocks with European interests.[15]

Public works projects comprised another focus for investment. According to David Landes, "The real stakes lay in contracts and concessions for the construction of public works and the creation of public services." His comments

---

11   Fawaz (note 8, supra), p. 86; Owen (note 9, supra), pp. 86–88.
12   C.R. Conder, *Heth and Moab, Explorations in Syria in 1881 and 1882*, London 1883, p. 368.
13   Schölch (note 5, supra), pp. 25–26; Owen (note 9, supra), p. 175.
14   Owen (note 9, supra), p. 157.
15   D.S. Landes, *Bankers and Pashas — International Finance and Economic Imperialism in Egypt*, London 1958, pp. 61–63; N. Verney & G. Dambmann, *Les puissances étrangères dans le Levant en Syrie et en Palestine*, Paris 1900, pp. 166–172.

about the public works in Egypt are equally applicable to the entire Ottoman Empire:

> All were designed to exploit the needs of Egypt and the weakness and ignorance of the Egyptian government. All aimed at making the most of a good thing, imposing one-sided conditions and charging exorbitant fees. All were intended to yield exceptional, even fabulous profits, although it must be admitted that results did not always meet expectations, and it goes without saying that none was expected to show a loss.... Those who invested in Egyptian ventures had no intention of venturing their money and where the normal returns were not sufficient there were always ways to convince the Viceroy that he owed it to his credit, to his people and to fair play to save the skin of his guests.[16]

Local entrepreneurs found unlimited areas in which to invest their newly amassed wealth. Starting at the beginning of the nineteenth century as middlemen for foreign merchants, these people developed into a wealthy class engaging in diversified fields of commerce, finance, industry and development. They became a dominant force in the Middle Eastern economy and brought about changes in the landscape of the region.

THE CASE STUDY OF JOSEPH NAVON BEY

Biographical Outline

Joseph Navon Bey can be considered a member of the local entrepreneur class. He was a scion of the prominent Sephardi families Navon and Amzalak. Branches of the Navon family were active in various spheres in Palestine: Jewish communal leadership, local government, and trade and commerce. The Amzalaks were considered among the wealthiest in Jerusalem. They too were involved in local government, trade and commerce, as well as representation of foreign governments.[17]

Joseph Navon was born in Jerusalem in 1858. His family, which originated in Turkey and included rabbis, scholars and businessmen, had strong roots in the city. He studied at a yeshiva in Jerusalem and at the age of thirteen was sent to

---

16   Landes (note 15, supra), p. 98.

17   Y. Ben-Arieh, *A City Reflected in Times — Jerusalem in the Nineteenth Century: The Old City*, Jerusalem 1977, pp. 151, 368 (Hebrew); R. Kark, "Activities of the Jerusalem Municipality in the Ottoman Period," *Cathedra*, 6 (December 1977), pp. 77–79 (Hebrew); Central Zionist Archives, Jerusalem (hereafter: CZA), A152, Joseph Navon Archives, file 9/4.

Son Excellence J. NAVON BEY

Fig. 1

France, where he received a secular education. Upon his return to Palestine in 1874, Navon began his activities in commerce, representing the interests of his father and his uncle, Haim Amzalak. A few years later he purchased the largest trading house in Jerusalem. Navon was also involved in banking, at first as an employee of Johannes Frutiger, the Swiss-German banker, and later as a partner in this same financial institution.[18] (See Fig. 1)

18   CZA, A152/1, A152/6/7, A152/9/14, A152/11/4; Israel State Archives (hereafter: ISA), British Foreign Office, file 371–114585; *Hamagid*, 5 (February 4, 1886), p. 42; *Havatzelet*, 39 (August 19, 1881), pp. 295–296.

Navon engaged in land transactions for personal investment purposes, and in the capacity of representative of individuals and groups, among them the Ottoman Government, the Frutiger Company, and the settlers of the Jewish agricultural colonies of Petah Tiqwa and Rishon leTziyyon.[19]

His activities did not stop with the purchase of these land holdings, for he was also involved in their development. In partnership with Frutiger and Shalom Konstrum, Navon developed lands along Jaffa Road and in Abu Tor, through the construction of the first commercial neighborhoods in Jerusalem: Mahane Yehuda (1887) and Beit Yosef (1887). He also proposed additional schemes, including the erection of a hotel on his holdings near the Jerusalem railway station.[20] (See Figs. 2 and 3)

By 1885, Navon had become involved in public works. He sought to gain the concession for a railway system in Palestine. After three years of negotiations, in 1888 the Sublime Porte in Constantinople granted Navon the exclusive right to construct and operate a railway line from Jaffa to Jerusalem with the option for building extensions to Gaza and Nablus. Unable to find backers among Palestinian and European Jewry, Navon sold his concession in 1890 to a French company, but retained shares in the railroad. The Jerusalem–Jaffa railroad was completed and inaugurated in 1892.[21] (See Fig. 4)

Navon's endeavors in the sphere of public works included attempts to promote the Jaffa area. He proposed two projects, one for the construction of a modern deep-water port for Jaffa, which would be the logical continuation of the railway, and the second for the development and irrigation of lands in the environs of Jaffa through exploitation of water from the Yarkon River. These plans were put forward in 1893–1894, and Navon received an Ottoman concession for building the port. Neither project, however, was ever realized by him.[22]

---

19   CZA, J41, Mikve Yisrael Archives, file 62; CZA, A152/8/2; *Le Renouveau*, 7 (May 6, 1927), p. 2, and 8 (May 13, 1927), p. 1.

20   Jerusalem Municipal Archives, Beit Yosef File; CZA, A152/7/1, A152/7/2, A152/8/2; *Havatzelet*, 34 (July 15, 1887), pp. 256, 264, and 26 (May 2, 1888), p. 193.

21   CZA, A152/6/1; A.Y. Loutfy Bey, *Projet d'une Ligne de Chemin de Fer Reliant L'Égypte à la Syrie, Note sur à la Société Khédivail de Géographie du Caire 20 Mars 1891*, Cairo 1891; S. Merrill, "The Jaffa and Jerusalem Railway," *Scribner's Magazine*, XIII, No. 3 (March 1893), pp. 295–297; J. Thobie, "Les intérêts économiques, financiers et politiques dans la partie Asiatique de l'Empire Ottoman de 1895 à 1914," doctoral dissertation submitted to the University of Paris, Paris 1973, pp. 203–207.

22   S. Avitzur, "The First Project for the Intensive Exploitation of the Yarkon Waters (the Frangiya–Navon Scheme of 1893)," *Museum Ha'aretz Yearbook*, 6 (1964), pp. 80–89 (Hebrew); idem, "Earliest Projects for Improved Harbour Facilities," Museum Ha'aretz

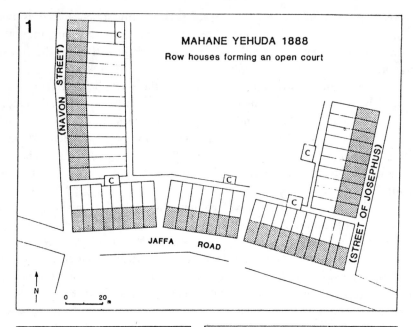

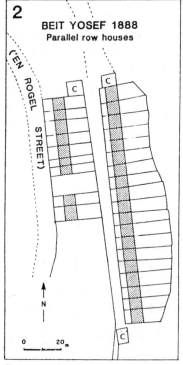

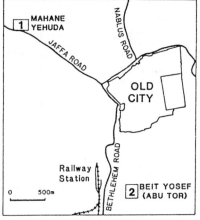

Fig. 2

BASIC DWELLING – MAHANE YEHUDA

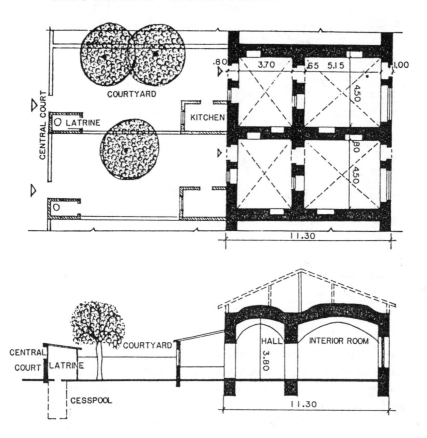

BASIC DWELLING – BEIT YOSEF

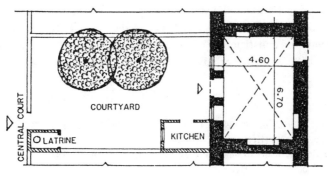

Fig. 3

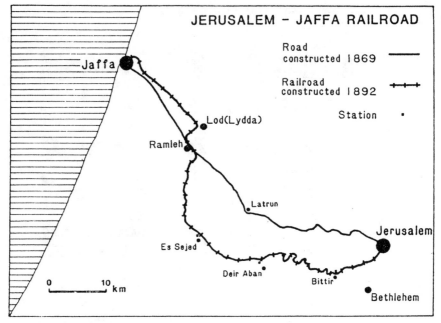

Fig. 4

In 1894 Navon left Palestine due to insolvency. His predicament was not unique, as during this same period two leading local bankers also went bankrupt: Peter Bergheim in 1892 and Frutiger in 1896. These business failures resulted mainly from the prohibition that had been issued by the Ottoman government against the sale of land to Jews. With regard to Navon and Frutiger, financial losses from the investment in the Jerusalem–Jaffa railroad were also a major factor.[23]

Navon resided in London and Paris until his death in 1934. While in Europe, he continued his financial activities, some of which were connected with Palestine. Of note was his scheme, between the years 1927; and 1930, for the development and construction of a garden city to be called Bet Yosef on Mount Canaan near Safed. It never advanced beyond the planning stages.[24]

Bulletin, 7 (1965), pp. 30–39; R. Kark, *Jaffa — A City in Evolution 1799–1917*, Jerusalem 1984, pp. 208–210 (Hebrew); CZA, A152/6/3.

23   ISA, RG67, German Consulate in Jerusalem Archives, files 456 and 429; CZA, A152/12/4 and A152/12/5.

24   CZA, A152/6/6; *Le Renouveau*, 15 (July 17, 1927), pp. 4–5.

Two Examples of Rational Explanation — Commercial Neighborhoods in Jerusalem and the Jaffa–Jerusalem Railroad

Navon's primary motive in developing commercial neighborhoods in Jerusalem was to make a profit, and a sizable one. He witnessed the fast growth of the city's population during the 1880's, which, according to a contemporary estimate, increased by 70%.[25] Thanks to his investment in the local land market he was cognizant of the rapidly rising prices, which increased more than sixfold at the time.[26] He hoped to capitalize on the resale of tracts which he had purchased earlier at low prices. Additional gains could be made by marking up the building costs on houses, with the profits being reinvested in mortgages on these same homes at 6% per annum for a period of ten to thirteen years.[27]

Navon was confident that his analysis of the situation would yield high profits. In the case of Mahane Yehuda he did dispose of all the houses he had planned to sell — fifty in number — within days after they were put on the market.[28] With Beit Yosef he was less successful. The geographical location of this neighborhood — which was not particularly desirable — had not been taken into account, so that the profit margin turned out to be lower. Only half of the houses planned were actually constructed.[29] Nevertheless, on the whole his perception of the situation was very close to the existing reality.

In the case of the Jaffa–Jerusalem railroad, Navon became involved in a large-scale project — a fact that he never seemed to completely comprehend. Plans for the railroad, motivated by a desire for external political control on contacts and the development of potential markets, as well as by religious ideology, had been repeatedly put forward in the years 1856, 1857, 1862, 1864, 1872 and 1889; and Ottoman concessions were granted in 1856, 1862 and 1872. These projects, however, were never implemented.[30]

25   M. Eliav, "The Jewish Community in Jerusalem in the Late Ottoman Period (1815–1914)," E. Shaltiel (ed.), *Jerusalem in the Modern Period*, Jerusalem 1981, p. 162 (Hebrew); Y. Ben-Arieh, *A City Reflected in Its Times*, Part II: *New Jerusalem — the Beginnings*, Jerusalem 1979, pp. 233–236 (Hebrew).

26   Verney (note 15, supra), p. 193.

27   J. Glass, "Commercial Neighbourhoods in Jerusalem at the End of the Ottoman Period," seminar paper submitted to the Geography Department of the Hebrew University, Jerusalem 1985; CZA, A152/7/1, A152/7/2 and A152/8/2; *Havatzelet*, 34 (July 15, 1887), pp. 257, 264.

28   *Havatzelet*, 26 (May 2, 1888), p. 193; CZA, A152/7/1 and A152/7/2; Glass (note 27, supra), pp. 22–24; Ben-Arieh (note 25, supra), pp. 230–232.

29   CZA, A152/8/2; M. Eliav, *The Jews of Palestine in German Policy*, Tel Aviv 1973, p. 123 (Hebrew); Glass (note 27, supra), pp. 7–10.

30   R. Kark, "Transportation in Nineteenth Century Palestine — Reintroduction of the Wheel" (see this volume); idem (note 22, supra), pp. 199–200.

As early as 1884 Navon was already engaged in promoting plans for the construction of his railroad. He spent the following years in Constantinople, meeting with ministers, statesmen and notables, attempting through pressure, connections and even bribery to win this concession. On October 28, 1888 a firman was issued by the Sublime Porte granting Navon a seventy-one year concession for the construction and operation of a railroad from Jaffa to Jerusalem, with the right, during the first four years, to add extensions from a desired point on the main line to Nablus and Gaza respectively.[31] The price that he paid is believed to be 5,000 Turkish liras.[32]

Navon thought that he would be able to raise financial backing for this project, or at least sell the concession at a profit. He solicited investment from Jewry in Europe and Palestine, but the capital needed exceeded the sum estimated in preliminary studies.[33] He sold his concession in 1893 for one million francs and the railroad was taken over by the newly founded Société du Chemin de Fer de Jaffa à Jérusalem et Prolongements.[34]

Navon suffered from the illusion that his extravagant scheme would appear lucrative in the eyes of investors, and therefore be profitable for himself. In fact, however, matters turned out quite to the contrary; he suffered great losses which brought about his own financial demise.

The biography of Navon has added to our knowledge of his actions and our understanding of them, thus facilitating a rational explanation of these activities. In many cases his intentions were confused and misguided by incorrect diagnoses of situations. His theoretical notions of having the ability and means to complete certain projects proved to be unfounded.

Navon played an important role in the development of the landscape of Palestine. He initiated ideas of modernization, but lacked the skill and know-how to carry them through to completion.

This study of Navon is merely the first step toward a greater understanding of the development and conditions of the local entrepreneur class. Their actions and rational thought processes were similar to those of the greater group to which they belonged. Lucien Fèbvre, the French geographer, in his work *La Terre et l'Évolution Humaine*, writes:

---

31 CZA, A152/6/1; Thobie (note 21, supra), p. 204.
32 P. Pick, "The Railway Line between Jaffa and Jerusalem," E. Schiller (ed.), *Zev Vilnay's Jubilee Volume*, Jerusalem 1984, p. 173 (Hebrew).
33 Thobie (note 21, supra), pp. 186–199, 201–204; C. Issawi, *The Economic History of the Middle East, 1800–1914*, Chicago 1966, p. 256; *Hamagid*, 1 (January 4, 1889), pp. 5–6.
34 *Havatzelet*, 9 (December 20, 1889), p. 67; Thobie (note 21, supra), p. 204.

When we are in possession of a few more local monographs — then and only then, by grouping their data by minutely confronting and comparing them, we shall be able to consider the subject as a whole, and take a new and decisive step forward. To proceed otherwise, would be merely to start, armed with two or three rough and simple ideas, on a kind of rapid excursion. It would be in most cases, to pass by everything that is particular, individual, irregular — that is to say, everything, on the whole, that is most interesting.[35]

35   L. Fèbvre, in: A. Gide, *The Counterfeiters*, Harmondsworth 1975, p. 199.

INTRODUCING MODERN AGRICULTURE INTO NINETEENTH-CENTURY PALESTINE: THE GERMAN TEMPLERS

NAFTALI THALMANN

INITIAL ATTEMPTS AT AGRICULTURAL SETTLEMENT

Three attempts at agricultural settlement in Palestine were carried out by Christian groups in the 1850's and 1860's. During the years 1852–1858 a group of American Seventh Day Adventists headed by Clorinda Minor joined a group of European settlers in the village of Artas in the Bethlehem subdistrict, and later moved to Jaffa, where they established the first American colony — "Mount Hope." Between the years 1866–1868 an American Church of the Messiah group led by the evangelist George Adams settled in Jaffa outside of the city walls. They dabbled in agriculture and set up a small settlement, which they abandoned in 1869, selling it to the Tempelgesellschaft — a German Christian organization that over the years founded a total of seven colonies in Palestine known as the "German colonies."

All three of these Christian sects embraced millenarian views, the pursuit of social and religious betterment, and the belief that the Holy Land was destined for the ingathering of God's people and for agricultural settlement.[1] While both of the American groups failed, due to difficult environmental conditions and a lack of social cohesion, the Templer settlements came to possess many unique features, and achieved notable success.

Ben-Artzi has noted the influence of the German Templers on the development of various spheres of life in Palestine.[2] In describing the agricultural enterprise in the German colonies from their founding until the outbreak of World War I, this article shall attempt to illuminate the Templers' role in laying the foundations for modern West-European agriculture in Palestine, where traditional Middle Eastern methods had heretofore prevailed.

---

1   R. Kark, "Millenarism and Agricultural Settlement in the Holy Land in the Nineteenth Century", *Journal of Historical Geography*, 9 (1983), pp. 47–62.

2   Y. Ben-Artzi, "Traditional and Modern Rural Settlement Types in Eretz-Israel in the Modern Era," in this volume.

THE TEMPLERS AND AGRICULTURE

The Tempelgesellschaft, conceived of and founded by Christoph Hoffmann, arose in the wake of the political and social turmoil in Europe in the first half of the nineteenth century. In 1875 Hoffmann, then the head of the German colony in Jaffa, published his book *Occident und Orient*, which served as the group's manifesto. The work delineates the Templers' goals and the road they chose to follow, as a new society living in the spirit of pristine Christianity and functioning outside the framework of the official churches, which they saw as one source of the political and social unrest of the period. The Templers strove to establish communities of their own, but felt that this could not be accomplished in Europe. They also ruled out colonization in America, and on both ideological and practical levels opted for settlement in Palestine. Their declared goal was the "uplifting of the East" ("*Emporhebung des Morgenlandes*") from out of its poverty, oppression and decay, and the molding of a respectable form of human existence, to serve as a model of true Christian life for the nations of Europe.

Agriculture and rural settlement played an important role in this scheme. Hoffmann viewed agriculture as vital for the economic survival of the settlement, claiming that the colony could achieve stability and independence only if the number of farmers far exceeded that of workers engaged in all other occupations. Although quite familiar with the bleak conditions of farming in Palestine stemming from centuries of desolation and neglect, he felt that there was enough fertile land to set up numerous colonies. This, however, would demand cooperation with the local populace, and the adoption of modern techniques, new crops, and animals to provide manure to be used as organic fertilizer. In addition to its economic virtues, agriculture provided the means for transferring European culture to the East, thus enhancing the material well-being of the population in this underdeveloped part of the world. The achievements of the German colonies, Hoffmann thought, would be emulated by the local residents.[3]

Owners of small and medium-sized farms, mainly from the southern and western parts of Germany, and viticulturists from the Neckar and Rems valleys, comprised a sizable portion of the Tempelgesellschaft.[4] The first generation of Templer farmers reaching Palestine brought with them experience and a tradition based on the West-European school of agriculture, built around the type of mixed farming and small family farms prevalent in Württemberg, Baden and Bavaria. This agricultural pattern had evolved from the breaking up of large farms as part of the agrarian reforms of nineteenth-century Germany. Growing

---

3   C. Hoffmann, *Occident und Orient*, Stuttgart 1875.
4   H. Seibt, *Moderne Kolonisation in Palästina*, I, Stuttgart 1933.

industrialization and the expansion of urban centers stimulated the development of mixed farming that incorporated branches such as beef and dairy cattle, vegetables, orchards, and vineyards and industrial crops. By utilizing family manpower and eliminating middleman fees, farmers endeavored to supply their own daily needs and achieve independence.[5]

The Templers were simple people, many of them with limited education. Whatever knowledge they had of agriculture derived mainly from the practical experience they had acquired in their homeland. They did, however, benefit from the advice of experts and from their ties with other countries, especially Germany, both directly and via the German Consulate in Palestine. The Templers were joined during the early years of colonization by settlers of German origin living in North America and in southern Russia — groups that had emigrated from Germany for ideological reasons similar to those that later prompted the Templers to abandon their homeland. These newcomers brought with them experience and modern agricultural techniques. Apparently this knowledge and expertise, along with the prevailing environmental conditions, allowed the settlers to set the stage for the foundation of modern agriculture in Palestine — a process described below.

FIRST STEPS OF AGRICULTURAL SETTLEMENT

The settlement enterprise was launched in 1869 when a group of Templers who had reached Haifa purchased plots of land in the western part of the city, at the foot of Mount Carmel. The Templers started growing assorted vegetables on the plots adjacent to their homes, and at an early stage began to keep domesticated animals. They purchased around 180 dunams of land, refraining from acquiring larger tracts because the Damascus District Governor had promised them — through the mediation of German Consul Theodor Weber — other lands in the vicinity. This promise, however, was never fulfilled, partially because of opposition by the Carmelite monks, their French neighbors. As this proposed solution failed to materialize, and as the prices demanded by the Haifa Arabs were prohibitive, the Templers rented some 2,160 dunams of fertile land streching over the wide plain westward of the colony, where they began to grow crops, some of which were used for fodder. The situation changed in 1874 when the Templers in Haifa were presented with an opportunity to acquire approximately 1,440 dunams from the Arab village of Tira. This transaction led to a lowering of land prices in the area, at which point the settlers bought an additional 180

---

5   M. Hecht, *Die Badische Landwirtschaft am Anfang des 20. Jahrhunderts*, Karlsruhe 1903.

dunams on the Carmel slopes and an olive grove covering 324 dunams to the east, at the foot of the mountain. The viticulturists who had brought grapevines with them from Germany planted vineyards on the mountain's slopes. The German colony in Haifa took on the appearance of a small rural settlement, and its life-style came to resemble that of a typical Swabian village.

In the same year that the German colony was founded in Haifa, another was established in Jaffa.[6] Here the environmental conditions made survival easier than in Haifa. As a port of great significance for foreign trade, and as the point of debarkation for sea travelers to Palestine, Jaffa was thriving economically. Its population came to include a large concentration of Europeans. These circumstances, ideal for the tradesmen and merchants among the settlers, encouraged the development of occupations chiefly urban in nature, but were far less favorable for the farmers. The German colony (the former American colony) was surrounded by citrus and pomegranate groves, and vacant land was unavailable. On the northern periphery of the Jaffa groves, some three kilometers from the colony, there were four farms where land could be worked: the Model Farm, Anglican mission property equipped with machinery and managed by one of the Templers; a farm beneath "Mount Hope" that was leased to a man whose initial tasks were reactivating the machinery and tilling the soil; and two privately-owned farms that had been bought from Arabs — one belonging to Conrad Röhm, which included fields, orange and pomegranate saplings, pumping wells, a water tank for irrigating the groves, and homes; and the other owned by the Templer Georg Günthner, which was in worse shape and required a large capital investment and much time to be rehabilitated. These four farms were all contiguous, and their combined area totaled 720 dunams.

Farmers and winegrowers applied increasing pressure on the Tempelgesellschaft leadership to find and acquire lands. Discussions were held over the proposal to purchase tracts in the area of the Yarkon River, but Hoffmann opposed the idea, arguing that there were not yet enough families or sufficient means for its implementation. On ideological grounds as well he preferred to concentrate the available resources in the Jaffa colony, designed to be a mission station. Finally, however, Hoffmann succumbed to swelling pressure by the farmers, and in 1871 the Tempelgesellschaft purchased 500 dunams near the Yarkon, slated to be a new colony. Planning got under way immediately, and within three years of the first settlement in Haifa there arose a third Templer colony: Sarona (in the area of present-day Tel Aviv) — the first purely agricultural colony in Palestine.

6   A. Carmel, *The Colonization of Germans in Palestine at the End of the Ottoman Period*, Jerusalem 1973, pp. 27–31 (Hebrew). This is the most comprehensive work on the Templer colonies and the political aspects of the Temple Movement in Palestine.

The German colonies in Haifa and Jaffa, designed from the outset as "reception centers," gradually turned into centers of trade, craftsmanship and industry, due to their proximity to the sea.

The early stages of settlement in Sarona were arduous. Survival hinged on the investment of enormous means and the acquisition of more land per farm unit. It became necessary to experiment on ways to increase efficiency and improve quality — and only time would tell if these endeavors were worthwhile.

A central problem confronting the Templer farmers was a lack of natural pastures, and the attempts at growing fodder crops met with only partial success. Since the number of barnyard animals that could be raised was therefore limited, the quantity of manure produced — so crucial for land enrichment — was also restricted, and consequently portions of the fields had to be left fallow. This created the need for larger fields — as was the case with the traditional Arab system of agriculture. Besides these difficulties, the Templers in Sarona also faced severe adjustment problems caused by isolation from the majority population, lack of experience, and climatic conditions demanding a life-style different from the one to which they had been accustomed in their homeland.[7] Despite these handicaps, within a few years Sarona became a prosperous village. Each home was encompassed by a 1.5-dunam garden, divided into sections for flowers, vegetables, and fruit trees — similar to the home gardens the German housewives had known in Europe. The village was surrounded by vineyards and by fields of grain such as wheat and barley (see Fig. 1).

MODERN AGRICULTURE IN THE TEMPLER FARMS

West-European agriculture in general, and that of Germany in particular, had undergone numerous changes in the nineteenth century. Rational planning had begun to take hold, at first in the large farms, and later in small and medium-sized ones. Achievements of the past, based primarily on experience, were now guided and reinforced by scientific principles, making it possible to operate a modern, advanced farm.[8]

As mentioned, the Templer farm in Palestine was from its inception based on intensive, mixed farming of the type the settlers had known in Europe. It rested on three fundamentals:

1.   a modern crop-rotation system with variegated crops;
2.   manuring and fertilization;

7   *Warte des Tempels*, 31 (July 30, 1874), pp. 122–123.
8   T. Goltz, *Geschichte der Deutschen Landwirtschaft*, II, Stuttgart 1903.

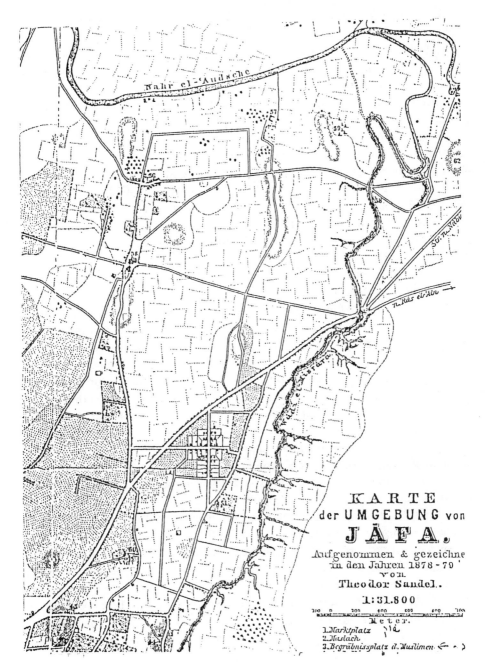

Fig. 1

3. new crops, raising of animals, and improvement of strains for plant proliferation.

These three fundamentals were absent from the traditional Arab farm. In the *musha'* system that was practiced by most of the fellaheen, land was held in common by all the peasants of the village, and was distributed to them by lottery. Private initiative was thus squelched, and the land exploited and impoverished. Seeds were planted on the traditional Arab farms in biannual cycles of winter and summer crops, and much of the land remained fallow. The fellah made no use of fertilizer, and manure was scarce since cattle farming was limited in scope, and barn animals were not raised. It was not customary to plant fodder crops. Seeds of the local "Balladi" varieties were used, as well as local animal stocks — despite their low productivity. The climatic, soil and hydrological conditions in Haifa — and even more so in Sarona — favored the development of various branches of horticulture, as well as cattle and dairy farming, which became central to agriculture in the German colonies.

Cereals and other field crops were grown in all the colonies, initially in wide areas as a balancing component in the crop rotation. The farmers needed straw for upholstery and fodder; grain for cattle feed; and flour for homemade bread. The area of the field crops was gradually reduced upon the expansion of other branches that supplied fresh produce to the steadily growing city population.

Vineyards stretched over broad tracts of land in all the colonies. Even in the German colony in Jerusalem, which had no commercial agriculture, there were vineyards with the finest quality grapevines.[9] The professionalism of the German winegrowers led to agronomical achievements in this branch, and created a reputation for their wine industries (see Fig. 2). Toward the end of the nineteenth century the viticultural branch underwent severe crises; in Haifa it failed agriculturally and elsewhere economic pressures made it necessary to uproot the vineyards and plant citrus groves in their stead, as citrus had replaced the vineyards as the most profitable branch.

The Templers grew *vegetables* both in their watered home gardens and in fields, some of which were irrigated while others received rainwater only. They introduced various species of European plants and grew local vegetables — especially gourds — having brought with them seeds of the finest quality, as well as collecting seeds of the local variety.[10] The home gardens in all the colonies excelled in their assortment of vegetables and spices. The importance of vegetables increased steadily as the demand in cities rose. The Templers played a major role in introducing potatoes as a commercial crop in Palestine.

9   Israel State Archive (hereafter: ISA), 67/456.
10   *Warte des Tempels*, 2 (January 12, 1871), pp. 7–8.

SEAL OF THE GERMAN COLONY-HAIFA

FROM:ISA,90,CONTAINER P/683

Fig. 2

It seems that the raising of *green fodder crops*, to compensate for the lack of grazing land, was their most important agricultural achievement. At first the Templers of Haifa harvested grasses in the Kishon Valley and in Sarona near the Yarkon, where they prepared the hay — which they then had to transport, with great difficulty, to the colony. However, once clover was introduced as a winter crop and corn as a summer crop, and these were supplemented by the cultivation of fodder beet, the Templers could ensure a year-round supply. As mentioned above, *barnyard animals* were the central branch of the Templer farm in all the agricultural colonies, as they provided organic fertilizer, in addition to the beef and dairy products that were marketed to the cities. The Germans reared a local breed of cattle, achieving notable success through selection, improved breeding conditions and cross-breeding with mating bulls they had brought from northern Europe.[11]

The Templers also raised sheep, goats, pigs, assorted fowl, work animals and bees. These usually served household needs, but a small number of farmers used them commercially.

In the 1870's and 1880's the farms in the Haifa and Sarona colonies stabilized, and developed in accordance with the farmers' capabilities and means (see Fig. 3). In the following two decades, however, economic and social crises besetting

11   Report on the economic conditions in Wilhelma, composed by F. Keller, 1912, ISA, 67/1578.

98

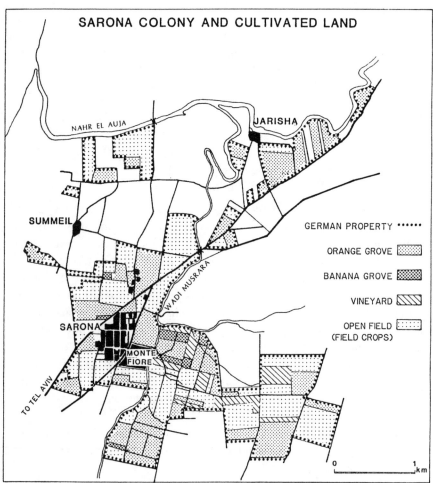

SARONA COLONY AND CULTIVATED LAND

NAHR EL AUJA

JARISHA

SUMMEIL

WADI MUSRARA

SARONA

MONTE FIORE

TO TEL AVIV

GERMAN PROPERTY ••••••

ORANGE GROVE

BANANA GROVE

VINEYARD

OPEN FIELD
(FIELD CROPS)

0   1
                     km

Fig. 3

AFTER   IMBERGER,KARL,DIE DEUTSCHEN LANDWIRTSCHAFTLICHEN
KOLONIEN IN PALÄSTINA, OEHRINGEN,1938

the Tempelgesellschaft, and the inability to enlarge the existing colonies, sparked a search for new resources that would allow for expansion and thereby solve the problem of the young generation. With the support of circles in Germany, three new colonies were founded at the turn of the century, all of them agricultural: Wilhelma (for those coming from the Jerusalem and Sarona colonies), Bethlehem in the Galilee, and Waldheim (for those coming from the German colony in Haifa).

These new settlements had a significant advantage, as they benefited from the experience accumulated over the years in the older colonies. Also, they came into existence during a period of greater inclination toward modern scientific agriculture. Reports in the periodic journals and in documents became more objective and professional. Commercial ties were established with foreign parties via the consulates and the urban shops partially under German ownership. The Templers obtained the latest in equipment and machinery for tilling the soil, irrigating, and turning out finished products — as well as fertilizers and pest-control equipment. An agricultural school was set up in Wilhelma to train and educate young farmers and to keep the veterans abreast of the latest developments (see Fig. 4).[12] Experimentation took place on different types of crops and cattle. In Wilhelma, Jaffa and Sarona a cooperative association was formed in order to institutionalize the grape-farming and wine-making industries, and to regulate the marketing (see Fig. 5). Following suit were the cattle farmers, who established cooperative dairies, and the citrus growers, who founded the marketing firm DOPEG. All of these organizations were registered as cooperatives with the German Consulate, and became official associations enjoying legal rights and government support.

By the eve of World War I four German agricultural colonies, including the Neuhardthof Farm near Tira, had become prosperous, well-organized villages with modern West-European agriculture and diverse craftsmen who were employed in every advanced village. As such, the colonies changed the face of rural Palestine.[13]

The German colonies in Haifa, Jaffa and Jerusalem lost their rural character with time, and turned into city neighborhoods with unique characteristics.

PENETRATION OF MODERN AGRICULTURE INTO PALESTINE

How and to what extent did the agricultural milieu which the Templers had transplanted and refined in Palestine affect the indigenous rural population and

12   Letter from Dr. Brode to the Chancellor of the Reich, February 3, 1914, ISA, 67/1532A.
13   Ben-Artzi (note 2, supra).

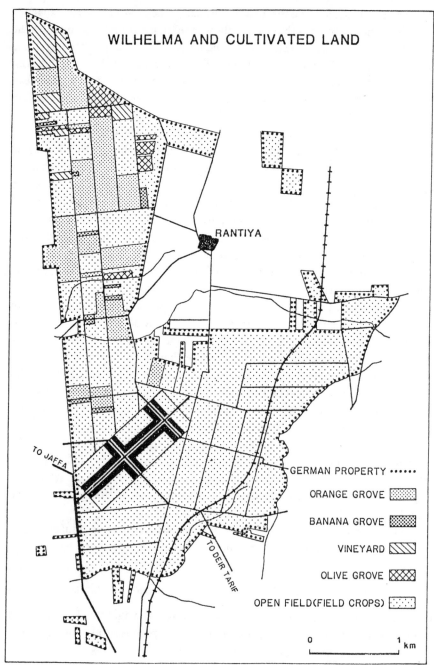

WILHELMA AND CULTIVATED LAND

RANTIYA

TO JAFFA

TO DEIR TARIF

GERMAN PROPERTY ······
ORANGE GROVE
BANANA GROVE
VINEYARD
OLIVE GROVE
OPEN FIELD(FIELD CROPS)

0　　　　　　　1 km

Fig. 4　　　　AFTER IMBERGER,KARL,DIE DEUTSCHEN LANDWIRTSCHAFTLICHEN
KOLONIEN IN PALASTINA,OEHRINGEN,1938

TRADE MARK ON WINE BOTTLES OF THE
UNITED WINEGROWER ASSOCIATION
SARONA – JAFFA – JERUSALEM

Fig. 5   FROM "WARTE DES TEMPELS",No 20,MAY,19,1892

the development of agriculture in the area? The answer should take into account both human and geographical factors.

The colonies were few in number, and there were only around 2,200 settlers on the eve of World War I. The geographical distribution of the settlements was confined to two narrow strips — one in the north: Neuhardthof–Haifa–Waldheim and Galilean Bethlehem; and the other in the south: Jaffa–Sarona–Wilhelma–Jerusalem. These areas contained relatively few permanent Arab agricultural settlements.

From the moment they appeared in Palestine the Templers encountered animosity and at times violence on the part of the indigenous Arab population, stemming from an inveterate xenophobia. The local residents looked upon the picturesque and orderly colonies with a jaundiced eye, regarding the German settlers as intruders who had encroached upon land and property rightfully theirs, thus usurping their source of livelihood. The Arabs felt exploited, and rankled at the strict demands made of the servants and workers on Templer farms, and the stern attitude displayed toward these employees.[14] The Templers, for their part, regarded the local Arab population with misgivings tinged with scorn and disgust at their character and life-style. With the fading of the ideals of

---

14   P. Sauer, *Uns rief das Heilige Land*, Stuttgart 1985, pp. 130–131. The book recounts the history of the Temple Society from its beginnings until the evacuation following World War II.

the founding generation, economic ambitions and religious and national views led to the Templers' isolating themselves in their colonies and resisting the integration of outsiders.[15]

As a result, contact between these two communities was severely limited. Nevertheless, the mutual influence, both direct and indirect, did not vanish. A sizable number of permanent and seasonal workers from the neighboring villages were employed on the Templer farms, and upon returning home they copied many of the practices and customs they had learned from the Germans. The Arabs started to utilize modern vineyard planting techniques, the German system of planting potatoes, and fertilizer. They tilled their soil with diligence and industry — qualities they had acquired from their employers. Productivity levels rose markedly. They borrowed the German methods of raising cattle, and began harnessing horses to wagons. Conversely, the Templers, being experienced farmers, were able to familiarize themselves with local practices and crops — and to take advantage of them. They adapted local fruit species and cattle of the neighboring countries to the conditions on their farms. They learned from the Arabs how to prepare foods from vegetables. The Europeans consulted with the Arabs about grapevines, and bought olives and grapes from them to be used in their farming industries. The Templers even tilled the Arab fields with the advanced machinery that had been brought over from Europe.

Mutual ambivalence marked the relationship between the Templers and the Jews. Some felt the two groups to be rivals and competitors — religiously, socially and economically — but nonetheless sharers of a common fate; both camps had to contend with the vagaries of Ottoman rule and Arab hostility.[16] Still, with regard to achievement in the realm of settlement activities, mutual admiration prevailed, as attested to by numerous chronicles. The Petah Tiqwa settlers had ties with the Sarona community, and later with that of neighboring Wilhelma. The members of the German colony in Haifa were involved in the affairs of Zikhron Ya'aqov. The Templers established connections with the Jewish winegrowers, and joined forces with them in petitioning the administration to ease the wine taxes. There was cooperation regarding other professional aspects of agriculture as well, such as the search for disease-resistant species of grapevine. The Jews were major consumers of agricultural produce from the German colonies, and trade with them greatly contributed to the colonies' prosperity. The Jewish settlers learned from the Templers what it meant to lead the life of a farmer, and from German women occupations such as

15   Letter from J. Dyck to the German Vice-Consul in Jaffa, July 29, 1909, ISA, 67/174I.
16   Carmel (note 6, supra), pp. 198–225.

raising fowl and vegetables in home gardens.[17] Such were the initial contacts in the last decades of the nineteenth century.

In the first decade of the twentieth century, with the establishment of the Jewish "Palestine Bureau," closer links were formed between the Zionists and the Templers. Otto Warburg, Arthur Ruppin and Max Bodenheimer, disciples of the German agricultural school, saw the Templers' colonies as exemplary models for modern agricultural settlement in Palestine. While residing in Ben Shemen, the agronomist Yizhak Elazari-Volcani (Wilkansky), father of Jewish agricultural research and conceiver of modern farming's diversified structure, established strong professional ties with the Templers, especially those at Wilhelma, and learned from them how to manage a family mixed farm and to maintain various modern branches of agriculture under conditions prevailing in Palestine. In 1928 he published an article entitled "Modern Mixed Farming in Palestine" — a plan based on data from the German colonies. This plan formed a basis for modern Zionist agricultural settlement.[18]

CONCLUSION

The appearance of the German Templers in Palestine was one of the most significant phenomena in the process of European penetration into the area in the second half of the nineteenth century. While the European powers were operating mainly in the large cities through their church and state establishments, setting up educational, health and welfare institutions,[19] The Tempelgesellschaft was realizing its settlement ideal by establishing communities and colonies. The Templers were involved in diverse areas of life, and attained important achievements, especially in the realm of agricultural settlement.

Their accomplishments evidently derived from a successful combination of *environmental and human factors*. Their colonies were located in areas where agronomic and climatic conditions favored mixed farming centered around barnyard animals. They had acquired diverse types of land, whose fertility they increased by using fertilizer and advanced tilling methods. Available water sources enabled them to irrigate a sizable portion of their crops, introduce new types of vegetables and fodder crops, expand vineyards and citrus groves, and

17   *Warte des Tempels*, 18 (May 15, 1911), p. 141.

18   Y. Elazari-Volcani, "Modern Mixed Farming in Palestine (The German Farm)," *Hassadeh*, 4 (1928), pp. 119–131, 193–201, 273–280, 326–337 (Hebrew).

19   N. Thalmann, "The Influence of the Germans (except the Templers) upon the Development of Land Settlement in Nineteenth Century Palestine till the First World War," M.A. Thesis, the Hebrew University, Jerusalem 1980 (Hebrew).

increase productivity. Their proximity to the developing cities and convenient access roads opened up markets, especially where the population was mostly of European origin.

The settlers were devout and diligent. Thanks to their professional agricultural knowledge and experience, they understood how to adapt local methods and crops to their farms. They established in their colonies a network of administrative institutions and organized communal life in which each individual carved out his own economic and social niche. The German Consulate in Palestine aided them in legal and administrative matters, represented them before the institutions of the Ottoman authorities, and fostered commercial and political ties for them with the German government. The Templers maintained close ties with their mother country. All of the above factors contributed to their success.

Their deeds paved the way for West-European agriculture in Palestine, which became the basis for the development of modern mixed farming in this area. Their arrival in the nineteenth century marked one of the high points of European activities in Palestine, and an important contribution to the processes of modernization in this period.

THE ANGLICAN MISSIONARY SOCIETIES IN JERUSALEM: ACTIVITIES AND IMPACT

SHAUL SAPIR

INTRODUCTION

Napoleon's invasion of Egypt in 1798 and his excursion into Palestine during the first half of 1799 precipitated major political, religious and scientific developments, and marked the inception of an era of renewed interest in the Middle East on the part of the Western powers. Although barely discernible at first, this trend gained momentum during the nineteenth century, and found concrete political expression during the period of Egyptian rule over Palestine from 1831 to 1840.

The Anglican Mission widened its involvement in the area, and the successful establishment of a permanent base in Jerusalem in 1833, following years of failure, was a harbinger of this development.[1] Five years later, European interests and influence in Palestine, especially in Jerusalem, expanded with the inauguration of the British Consulate in Jerusalem.

Anglican activity in Palestine was part of a worldwide missionary campaign that flourished in the wake of the Napoleonic Wars in Europe and the Orient. Western penetration into the area was further accelerated when England, Austria, Prussia and Russia defeated the Egyptian regime in 1840 and paved the way for the restoration of Ottoman rule.

This article shall examine the various undertakings of the Anglican Mission in Jerusalem, along with its physical and cultural contribution toward the shaping of the urban landscape from the early nineteenth century to the outbreak of World War I in 1914. The three missionary societies and the institutions that they established are categorized in accordance with the functions they fulfilled. Finally, the impact of Anglican construction on the development of Jerusalem

---

1   For a more detailed study, see: S. Sapir, "The Contribution of the Anglican Missionary Societies toward the Development of Jerusalem at the End of the Ottoman Empire," M.A. thesis, the Hebrew University, Jerusalem 1979 (Hebrew).

and its image toward the end of the Ottoman Empire shall be explored in the context of European construction overall.[2]

HISTORICAL BACKGROUND

In the early nineteenth century the Protestant Church was totally unrepresented in Palestine, and its first official representatives arrived only in the 1820's, accompanied by American, English and German missionaries. The first Anglican missionaries were sent under the auspices of the London Society for Promoting Christianity amongst the Jews, known as the London Jews Society (L.J.S.), or the London Society for short. This organization had been founded in London in 1809, with the goal of propagating Christianity among Jews wherever they might live.[3]

In the 1830's the Anglican missionaries from the L.J.S. solidified their position in Palestine, particularly in Jerusalem, with the establishment of their permanent center in 1833. This breakthrough was made possible by a combination of three factors: changes in the political status of Palestine in the wake of its conquest by Muhammad Ali and Ibrahim Pasha, the rulers of Egypt; the opening of the British Consulate in Jerusalem in 1838;[4] and the founding in 1841 of the Joint Bishopric for the Anglican Church of Great Britain and the Lutheran Church of Prussia.[5]

The Joint Bishopric was headed at first by Michael Solomon Alexander, a Jewish proselyte who reached Jerusalem in January 1842.[6] He died in 1845, and the following year Samuel Gobat was appointed as his successor.[7] Under his leadership, the Anglican Mission in Jerusalem underwent major changes, especially in the area of education. Gobat also greatly advanced the evangelical cause by inviting a second Anglican missionary society to operate in the land in 1851 — the Church Missionary Society (C.M.S.). It had been founded in

2   The article in the present volume is primarily based on the final chapter and the conclusions of the above dissertation (note 1). For an elaboration and evaluation of the sources of Anglican activity in Jerusalem, see: S. Sapir, "Historical Sources Relating to the Anglican Missionary Societies' Activities in Jerusalem and Palestine toward the End of Ottoman Rule," *Cathedra*, 19 (April 1981), pp. 155–170 (Hebrew).

3   W.T. Gidney, *Missions to Jews, a Handbook of Reasons, Facts and Figures*, London 1897, p. 76; T.D. Halsted, *Our Missions, Being a History of the Principle Transactions of the L.S.P.C.J., from Its Foundation to the Present Year*, London 1866.

4   A.M. Hyamson, *The British Consulate in Jerusalem in Relation to the Jews of Palestine 1838–1914*, I, London 1939, p. ix.

5   W.H. Hechler, *The Jerusalem Bishopric — Documents with Translations*, London 1883.

6   M.W. Corey, *From Rabbi to Bishop*, London (n.d.).

7   Samuel Gobat, *Bishop of Jerusalem, His Life and Work*, London 1884 (author not listed).

London in 1799, and in Palestine it mainly functioned among Muslims and members of various church denominations.[8]

Upon Gobat's demise in 1879 Joseph Barclay was appointed as the third head of the Joint Bishopric.[9] Barclay's death two years later marked the end of the Joint Bishopric's operations, even though the official disbanding of the institution did not take place until 1886.

A year later, in 1887, George Francis Popham Blyth was designated the first bishop in Jerusalem for the Anglican Church on its own. His efforts were largely devoted to the founding of a new missionary society — the Jerusalem and the East Mission (J.E.M.), whose spiritual and administrative center was in Jerusalem.[10] Blyth also established a network of institutions in the fields of religion, health and education in various locations throughout Palestine, including the impressive St. George's College in Jerusalem (see Fig. 1).[11]

SCOPE AND CHARACTER OF ACTIVITIES

The Anglican Mission in Jerusalem established a wide range of public institutions, including churches, hostels, schools, and philanthropic bodies providing health and welfare services on a voluntary basis to city residents of all faiths. Initially the activity was mainly conducted in rented structures, whereas by the end of the period under study most of the buildings used by the Anglicans were owned by them, both within and beyond the Old City walls. The following is a survey of the various institutions founded by the societies.

Churches
These buildings were erected at approximately twenty-five-year intervals. The first one to be established was Christ Church, belonging to the L.J.S. Built during the 1840's and opened in 1849, this church was one of the first modern structures in Jerusalem. It merited a choice location within the Old City — opposite David's Citadel by the Jaffa Gate, in close proximity to the Jewish Quarter. It holds a special place in history as the first Protestant church constructed throughout the Ottoman Empire (see Plate 1).[12]

8   E. Stock, *The History of the Church Missionary Society, Its Environment, Its Men and Its Work*, II, London 1899.

9   Joseph Barclay, *Third Anglican Bishop of Jerusalem*, London 1883 (author not listed).

10 A.L. Tibawi, *British Interests in Palestine, 1800–1901*, Oxford 1961, pp. 224–254.

11 S. Sapir, "Bishop Blyth and His Jerusalem Legacy: St. George's College," *Cathedra*, 46 (December 1987), pp. 45–64 (Hebrew).

12 S. Sapir, "The First Anglican Church in Jerusalem," E. Schiller (ed.), *Zev Vilnay Book*, II, Jerusalem 1987, pp. 50–57 (Hebrew).

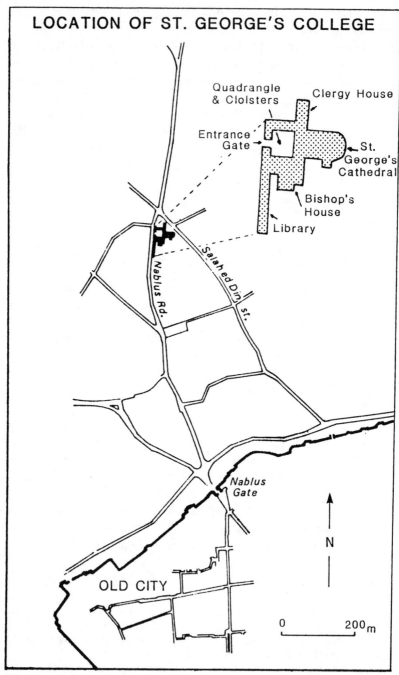

Fig. 1

Around twenty-five years later, in 1874, the second Anglican church, St. Paul's, was built by the C.M.S. It was located outside of the walls, on a street named St. Paul Street (now Shivtei Yisrael),[13] where it remains to this day (see Plate 2).

After roughly another quarter of a century, in 1898, the third Anglican church was completed. Named St. George, it was located on the campus of St. George's College, outside the walls, near the intersection of Nablus Road and Salah ed-Din Street. This church was larger and stylistically more impressive than the others; it became the central church of the Anglican community in Jerusalem, and was also known as the Anglican Cathedral (see Plate 3).[14]

Hostels for Pilgrims

None of the Anglican societies excelled in the construction of hostels. A source from the early twentieth century noted that all of the churches, whether Greek Orthodox, Russian, Abyssinian, Coptic, German, Austrian or French, had lodging facilities to offer foreign guests — with the exception of the Anglican Church.[15] In an effort to rectify this situation, Bishop Blyth established a small hostel called the Clergy House in St. George's College campus, but it contained only a few rooms, which were reserved for scholars or prominent clergymen visiting the city. The lack of full-fledged hostels can probably be explained by the fact that there were few Anglican pilgrims to the Holy Land, relative to the Germans, French and Russians.[16]

Educational Institutions

The establishment of schools by the three Anglican societies was restricted both by limited demand on the part of the population, and by hostility on the part of the Ottoman regime.[17] Nevertheless, the network of Anglican educational institutions expanded, and progress in this area received wide coverage in the journals of the three societies.

Priority was given to education for the young, and separate schools were founded for boys and for girls. For the young adult population, seminars,

---

13   Stock (note 8, supra), III, p. 3; Hechler (note 5, supra), p. 74.

14   Y. Ben-Arieh, *Jerusalem in the 19th Century, The Emergence of the New City*, Jerusalem 1986, pp. 325–326.

15   A. Goodrich-Freer, *Inner Jerusalem*, London 1904, p. 205.

16   Y. Ben-Arieh, *Jerusalem in the 19th Century, The Old City*, Jerusalem 1984, pp. 181–201, 250–264; idem (note 14, supra), pp. 276–348.

17   It is noteworthy that in 1850 the Protestant Church received recognition and an official standing in the Ottoman Empire. See: J. Richter, *A History of Protestant Missions in the Near East*, Edinburgh-London 1910, p. 240.

colleges, and trade schools, including workshops and farming projects, were set up for teenagers and adults. Great stress was placed on dormitories for orphans and for students who lived outside of Jerusalem. These dormitories were usually attached to the educational institutions.[18]

Educational activity got under way at a late stage, relative to health and welfare operations.[19] This is probably because in the field of education it was more difficult to overcome opposition on the part of the local populations, mainly Jewish and Muslim, whose antagonism stemmed largely from the fact that Anglican schooling was offered gratis and was therefore luring. However, once the first schools were opened, their role in the Anglican Mission steadily grew, and they even wound up competing with one another over quality of education and the number of students.

Workshops

All three societies created and cultivated frameworks in which various trades were taught. These programs were especially popular among women, whose wages were set on a piecework basis. The L.J.S. founded a number of frameworks specifically for young Jewish women, known collectively as the Jewesses' Institution, which included the Industrial (or Working) School.[20] It also hired young men to work in the renowned workshop it had set up in the early 1840's, the House of Industry, which was moved to a rented structure near the Tomb of the Kings at the end of the 1880's.[21] Indeed, all three societies located most of their workshops in rented buildings.

Welfare

Among the variegated activities in this realm, the most important was the distribution of clothes, food and water to the needy, along with gift packages sent by mission supporters in Great Britain. Visits were paid to the homes of the ill, especially by members of the J.E.M.[22]

---

18   W.T. Gidney, *Sites and Scenes: A Description of Missions to Jews in Eastern Lands*, II, London 1898, pp. 84–88.

19   The first Girls' School was established by the L.J.S. in 1848. See: *Jewish Intelligence* (hereafter: *JI*) (1888), p. 156. The first Boy's School was founded by Gobat in 1847. See: Gidney (note 18, supra), pp. 84–85.

20   W.T. Gidney, *The History of the London Society for Promoting Christianity Amongst the Jews from 1809 to 1908*, London 1908, pp. 297–298; A. Rhodes, *Jerusalem as It Is*, London 1865, p. 456.

21   *JI* (1887), p. 182; *ibid.* (1888), pp. 143, 145; *ibid.* (1890), pp. 122–124. These journals contain comprehensive information on the subject at hand.

22   *Jerusalem and the East Mission Fund* (hereafter: *JEMF*) — *Annual Reports* (from various

Dormitories called Inquirers' Homes were set up for converts and the homeless. The L.J.S. was especially enterprising in this area. It devoted ceaseless efforts to accommodating Jews reaching Jerusalem during the First Aliya (1882–1904), and even established a special fund to assist these people, called the Refugees' Aid Society.[23]

In truth, every branch of Anglican missionary activity can be considered a form of welfare. Furthermore, in every branch, material resources were used as a means of achieving spiritual goals.

Health

In this field, as in most, it was the L.J.S. that took the initiative. Anglican medical care started in 1824 with the arrival in Jerusalem of the sect's first missionary doctor, Edward George Dalton, under the auspices of the L.J.S.[24] However, it came to an abrupt halt upon Dalton's death the following year. It was renewed only in 1838 when the proselyte Jewish doctor, A. Gerstmann, arrived in the city.[25] In 1842 a hospital with an outpatient clinic and twelve beds (the number later grew to sixteen), which came to be known as the Anglican Mission Hospital or simply the Anglican Hospital, was opened in a rented building.[26] Not until 1897 did this institution move to its present location in a building on Prophets Street. The new, horseshoe-shaped structure contained a modern pharmacy which, along with the clinic, attracted hundreds of people each week (see Fig. 2 and Plate 4).[27] Although initially intended to serve mainly the Jewish population, it accepted needy patients from other faiths as well, in addition to pilgrims and tourists (mostly British).

Documents of the C.M.S. offer no evidence that this group conducted any activities of this sort in Jerusalem, although its members did engage in medical missionary work in other cities in Palestine, and occasionally even established large hospitals — the most spacious of these being the one built in Nablus in 1891, with sixty beds.[28] In Jerusalem, missionary health services were dominated

years); *Bible Lands — Quarterly Paper of the Jerusalem and the East Mission* (hereafter: *BL*) (from various years).

23 *JI* (1886), pp. 77, 187; *ibid.* (1887), p. 76; *Jewish Missionary Intelligence* (hereafter: *JMI*) (1897), p. 137.

24 *JI* (1874), p. 50; Halsted (note 3, supra), p. 145; A.A. Bonar & R.M. Mc'Cheyne, *Narrative of a Mission to the Jews from the Church of Scotland in 1839*, Edinburgh 1842, p. 169.

25 *JI* (1839), pp. 107–108, 143–144; W.H. Bartlett, *Jerusalem Revisited*, London 1855, pp. 59–61.

26 *JI* (1883), p. 156; *ibid.* (1889), p. 113; *JMI* (1897), p. 103; G. Williams, *The Holy City, Historical, Topographical and Antiquarian Notices of Jerusalem*, II, London 1849, p. 23.

27 Sapir (note 1, supra), pp. 55–68.

28 Richter (note 17, supra), p. 252.

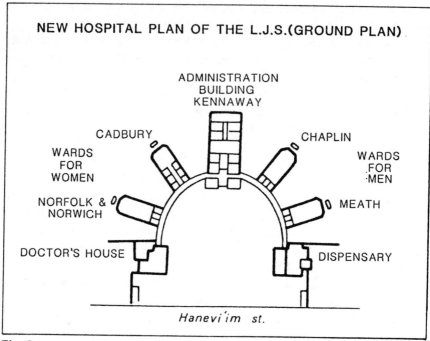

NEW HOSPITAL PLAN OF THE L.J.S.(GROUND PLAN)

ADMINISTRATION
BUILDING
KENNAWAY

CADBURY   CHAPLIN

WARDS   WARDS
FOR   FOR
WOMEN   MEN

NORFOLK &   MEATH
NORWICH

DOCTOR'S HOUSE   DISPENSARY

Hanevi'im st.

Fig. 2

by the L.J.S. and the J.E.M, although the latter society did not commence operations in this sphere until 1903.[29]

The primary importance of these initiatives in the field of health, which had first been spurned by the majority of the population, lay in the fact that they eventually softened opposition to missionary operations in general, thus paving the way for other Anglican endeavors.

Other Activities

The Anglicans operated bookstores that distributed mainly the Old and the New Testament and biblical commentaries, either produced by local printing houses or specially sent over from Great Britain and other centers in Europe. In addition, cards with prayers inscribed on them were handed out by itinerant missionaries in various communities throughout Palestine.[30]

29   *BL*, 20 (April 1904), p. 50; *ibid.*, 22 (October 1904), p. 88; *JEMF* (1904), p. 17.
30   *Proceedings of the Church Missionary Society for Africa and the East, the Annual Report of the Committee (1892/1893)*, p. 67; *The Church Missionary Gleaner* (hereafter: *CMG*) (August 1893), p. 124.

To the best of our knowledge, at least two of the societies owned printing houses in Jerusalem. The one run by the C.M.S. printed everything the society needed for its Jerusalem operations, and provided the material used at its missionary stations throughout the land. British Consulate correspondence indicates that the L.J.S. also had its own printing press.[31] According to documents of the society, this press appears to have been part of a workshop that also included other trades.[32]

SPATIAL ASPECTS

Moving out of the Old City Walls

The first signs of movement in this direction by the inhabitants of Jerusalem — among them the Anglicans — appeared in the 1850's, signaling a trend that was to characterize the city in the modern era. Most of the Anglican institutions had been founded by the L.J.S. when it launched its Jerusalem operations, which were mainly conducted in rented structures in the Old City. In the latter half of the nineteenth century the Anglicans began to abandon the old edifices and transfer their activities to new buildings outside the Old City walls. A number of the institutions, however, such as Christ Church, remained behind.

The area outside the walls had more open spaces and a more salubrious atmosphere than the filthy and densely crowded Old City. This allowed for spacious and well-ventilated construction planned in accordance with ideas and standards imported from abroad. On the other hand, the translocation entailed risks, such as attacks by Bedouins or other hostile elements.

The first Anglican missionary society to move outside the walls was the C.M.S, and the first institution it set up was the Gobat School, built through the initiative of Bishop Gobat (see Plate 5).[33] This society later erected St. Paul's Church opposite its administrative center.

The L.J.S. also began to shift its operations to the new areas, where, by the early 1860's, it already ran a rest home for its members, called the Sanatorium. The structure stood on an elevated area named the Heights of Godfrey, on Prophets Street. Not far from there it set up what was called the Community House, run today by the Finnish Messianic Center.[34] The J.E.M. was spared the

31   British Consulate report from March 15, 1899, Israel State Archives, Jerusalem, 123/1/5.
32   *JI* (1890), pp. 123–124.
33   Stock (note 8, supra), III, pp. 117–121; Richter (note 17, supra), pp. 248–250.
34   Ben-Arieh (note 14, supra), pp. 137, 319.

need to expand beyond the Old City, as its institutions had been founded outside the walls from outset.

The three societies adapted themselves to the pattern of movement from the Old City to the new areas in the second half of the nineteenth century, which had been established by both the local populace and the other Western powers.

Geographical Distribution of the Missionary Centers

The L.J.S. had two distinct centers of activity, each in a different part of the city. The first was the important complex in the Old City, which combined religious, administrative and educational institutions. Founded by the Danish missionary activist John Nicolayson, it was the initial core of Anglican operations in Jerusalem. The complex remained within the confines of the Old City because of its proximity and accessibility to the Jewish Quarter.[35]

The L.J.S.'s second center was the Sanatorium region northwest of the Old City. In this complex were concentrated the health and welfare institutions, and some of the schools, the most important of which was the large Girls' School. Like its predecessor, it adjoined an area of increasing Jewish activity — the new Jewish neighborhoods outside the walls. Its location can hardly be considered coincidental, since Jews comprised the society's primary target population.

Similarly, the C.M.S. had two main complexes. The first, from a chronological standpoint, was the Gobat Boys' School, which included the Diocesan Boys' School with accompanying dormitory, and the Preparandi Class (later the English College), where young ministers were trained to be teachers.[36]

The society's other, and more important center was the area divided by St. Paul's Street into two parts: to the east, St. Paul's Church, and to the west, the administrative headquarters. Although the C.M.S. had other buildings linked to its ramified operations, they were mostly rented, and some of them are today difficult to locate.

In the case of the J.E.M., St. George's College served as a focal point for missionary work not only among residents of the city, but also among Anglican pilgrims and tourists, especially toward the end of Blyth's reign as bishop in Jerusalem. In addition, the complex functioned as the focus of administrative,

---

35 H.C. Frus, *Hans Nicolajsen En Dansk Jodemissionaer fra forriage Aarhundrede*, Copenhagen 1949 (Danish).

36 The Gobat School building exists to the present day and is now called "the American Institute of Holy Land Studies."

religious and educational activities in all of the major settlements in Palestine, as well as for other Middle East lands.[37]

Evidently the distribution of Anglican centers was dictated by well-defined guidelines. This holds true especially for the L.J.S., which sought to remain close to the Jewish population. The considerations of the other two societies are more difficult to pinpoint, but it is reasonable to conjecture that they too sought locations near their target populations. Occasionally the purchases were determined by land availability, even though the locations were strategically undesirable, as was the case with the Gobat School. (See Fig. 3).

ARCHITECTURAL STYLE AND FEATURES

The architectural styles that the societies selected differed in accordance with the functions of the buildings.[38] For example, the three churches erected by the Anglican societies were modeled after buildings in England, while local or eastern elements of any sort were nearly totally absent. One exception was the local building material that was used, which was mainly stone (see Plates 1–3).[39]

The architects employed by the Anglican societies to design the churches showed a clear preference for outstanding British models extant since the Middle Ages, or more modern versions patterned after these same prototypes. Hence the Gothic style, then called neo-Gothic or Victorian, was most prevalent. Occasionally innovations introduced by these societies — such as the use of chiseled stone — served as models to be emulated by other groups engaged in construction.[40]

As for the buildings designed for secular purposes, the architecture was quite different, as exemplified by the hospital erected by the L.J.S. Its architect was A. Beresford Pite, who was appointed president of the Association of Architects in England in the course of his work on the society's hospital. The building was designed in accordance with the Detached Pavillion Plan (see Fig. 2 and Plate

---

37 Sapir (note 1, supra), pp. 85–138.

38 For general aspects of the architecture of European buildings in Jerusalem, see: D. Kroyanker, *Jerusalem Architecture — Periods and Styles*, Jerusalem 1987 (Hebrew); Y. Karmon, "Changes in the Urban Landscape of Jerusalem in the Nineteenth Century," *Cathedra*, 6 (December 1977), pp. 38–73 (Hebrew).

39 Stone construction constitutes a popular common denominator. It is the element that, more than any other, guarantees a blend of old and new, forming a connection between the present and the historical past. It also contributes to stylistic uniformity and maintains structural quality.

40 *BL*, 43 (January 1910), p. 149.

LAYOUT OF THE MAIN INSTITUTIONS & BUILDINGS OF THE THREE
ANGLICAN SOCIETIES IN JERUSALEM : 1833–1914

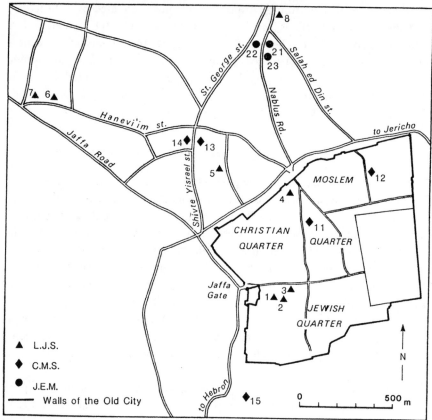

Fig. 3

4),[41] and architecturally it was planned in the "Integrated" or "Eclectic" style in
which features borrowed from similar institutions in Great Britain were
combined with local elements such as arches, vaults, domes, and local stone
exterior. Once the edifice was completed in 1897, it gained recognition as one of
the most handsome hospital buildings constructed outside of Great Britain.
Similarly, in other structures erected for secular endeavors, such as the Gobat
School and the new Girls' School, the local influence was blatant (see Plate 5).

Probably the most impressive architectural contribution by the Anglicans in
Jerusalem was St. George's College, designed by the architect George Jeffrey.

41   *JMI* (1897), p. 105.

Bishop Blyth was interested in having all the buildings in the complex patterned after the Old English style, and as the idea met with Jeffrey's approval, he attempted to implement this plan. In one of his reports he noted that the architecture was identical to that of the buildings at Cambridge University and Oxford University, particularly the New College at Oxford (see Plate 6).[42]

Upon close inspection, it becomes apparent that the imported model was dominant, especially in the case of St. George's College. Many descriptions compare the building and the entire campus to those of the old universities in England.[43] Evidently Blyth succeeded in transferring this architectural heritage to Jerusalem, on a small scale, so that St. George's College might quite accurately be referred to as "Little Oxford."

The phenomenon of stylistic importation was especially prominent in the Anglican religious edifices in Jerusalem, as it was in churches built by the other Western powers throughout the city.[44] As a result of this grafting process, the urban landscape of Jerusalem, initially typically Middle Eastern, was transformed into a harmonious blend of Middle-Eastern and West-European styles.

CONCLUSION

The activity of the three Anglican missionary societies in Jerusalem was the primary expression of British involvement in the city during the nineteenth century. The geographical impact of the Anglican Mission surpassed that of other British institutions, such as the British Consulate, research groups like the Palestine Exploration Fund, and voluntary bodies like the Order of St. John, which constructed the Opthalmic Hospital opposite Mount Zion.[45]

The Anglican construction in Jerusalem did not excel either quantitatively or physically, in comparison with that of the other European powers active at the same time, such as Russia, France and Germany. The financial resources of the Anglican societies were relatively meager, and these were raised through contributions by supporters at Sunday prayer services or special religious events taking place at the Anglican centers in Great Britain. British Government support for the Anglicans' endeavors abroad was practically nil.[46]

---

42 *JEMF* (1897), pp. 18–19.

43 *BL*, 52 (April 1912), p. 49; *ibid.*, 53 (July 1912), p. 65.

44 For a comparative description of various styles of European buildings, see Jeffrey's article in *BL*, 45 (July 1910), pp. 181–183.

45 On the architecture of the building, see: Kroyanker (note 38, *supra*), pp. 411–417.

46 E. Blyth, *When We Lived in Jerusalem*, London 1927, p. 150.

Nevertheless, the Anglican missionary societies made a major impact on the city, especially because they were pioneers in many fields, and their example was followed by other religious activists.[47] For instance, it was due to their influence that the first Protestant church in the entire Middle East was founded in Jerusalem, and that the Joint Protestant Bishopric was established — a development that precipitated the renewal of the patriarchies of the older Churches in the city.

This pioneering spirit is apparent in the construction that took place outside of the Old City walls. One of the first public buildings erected beyond the walls was the Gobat School, built by the Anglicans as early as the mid-1850's.

The Anglicans established the first modern clinic and pharmacy in Jerusalem. They brought over the first male and female doctors, and their physicians initiated house calls. They also set up the first workshop in the city, which trained young people in olive wood craft and in chiseling stone.[48] Thus the Anglicans were groundbreakers in the field of philanthropic public service institutions in Jerusalem, especially in the spheres of education, handicrafts, welfare and health.

These institutions made an important contribution to the modern development of the city, as they set in motion a chain reaction among the various ethnic and religious groups. Anglican missionary operations in Jerusalem reached their peak at the end of the nineteenth and in the early twentieth century, at a time when all three missionary societies were active simultaneously. This period coincided with the peak of development and construction in Jerusalem as a whole, in which other Christian and European circles also vigorously participated. Various nations and religious groups competed for the establishment of philanthropic institutions such as schools and hostels, while Church denominations vied for the privilege of founding churches and monasteries. By the end of the period under study there was hardly a foreign power involved in the area that did not operate a public service institution in one of the fields in which the Anglicans had led the way.[49] Thus Jerusalem became a metropolis of foreign philanthropic activity prior to World War I.

Each group, of course, had its own objectives, but they all contributed to the great leap forward in Jerusalem's development, especially beyond the Old City

---

47   The question of which group was the first must be treated with extreme caution. My determination is based on both early Anglican sources and on various other documents published at a later date.

48   Gidney (note 3, supra), p. 609.

49   *JI* (1886), pp. 83, 85; *CMG* (February 1897), p. 21; J. Neil, *Palestine Re-peopled*, London 1877, p. 21.

walls. The achievements of one party sparked similar or even more intensive endeavors on the part of rival groups. All three Anglican missionary societies left their individual mark on the resurgent city of Jerusalem toward the close of the Ottoman era — a phenomenon that is clearly evidenced in its urban landscape to this very day.

THE BAHAI CENTER IN ISRAEL

IDIT LUZIA

INTRODUCTION*

This article discusses the development of the Bahai Center in Israel. In a curious twist of fate, the members of a religious sect reached Palestine against their will, and precisely the severance from their religious origins, coupled with the conditions prevailing in their new land, precipitated the development of a new, independent faith. The evolvement of this novel religious philosophy and the course staked out by its luminaries brought about significant and permanent geographical changes in the land.

The Bahai faith originates from the Shiite branch of Islam. According to the Shiite faith, Muhammad ascended to heaven, entrusting the divine message to a dynasty of twelve Imams, the last of whom disappeared. Members of the Shaiha sect, which belongs to this branch of Islam, believe that there is a man (Bab = gate) who forms a link between the missing Imam and his disciples.

Mirza Ali Muhammad, a member of this sect, formulated the tenets that eventually resulted in the founding of the Bahai sect. In 1814 he declared himself to be the contemporary Bab. His ideas generated widespread opposition, and in 1850 he was executed. Mirza Ali Muhammad had selected as his successor Mirza Ihye, nicknamed Zabah Izal (dawn of eternity), but the latter was not accepted by many of the Bab's followers. Mirza Ihye was forced to flee from Persia in 1852 in the wake of an attempt by the Babis to assassinate the shah. He escaped to Baghdad, which was under Ottoman rule, finding refuge with his stepbrother Mirza Husain Ali. Responding to pressure by the Persian authorities, the Ottoman government exiled the two men to Constantinople, and from there to Adrianople, which they reached in 1866. There Mirza Husain Ali declared that Mirza Ali Muhammad had heralded the coming of a prophet, and that he himself was this prophet. He dubbed himself Baha'u'llah (splendor of God). This pronouncement triggered a dispute between the stepbrothers, and the Ottoman

*   I wish to thank Ruth Kark for her guidance and Michael Sebbane for his helpful comments.

regime exiled Zabah Izal to Cyprus, where he died in 1912, without any followers.[1]

Baha'u'llah was exiled to Acre in the company of his disciples. There he developed the ideas concerning the Bab to such an extent that they now lay indubitably beyond the framework of Islam. His doctrine included: continuity between the prophets of the various religions; equality of all humans regardless of race or sex; peace and unity among all mankind; aesthetic cultivation of the landscape and the environment in order to create an atmosphere suitable for true unification with God.

Our discussion shall proceed from Baha'u'llah's arrival in Palestine. The process in which the Bahais gained a foothold in the land shall be divided into three chronological periods, coinciding with the reigns of the various spiritual leaders. The reason for this division is that each leadership stressed different themes and guided the sect along different lines, considerably influencing the geographical features in the process.

During the first period the sect was headed by its prophet Baha'u'llah. Upon his death he was succeeded by his son Abbas Effendi, known as Abdul-Baha (the servant of splendor). From this time on the leadership ceased to possess an aura of holiness. Next in the line of succession was Abbas Effendi's grandson Shogi Effendi Rabani (the guard). His death marked the end of one-man leadership. Shogi Effendi gave instructions to establish the Universal Bahai Assembly until the election of the heads of the Universal House of Justice, the central body of the sect worldwide, elected through democratic process.[2]

THE FIRST PERIOD: GAINING A FOOTHOLD

Unlike other religious movements, the Bahais reached Palestine as a result of external coercion.[3] They exploited the religious connotations of the environment in order to entrench themselves and expand the movement. Baha'u'llah arrived in Palestine in August 1868, and was imprisoned in the Acre Citadel along with eighty of his disciples.[4] The same citadel was used as the headquarters for the Turkish army stationed in the area, and in 1870, following an overall redeployment of Turkish troops, the army needed additional room in the citadel and released some of the prisoners, including Baha'u'llah and his followers.

---

1   W. Miller, *Bahai Faith*, California 1978.
2   Y. Friedler, "The Bahai Faith," *The Jerusalem Post*, May 15, 1983.
3   At that time Acre served as a place where prisoners of the Ottoman Empire were exiled.
4   D.S. Ruhe, *Door of Hope*, Oxford 1981.

Nevertheless, they were forbidden to leave the city, and so they moved into Khan el-O'mdan and into homes rented from Muslims in Acre's Crusader Quarter.[5]

It is noteworthy that the Babis conducted business with the Muslims despite the animosity that the latter displayed toward them. Being the owners of nearly all of the property in the city, the Muslims evidently consented to rent homes to the Babis out of purely economic considerations.

It was at this stage that Baha'u'llah composed the book of religious tenets that became the cornerstone of the new faith. During this same period his son, Abbas Effendi, who was the administrative director of the sect, began to form ties with members of the upper class having close connections to the Ottoman administration. In parallel the Babis started to settle outside the city, even though they had yet to receive official permission to do so.[6] In 1875 Abbas Effendi rented from the descendants of Abdullah Pasha, who had been the governor of Acre from 1819 to 1831, three estates east of the city, through which the Ne'eman River flowed.[7] The eastern area was Ridvan Park, designed as a resort for Baha'u'llah and a pilgrimage site for his disciples. This was the first park in Palestine planned by the Babis. It was designed by a gardener brought from Persia especially for this purpose, and patterned after the Persian parks. The other two estates were used for agriculture. The Babis purchased all three in 1881. The western estate — the Paradise Garden — was cultivated by the Babi brothers Jimshad and Hassan Paradise, while the northern one (Ashraf Garden) was acquired by Mullah Abu-Talib, who later bequeathed the land to the Bahai faith.[8]

In 1877 the governor of Acre declared Baha'u'llah's prison term to be over, and the Babi leader was thus free to move at will. Abbas searched for a place of residence for his father in the rural areas adjacent to Acre. In his writings Abbas noted that Baha'u'llah longed for rural life,[9] but apparently there were additional factors favoring a move in this direction. For instance, Baha'u'llah could operate more freely if he were far removed from the eye of the authorities. Abbas Effendi rented the Mazra'ah estate north of Acre from the wealthy Sawfat family,[10] and

5   *Ibid.*, pp. 75–76.
6   H.M. Baluzi, *Bahaullah, The King of Glory*, Oxford 1980.
7   This is according to an interview in July 1984 with Mr. Paradise, a member of the clan that cultivated the land from the start of the settlement.
8   Z. Ilan, *Tourist Sites in Eretz-Israel, Guide to the Northern Region*, Tel Aviv 1983 (Hebrew).
9   J.E. Esselmont, *Bahaullah and the New Era*, N.Y. 1927.
10   They were opposed to the Bahais, but evidently because they did not make use of Mazra'ah, they consented to lease it.

the home on this estate had been built by Abdullah Pasha's father.[11] The Babis did not plan the park around the home even though the leader of the sect resided there, and it seems that it was clear from the outset that the stay at Mazra'ah would be brief, since the place was too small for all the members of the family. The Babis had yet to undertake independent construction. They began to buy land upon moving beyond the city limits. Throughout the history of the Bahais in Palestine, never was the process of land acquisition as rapid and intensive as in the days of Baha'u'llah. The spiritual leader was probably seeking to ensure the status and position of the sect, which was still in its formative stage.

Land was purchased in two areas: 1) the Zebulun Valley and 2) the Jordan Valley and the area east of the Sea of Galilee. Around 550 dunams were acquired at Jidru in the Zebulun Valley, and on a private basis members of the sect purchased another 120 dunams in Junaynih, cultivated them for agriculture and landscaped parks, and later transferred them to the sect. Probably because favorable geographical conditions prevailed and there was no problem of water supply, the cultivation of these tracts was performed from the start by members of the sect rather than by local land tenants.[12] The area selected by the Babis in the Jordan Valley was not contiguous with the Zebulun Valley settlements, and it is probable that because of the small demand for these lands the price was attractively low. The area had been neglected for a protracted period, and its residents suffered attacks by Bedouin tribes lodging in the vicinity. This location offered the additional advantage of being located near the town of Tiberias and not far from the sect's center in Acre, while at the same time lying far enough away from other cities to avoid harassment by the authorities. Four sites were located in this area: Nuqaib, Samara, Umm Juni and Adassiya. Around 13,000 dunams were purchased in Nuqaib, 12,500 in Samara, 5,600 in Umm Juni, and 1,100 in Adassiya (which was settled at a later stage) — a total of some 32,200 dunams. According to sources from this period, the villages were undeveloped, and the lands worked by fallah land tenants, who had resided on the site prior to the arrival of the Babis.[13] (See Figs 1 and 2)

In 1879 Baha'u'llah moved from Mazra'ah to Bahji (Persian for park or

11 "Bahai Holy Places at the World Center," The Universal House of Justice, Haifa (1968); Map of El Mazraa, Acre, sub-dist. surveyed in 1930, 'Survey of Palestine, September 1932, Jewish National Fund Maps Archive (hereafter: JNF Archive), File 54, Map 312, at the Hebrew University Map Library, Jerusalem.

12 Maps 1:15,000, Nahariyya sheet, Survey of Israel; Plan des Villages de Kafratta, Medjdel et Jedro, Maps 1:2000, JNF Archive, File 17, map no. 7094.

13 Central Zionist Archives, Jerusalem, En Gev File, S25/2795; Northern District: sub-dist. Tiberias, Village Nuqaib, JNF Archive, File 19, Map 1178.

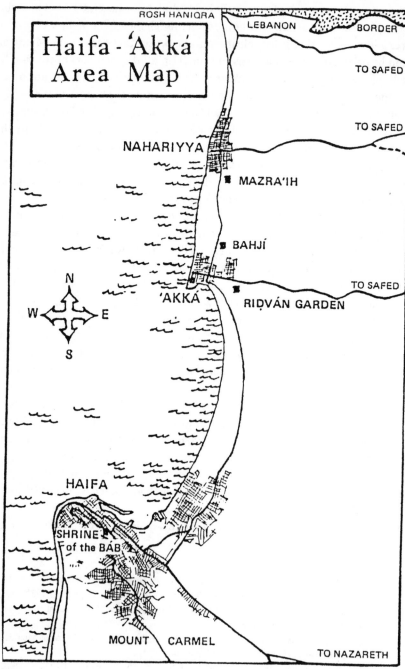

Fig. 1

SITES ON THE JORDAN RIFT
AND NEAR THE SEA OF GALILEE

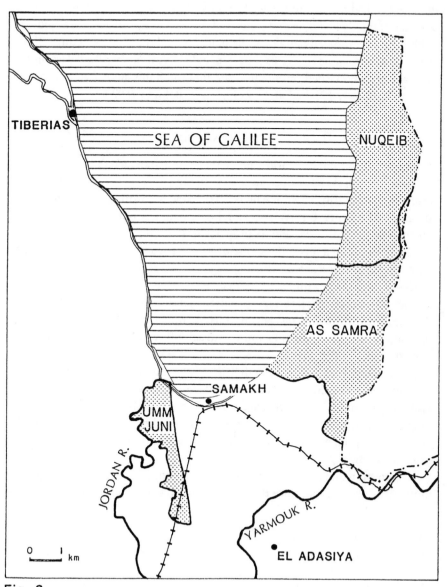

Fig. 2

pleasure), which like Mazra'ah was a rural estate. Bahji had been built by Sulayman Pasha (governor of the Acre District from 1805 to 1819), and had become the summer resort of his successor Abdullah Pasha. It included a large one-storey home encompassed by a number of structures and a garden. In 1840 the home was sold to Udi Khammar, a merchant from Acre who expanded the building and added a storey to it. The renovations ended in 1870 but by 1878 the Khammar family had already abandoned the site because of a cholera epidemic. Abbas Effendi took advantage of the panic, rented the estate and immediately afterwards purchased it. At this time it included five dunams,[14] and descriptions by travelers who visited the site indicate that the Babis cultivated the grounds diligently. Baha'u'llah died and was buried in Bahji in 1892.[15]

LAND PURCHASE ON MOUNT CARMEL

Personnel of the Bahai World Center relate that Baha'u'llah had, in his will, declared his son Abbas as his successor. In fact, a struggle broke out over the leadership, primarily between Abbas Effendi and his brother Muhammad Quli. It ended in victory for Abbas, and his triumph was to have far-reaching repercussions for the sect and its property in Palestine.

Abbas Effendi changed the name of the sect from the Babis to the Bahais (after their prophet Baha'u'llah), and began to adapt the sect's ideas to Western modes of thinking. He forged ties with diverse influential circles outside the sect, thus greatly facilitating its efforts to entrench itself in Palestine. In 1898 the first Bahai pilgrims from the West began to arrive, which greatly helped to propagate the faith in several continents and to attract a flow of financial contributions from disciples in the West.[16]

In that same year Abbas Effendi ordered the remains of the Bab, Mirza Ali Muhammad, to be disinterred and brought from Persia to Palestine. He inquired into the possibility of purchasing a burial site on Mount Carmel, with the intention of turning it into a world center. According to Bahai tradition, this decision had been made by Baha'u'llah himself, and it was he who selected the exact location.

The question that arises is why Haifa was chosen. The selection of Palestine is more easily understood, since Baha'u'llah resided in the land in the latter part of

---

14   A. Kitchner, *The Survey of Western Palestine*, I, London 1881; Haifa-Acre Area Map, Bahai World Center, 1984.

15   M. Moojan (ed.), *The Bahi and the Bahai Religions, 1844–1944*, Oxford 1981.

16   M. Kapelyuk, "The Bahais, Their Beliefs and Their Movement," *Carmelit* (1954) (Hebrew).

his life, when his standing reached a peak. Moreover, this was the Holy Land for the three monotheistic faiths, which imbued the land with a strong religious character.

Ostensibly it was only natural that Jerusalem, the center of Judaism, Christianity and Islam, be selected by the Bahais. On the other hand, the fact that the large faiths had already entrenched themselves in this city posed potential difficulties for the new sect. Furthermore, Jerusalem would have been distant and isolated from the existing center in Acre, unlike Haifa, which belonged to the same administrative district as Acre. Furthermore, the Bahais were already familiar to the populace of the Haifa area, and despite its limitations it was clear that this area would continue to serve as a focal point for pilgrimages after the death of Baha'u'llah.

The selection of Haifa in preference to Acre also stemmed from the changes that had been occurring in the two cities. Acre had begun to deteriorate, and Haifa to develop. At the beginning of the nineteenth century Acre had been the capital of the Northern District, but at mid-century the center of the Ottoman administration had been moved to Sidon, and during the 1860's to Beirut. The volume of goods passing through the Acre port — which had been the hub of economic activity — began to dwindle from mid-century onward, as it was not a deep-water port, nor was it sufficiently protected to provide safe anchorage for the steamships that had started to sail in the Mediterranean.

In Haifa, by contrast, several attractive elements had emerged. In 1858 construction was undertaken outside of the walls; in 1859 the Russians built a quay in the port; in 1868 the Templers arrived, bringing with them a new style of building; and in the 1880's the Jews appeared on the scene, also contributing to the construction of the city. Apart from these factors, Haifa possessed a religious attraction for the Bahais as well — according to various traditions the cave of Elijah, who was accepted by the Bahais as one of their prophets, was located near the city.[17]

Abbas Effendi attempted to purchase the cave site from a Muslim, who was reluctant to sell property to the Bahais. This endeavor on his part, and the ties that he had managed to forge with the governor of Acre, aroused the suspicion of the authorities and in 1901 he was arrested and imprisoned. While his sentence was drawing to a close in 1908, Abbas Effendi succeeded through his disciples in acquiring around ten dunams of land on Mount Carmel. The Bahais specifically selected a locality near the Templer colony. The Templers had reached the area in the early 1860's, and had stressed the aesthetic appearance of

---

17   L. Oliphant, *Haifa — Life in Modern Palestine*, N.Y. 1887.

the neighborhood they established — which attracted the Bahais, for whom aesthetics were a central spiritual theme.

The first Bahai construction on the Carmel — and in fact the first building they erected in all of Palestine — was Abbas Effendi's home, into which he moved in 1910. A year before, in 1909, the bones of the Bab were reinterred on the Carmel. Above the tomb a square structure was erected, which served as a place for meetings and communion. In this same year a hospice was built in Templer style for pilgrims from the East, and another one for those from the West. The latter construction was completed only after Abbas Effendi's death. This separation between East and West constituted a contradiction to the Bahai precepts of unity and equality among all humans, but it was maintained, evidently because the differences were so substantial and Abbas Effendi understood that the ideals of the faith could be realized only in stages.[18]

At the same time there were changes in the property that the Bahais had acquired before Abbas Effendi became their leader. Bahji turned into a stronghold of his opponents, although he continued to pay occasional visits to the place in the company of pilgrims, and to lodge in the teahouse that he had been renting. Contemporary sources attest to the fact that the place was largely neglected and run-down.[19] In Paradise Garden Abbas Effendi added a room on the top floor of the gardener's home, where he himself resided every so often.[20] In the Jordan Valley the Bahais began to sell land to Jews, evidently for both economic reasons — the land was still worked by tenant farmers, who had introduced no improvements in their techniques — and security reasons — the Bedouin tribes persisted in their raids. In addition, the Jews had begun to take an interest in the area, and made attractive offers. Contemporary accounts note the difficulties inherent in cultivating the land, and the unenviable plight of the fellaheen victimized by the Bedouin incursions.

Umm Juni and Samara were sold during the first decade of the twentieth century. Adassiya was retained, and in 1909 Abbas sent thirty Bahai families to settle there.

The establishment of the village of Adassiya was exceptional in the process of land settlement in Palestine, as it was the first and only attempt by the Bahais to found a village of their own and to cultivate the soil by themselves.[21] This enterprise seems perplexing in light of the opposite trend that was unfolding

---

18   JNF Archive, File 54, Map 7195; Ruhe (note 4, supra), pp. 150–155.
19   A. Aaronsohn, *Acre*, Tel Aviv 1925 (Hebrew).
20   According to Mr. Paradise's testimony.
21   J. Thon (ed.), *The Warburg Book*, Tel Aviv 1948 (Hebrew).

simultaneously: the sale of land by the Bahais. It is probable that Adassiya, which was located at some distance from the other cultivated lands in the area, aroused no interest among the Jewish institutions, and Abbas Effendi, finding no way to sell it, opted to develop the site. Furthermore, this settlement provided an additional source of income for the Bahais concentrated around Haifa and Acre. Another explanation for Abbas' reluctance to forfeit this land was its location — on the Yarmuk River and near the Hejaz railroad track. Because this was a strategic location it could be exploited as a bargaining card to attain administrative advantages for the sect. If indeed this was Abbas' primary motivation, then the plan went awry with the signing of the Sykes–Picot treaty in 1916, which fixed the Jordan River as the boundary between the British Mandate in Palestine and the Hashemite kingdom. Abbas' decision to have the Bahais themselves perform the labor probably stemmed from the fact that they were more likely to employ the methods he had instituted for cultivating the land than were the land tenants who, having little motivation, used antiquated methods.

Between 1910 and 1913 Abbas toured Egypt and Europe on a preaching mission. With the outbreak of World War I in 1914, the Bahais — like the other minorities — feared being drafted into the Turkish army. They were also wary of the possibility that animosity toward them would be augmented by war tensions. Abbas exploited his ties with the Druze and moved his people to the village of Abu Sinan. Later in that year, as the intensity of the initial pandemonium waned, they returned to their homes.

The British conquest of Palestine greatly ameliorated the Bahais' position and in 1919 a new wave of pilgrims arrived. Abbas Effendi died in his home in November 1912, and was buried in an alcove dug near the grave of the Bab.[22]

BUILDING THE CARMEL CENTER

The period of Shogi Effendi's leadership got under way amid turmoil in the Bahai world. Even though Abbas Effendi had appointed him as his successor, Shogi had studied outside of Palestine for a long period (in the American University of Beirut and in London), and he was only twenty-five when his grandfather died. His Western education and young age aroused skepticism as to his ability to lead the sect. In 1922 a struggle over the ownership of Bahji was waged between Shogi Effendi, his uncle Muhammad Ali, and Baha'u'llah's grandson Hussain Afnan. The matter was brought before a British court, which

---

22 Kapelyuk (note 16, supra), pp. 221–215.

ruled in favor of Shogi. In the wake of this affair he had many of his opponents, branded "violators of the faith," deported from Palestine.

In 1929 the British officially recognized the Bahai faith as independent, which facilitated Shogi Effendi's operations. From then on he concentrated on turning the property in Palestine into an impressive Bahai World Center, without settlement. He also introduced a form of democratic leadership, which was exceptional in religious frameworks. This initiative was apparently inspired by liberal Western ideas he had absorbed in the course of his studies.[23]

During this period most of the remaining Bahai lands in the Jordan Valley were sold to Jews. Not included in these deals were around 200 dunams in Nuqaib, where the Bahais continued to reside until 1948, and Adassiya, which could not be sold because of the partition plan.[24] In contrast to the situation in the Jordan Valley, the holdings in the Zebulun Valley and Haifa underwent development. The land at Jidru and the remaining tracts in Nuqaib were transferred in 1953 to the government of Israel in exchange for land in Bahji. Ridvan Park, Paradise Garden and Ashraf Garden have been cultivated up to the present day. The British general McNeill took up residence in Mazra'ah in 1931, and his wife described the place as "old and neglected." The McNeill family renovated the home without altering its structure. General McNeill left Mazra'ah in 1947 following his wife's death. In 1950 Shogi Effendi appealed to the prime minister at the time, David Ben-Gurion, to recognize the right of the Bahais to the site, and he received approval to lease it. In deals taking place in 1980 and 1983, the site was purchased by the legatees of Abdullah Pasha, along with additional land that had been acquired in 1980 by the Bahai community.

It was also Shogi Effendi who planned the circular garden with a home in its center in Bahji (see Plate 1). This garden integrated Eastern and Western elements. There were Persian symbols, such as eagles, the symbol of strength, and peacocks, the bird of paradise. The circle was divided into quadrants, in the tradition of the Persian garden. On the other hand, there were amphoras and pillars with Corinthian capitals, which originated in classical Greece but which were also very characteristic of the English garden.[25]

Along the Carmel land purchase continued in the framework of the development of the World Center, and Shogi Effendi also expanded the structure above the graves of the Bab and Abbas Effendi. Between 1949 and 1953 the edifice that exists today was erected (see Plate 2).[26] Here too, diverse styles were

23   H. Zimer, *A Fraudulent Testament, Germany Free Bahais*, West Germany 1973.
24   H. Eugene, *East of Jordan*, Jerusalem 1966.
25   Ruhe (note 4, supra), pp. 90–94.
26   Y. Rawley (ed.), *Haifa 1954*, Development Division of the Haifa Municipality (Hebrew).

incorporated: marble pillars from the West and a dome from the East, Oriental interior design, and a garden containing the same elements as the other Bahai gardens.[27] The erection of this large building constituted a turning point in the nature of Bahai construction, as it represented a considerable financial investment. The funds were gathered through contributions by members of the sect throughout the world, and from land sales.

The hospice for Bahai pilgrims from the West was completed in 1923. Between 1951 and 1963 the World Bahai Council resided there, and from 1963 to 1983 members of the Universal House of Justice lodged in the building.

In the years 1953–1975 the Bahai Archive was built, and Shogi Effendi ordered it to be designed like the Parthenon (see Plate 3).[28] Greek architecture was regarded in the West as the epitome of culture, and the selection of the Parthenon as a model reflected Shogi's esteem for classical civilization and his desire for integration on a world scale.

The Universal House of Justice was built from 1975 to 1982. The idea had been suggested earlier by Shogi Effendi, but the execution was postponed until after his death, evidently due to a lack of funds. This structure is located next to the archive, and it too was built in classical Greek style so that the two buildings would be congruous. Nevertheless, the Universal House of Justice was built with a dome — once again, in order to blend diverse styles (see Plate 4). The garden containing these buildings is a continuation of the one around the cave of the Bab, and it strongly resembles the garden in Bahji. Here too, a circle is divided by boulevards into quadrants, the novelty being a hanging garden in the tradition of ancient Persia.[29] Today the lands held by the Bahais on the Carmel total approximately 300 dunams.[30]

CONCLUSION

Upon arriving in Palestine the Bahais encountered a hostile Muslim majority who impeded their efforts to conduct negotiations for real estate. Consequently they had to take advantage of opportunities that arose and to acquire property considered undesirable by the owners. From the start the Bahais handled their financial affairs efficiently, which enabled them to establish a solid economic base. The imprisonment of Bahai figures marked the peak of official control over the operation of the sect, but even afterwards the Bahais were subject to

27   E. Forada, *Faiths of the World — Ancient Iran*, Tel Aviv 1964 (Hebrew).

28   M. Brouskari, *The Acropolis Greek Sarantopulus*, Greece 1978.

29   D.N. Wilber, *Persian Gardens and Garden Pavilions*, Washington 1979.

30   Miller (note 1, supra), p. 298.

direct supervision. Although the Turks ruled the land until close to Abbas Effendi's death, he managed to create an effective public relations network both in Palestine and abroad. With the British conquest came a relaxation of governmental pressure, and the Bahais began to operate openly.

The Bahais selected two districts in which to settle:

1. The northern coastal plane, where the geographical conditions were favorable. Settlement was begun on a small scale, and was characterized by self-labor. Its scope was evidently limited by the existence of rural holdings in the area owned by the local aristocracy, and of well-established Arab villages.

The period of Baha'u'llah's leadership was characterized by the rental and purchase of structures and land in the vicinity of Acre, evidently intended to create a basis that would safeguard the standing of the sect in Palestine.

During Abbas Effendi's leadership sites in this area were neglected, in the wake of struggles over ownership rights within the sect. On the other hand, lands were purchased and construction initiated in Haifa.

During the final period the Haifa site underwent intensive development including the acquisition of small contiguous lots on the Carmel. A similar process occurred in Acre and its environs, as the Bahais purchased holy sites they had rented in the past, and cultivated those already in their hands, as part of the consolidation of the World Center. These sites were developed only as focal points for pilgrimage, and not for settlement. The plan was for only the world leadership and the staff of the Center's ancillary services to reside in Palestine.

2. The second area that the Bahais gained possession of was in the northern Jordan Valley and the region east of the Sea of Galilee. The lands were bought during the first period. Although the geographical conditions were not favorable, the scope of the purchase was large, which indicates that political considerations and economic contingencies were the dominant factors behind the decision to acquire realty in this area.

Settlement was agricultural in nature, and the land was initially cultivated by tenant farmers. In the second period land sales were initiated, and in parallel an attempt was made to settle Bahai families on the tracts that were retained. During the last period nearly all of these lands were sold. One striking feature of the Bahai community throughout its history in Palestine was its small size, which never exceeded several hundred members. There were a number of reasons why the community in Palestine never expanded: historical events not directly related to the sect, a hostile administration, internal struggles within the sect, and a leadership that consciously limited demographic development.

TRADITIONAL AND MODERN RURAL SETTLEMENT TYPES IN ERETZ-ISRAEL IN THE MODERN ERA

YOSSI BEN-ARTZI

INTRODUCTION

In the modern era, rural settlement has played a far more central and significant role in Eretz-Israel than in nearly any other area of the world, and it has been the most crucial element in modern Jewish settlement there. While the Western world in the nineteenth century witnessed accelerated modernization, urbanization and industrialization that induced millions to move from rural areas to the city, village life and agriculture remained the basis of Palestine's economy. Even when the developments sweeping Europe and America began to make their mark in Eretz-Israel, rural settlement — of both traditional and modern types — continued to dominate large geographic regions.

Moreover, the renewed Jewish settlement movement regarded rural living as an ideal, and as a symbol of national revival and the return to the land of the forefathers. During the early years of the Zionist movement nationalistic aspirations revolved around a return to the soil, the creation of Hebrew villages and the molding of an archetypal rural Jew who sustains himself by tilling his own fields. These ideals held sway even when it became apparent, early on, that a decisive majority of Jewish immigrants were drawn to the cities; at least up to this last generation, the settlement policy of the Zionist movement and the State of Israel has favored rural over urban settlement.[1]

It is natural, then, that scholars from a wide range of disciplines — history, architecture, sociology and education, to name a few — have concentrated on the various types of rural settlement, and their development and changes over the years, and have greatly broadened our understanding with regard to many aspects of this historical phenomenon. Geographers have also been naturally attracted to this sphere, and have enhanced our knowledge both about distribution patterns and about the link between the underlying ideology of

---

[1] This phenomenon in the history of Jewish settlement in Palestine is explained in E. Cohen, *The City in the Zionist Ideology*, Jerusalem 1970.

various settlement types and their emergence on the landscape. Other researchers have dealt with the farm economy and the material culture of the rural settlement, while a small number have explored non-Jewish agricultural settlement and its evolution.

Historical geographers specializing in rural life have had to chart the most appropriate course among the myriad topics and issues begging investigation. While those engaged in the study of urban life have mainly focused on the development of the city and the changes in its functions, historical geographers investigating the rural sector have tackled issues that have been ideological, social, material, economic or essentially historical in nature. The historical geographers find themselves working side-by-side with researchers from the other disciplines involved, in the course of studying such settlement-related issues as the multiple branches of agriculture, land acquisition, organizational and ideological changes, etc. It seems that with regard to only one sphere do the geographers lack partners and offer a totally unique contribution to the study of rural life in Eretz-Israel; this is the physical sphere, entailing the emergence of the settlements on the landscape, the differences between one settlement and another, and the connection between the circumstances of their establishment and the location selected.

Thus the primary objects of historical-geographical investigation are those basic elements which can be compared to equivalent ones existing elsewhere in the world, such as location, the rural house, farmsteads, field division, settlement patterns and layouts. This perception has found expression in a number of studies,[2] including the one at hand, which shall attempt to describe the main settlement types that have evolved on the landscape of Eretz-Israel in the modern period, i.e. the nineteenth century and early twentieth century.

THE TRADITIONAL SETTLEMENT

Because the concept of "time" is relative, the definition of a "traditional settlement" is tempered by one's historical perspective. Changes and developments in Eretz-Israel have come about so rapidly in the past hundred years that even relatively new settlement types like the moshava are liable to be perceived as traditional. However, by adopting a broader perspective one realizes that only the Arab village constitutes a truly traditional settlement type. The Arab village in Palestine of the nineteenth century reflected on the one hand the

---

2   Y. Ben-Artzi, *The Moshava on the Palestinian Landscape 1882–1914*, Jerusalem 1988 (Hebrew).

long-term process of man's adapting to his environment and on the other hand his attempt to shape the landscape as he saw fit. It appears that in a number of respects he also conveyed to us an earlier heritage, stemming from ancient times.

The settlement pattern of the Arab village had a clustered and agglomerated structure, and there were no signs of prior planning. The network of streets and alleys was crowded, sinuous, and fraught with dead ends. The pattern was evidently dictated by the building activity itself, as it did not clearly demarcate space for houses and yards. Homes had been built for generations, with just enough room left for a narrow passageway between one building and the next. Repetition of this layout over hundreds of years resulted in the creation of a typical agglomerated pattern. The domiciles were a characteristic product of folk architecture.[3] The building material, which was local, blended in well with the rock outcrops in the vicinity. Stone was widely used in hilly areas, while adobe was utilized in the plains. (See Plate 1)

The farmer's house and yard formed one integral unit, with people and animals crowded together under the same roof. The homes averaged 25 sq. m. in size, and had several levels, each designed for a different purpose: storage of tools and livestock, living quarters and sleeping quarters. When the family grew, the residents generally added rooms in various sections of the yard, which was always surrounded by a large wall with a single narrow opening for an exit. Most of the built-up area was an agglomeration of yards and domiciles, and only a few public buildings were constructed as independent entities. Even the village mosque was often no more than an expanded residence, and as a rule it hardly rose above the rest of the structures — unlike the situation in many other rural settings, such as traditional Europe, where church towers loom prominently above the surrounding buildings. Such important institutions as the *mad'afa* (guest chamber) were either maintained jointly by the villagers or passed from one family to the next on a rotating basis. Similarly, the well, spring and central threshing floor were held as common property. Other institutions, such as schools and community buildings, were completely absent from the traditional village until recently.

The farm in the Arab village developed over generations, constantly adapting itself to the particular soil conditions, climate and location. Most of the agricultural branches were seasonal. The physical conditions dictated the nature of the crops, the size of the fields and the time assigned for work. Man's impact

---

3   See: T. Canaan, "The Palestinian Arab House: Its Architecture and Folklore," *Journal of the Palestine Oriental Society*, XII (1932), pp. 223–247, and XIII (1933), pp. 1–28; G. Dalman, *Arbeit und Sitte in Palästina*, VII, Gutersloh 1928. This volume focuses on the Arab village and home.

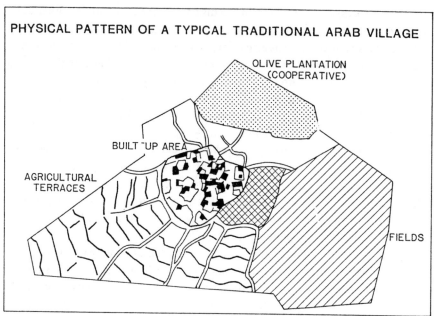

Fig. 1

on this tradition was essentially limited to building terraces to prevent erosion on hilly terrain, and channeling water to the soil. No large-scale, European-style activities to gain mastery over the land — such as drying swamps, controlling pests or developing rocky areas — were carried out, whether by the authorities or through local initiative. Hence most of the citrus and field crops were extensive, while only a few — mainly vegetables — were grown through irrigation. Nevertheless, this was not merely subsistence farming, since produce was accepted in lieu of taxes and exchanged for utensils and equipment — and some of it was even exported to neighboring countries.

The system of land ownership and parcellation was complex, and rooted in ancient agrarian systems.[4] Most of the land was owned by the government or charitable institutions, and a large portion of it was untilled. The farmers' fear of taxes and of army recruitment prompted them to register the lands in the name of landholders who could protect them, or else to practice the *musha'* system

---

4   See: G. Baer, *Introduction to the History of Agrarian Relations in the Middle East 1800–1970*, Tel Aviv 1971; S. Bergheim, "Land Tenure in Palestine," *Palestine Exploration Fund Quarterly Statement*, XVI (1894), pp. 191–199.

whereby they were held in the name of the entire village and redistributed every year. This somewhat resembles the "open field," and not until the end of the eighteenth century were tracts assigned to specific families rather than being constantly rotated. Because the area to be cultivated was defined not by dimensions but by the *fedan*, or tillable unit, its size differed from one region to the next, in accordance with the quality of the soil and the nature of the crops. Thus a unique mosaic of land ownership was created, characterized by a division into large plots that were then subdivided into long and narrow strips for tilling.

The settlement pattern, construction layout and street network, together with the fields and citrus groves, lent the traditional village in Eretz-Israel a distinct appearance. Like its European counterparts, it became integrally woven into the landscape, adhering to its contours and bound by its limitations. It served to convey into the present the heritage of the past, the conditions prevailing during the hundreds of years when the village took shape, and the relationship between man and his environment over this period. It should come as no surprise, then, that the general appearance and the internal make-up of the traditional village infused the modern-day travelers and reseachers who reached Palestine with enthusiasm — just as, to an equal degree, they deterred the newly arrived settlers, Jewish and Christian alike. The latter rejected the crowded traditional settlement type out of hand, and sought new ones.

THE GERMAN COLONY

In the mid-1800's the Holy Land became not only a destination for pilgrimages and an object of "rediscovery," but also an ideal for various Christian groups who, through settling in Eretz-Israel, strove to prepare the land for the Second Coming — and thereby hasten this event.[5] Most of these groups were tiny, and made little impact on the country's landscape. The only one that managed to stamp its own imprint — and even to influence the local Arab residents and the Jewish settlers — was the German Templers. Their faith, an outgrowth of southern- German pietism, was strongly influenced by the theologian Christoph Hoffmann. This sect was first organized in the form of "Friends of Jerusalem" associations, and later as the Tempelgesellschaft ("Temple Association"). Most of its members came from Württemberg, and its declared goal was to mend the Church and the world through settling in the Holy Land and preparing it for the

---

5   See: R. Kark, "Millenarism and Agricultural Settlement in the Holy Land in the Nineteenth Century," *Journal of Historical Geography*, IX (1983), pp. 47–62; M. Verete, "The Restoration of the Jews in English Protestant Thought 1790–1840," *Middle Eastern Studies*, VIII (1972), pp. 3–10.

Second Coming. Such action was meant to serve as a model of true, pristine Christianity.[6]

In 1869 the Templers laid the cornerstone for the first colonies in Palestine — initially in Haifa, and later in Jaffa. In 1871 they established the agricultural colony Sarona (today in the center of Tel Aviv) and in 1873 they also began to settle in the vicinity of Jerusalem. Thirty years later, inspired by success, they established colonies for the second generation, and also acquired holdings in various cities, where they ran hotels and flour mills. Over the years the Templers gained unusual influence over daily affairs in Palestine, and served as a model for the other residents to emulate. They were innovative pioneers in many areas: transportation, hotels, agriculture, industry, construction, medicine and research. Despite their small numbers (around 1,800 people in 1914), they maintained primacy in these fields, and created well-established communities that earned the admiration of all.

From a strictly "settlement" standpoint, the Templers exerted a powerful influence over their neighbors, and their colonies constituted a new settlement type on the landscape of Eretz-Israel. As far back as the establishment of their first colony in Haifa, it was apparent that they sought to create a new landscape, completely different from both the traditional one around them and the one they had known in Germany. Their desire to fashion a model of a spacious and modern settlement guided the planning of the colony's shape, streets and buildings. (See Plate 2)

The Haifa colony typifies the Templer stettlement pattern. From the outset it was decided that the colony would be set off at a distance from the crowded, walled city, and would be located near the agricultural land the Templers had acquired. In the center of the area earmarked for construction, a straight road was built with amazing precision. It linked the coast with the slope of Mount Carmel, and its width — 35 meters — was unprecedented in Eretz-Israel. Parallel to it two narrower streets were laid, and thus a "Strassendorf" settlement pattern was created, with a network of additional parallel streets and perpendicular alleys. The residences were allotted in accordance with the usage assigned to the land: in the upper part near the mountain, where the tracts were intended for vineyards "like on the banks of the Neckar," plots were given to viticulturists. In the lower portion, close to the sea and the main road from Haifa to Jaffa, hotels, shops, a soap factory and a central public building were erected. In the middle, along the central avenue, the remainder of the homes were built — some of them owned by farmers and others by craftsmen. (See Plate 3)

---

6   The most comprehensive research about the role of this movement in Palestine is A. Carmel, *Die Siedlungen der Württembergischen Templer in Palästina 1868–1918*, Stuttgart 1973.

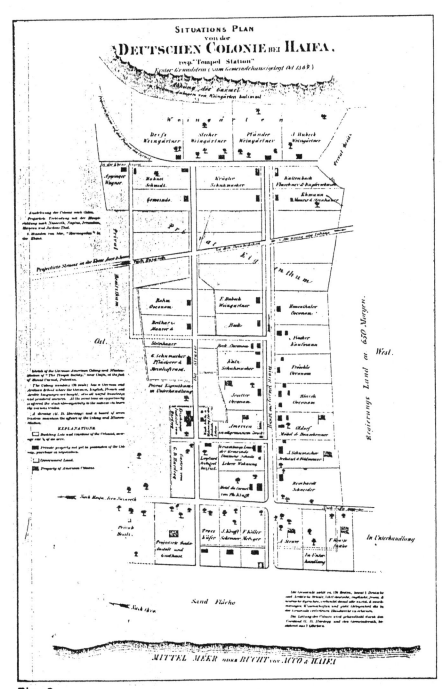

Fig. 2

The houses were built at precise, equal distances from one another and from the sides of the central thoroughfare. These were actually "urban" homes with two storeys: a ground floor with a kitchen and living room, and an upper floor with bedrooms. The construction was massive and sturdy, and local stone was the primary building material. With time tiled roofs were added, which allowed for another floor. The style was neither European nor Oriental, but a unique blend of elements from both of these cultures. The large yards contained extra living quarters, barns, storerooms and wells. Decorative trees on the sides of the road, along with the gardens near the homes, helped create the charming image of a broad, attractive boulevard. The sole public building served as both a community center (there was no church) and school. The large structures such as the hotel and soap factory featured architectonic innovations, while highlighting the unique geographical setting. It is understandable, then, why Lawrence Oliphant, who resided in this colony from 1883 to 1886, should write: "Leaving the town by the western gateway...about a mile...we suddenly find ourselves apparently transported into the heart of Europe."[7]

Following the Haifa model but constantly adjusting to local conditions, the Templers established colonies in Jaffa (1869), Sarona (1871), Jerusalem (1873), Wilhelma (1902), Galilean Bethlehem (1906), and Waldheim (1907). In addition to their role in modernizing the economy of Palestine, they also contributed to shaping the landscape of the region, at least in those few colonies in which they were active. (See Plate 4)

Indeed people flocked from far and near to see the new "wonder" that had sprung up on the landscape of Palestine, and before long wealthy Arabs who built homes in new parts of Haifa began copying the Germans. The Templer colonies, as the first truly planned settlements in modern Palestine, were exemplary models that inspired the local Arabs, the Turkish rulers, and most of all the Jews, who in 1882 began reaching Palestine in large numbers with a goal similar to that of the Germans: settlement in agricultural colonies.[8] The Templers' success in establishing themselves in Palestine and in introducing modern agriculture proved to the founders of the first moshavot that their hope to strike roots in Palestine and to forge a generation of Jewish farmers was not entirely unfounded.

7   L. Oliphant, *Haifa, or Life in Modern Palestine*, London-Edinburgh 1887, p. 20.
8   For more on this impact and the linkage between Jewish and Templer settlers, see: Ben-Artzi (supra, note 2), pp. 250–255.

THE JEWISH MOSHAVA

During the years 1882–1914 thirty communities of the settlement type called moshava were established in Palestine. These were set up through the initiative of organizations and settlers from diverse countries of origin, mostly East European. Unlike the Templer venture, this was not an enterprise organized and run by one central body, and consequently the settlements differed one from another. This diversity stemmed from the nature of the settlers, the goals of the organizational elements behind the scenes, the period and regional differences. Nevertheless, the distinctions notwithstanding, all of these moshavot were based on the principle that private farmers should own the land and means of production, and that cooperation between them would be on a voluntary and ad hoc basis.

Much criticism was leveled at the moshavot at various stages of their development, from both economic and ideological standpoints. It focused primarily on three issues: the strong dependence of the settlers on some external agent, such as Baron Rothschild and the Jewish Colonization Association; the economic failures; and the dissipation of the spirit that had characterized the settlements at the time of their founding. Jewish rural settlement set as its goal the creation of a new type of Jew — a farmer tilling his own fields and supporting himself from them, who along with his peers would lay the foundation for a Hebrew national revival in the land of the forefathers. In reality there were numerous signs of deviation from this path — from the employment of salaried workers, mainly Arabs, to the negation of the values held dear by the founders. Nevertheless, despite the criticism, the moshava was the primary Zionist achievement in Palestine, at least until World War I, and its imprint on the landscape was the most concrete sign of the Jewish presence in Eretz-Israel. The unique physical qualities of the moshavot throughout the land were apparent, as this description by a traveler demonstrates:

> For of a person traveling through Palestine, the moshavot will be a sort of magical vision; as he moves through huge desolate areas, climbs the mountains and descends into the valleys following no beaten path, the appearance of things suddenly begins to change, and before him are beaten paths and comely, marvelous moshavot decked in their attractive buildings, straight and wide streets, vineyards and citrus groves.[9]

This imprint on the landscape was not achieved at once, nor was it the product of any master plan. Nevertheless, the physical features of the Jewish moshava do

---

9   A.S. Hirschberg, *The Way of the New Yishuv in Eretz-Israel*, Wilna 1901, p. 27 (Hebrew).

clearly reflect advanced planning, as a result of which this type of agricultural settlement gained a modern character.[10] In only four out of the first thirty moshavot was the physical pattern haphazard; in the rest two different types emerged: "compact" and "spacious." (See Plates 5 and 6).

The compact type is typical of all the moshavot built and supported by the administrations set up by the Baron Rothschild or the Jewish Colonization Association. Their engineers designed various layouts — such as the "Strassendorf," the T-shaped village, and the hamlet built on only one side of the street — but all of them possessed several common features: the living quarters and yards were built in the same shape, in groups of six to nine units, enclosed by an outer stone fence that was created by the junction of the back walls of the barns and the storage rooms. Thus a sort of crowded "yard settlement" came into existence, in which each farmer had a private farm adjacent to that of his neighbor's. In each moshava of this type numerous public buildings were erected at the outset: synagogue, bathhouse, administrative quarters, pharmacy and doctor's residence. Even in the smallest of the moshavot these public structures played a far more prominent role than they did in any other settlement type in Palestine. Throughout the land the living quarters and yard had a uniform pattern, usually containing a home with a kitchen and two other rooms, and separate stables, barn and storage room. (See Plates 7 and 8).

The spacious type was characteristic of all the settlement associations of Hovevei Zion, which were not always supported by a central body, The planners were lavish in their allotment of land for living quarters. There was no uniformity in the homes, which were constructed in accordance with each owner's personal taste and ability, and the means at his disposal. The yards were unenclosed. There were few public buildings, and these were erected relatively late. The area on which these moshavot stood exceeded the dimensions prescribed by bureaucratic specifications. As a rule, the administrations' moshavot were standard in all regards, while heterogeneity and individuality characterized the moshavot free of centralized planning.

After struggling for existence for several years — each type after its own fashion — the moshavot eventually molded a new rural landscape in Palestine. While the Templers were pioneers of the modern settlement, they failed to develop a widespread network of communities, and contented themselves with seven colonies, some of them urban. By contrast, Jewish settlement spread to

10   Y. Ben-Artzi, "The Jewish Moshavot and the Beginning of Physical Planning in Israel," Y. Ben-Arieh, Y. Ben-Artzi & H. Goren (eds.), *Essays in Settlement Historical Geography in Israel*, Jerusalem 1987 (Hebrew).

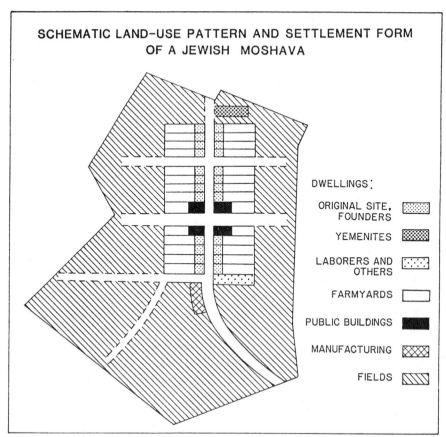

SCHEMATIC LAND-USE PATTERN AND SETTLEMENT FORM
OF A JEWISH MOSHAVA

DWELLINGS :

ORIGINAL SITE,
FOUNDERS

YEMENITES

LABORERS AND
OTHERS

FARMYARDS

PUBLIC BUILDINGS

MANUFACTURING

FIELDS

Fig. 3

every part of the country. In Upper and Lower Galilee, the southern Carmel, and most of all the Judean coastal plain, the moshava formed a sort of "European island" in the eastern landscape. Modern living quarters and yards, albeit quite modest in comparison with those of the Templers; numerous public buildings and gardens; the first factories in the region; tilled fields alongside thousands of dunams of citrus groves — all this created a unique character that distinguished the moshava from the hundreds of traditional villages in the area. The attention of travelers was drawn to the "modern cultural islands," and the local Arab residents frequented the moshava and benefited from the services it provided.

Until 1914 the moshavot entrenched themselves demographically, economically and agriculturally. From three small communities totaling 150–160 families in 1882, their number increased to thirty with 8,000 people in the prewar years. The last of them were founded between 1901 and 1908, and a hierarchy was created in terms of size and economic standing. The veteran settlements grew large and well-established, while their population became diversified; the membership that originally comprised only independent farmers came to include farm hands, merchants, providers of various services, and even prototype industrial initiators. As early as the 1910's the broadened economic base and increased population imparted a distinctly urban quality to moshavot such as Petah Tiqwa. The younger and smaller ones, on the other hand, retained their markedly rural character, were inhabited mainly by farmers and manual laborers, and struggled for years to come to consolidate their economy.

OTHER SETTLEMENT TYPES — INITIAL EXPERIMENTS

As the Second Aliya (wave of immigration to Eretz-Israel), beginning in 1904, marked a change in the immigrant population's make-up and ideology, these newcomers strove to create novel settlement types. They "accused" the moshava of deviating from its initial ideological path. Many of them felt that urbanization, the altered economic structure, and the growth of hired labor — including a large number of Arabs — combined to disqualify the moshava from serving as a model for the Zionist movement seeking to settle masses of people on the land and produce a generation of self-supporting Jewish farmers. From 1908 onward, the Zionist movement did not establish a single additional moshava; rather, its efforts were concentrated on developing alternative settlement types.[11]

The bearers of this new spirit were farm workers, for the most part young Jews from Eastern Europe, who held a clearly defined socialistic world view. Moreover, the various settlement associations wished to find frameworks appropriate for both workers with families and middle-class Jews from abroad. Between 1908 and 1914 at least three new settlement types were attempted, and nationally owned farms were established where agronomic experiments were conducted, an agricultural labor force was trained, and forests and woods were planted.

The three major settlement types that were tried differed greatly from one another, and each was designed for a different population. The first was intended as a solution for veteran laborers in Palestine who had families and a small amount of capital. Land was purchased for them, and for the first time settlement was based on the fundamentals of self-employment, Hebrew labor and mutual assistance. This type was called a *moshav po'alim* (agricultural-laborers'

---

11 For more about the organizational and ideological problems of the moshavot, see: D. Weintraub, M. Lissak & Y. Azmon, *Moshava, Kibbutz and Moshav: Patterns of Jewish Rural Settlements and Development in Palestine*, Ithaca-London 1969.

settlement), since the settlers were to continue working as salaried employees of farm owners in the large moshavot, while running small 15-dunam supplementary farms for themselves. There was minimal cooperativeness, along with a large degree of reliance upon the already-existing services provided by nearby moshavot. Within a short time it transpired that this settlement type had failed, because it was based on the concept that an individual could somehow fuse the traits of a wage earner with those of an independent landowner. The privately owned land did not suffice to sustain an agricultural economy, and anyone who diligently performed his duties as a hired laborer was perforce compelled to neglect his own land. This failure gave rise to the idea of a *moshav ovdim* (laborers' settlement), first founded in 1921, which was to become the dominant type of Jewish settlement in Palestine.

In 1909 the most revolutionary experiment in Jewish settlement, especially from a social standpoint, got under way. Little did its initiators realize that their idea would blossom into a major contribution to world society — the *kvutza* — a collective settlement whose settlers were homogeneous, united in their social outlook, and totally committed to the principles of cooperation, equality and mutual assistance. Such a framework especially suited young workers without families. Although variations of the kvutza took hold in cities, only after evolving into the kibbutz settlement type after World War I did this framework begin to attract masses of people.

Shortly before World War I an attempt was made to organize yet another settlement type, the *achuza*. This was to be owned by an association of small capitalists living abroad, who would employ laborers to work their land until it should bear fruit, at which time they would immigrate to Palestine and receive an operative farm. This idea spread through Jewish communities from Russia to the U.S.A., and around five such *achuzot* were founded from 1911 to 1914. The world war and the ensuing severance of the links with Palestine, along with pessimistic economic prognoses, nipped this new venture in the bud.

On the eve of World War I there were about fifty Jewish settlement sites in Palestine, with a total population of approximately 12,500. Thirty of these were moshavot, and the remainder merely embryonic forms of various other settlement types. Following the war, hundreds of additional sites were prepared, most of them based on the moshav or kibbutz idea — thus creating the false notion that the origins and main thrust of Jewish settlement in Palestine derive from precisely these two types. However, the above review demonstrates that for its first forty years, i.e. up to World War I, the Jewish settlement enterprise in Palestine was based primarily on the moshava type, which constituted the primary Jewish imprint on the landscape during this initial period.

Conclusion

The settlement scene in Palestine up to World War I remained essentially traditional. The urban landscape was dominated by approximations of traditional Oriental cities, coexisting with relatively modern quarters, while the rural landscape was ruled by the traditional Arab village, with all of its characteristic features. However, it is precisely against this backdrop that the new settlement types established by the Christians and Jews stood out so prominently. These new villages formed the keenest expression of the internal changes which the population and mode of living in Palestine underwent during the nineteenth century. The physical aspects — the village type, its streets, homes and fields — lucidly reflected the aspirations and ideological motivations of the founders.

In seeking to fashion an exemplary model of a modern, culturally advanced, Christian society, the Templers made sure that their settlements acquired a European appearance. Even so, they were unsuccessful in attracting masses in their wake, and their seven colonies remained a small minority vis-à-vis the extensive network of new Jewish settlements.

Jewish settlement, like that of the Christians, had ideological motivations at its heart, but unlike the Templers the Jews did not seek to influence the local Arab residents. They regarded their goal of returning to the homeland as contingent on a return to the soil — on the creation of a "Jewish farmer" as the bearer of the national ideal. Consequently, the rural village gained undisputed priority in Zionist immigration and settlement policy. For fourteen years the Jewish organizations searched for a form of social and organizational settlement befitting the goal of massive Jewish immigration. As a result, physical patterns for diverse settlement types were designed, and although it was in the 1920's and 1930's that ideology and physical layout were matched most successfully, the origins of the new types lie in the pre-World War I period. Over time, the Jewish settlements, which still constituted a minority vis-à-vis the traditional villages, became a unique feature on the landscape, standing out as "islands" of modernization and development. When they proliferated and a certain balance was struck between them and the Arab villages, the settlement mosaic characteristic of Eretz-Israel — an intermingling of the modern and the traditional — came into being.

CULTURAL LANDSCAPE OF PRE-ZIONIST SETTLEMENTS

RAN AARONSOHN

INTRODUCTION

The emergence of a modern national Jewish identity took on several forms. The establishment of the Zionist movement by Theodor Herzl in 1897 marked the key step toward political realization of national goals. A wave of Aliya (Jewish immigration to the Holy Land) which had started fifteen years earlier laid the foundations of what later came to be termed practical Zionism. Although the immigration of Jews to Eretz-Israel had never ceased from the time of the Exile (70 C.E.), this particular influx was considered to be a new type of aliya, and was therefore called the "First Aliya."

During the First Aliya (1882–1904) an important element was added to the landscape of Palestine: Jewish agricultural settlements. At the outset of this period, there was only one settlement of this sort, the agricultural school of Mikve Yisrael, which had been founded in 1870 by the Alliance Israélite Universelle. By the year 1890 another twelve had been established, and the total reached twenty-eight by 1904. All of them had been patterned after European villages, being based on privately-owned farms, in a settlement type that until the present day has been called the moshava.

It was the moshava that characterized the First Aliya, in contrast to the exclusively urban communities set up by earlier immigrants to Eretz-Israel. Indeed, the moshava has come to symbolize the First Aliya in the public mind and in historiographic research up to the present.

The scope, however, of the moshavot was limited by the period's end in 1904. Their population is estimated at 5,500, from among approximately 55,000 Jews in Palestine (as compared to around 25,000 Jews at the outset of the period in 1882), and a total population of nearly 500,000. The amount of land owned by the twenty-eight moshavot was relatively small, around 1/4 million dunams.[1]

---

1   R. Aaronsohn, "Building the Land: Stages in First Aliya Colonisation," L.I. Levine (ed.), *The Jerusalem Cathedra*, 3, Jerusalem-Detroit 1983, pp. 197–227. Cf. G. Smith, "Jewish Settlement

147

Therefore, from today's perspective this settlement type in Palestine appears to be relatively marginal, in spatial and physical terms (see Fig. 1).

However, the moshava did play a central role in molding the human values of the country's population as a whole. Its achievements in this regard stemmed from a combination of factors: the ideology upon which it was based, the settlement bodies involved in its development, and the new society and cultural-organizational tools that it produced. This article analyzes the human fabric of the first moshavot, with a view toward the theme of continuity vis-à-vis innovation — i.e. the transplantation of the traditional life abroad vis-à-vis the germination of a new, modern, national life. Thus the question to be explored here is to what extent the new cultural landscape created by the First Aliya was in fact primary and original.

POPULATION AND SOCIETY

During the twenty-two years that elapsed from 1882 to 1904, it is estimated that between thirty to fifty thousand Jews immigrated to Palestine. Those who settled in moshavot or in newly-built cities, such as Jaffa and Haifa, formed the core of the new *yishuv* (national Jewish community). The sources, although vague and incomplete, generally indicate that aliya was continual, but marked by fluctuations. The two most significant waves reached the country in 1882 and 1891, precipitating two surges of settlement.[2] Although the rate of emigration from Palestine at the time is unknown, it too was evidently marked by rises and falls, and seems to have peaked after 1900. Even so, in the first four years of the twentieth century seven new moshavot were established, whose members came largely from the ranks of the already-existing moshavot (see Table 1).

The population in these agricultural settlements can be divided into three main categories, two of which consist of permanent settlers — the enfranchised "citizens" and the "residents" — and the third of temporary workers. The citizen grouping was composed of land owners, who formed the core of the moshava population. These were the policy makers, entitled to vote for and be elected to the various committees and associations. They included mainly farmers, but also craftsmen and civil service employees who had lived in the moshava for at least three years and had acquired land, thereby gaining suffrage.

The second category consisted of all the others who resided permanently in

in Palestine between 1882 and 1948," A. Lemon & N. Pollock (eds.), *Studies on Overseas Settlement and Population*, London 1980, pp. 301–307.

2   *Ibid.*; A. Bein, *The Return to the Soil*, Jerusalem 1952, pp. 4–17.

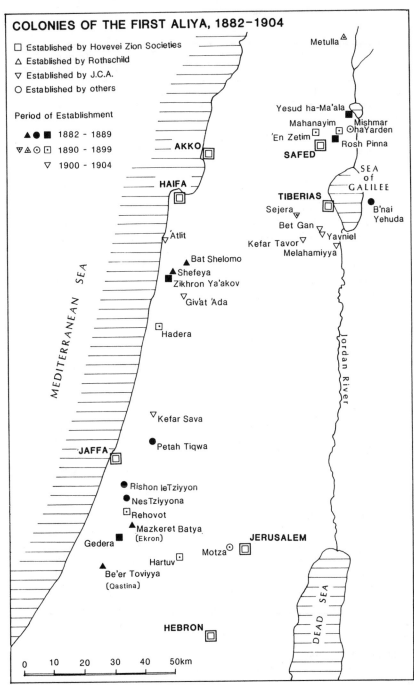

COLONIES OF THE FIRST ALIYA, 1882–1904

☐ Established by Hovevei Zion Societies
△ Established by Rothschild
▽ Established by J.C.A.
○ Established by others

Period of Establishment

▲●■ 1882 – 1889
▽△⊙⊡ 1890 – 1899
▽ 1900 – 1904

Metulla △

Yesud ha-Ma'ala ■
Mahanayim ⊡   Mishmar
'En Zetim ⊡   ○ haYarden ■
SAFED   ⊡ Rosh Pinna

MEDITERRANEAN SEA

AKKO ▣

HAIFA ▣

SEA
of
GALILEE

TIBERIAS
Sejera ▽   ▣   ● B'nai
Bet Gan ▽   Yehuda
Kefar Tavor ▽ ▽ Yavniel
Melahamiyya ▽

'Atlit

▲ Bat Shelomo
▲ Shefeya
■ Zikhron Ya'akov
▽ Giv'at 'Ada

⊡ Hadera

Jordan River

▽ Kefar Sava

JAFFA
▣

● Petah Tiqwa

● Rishon leTziyyon
● Nes Tziyyona
⊡ Rehovot
▲ Mazkeret Batya
(Ekron)
Gedera ■
Hartuv ⊡
Motza ○
JERUSALEM ▣

▲ Be'er Toviyya
(Qastina)

DEAD SEA

HEBRON ▣

0   10   20   30   40   50km

FIG. 1

Table I
First Aliya Moshavot (1882–1904)

Moshava (in chron-ological order)	Founding Year	Founding Organization	Residents 1904	Territory 1904 (in dunams)
Rishon leTziyyon	1882	H.Z.* — Individuals	626	6,828
Rosh Pinna	1882	H.Z. — Rumanian Society	512	4,689
Zikhron Ya'aqov	1882	H.Z. — Central Ru-manian Society	871	7,194
Petah Tiqwa	1882	Individuals from Jerusalem	818	13,859
Mazkeret Batya (Ekron)	1883	B.R.**	231	4,260
Nes Tziyyona	1883	H.Z — Individual	137	1,369
Yesud haMa'ala	1883	H.Z. — Polish Society	230	11,000
Gedera	1884	H.Z. — Central Russian Society	114	3,368
Bat Shelomo	1888	B.R.	116	2,534
Be'er Toviyya (Qastina)	1888	B.R.	123	5,623
B'nai Yehuda	1888	Society from Safed	49	3,500
Shefeya	1889	B.R.	128	8,518
Rehovot	1890	H.Z. — Society & Individuals	222	10,652
Mishmar haYarden	1891	Local Individuals	110	4,400
Hadera	1891	H.Z. — Russian Societies	152	29,280
'En Zeytim	1892	H.Z. — Russian Society	37	5,800
Motza	1894	Society from Jerusalem	28	510
Hartuv	1895	H.Z. — Bulgarian Society	75	4,350
Metulla	1896	B.R.	284	12,800
Mahanayim	1899	H.Z. — Russian Society	67	5,857
Sejera	1899	JCA+	150	18,000
Atlit	1901	JCA	15	7,000
Kefar Tavor	1901	JCA	150	4,000
Yavne'el	1901	JCA	200	19,000
Melahemiyya	1901	JCA	100	8,000
Bet Gan	1903	JCA	± 100	20,000
Giv'at Ada	1903	JCA	35	5,000
Kefar Saba	1904	JCA	± 3	7,500
Total (approx.)			±5,500	235,000

*   Hovevei Zion.

** Baron Rothschild.

+   Jewish Colonization Association.

Sources for residents and territory: R. Aaronsohn, *The Jerusalem Cathedra*, 3, Jerusalem-Detroit 1983, p. 273.

the moshavot, but who, as they did not own land, were disfranchised. This group can be classified into three subdivisions: 1) craftsmen who lived in rented buildings on the moshavot; 2) various administrators and civil servants who resided in office quarters owned by the administration, or in public community buildings; 3) permanent Jewish workers who lived in structures made available by their employers. Most of the residents were married, and along with their families they comprised a significant percentage of the moshava population (see Table 2).

Table II
Internal Social Structure in Selected Moshavot. The "Judean Colonies," 1891 & 1900

| Moshava | 1891* | | | | 1900** | | |
	Farmers	Workers	Others	Total	Farmers	Workers & Others	Total
Rishon leTziyyon	219	60	80	359	404	222	626
Petah Tiqwa	250	20	217	487	649	169	818
Ekron	167	—	48	215	179	52	231
Nes Tziyyona	54	39	13	106	86	33	119
Gedera	37	6	12	55	80	34	114
Be'er Toviyya	—	5	35	40	114	10	124

* According to data compiled by Barzilai, appearing in D. Gurevitch & A. Graetz, *Hebrew Agricultural Settlement in Palestine — General Survey and Statistical Data*, Jerusalem 1938, Table 30 (Hebrew).

** According to data compiled by Meirovitch, appearing in Y. Ben-Arieh & Y. Bartal (eds.), *The History of Eretz-Israel*, VIII, Jerusalem 1983, p. 288 (Hebrew).

The third and final grouping included the Jewish and Arab workers who were considered temporary, and were evidently not recorded in the censuses. Their numbers varied, as some of them were seasonal laborers. According to one of the sources, there were around 1,600 Jewish workers on moshavot in the year 1900.[3] It is likely that the number of Arab workers — some of whom were fellaheen from neighboring villages who supplemented their income through part-time work on the Hebrew moshavot, while others had moved with their families onto

---

3   R. Aaronsohn, "The Jewish Colonies at Their Inception and the Contribution of Baron Rothschild to Their Development," Ph.D. thesis, Hebrew University, Jerusalem 1985, pp. 357–362 (Hebrew); I. Kollatt, "Jewish Laborers of the First Aliya," M. Eliav (ed.), *The First Aliya*, I, Jerusalem 1981, pp. 337–382 (Hebrew).

the land of the farmers who employed them — was no lower than this, and perhaps even higher.

The typical settlers were middle-aged and middle-class people with families. Most were formerly small merchants, craftsmen or low-ranking public servants, conservative and religious. They had banded together in one of the numerous colonization associations that had sprouted in Eastern Europe during the last two decades of the nineteenth century — mostly in Czarist Russia (which then included large parts of Poland), and to a lesser degree in Romania, Bulgaria and the neighboring countries.[4] Besides the desire to support themselves through manual labor in Eretz-Israel, and a blend of religious and national ideas, most of the immigrants also brought with them a modest sum of money. They planned to use this private capital to acquire plots of land and to support their families until crops could be raised.

The majority of the residents aspired to become farm owners, as did the salaried workers, who were not imbued with class consciousness. Both of these groups, however, lacked the capital necessary for the purchase of land. Notable among the salaried workers were the members of Bilu, a small but dynamic organization of young, secular and educated bachelors who were among the first immigrants in 1882. They held narodnik- socialistic views on the one hand, while on the other hand they had a far higher level of national consciousness than the rest of the paid laborers or the other settlers. The Biluim became independent farmers on their own moshava from the outset of the First Aliya.[5]

The average population of a moshava ranged from nearly 170 people in 1890 to 200 in 1900, with sizable deviations (see Tables 1 & 2). Families averaged slightly over five members. There were differences not only between moshavot but also between the social categories, especially the citizens and the residents. Most of the families of farmers resembled the extended families of traditional East European society, and numbered over six members on an average; in several of the moshavot the typical family had ten members. By contrast, the average size of a resident's family was three.

The social stratification was complex, as the sub-categories formed a variegated human fabric. Besides the class division, there was also a clear distinction between new immigrants and the veteran settlers, who may have been in Palestine merely five years longer than the new arrivals. Another division was between people of different origins, expressed mainly in the cultural differences

---

4   D. Weintraub et al., *Moshava, Kibbutz and Moshav, Patterns of Jewish Rural Settlement in Israel*, London-Ithaca 1969.

5   C. Chissin, *A Palestine Diary*, New York 1976; S. Laskov, *The Biluim*, Jerusalem 1979 (Hebrew).

between various countries in Eastern Europe. The number of Jews from other parts of the world, such as the Middle East and North Africa, was negligible, and these people were scattered throughout the moshavot.

The group of young adults stood out particularly in four central moshavot that were both the oldest and the largest such settlements — hence the high number of farmers' children who reached maturity, and the concentration of experienced permanent Jewish workers. The relative size of this group, consisting of those who had grown up in villages in Palestine but who lacked the capital or means of production to set up their own farms, increased during the First Aliya years. The dilemma was partially solved when these people, along with salaried workers, populated nine moshavot founded during this period. These moshavot, like most other First Aliya settlements, were established by three central bodies: Hovevei Zion, Baron Edmond de Rothschild and his staff, and the Jewish Colonization Association.

THE SETTLEMENT ESTABLISHMENT

The ardent desire to abandon Eastern Europe led the Jews to create a spontaneous mass immigration movement from the 1880's onward, and the First Aliya should be seen in this context. Most of the Jews, however, turned to Western Europe and beyond, to the New World, especially the United States. Millions of westward-bound Jews were aided by philanthropic organizations, particularly the Alliance Israélite Universelle, the most important international Jewish organization at the time. The minority who headed for Palestine were not assisted by any institutional body, nor did Palestine offer them any material advantages. These immigrants had to surmount both the harsh conditions of the area, whose economic and technological development lagged far behind that of the West, and the obstacles imposed by the Ottoman regime, which opposed Jewish immigration and settlement. Jews turning to agriculture faced two additional handicaps: a dearth of capital essential for the establishment of new settlements, and a lack of prior experience in working the land.[6]

These and other difficulties, along with the need of each religious Jew for such basics as a quorum of ten Jewish men for prayers, a ritual bath and kosher food, prompted the intending settlers to form group frameworks. These were initially organized at the local level only, as several dozen members of the Jewish

---

6   D. Gil'adi, "The Agronomic Development of the Old Colonies in Palestine (1882–1914)," M. Ma'oz (ed.), *Studies on Palestine during the Ottoman Period*, Jerusalem 1975, p. 175; N.T. Mandel, *The Arabs and Zionism before World War I*, Berkeley 1976, pp. 1–23.

community in an East European town formed an organization for immigration to Palestine and settlement there. Tens of such associations, working separately, handled the   necessary arrangements and supported a particular moshava. Initially the term "Hovevei Zion" referred to these associations in general; only in 1884 an umbrella organization of the same name was founded in Russia. Even then, however, the individual associations continued to function in parallel.[7]

The oppressive objective and subjective conditions in which the settlers operated affected every sphere of life, delayed the development of the moshavot and drained the community's financial resources. The budget that had been estimated for each moshava prior to the settlers' arrival proved to be highly inaccurate. On the one hand, expenses were immeasurably greater than planned, especially with regard to development, infrastructure and public services. On the other hand, income fell short of what was anticipated. It is no wonder, then, that shortly after the founding of the first moshavot, all of the settlements faced a serious crisis. When it finally became clear that no salvation was forthcoming, either from traditional cash crops and subsistence agriculture or from Hovevei Zion in Eastern Europe whose resources were meager, the settlers requested aid from the wealthy Jews of Western Europe.

The first moshava to receive assistance was the first one founded, Rishon leTziyyon, which in mid-1883 came under the auspices of Baron Edmond de Rothschild from Paris. With the exception of Gedera, the Bilu settlement that remained "autonomous" under the auspices of Hovevei Zion, all of the other moshavot were granted Rothschild's patronage till 1890, and were then referred to as "the Baron's moshavot." Rothschild paid the colonies' debts and initiated development projects in all spheres of life. His Palestine operations were executed by a network of agents known as "the Baron's Staff" or simply "the Administration." Vast sums of money were injected into the settlement enterprise from his private savings, over the objections of his family and social circle. The Baron's Staff consisted of hundreds of employees of three different types: administrators, clerks and executives; technical experts such as agricultural advisors and engineers; and, most numerous of all, community workers such as teachers, doctors and rabbis.

The substantial development that the Baron's moshavot underwent, spurred by Rothschild's capital and the work of his agents, was physically expressed in infrastructure and high-level construction of spacious residential units and

---

7   W. Laqueur, *A History of Zionism*, London 1972; I. Klausner, *Love of Zion in Romania*, Jerusalem 1958 (Hebrew); idem, *The Zion-bound Movement in Russia*, I, II and III, Jerusalem 1962–1965 (Hebrew); D. Vital, *The Origins of Zionism*, Oxford 1975, pp. 378–385.

dozens of public buildings. From the standpoint of the farm economy, his greatest contributions were expanding the moshavot lands, gearing for commercial agriculture by basing it on groves (especially vineyards) and establishing modern processing plants, whose products were exported to Europe; the most notable of these were the wine presses at Rishon leTziyyon and Zikhron Ya'aqov, which have been in operation up to the present. On the social plane there was a marked improvement in public services, a rise in the standard and quality of living, and a substantial population growth among farmers, "administrators," and hired laborers. These changes were most striking in Rishon leTziyyon, which became the center for the Baron's Staff, and in many respects the focus of cultural life on the moshavot. (See Plates 1 and 2).

On the other hand, "rebellions" broke out among the settlers who aspired to preserve their economic independence and free spirit vis-à-vis the Baron's Administration. The Baron's auspices had deprived the settlers of responsibility for their own farms and lives, for good or for bad. Some of the benefits bestowed by the system, such as income subsidies in the form of permanently inflated prices for agricultural produce, as well as direct financial aid to the farmers, created an artificial support system with built-in distortions. The Baron's Staff, whose members received monthly salaries from Paris, constituted a privileged "class" among the settlers. They formed a tough centralistic system and adopted Rothschild's patriarchal-philanthropic approach. Contrary to the commonly held view, the background of most members of the Baron's Administration was identical to that of the population that they served; there were almost no Christians (barring a few French experts) and relatively few French-speakers (employees of the Alliance Israélite Universelle and graduates of its schools), and most of the personnel were Jewish immigrants from Eastern Europe. Nevertheless, the system bred alienation between members of the Administration and the farmers who were subordinate to them and required their services. From here the way was short to charges of incompetence, favoritism and corruption.[8]

The "rebellions" were abortive, and the Baron's regime entrenched itself. In fact, not only were his eleven moshavot under its direct auspices, but the other Jewish rural settlements (including the "autonomous" Hovevei Zion colonies of the 1890's) were also largely, if more informally, dependent on the system. Essentially the Baron took upon himself the responsibility for all Jewish agricultural settlement in Palestine.

---

8 I. Margalith, *Le Baron Edmond de Rothschild et la Colonisation Juive en Palestine (1882–1899)*, Paris 1957, pp. 91ff.; S. Schama, *Two Rothschilds and the Land of Israel*, London 1978, pp. 54–134.

Continuing to operate in the Baron's shadow were several additional bodies, such as the "old *yishuv*" organizations that established two moshavot during the First Aliya period, and the Hovevei Zion associations.[9] Various groups within the latter framework set up another six moshavot during the 1890's. By the turn of the century the approximately 140 Hovevei Zion associations throughout Europe had a membership of between ten to fourteen thousand, from whose ranks came the founders of these moshavot and most of the other immigrants to Palestine. The operational work in Palestine was carried out by the "Hovevei Zion Executive Committee," situated in Jaffa, and the spiritual message was conveyed by members of B'nei Moshe, an elitist association belonging to Hovevei Zion and headed by Ahad Ha'am. It stressed the importance of cultural ("moral") advancement vis-à-vis the actual work. Hovevei Zion's activities within the older moshavot, the settlement nucleus, were reduced to marginal areas, and mainly took the form of moral support and spiritual inspiration.

The year 1900, though, saw an important organizational change in Palestine. At the turn of the century Baron Rothschild decided to withdraw from the direct administration of the moshavot. Although the motivation for such a decision at this particular time is unclear, it seems to have been related to the economic situation of the moshavot. After eighteen years of work, during which Rothschild invested an estimated forty million francs — nearly twenty times the sum expended by all of the Hovevei Zion associations combined during the same period — the moshavot were as far from economic independence as ever. On January 1, 1900, the Baron transferred all of his property in Palestine, and with it the administration of his moshavot, to the Jewish Colonization Association (JCA). The French philanthropist contributed an additional fifteen million francs to bolster the economy of the moshavot, and was appointed the head of a new JCA department charged with handling settlement affairs in Palestine.[10]

The JCA had been founded by Baron Hirsh in 1891. It was active in various countries, especially Argentina. From the year 1896 it began operating in Palestine on a limited basis, in four moshavot not under Rothschild's auspices. Once the JCA took over the administration of the settlement operations in 1900, it hastened to apply its liberal principles: responsiveness to market laws and closure of foundering enterprises, thrift in expenditures and balanced accounts, minimal administrative apparatus and reduction of manpower. This policy

9   Even though the Zionist Organization was founded in 1897, its institutions only began operating in Palestine around a decade later, i.e. after the period under discussion. See: Bein (note 2, supra), pp. 11–25.

10   Schama (note 8, supra), pp. 134–136.

found immediate expression in a curtailment of financial aid to private farmers, termination of subsidies, a decrease in the number of clerks and public service employees, and a general slowdown of economic activity.

The frugal policy of the JCA led to unemployment and a concomitant psychological crisis at the start of the century, which caused many young people, the children of farmers and workers, to emigrate from Palestine. The crisis persisted even after 1904, when the First Aliya drew to a close, and it was not until the Second Aliya period that the moshavot were to extricate themselves from it, with renewed vigor. Nonetheless, already in the first four years of the twentieth century, in the framework of its curative measures for the moshavot, the JCA created a new settlement reality. It established an agricultural training farm and seven moshavot of a new type. These new communities were based on grain crops, and their members were mostly from the weaker social classes in the existing settlements (workers, children of settlers, or independent farmers whose land holdings were small). The founders of the new moshavot received relatively large plots of land, which they worked in the capacity of tenant farmers, under the JCA's supervision from a distance. The JCA continued to administer the settlement enterprise in the following decades.[11]

CULTURE, EDUCATION AND LANGUAGE

At the center of cultural life on the moshava stood religion, an inseparable part of the daily life of most of the settlers. Behavioral norms and life-styles were Orthodox and traditional, even though individuals in most of the moshavot, and entire groups in a few of them (consisting mainly of workers like the Biluim, and the second generation among the independent farmers), adopted a relatively "free" life-style.

Similarly, in continuation of the way of life practiced abroad, most of the holidays and special events were of a religious or at least traditional character. Still, in the course of the First Aliya, modern, nonreligious cultural institutions and activities took shape and gained popularity. These included secular public libraries in most of the moshavot, bands for wind instruments, celebrations and dances, amateur theater, sports competitions, etc.[12] (See Plates 3 and 4).

Other cultural activities, which were unique to Palestine and the new agricultural settlement experience, may be viewed in the context of heightened

11 *Ibid.*, pp. 136ff.; T. Norman, *An Outstretched Arm, a History of the Jewish Colonization Association*, London 1985.
12 Aaronsohn (note 3, supra), pp. 382–390.

secular national consciousness: renewal of agricultural holidays to mark the harvest and vintage, which had been celebrated during the First and the Second Temple periods; renewed celebration of Tu Bishvat, the New Year for Trees; ceremonies upon the establishment of new settlements; development of a tradition of organized trips to historical-national sites throughout the land; and songs in Hebrew, some of which expressed the national renascence and later were adopted as the anthems of particular moshavot. One of the songs, *Hatikva* ("The Hope"), later became the national anthem. Another national symbol was the blue-and-white striped flag with the Star of David at its center, first flown in Rishon leTziyyon in 1885 at the celebrations marking the third anniversary of the first moshava.

Two distinct trends crystallized in the field of education: traditional and new.[13] The traditional schools, modeled after the old Heder and Talmud Torah, were located in subleased structures such as synagogues or farmers' homes. The tutors hired were mainly yeshiva graduates from the old *yishuv* in Palestine. Only boys studied, and religious subjects were taught almost exclusively. The language used was the one the new immigrants had brought with them from Eastern Europe: Yiddish. This framework was nearly identical to the religious educational system in the Diaspora and the old communities in Palestine. It was instituted in the moshavot from the outset, and continued to function in most of them throughout the period in question, as well as afterwards.

Already in the 1880's a parallel system, modern in both content and form, began to sprout in the larger of the Baron's moshavot. Physically, the new system was revolutionary, since spacious buildings were designed and constructed as schools, and they contained modern furniture, equipment and pedagogical aids such as atlases and wall maps. Girls were admitted, the staff was for the first time composed of professional teachers, and administrative and supervisory positions were added.

The most fundamental change was in the curriculum. The syllabus was extended beyond religious subjects, to include on the one hand theoretical subjects such as math, science and geography, and on the other hand trades like wood craft and sewing, or enrichment courses such as singing and gym. This was part of a comprehensive curriculum set in schools of the Baron's moshavot, ten years after the First Aliya had begun. (See Plate 5).

Another innovation was the teaching of some of the secular subjects in Hebrew (the religious subjects had traditionally been taught in the Holy Tongue).

---

13   *Ibid.*, pp. 374–382; R. Elboim-Dror, *Hebrew Education in Eretz-Israel*, I, Jerusalem 1986, pp. 122–215 (Hebrew).

The first school to implement this change opened in Rishon leTziyyon in 1887. Hebrew was studied in parallel with Arabic and French, initially through translation from Yiddish, but shortly thereafter through the "Hebrew in Hebrew" method. Also helping to spread the once-dead language were Hebrew printings of study texts and other books, composed mainly by moshavot teachers, some of them retired. During the 1890's some of the teachers formed a voluntary pedagogical body, with the aim of promoting studies in Hebrew and integrating them into a comprehensive curriculum with a national character.[14]

Activity in the educational domain produced immediate results in the field. The ancient language was used not only by students in their daily affairs, but also here and there by the settlers as a living language, from the end of the first decade of settlement. In a few of the moshavot, organizations were established in parallel with sister bodies in Jerusalem, to promote the Hebrew language. True, the process was long and arduous. The struggle for the primacy of Hebrew as opposed to French, the international language (used in Palestine even before the Baron's Administration had designated it "the language of culture" on the moshavot), and Yiddish, the spoken tongue of the East European immigrants, was not won until the Second Aliya period. Still, phenomena such as a national culture intentionally revolving around the Hebrew language, and the new status of Hebrew as the "national language" and the native tongue of the new generation, were clearly present in the moshavot of the First Aliya period.

ORGANIZATIONAL STRUCTURE AND PUBLIC ACTIVITY

One basic structural problem characterizing the settlement enterprise from the outset was the fact that no inter-moshava society ever emerged, and no central, national institution was created to coordinate the network of colonies. Perhaps this decentralization stemmed from the individualistic character of the settlers, and the lack of unifying social concepts. The moshavot's administrative and material dependence on the French Baron and international Jewish organizations also militated against their being organized on anything but the local level. Rothschild, and the JCA in his footsteps, even developed hierarchical systems that encompassed large portions of the new settlement enterprise, but whose apex lay outside it: the supervisors resided in the Middle East but not in the moshavot, and the general directors and governors managed the operations from Europe (see Fig. 2). As for Hovevei Zion, all of its organizational work

---

14   S. Haramati, "The Revival of Hebrew as a Spoken Language in the Settlements," *The First Aliya*, I (note 3, supra), pp. 427–446.

SPATIAL & FUNCTIONAL HIERARCHY:
THE MOSHAVOT & THE BARON'S ADMINISTRATION.

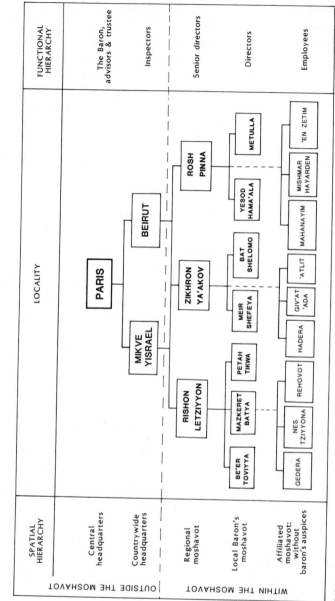

FIG. 2

took place abroad, which is where its leaders, including Ahad Ha'am, elected to remain. Only local branches were set up in Palestine.

Most of the moshavot were organized on the local level as autonomous communities. They were subject to by-laws that set behavioral norms and ground rules governing the relationship between citizens and residents and delineating the internal administrative structure: membership meetings, committees, positions. These bodies managed the affairs of the moshavot in an intensive fashion during the first and inevitably problematic year of settlement on the land, mainly in a cooperative format called a "commune." Afterwards the organization took the form of committees that convened irregularly, especially in the Baron's moshavot, where the actual administration was mainly performed by his staff.

In contrast to the minuscule influence of the committees over time was the profound impact of many and varied groups serving specific sectors.[15] The joint social activity they sponsored was spontaneous in nature, in that it stemmed from the settlers' own initiative rather than that of the supporting organizations. Although these organizations strictly supervised and restricted the moshavot committees, they allowed the social groups a free hand. Because the Baron's moshavot had reached a higher level of development than the others, the activity in these colonies was more inclusive and advanced than in the other Jewish settlements in Palestine.

The traditional societies for religious study, the hosting of guests, burial, etc. constituted the center of social activity in all of the moshavot. Nevertheless, public endeavors of a new variety, based on actual needs, began to develop in many of these settlements. For example, groups for guarding the moshava were formed, with all of the settlers participating on a rotating basis. In several of the Baron's moshavot, societies sprang up to promote various concepts related to the national revival in Palestine. These included the above-mentioned societies for the promotion of the Hebrew language, and the Jewish National Fund, originally set up in 1889 in Rishon leTziyyon for the sake of land acquisition and settlement. This latter organization, in an altered form, is still active at present.

One type of organization geared to a specific sector of society was the labor unions. The first of these was founded as early as 1887 (although it soon disbanded), and others followed in the 1890's. The workers were also the first to attempt to organize in a national framework, when, in 1899, 530 of them from various moshavot registered as members of a central organization. Activity geared to a particular branch of the economy got under way in 1896, when

---

15   Aaronsohn (note 3, supra), pp. 363–374.

Hovevei Zion, with the Baron's approval, founded the Carmel Company to handle the marketing in Europe of vineyard products. Four years later citrus growers from the southern coastal plain (the "Judean Colonies") founded a cooperative called Pardes to market their produce. In 1903 around sixty delegates from all of the Jewish institutions in the land convened in Zikhron Ya'aqov to establish the Federation of Teachers, the first trade union in Palestine.[16] Carmel, Pardes and the Federation of Teachers are still in existence. (See Plate 6).

Thus, despite the difficulties, the trend toward national settlement organizations began to take shape at the turn of the century. It gained momentum in 1897 with the founding of the World Zionist Organization in Basel, and the launching of Herzl's political Zionism. This led to the establishment of separate Zionist associations in several of the moshavot, which united in 1902 as the Committee of the Associated Zionist Societies in Palestine. The committee had a membership of three thousand, including many city-dwellers. The following year the Palestine Convocation, a body claiming to represent all of the diverse components of the new *yishuv*, assembled in Zikhron Ya'aqov. Half of the sixty-seven delegates attending were from cities, and the other half from the moshavot.[17] Even though the organization that was founded by the Palestine Convocation never implemented its resolutions, the assembly, taking place just as the First Aliya period was drawing to a close, may be viewed as the new settlers' first attempt at an organization with permanent national representation supported largely by the moshavot.

CONCLUSION

The cultural landscape in the moshavot of the First Aliya was not uniform. Old and new elements, imported and local, were mingled together in every sphere of life. On the social plane, for example, a class structure like that in the East European Shtetel could be found, with its many non-agricultural occupations, social and economic gaps, etc. Education and certain aspects of the life-style were also largely a continuation of the traditional life abroad. One of the significant obstacles in the way of creating a new national and social way of life was the lack of internal bonds between the moshavot, which deepened their dependence on various Jewish circles abroad that divided between them the actual management of the Jewish settlement enterprise. Organizational cleavage

16   D. Gil'adi & Y. Shavit, "The Organization of the Yishuv," Y. Ben-Arieh & I. Bartal (eds.), *The History of Eretz-Israel*, VIII, Jerusalem 1983, pp. 298–305 (Hebrew).

17   I. Kollatt, "The Organization of the Jewish Population and the Development of Its Political Consciousness Before World War I," *Studies on Palestine* (note 6, supra), pp. 211–223.

would continue to characterize the moshavot in the future, thereby reducing their relative role in the settlement landscape of the country, as well as on the cultural and political scene.[18]

On the other hand, there were clear signs of a budding native Hebrew culture in activities such as the development of a modern educational system, establishment of secular social organizations, and inauguration of national events. Especially notable was the culture that expressly revolved around the Hebrew language, and the process by which it became the argot of the entire new *yishuv*.

The driving force behind the establishment of the moshavot, and the unifying factor giving rise to a society with various unique features, was ideology. In the period preceding the Zionist movement, the ideology was inchoate, nebulous, and tinged with old aspirations, such as the return to and settlement of Eretz-Israel as the fulfillment of a divine commandment, and manual labor as a productive act in the spirit of the Enlightenment.[19] However, at its core were new ideas about the Jewish people returning to the Land of Israel for the sake of a secular-national renascence. When the seeds of these ideas germinated, the new elements in the cultural landscape of the First Aliya became dominant in the Jewish community in Palestine as a whole, even after the moshavot lost their standing and became a minor component of the settlement map.

18   The first kibbutz was established in 1909, and the first moshav in 1921. Following World War I, the kibbutz overtook the moshava as the most widespread form of Jewish rural settlement.

19   Cf. S. Ettinger & I. Bartal, "The First Aliya: Ideological Roots and Practical Accomplishments," L.I. Levine (ed.), *The Jerusalem Cathedra*, 2, Jerusalem–Detroit 1982, pp. 197–227.

PART III:

THE TWENTIETH CENTURY — NOMADISM AND RURAL SETTLEMENT

TRANSFORMATION IN ARAB RURAL SETTLEMENT IN PALESTINE

MOSHE BRAWER

INTRODUCTION

From the sixteenth century until the onset of the modern era in the 1870's, the basic geographical characteristics of the typical Arab village in Palestine remained essentially unaltered. In the latter half of the nineteenth century, changes heralding the beginning of transformation appeared. These were initially minor, slow, and limited to a small number of communities, and were reflected in the village's layout, social pattern, economy, standard of living, public services and relations with the environment. By the end of the 1920's, the majority of Arab villages had been affected.

While the typical Arab village remained in a state of almost complete stagnation for over three centuries, there was a significant decline in the extent and density of rural settlement. There is convincing evidence from the end of the sixteenth century that the number of villages and the extent of permanently-settled areas were far greater at that time than in the 1870's.[1] Many villages were abandoned during the seventeenth to the nineteenth century, most of them totally ruined, particularly in southern and eastern frontier zones facing arid Bedouin-dominated territory.[2]

According to W.D. Hütteroth, approximately 50% of the villages in the Hebron region, eastern Judea, Samaria and the central Jordan Valley were deserted during this period, as were 85% in the Bet She'an and eastern Jezreel Valleys, and 26% in the central coastal plain (Sharon) and the adjoining Samarian foothills. By contrast, the extent of this phenomenon in the central

---

1   There is ample evidence from the sixteenth century on the extent of settlement. See: W.D. Hütteroth & K. Abdulfattah, *Historical Geography of Palestine, Transjordan and Southern Syria in the Late 16th Century*, Erlangen 1977; D.H.K. Amiran, "Pattern of Settlement in Palestine," *Israel Exploration Journal*, III, nos. 2–4 (1953).

2   W.D. Hütteroth, "Schwankungen von Siedlungsdichte und Siedlungsgrenze in Palästina und Transjordanien seit dem 16. Jahrhundert," *Tagungsbericht und Wissenschaftliche Abhandlungen*, Deutscher Geographentag Kiel 1969, Wiesbaden 1970.

and northern highlands totaled only 9%, mostly in marginal areas.[3] Thus only minor changes took place in the number and density of villages in these latter regions, even during the period of maximum retreat in rural settlement in Palestine as a whole. Hence by the 1870's, the great majority of the rural population — which was nearly entirely Arab[4] — resided in this part of the country.

The number of villages and density of the rural population reached a nadir during the first half of the nineteenth century.[5] The late 1840's marked the beginning of a clear upward trend. Some of the abandoned villages were reinhabited and rebuilt. Several others, unmentioned in sixteenth-century records, sprang up, either in locations which were not settled during the 1500's, or, having taken on new names, on the sites of earlier villages.

Historical-geographical studies on this revival, and on Arab rural settlement in general, have thus far been few, and mainly concerned with the extent and density of settlement during various periods. While examining the processes of growth or decline in the number of villages, and their causes, along with the changing pattern of their spatial dispersion, they have paid scant attention to the geographical characteristics of the individual village. True, there is much descriptive information on the Arab village in nineteenth- and early twentieth-century studies, surveys and travel reports. A wealth of geographical, historical and other literature, such as the survey conducted by the Palestine Exploration Fund, provides a detailed and authentic picture of Arab villages immediately prior to, or during, the early stage of the modern era. Nevertheless, there is very little systematic historical-geographical research on the relationship between the typical village's physical and human properties, morphogenesis, evolution and the factors that produced its pre-modern semblance.

Sources

The actual process of transformation which the Arab village underwent from the 1870's onward can be traced through a variety of sources that grow in scope, detail and accuracy as one approaches World War I, and even more so during the period of British rule. These include surveys, reports, studies, cartographic material, aerial photographs from World War I up to the late 1940's, and both

---

3   *Ibid.*, p. 469.
4   Y. Ben-Arieh, "The Population of Palestine and Its Settlements Immediately Prior to the Initiation of the Zionist Colonization Project," Y. Ben-Arieh et al. (eds.), *Studies in the Geographical History of Settlement in Palestine*, Jerusalem 1987, pp. 3–14 (Hebrew).
5   Hütteroth (note 1, supra), pp. 62–63.

official and private documents. Cadastral and village maps produced by the Survey of Palestine (1925–1947) provide extensive information on the physical features of many villages, as well as on land ownership and utilization there. Field work we have carried out since 1967, which has covered 282 villages in the Galilee, Judea and Samaria, has made a most valuable contribution to this study, filling many of the gaps left by the above-mentioned sources. Records kept intermittently by headmen in some of the villages, especially in "village notebooks" introduced by the British in the 1930's, contain data on agricultural production, tax collection, public works, changes in land ownership and, occasionally, outstanding local events. Testimony by elders acquainted with oral traditions concerning the origins and history of the village was often the only source on these subjects. These people were also instrumental in chronicling the changes that had taken place in their village and its environs throughout their lifetime. With the assistance of these elders it was possible to reconstruct features of the village's physical layout, and the mode in which the social structure fitted into this pattern, before transformation got under way. Fortunately, in many villages, mainly in the central highland, the old nucleus was still in existence when this study began in the late 1960's. A close examination of such old village nuclei formed a substantial part of our field work, as it supplemented the knowledge we derived from all other sources.

THE VILLAGE AT THE START OF THE MODERN ERA

The 1870's are generally viewed as the beginning of a new era for rural Palestine, brought on by the introduction of modern European agricultural settlement (at first German and later Jewish), the rapidly-burgeoning activities of European Christian religious institutions, the influx of Christian pilgrims, the improvement and expansion of the interurban road network and later railways, the increase in the urban population and its demand for agricultural produce, and finally the growing strength and efficiency of the security services.

The Arab rural population of Palestine in the 1870's inhabited 673 villages. Of these, 516 appear in Ottoman census records from around three hundred years earlier. It may be assumed that many of the remaining 157 villages and hamlets had also existed in the sixteenth century, but that their names either had been erroneously recorded, or else had changed over time, especially if after the census was conducted the villages were abandoned and subsequently resettled. The majority of Arab villages in the 1870's, and those established in following decades — including the ones which cannot be traced back to the sixteenth century — were built on or near sites of antecedent settlements from much earlier periods. In the words of D.H.K. Amiran: "Research in archeology and historical geography has produced ample evidence to show that a large number, probably the large majority, of present-day village sites in the uplands of Palestine are the successors *in loco* of settlements known from biblical times and very often mentioned in the Bible itself."[6] This fact should be borne in mind in any examination of the morphogenesis of the Arab villages, especially those with physical features differing widely from the typical pattern.

The population of most Arab villages had increased either little or not at all since the sixteenth century.[7] Over 70% of the villages in the 1870's had fewer than 500 residents, and the majority under 250. There had hardly been any natural increase among the rural population during that period. Its total in the 1870's was estimated at 255,000, constituting 72% of the total settled population (i.e. excluding nomads) of Palestine.[8] Morevoer, a substantial portion of the inhabitants in certain towns, such as Hebron, Gaza, and Nablus, were engaged in agriculture, so that the actual percentage of what may be considered as rural population was actually higher.

THE DENSELY NUCLEATED PATTERN AND ITS MORPHOGENESIS

Nearly all Arab villages and hamlets of the 1870's, as well as most of those appearing on the Palestinian landscape up to the 1920's, consisted of haphazard clusters of low, one-storey houses. In this very compact type of *Haufendorf*, each village is made up of several blocks of houses with small courts, separated from each other by narrow, tortuous lanes. Each block was originally enclosed by the joining outer walls of the houses and courts. Buildings and fences on the outer perimeter were often constructed to meet defense requirements. Outward-facing walls were either windowless or had only small porthole-like windows placed high above the ground. Variations of this typical clustered pattern largely represented adaptations to the topographical and geographical features of the site. The nature of the locally-available building material, of which nearly all of the houses were constructed, was also an important factor in determining the appearance of the village. Settlements in the highlands and the adjoining foothills were built of local stone, mostly limestone quarried very close to the village site. Only some villages in eastern Galilee were built of local basalt. In parts of the coastal plain, a soft crumbly sandstone (*kurkar*), the only locally-available stone, was often used, while in the southern part of the coastal plain, mud bricks

---

6   Amiran (note 1, supra), p. 195; C.T. Wilson, *Peasant Life in The Holy Land*, London 1906, pp. 57–58.

7   *Ibid.*, p. 10; Hütteroth (note 1, supra), p. 47.

8   Ben-Arieh (note 4, supra), pp. 5–9.

and a mixture of mud and straw or shrub stems constituted the primary building material (see Plates 1 and 2).[9]

This densely-clustered pattern, which often incorporated elements inherent in the site, provided defense advantages against both external raids and internal frays. Security requirements played a decisive role in the pattern of most Arab villages, and in many cases also in the choice of site.[10]

Study of the morphogenesis of this typical clustered Arab village has yet to provide conclusive evidence on the circumstances under which it evolved and its relations to the patterns of antecedent villages. Excavations in existing Arab villages, mainly in connection with reconstruction work and replacement of old buildings by modern houses, have thus far been insufficient to expose the pattern of the ruined underlying settlement. The same applies to those abandoned and ruined during recent wars in Palestine. An attempt to excavate all the underlying strata of an Arab village ruined in 1948 is being undertaken at the time of this writing (1988) in the Samarian foothills.[11]

Archaeological research is generally aimed at eras much earlier than the one immediately preceding Ottoman rule. Far more light has been shed on the characteristics of rural settlements in biblical and post-biblical periods than on those whose ruins became the site of the recent generation of Arab villages. Excavations have revealed that during biblical and post-biblical times, up to the Crusader period, rural settlements in Palestine were clustered, in most cases extremely so, but there are clear indications that their layout was different from that of villages in recent centuries. Remnants of antecedent settlements are apparent in many of the Arab villages, consisting of partly-reconstructed walls, hewn stones, cisterns, canals and paved alleys. However, even where many such remains are conspicuous in old nuclei of contemporary villages, the extent to which the latter's patterns conform with those of the ruins on which they stand has yet to be studied.

There is good reason to assume that the typical pattern of the Arab village is the result of a combination of factors, including conditions dominating rural life in Palestine during the sixteenth to nineteenth centuries, traditions and practices inherited from previous generations or introduced from neighboring areas

---

9   A.J. Brawer, *Ha'aretz*, Tel Aviv 1928 (Hebrew), pp. 256–258; G. Robinson Lees, *Village Life in Palestine*, London 1905, pp. 75–79; Wilson (note 6, supra), pp. 58–60, 63–64.

10   Robinson Lees (note 9, supra), p. 75; Wilson (note 6, supra), p. 57; Hütteroth (note 1, supra), p. 47.

11   These excavations have been carried out under the direction of Dr. M. Fisher of the Department of Archaeology, Tel Aviv University, at the site of the village Muzeiriya, abandoned and in ruin since 1948.

(mainly Hejaz), and perhaps also the residual pattern of the antecedent settlement. In addition to meeting defense requirements and offering some climatic advantages, this layout was well suited to the social structure that prevailed until very recently, and to the traditional way of life of an Islamic rural society (see Plates 3 and 4).

DISPERSION AND CONSTRUCTION CHANGES

The transformation processes in the typical Arab village since the 1870's manifested themselves in its gradual dispersion, generally simultaneous with growth in population, innovative architecture and construction techniques, expansion and improvement of old buildings, erection of public buildings (mainly schools), and in some areas the initial stages of an infrastructure (roads, water supply, etc.). A more modern building style, which exploited new materials brought from afar (cement, iron, timber, glass) in addition to those procured near the village, produced a gradual change in the rural landscape. The buildings had merged naturally into the environment so long as local stone had been used exclusively, but this quality faded with growing use of "modern" materials. The massive masonry featuring thick walls and domed ceilings and roofs was replaced by much thinner, concrete-supported structures with flat or tiled roofs.[12]

In some villages the process of dispersion was linked with a gradual shift in the main site of the built-up area. This was particularly the case where the original advantages of the old site had lost their significance or even became disadvantages as a result of recent developments. Far-reaching improvements in security conditions, mainly after the establishment of the British administration in the 1920's, along with the concomitant suppression of Bedouin and bandit raids, and of violent conflicts both between and within villages, turned difficult accessibility into a disadvantage. Thus hilltop villages, known as the acropolis type, started to sprawl downhill, as nearly all new buildings were erected on an adjacent, much lower site. Similarly, the protective aspects of the extremely clustered pattern lost their usefulness. The main exceptions to the typical clustered Arab village of the 1870's were a few small, dispersed Bedouin settlements, established since the 1830's on the fringes of the rural areas. (See Fig. 1).[13]

The transformation processes in village pattern and building style were initially very slow, and limited to a small number of villages, mainly in the vicinity of

---

12   H. Kendall, *Village Development in Palestine During the British Mandate*, London 1949, p. 22; Wilson (note 6, supra), pp. 58–59, 71.
13   Amiran (note 1, supra), p. 255.

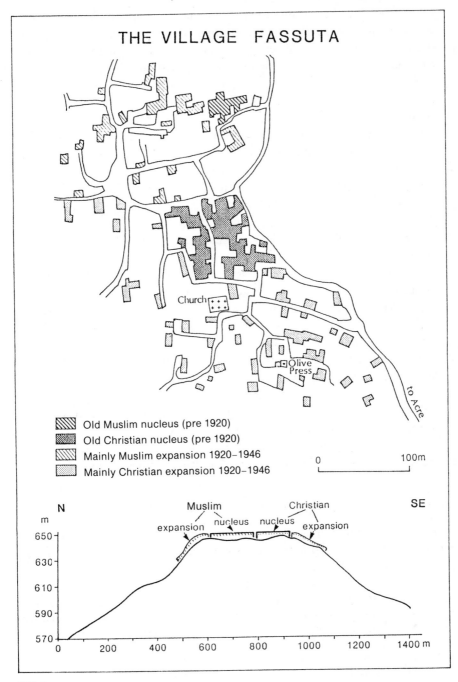

THE VILLAGE FASSUTA

Church

Olive
Press

to Acre

Old Muslim nucleus (pre 1920)
Old Christian nucleus (pre 1920)
Mainly Muslim expansion 1920–1946
Mainly Christian expansion 1920–1946

0   100m

N

m

Muslim   Christian

expansion   nucleus   nucleus   expansion

SE

650
630
610
590
570

0   200   400   600   800   1000   1200   1400 m

FIG 1

urban centers or along interurban communication arteries, especially those subject to improvement and modernization. The pace of dispersion and of the introduction of new architecture was more rapid in villages inhabited by Christian Arabs or on sites of interest to Christian religious institutions,[14] apparently as a result of the influence and material assistance of European church organizations, which became increasingly active in Palestine during the second half of the nineteenth century. The German Templer Society and Zionist modern rural settlements, which were established from the late 1860's onward, also hastened the initiation of transformation processes in some neighboring Arab villages.

One feature of dispersion that made its slow appearance about the turn of the century was the establishment of subsidiary outer hamlets, generally known by their Arabic name *hirba*. These had in many cases started as a few huts temporarily inhabited on outlying agricultural lands, especially during plowing and harvesting seasons.[15] The hamlets came into being mainly on the western and northern fringes of the central highland, on the periphery of cultivable lands owned by villages in the highlands, on the coastal plain, and in the Jezreel and Jordan Valleys. From the 1920's onward, many of these subsidiary settlements or *écarts* grew into independent villages. For example, the village of Deir el Ghusun in western Samaria, which apparently featured no permanently settled *hirba* at the end of the nineteenth century, had six of them by the early 1920's and nine by the mid-1930's, six of which subsequently developed into independent villages. The nearby village of Ya'bad, as well as Tubas in northeastern Samaria, each produced five outlying settlements during the same period. Where such a *hirba* was established within a comparatively short distance of the mother village, and both settlements developed and dispersed, the *hirba* became reabsorbed into the main village as one of its quarters (see Plate 5).

ACCELERATION IN TRANSFORMATION

The transformation of the physical characteristics of the Arab village gained momentum only in the 1930's, and not until the 1940's did this process spread to

---

14   E. Grant, *The Peasantry of Palestine*, New York 1907, pp. 44–45. The villages of Jifna and 'En Kerem (in the environs of Jerusalem), Abud (southwest Samaria), and Kafr Kanna (near Nazareth) are conspicuous examples of accelerated transformation precipitated by Christian organizations.

15   D. Grossman, "The Development of Subsidiary Settlements on the Fringes of Samaria — Processes and Factors," A. Shmueli et al. (eds.), *Judea and Samaria*, II, Jerusalem 1977, pp. 398–408 (Hebrew).

most highland areas. Nevertheless, change was slow, as a report on a special 1945 survey on the Arab village attests: "To the approaching visitor the most noticeable feature of the typical Arab village is the concentration of the houses in a thick cluster on the high stony ground of the village land."[16] According to this report, only 16% of the dwellings, containing 18% of the village population, were dispersed and lay outside the old congested village nucleus.[17]

The relationship between the pace of village transformation and development on the one hand, and the geographical properties of the environment of which the village formed a part, on the other hand, became more apparent as the extent and intensity of these processes grew. The substantial rise in population due to both natural increase and immigration, the growth of urban centers, the expansion and modernization of road and rail networks and transportation services, the introduction of new economic activities, the development and improvement of economic functions, and, finally, a number of additional countrywide and local changes in Palestine had a much stronger impact on villages in close contact with these developments than on "backwater" settlements. This phenomenon is well known from many other parts of the world, especially in underdeveloped countries,[18] but the situation in Palestine had unique qualities since this was the Holy Land, external elements were intensively involved and the area had been afflicted by much strife since the early 1920's. Thus while some villages, especially those in the vicinity of the main urban centers, on or near holy sites, or well placed on a main artery of communication, had lost most of their original layout and become largely dispersed by the end of the British Mandate period, others, particularly in parts of the highlands still inaccessible in the 1940's to modern transportation, were experiencing only the initial stage of departure from extreme nucleation.

There was also a conspicuous correlation between geographical factors and a shift in the site of the village, or at least the settlement nucleus, with the emergence of new conditions that made considerations of convenience more dominant than those of defense and social traditions in the choice of building ground. The rapid development of the "Citrus Belt" along much of the coastal plain during the 1920's and 1930's had a strong influence on villages within this area, and in the adjoining western foothills of the highlands. Here these villages developed dispersed "outliers" resembling more the typical Huerta settlements

16   Government of Palestine, "Survey of Social and Economic Conditions in Arab Villages 1944," *General Monthly Bulletin of Current Statistics* (September 1945), p. 561.

17   *Ibid.*, p. 562.

18   R. Abler et al., *Spatial Organization*, London 1972, p. 289.

of southern Spain than the traditional Palestinian Arab pattern. The dispersion in some of these villages encompassed over one-third of the dwellings, housing nearly 30% of the population.

While it is possible to reconstruct the layout and extent of the built-up area in many Arab villages around the turn of the century, the size of the respective populations can only be roughly estimated. Quantitative representations of the major transformation processes, especially dispersion, can therefore be made only from the early 1920's onward, following the first complete modern census in the area, conducted by the British authorities in 1922 (see Table I).[19]

The initial stages were marked not only by their slow pace but also by the short distance away from the clustered nucleus that people were willing to move. Frequently this range was initially so small that the process appeared more like a loosening of the extreme congestion than actual dispersion. In many villages the growth of the population and number of households up to the early 1940's resulted in the expansion of the clustered area rather than in dispersion and a change in pattern. Here again, as in other aspects of transformation, the nature and expression of this process depended largely on the geographical location and attributes of each village. Proximity and easy access to a major urban center led not only to a faster pace of transformation, but also to a much wider dispersion of the newly constructed dwellings (see Plate 6).

In none of the villages did the dispersion adhere to planning or any organized and directed form. A policy envisioning the imposition of basic planning rules on the expansion of the built-up areas in Arab villages was drawn up in the latter years of the British Mandate, but hardly put into practice.[20] Therefore, expansion and dispersion were sporadic, in accordance with local tendencies and the villagers' convenience. Thus the dispersed parts of many villages preserved the *Haufendorf* pattern, but in a much looser form. They consisted of small houses with fenced courts separated by open spaces on which, wherever possible, some vegetables and fruit trees were grown. In some villages, a substantial number of the dispersed houses were built along the road leading into the village or running through it, so that the new section came to resemble a *Strassedorf*. As transformation progressed, such villages developed a pattern consisting of three distinct sections: the old thickly-clustered nucleus; a belt with haphazardly-scattered, small new houses around the nucleated part; and a row of irregularly-

19   Due to the nature of nucleation and dispersion in the typical Arab village, neither the Demangeon nor the Zierhofer formula can be applied to measure the rate of dispersion which these villages underwent.

20   Kendall (note 12, supra), pp. 5–9.

TABLE I
Growth and Dispersion of Typical Arab Villages in Palestine During British Rule*

Village	Geographical Position**	Population Increase 1922–1947 (%)	Population Density Per dunam† Early 1920's	1946/47	Population Outside Nucleated Area 1946/47 (%)
Jerusalem Environs					
Abu Dis	I	110	24	12	25
Beit Hanina	I	80	28	16	18
Battir	I	110	28	14	15
Walaja	III	100	30	25	4
Hizma	II	60	23	14	10
Qatana	III	90	32	24	5
Central Highlands					
Tarqumiya	II	70	27	22	8
Surif	III	90	32	29	5
Ras Karkar	III	70	34	30	—
Sinjil	II	60	30	22	10
Beit Rima	III	70	26	24	6
Anabta	II	110	30	26	8
Western Foothills					
Ni'lin	III	30	38	30	4
Rantis	II	70	34	30	6
Shuweika	II	60	28	18	12
Kafr Yassif	I	70	24	16	18
Northern Highlands					
Tur'an	II	90	32	25	8
Reina	I	80	22	12	22
Fassuta	III	120	26	22	5
Jish	II	70	28	15	12

*   The built-up area of each village was measured by forming a polygon of lines connecting the extreme houses on each side of the village. Density figures for the early 1920's are rough estimates based, whenever possible, on World War I aerial photographs, field work, interviews and, in some villages, local documents. Density figures for 1946/47, as well as the percentage of dwellings outside the nucleated part, are based on village surveys (Government of Palestine) and sources similar to those used in the 1920's.

** Geographical Position: I = village within the vicinity and easy access of an urban center; II = village on or near an all-weather road (or railway) with regular transport service; III = isolated village.

1 dunam = 1,000 sq. m., or 1/10 hectare.

spaced dwellings lining the main route running into the village. This latter section was to develop into the modern village center, in most cases only from the 1950's onward. The trend toward the *Strassedorf* pattern was in some cases a dominant factor in the shift in the village site, particularly where a new modern highway was constructed in the vicinity, causing the settlement to gradually creep toward this main artery, along the connecting route. (See Fig. 2).[21]

SOCIAL AND AGRICULTURAL ASPECTS

Arab villagers, especially in the hilly regions, traditionally avoided the construction of houses on arable land, which is scarce and patchy. This practice affected the choice of village site and often the pattern of its built-up area. The villagers continued to adhere to this tradition during the first stages of the dispersion process. Only from the late 1940's, with the gradual decline in the role of agriculture as a nearly exclusive source of livelihood, ever more new outlying dwellings appeared on cultivable land. However, extensive incursions of rural, built-up areas into agricultural lands surrounding Arab villages did not become widespread until the 1960's. Until then, the extension and dispersion of highland villages had been mostly directed toward rocky areas or poor, stony soils. Where there was insufficient land of this type in close proximity to the settlement, the expansion was perforce pushed beyond cultivated areas and plantations, thus giving rise to a separate *écart*. Construction on solid rock had several advantages, in addition to sparing valuable arable land, so long as the traditional techniques and style were still in use.

One social aspect of transformation closely linked with the changes in physical pattern was the weakening of bonds within the clans. In its densely-clustered form, the village was divided into what can be described as quarters, each of which consisted of several blocks of houses and compounds. The population of each quarter was composed entirely of members of a single clan (*hammula*). Large ones often occupied more than one quarter, while small ones were at times confined to one block. The residential areas of each were clearly separated by lanes or open ground. Generally, the inhabitants of small villages were divided into two or three clans, and those of large villages into five or more.[22]

Villagers who did not belong to any of the clans usually associated with one of them, and resided within or around its quarter. With the progress of dispersion the practice of residence only within the exclusive area of one's *hammula* was

21   The villages of El Khadr, 'Azzun, Irtah and Mes-ha are good examples of such a development.
22   Kendall (note 12, supra), pp. 49–52.

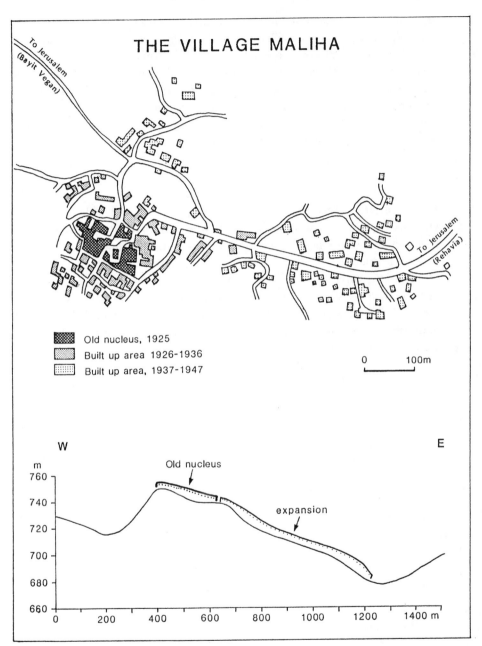

THE VILLAGE MALIHA

Old nucleus, 1925
Built up area 1926-1936
Built up area, 1937-1947

0   100m

FIG. 2

gradually abandoned. A population from diverse clans took up residence in the new dispersed parts of the village. A study of the loosening of the traditional rigid *hammula* framework should, however, also form part of a comprehensive survey of the socioeconomic transformation that took place in the villages at the time. There are clear indications that a close relationship existed between socioeconomic developments and change in the physical features of these villages. Sufficient information on this relationship is only available from the mid-1940's onward, and this topic merits a separate discussion.

CONCLUSION

For centuries, the geographical characteristics of the Arab village remained virtually unchanged. Not until the 1870's, when external forces began to play a more active role in Palestine, did the first signs of transformation appear. This process accelerated steadily, especially in the twentieth century. Numerous aspects of the rural landscape and life in the area — such as village pattern and density, the clan structure and economic framework — were altered beyond recognition. The interrelationship between these elements and the changes they underwent is a subject of great interest to historical geographers, and one that warrants further study.

THE NEGEV BEDOUIN: FROM NOMADISM
TO AGRICULTURE

JOSEPH BEN-DAVID

INTRODUCTION

With little fanfare, one of the most fascinating sociocultural processes ever is unfolding in the Middle East. The last of the nomadic Bedouin are undergoing a transition toward settlement and integration into the surrounding society. This development has attracted much attention in interdisciplinary studies, which regard the Bedouin as a living human laboratory. Scientific literature on nomads in general and the Bedouin in particular has expanded at an unprecedented pace, focusing primarily on the changes their society has undergone.

Traditionally, settled societies and nomadic ones have always been opposed to each other. The Bedouin have been stereotyped negatively as characters who regard any form of administration with contempt and leave nothing but ruin and bareness in their wake.[1] In truth, however, there is growing evidence that in addition to nomadic herding, they also engage in agriculture,[2] although such endeavors have been scanty, primitive and inconsistent, so that there has been no Bedouin agricultural economy per se.[3] It is hardly surprising that the Bedouin tried their hand at farming in rainy areas that have always been settled, such as

---

1 Although space limitations prevent an enumeration of the abundant sources dealing with the destructive influence of the Bedouin who moved from their natural desert habitat to the settled parts of Israel, the following works are especially noteworthy: A. Reifenberg, *The Struggle Between the Desert and the Sown*, Jerusalem 1955; M. Sharon, "The Bedouin in Palestine in the 18th and 19th Centuries," M.A. thesis, The Hebrew University, Jerusalem 1964 (Hebrew).

2 G. Baer, *The Arabs of the Middle East*, Tel Aviv 1973, p. 139 (Hebrew).

3 The subject of agriculture occupies only a tiny portion of the accounts on the Palestine Bedouin written by travelers and researchers, both because the phenomenon was not widespread and because it did not generate much interest. In view of the scantiness of such source material, one must search elsewhere for an explanation of the intriguing contrasts within their society; on the one hand the Bedouin scorned agriculture and farming, while on the other hand they were attracted to it. See: S. Avitzur, *Daily Life in Palestine in the 19th Century*, Tel Aviv 1977 (Hebrew); C.R. Conder, *Tent Work in Palestine*, London 1879.

the coastal plain, the Hula Valley, the Bet She'an Valley, etc.[4] Even in the arid Negev, sedentarization among the Bedouin stemmed from their "natural" tendency to integrate nomadic herding with small-scale agriculture. This was a gradual and continuous process that affected not only their economic structure, but their culture as well.

Modern sociology and anthropology are incomplete without the field of historical geography, which imparts a foundation and depth to these pursuits. In the words of Karl Marx:

> Social analysis is historical analysis, not an analysis that limits itself to one point in time. It is impossible to understand the present without relating to processes that took place in the past, through which the present took shape.[5]

This article aims to support the claim that economically, socially and culturally the process of Bedouin settlement in the Negev followed a natural, almost instinctive course, oriented toward agriculture. I have interviewed many tribal elders, and attached more credibility to oral traditions than to written sources; most of those questioned described events that they themselves had witnessed, or accounts that had been passed down by preceding generations. Their ages ranged from seventy to one hundred.

CULTURAL HETEROGENEITY

In turning to agriculture, the Bedouin were not obliged to relinquish one way of life for the sake of another, since the nomadic herding they had engaged in for centuries is simply one branch of Middle Eastern agriculture.[6] In other words, the Bedouin's nomadic life-style is not self-contained and opposed to sedentarization, but rather related to it. In many ways the Bedouin resemble agricultural villagers. Nomadism is part of the variegated mosaic of the Arab world, i.e. an economic system suited to desert conditions, within the framework

---

4   A close examination of the socioeconomic structure of the Ghawarnah tribes in the Bet She'an and Hula Valleys reveals that some of them were inclined toward agricultural settlement. See: I. Agmon, "The Bedouin Tribes in the Hula Valley and the Bet She'an Valley at the End of the Ottoman Period," *Cathedra*, 45, pp. 87–102 (Hebrew).

5   The quotation from Karl Marx is taken from: S. Avineri (ed.), *Early Writings*, Tel Aviv 1965 (Hebrew).

6   Baer (note 2, supra); F. Barth, "A General Perspective on Nomad-Sedentary Relations in the Middle East," C. Nelson (ed.), *The Desert and the Town: Nomads in the Wider Society*, Berkeley 1973, pp. 11–12.

of Middle East agriculture. This is illustrated by the following diagram (Fig. 1), which is applicable to the Bedouin of the Middle East in general, and those of the Negev in particular, both in the past and at present:

As the diagram demonstrates, two different secondary stages in the transition from nomadism to urbanization may arise simultaneously. Even once the final, urbanization stage is attained, secondary stages still exist: urbanization together with agriculture, and urbanization together with nomadism. Agriculture is the dominant intermediary element. In today's Middle East, all the secondary stages are unquestionably temporary in nature, and applicable to ever smaller portions of the Bedouin population in general, due to the accelerated sedentarization process.[7] Thus we are witnessing the last vestiges of traditional nomadism, which is being replaced by a sedentary life-style, whether agricultural or urban. Unlike the sedentarization process from early times up to the modern era, that of the twentieth century is irreversible.

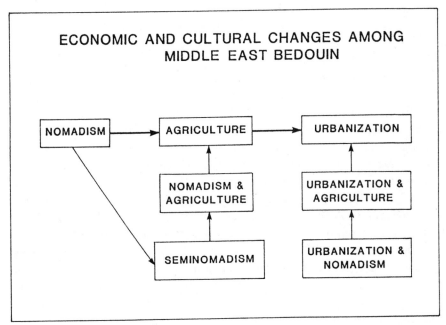

Fig. 1

---

7   A.A. Shamekh, *Spatial Patterns of Bedouin Settlement in Al-Qasim Region*, Saudi Arabia, Lexington, Ky. 1975. There is a striking similarity between the settlement processes and types among the Bedouin of Saudi Arabia, as described in Shamekh's book, and those among the Bedouin of the Negev, as delineated in my article. One difference, however, is the agricultural settlement planned by the Saudi Government, which to date has no parallel in Israel.

Despite the fact that the Bedouin have developed a distinct secondary culture, based on herding, their basic spiritual, ethnic and institutional concepts and values are no different from those of Arab culture in general. Sedentarization is a natural stage in the framework of the modern state, whereby the Bedouin undergo a transition from traditional economic systems to intensive ones, with regard to both livestock and agriculture.

The above theory, to which the Bedouin themselves adhere, is regarded unfavorably by modern governments, as it provides a basis for claims by nomadic tribes to lands they had possessed and made use of for generations. According to the laws of most states, the Bedouin have no land rights, but merely utilization privileges deriving from the fact that they have lived on the land for protracted periods. It is obvious that the problem transcends the legal sphere, and reflects the state's approach toward land and population in general. The Israel Government's settlement policy with regard to the Negev Bedouin has facilitated the creation of semi-urban communities, while ignoring their natural inclination toward agricultural villages.

BEDOUIN SETTLEMENT IN THE NEGEV: UNIVERSAL AND UNIQUE

Over the past two centuries, Bedouin society in the Middle East has undergone far-reaching changes, all of which fit into a single historical pattern.[8] Nevertheless, specific conditions within particular areas have influenced the Bedouin communities living there in different ways. The waning, and eventual disappearance, of nomadism, and its replacement by permanent settlement, are not unique to the nineteenth and twentieth centuries; in fact, this phenomenon has occurred throughout the history of the Arabs in the Middle East.[9] In the case of the Negev Bedouin, settlement was merely a phase, and not the final one, in an ongoing process. A succession of changes over the past century had a cumulative effect, and led toward sedentarization. The central factor was the character of the Ottoman regime. While during the first three hundred years of its rule this administration implemented a policy favorable to the Bedouin — encouraging them to immigrate to the country by making land readily available and allowing them complete freedom of movement — in its final years it attempted to restrict the Bedouin to particular Negev settlements.[10] (See Plate 1)

8   For a general survey of the changes that have taken place in the Arab world, see: M. Berger, *The Arab World Today*, New York 1964, p. 154.

9   For a detailed description of such settlement, see: R. Bulliet, "Sedentarization of Nomads in the Seventh Century: The Arabs of Basra and Kufa," P.C. Salzman (ed.), *When Nomads Settle*, Prager, N.Y. 1980, pp. 35–47.

10   Baer (Note 2, supra), pp. 145–146.

From the outset, the sedentarization process was marked by a shift from herding to agriculture, with economic changes preceding social ones. At a later stage permanent settlement types became institutionalized, and the signs of an agricultural way of life began to appear.[11] A determined government and various historical events combined to forge new conditions and challenges to which the Bedouin had to adjust. This is not to say that they were merely swept up by historical currents, and passively responded to trends rather than initiating them. Many members of the Bedouin community eagerly sought opportunities to alter their life-style. Only a minority of tribes, or parts thereof, insisted on preserving the nomadic tradition and culture, and even these are today beginning to move toward settlement.[12]

It is enlightening to view the changes in nomadic culture against a background of the varying political situation in the area, both because the administration in power always constituted a primary factor in this historiography, and because most of the documentation on this process was initiated by the ruling regime or with its backing.

Table I

Changes in Bedouin Culture according to Politial Periods: 1800–1948

1800–1857	1858–1917	1918–1948 Permanent Agricultural Settlement	From 1948
Nomadism	Seminomadism and Settlement		Modernization and Urbanization
Nomadic herding	1858 Ottoman Land Laws	Institutionalizing of agriculture and its commercial aspects	Founding of the State of Israel
Control of desert	Beersheva established as Bedouin capital	Land parcellation and legal insti- tutionalization	Territorial and economic changes
Appearance of fellaheen Seeking land within Bedouin society	Institutional- ization of tribal territory and settlements	Beginnings of spontaneous settlement	Beginnings of modern urbanization

11   *Ibid.*, pp. 147–148.
12   D. Stea, "Cultural Change and the Values of Environmental Designers," M. Buvinie (ed.), *American Values and Habitat*, Washington D.C. 1976. Although Stea discusses the American

Unlike Fig. 1, which presents a model of universal change, Table 1 focuses on the economic, cultural and settlement changes among the Negev Bedouin. What follows is a survey of each sub-period.

NOMADIC STAGE (1800–1857)

The first sub-period was the nomadic stage, characterized by all of the classic features of Bedouin society. The tribes monopolized one of the vital resources of the time, comparable in importance to oil in the modern world: camels. Not only did this animal provide the Bedouin with milk, meat, wool, and dung for fuel, it also served throughout the Middle East, for over a millennium, as the primary means of transportation through the desert. Merchants rented camels by the tens, hundreds or even thousands to form caravans, and hired Bedouin pack leaders and armed guards. These hired hands had to pay *hawa* (protection money) to tribes whose territory they crossed. Thus the camel afforded the Bedouin of the Middle East, the Sahara and other regions immeasurable economic and geopolitical advantages. (See Plate 2)

Under these circumstances, the Bedouin evinced no ambition to become fellaheen. They regarded themselves as superior to the latter — nobler, stronger, freer, more mobile and even more secure, as they always had the option of retreating from danger to their safe "home" in the desert expanses.

It is curious, then, that the Bedouin were induced to settle down precisely during this period. Some of the motivating factors are delineated by G. Baer, including a stable, orderly central government, land registration, new political regulations, and the spread of hired labor.[13] Two additional causes were a lessening of the relative advantage of the camel as a means of transportation, even before the introduction of modern alternatives into the Middle East, and an unexpected demand for agricultural land in the desert wilderness. The latter factor was partially the result of the movement of fellaheen from agricultural settlements to Bedouin territory, due to the political situation. With the end of Ibrahim Pasha's rule in Palestine and his return to Egypt in 1841, many Egyptians who had settled in the Holy Land were forced to abandon their farms and seek sources of livelihood elsewhere. The areas occupied by the Bedouin tribes in the Sinai and Negev deserts and used for grazing included cultivable lands. These frequently attracted fellaheen migrants who attached themselves to the Bedouin

Indians rather than the Bedouin, there are similarities between the changes that took place among the two groups.

13   Baer (note 2, supra), pp. 145–146.

tribes,[14] and today's fellaheen among the Bedouin are probably their descendants, as they are referred to by the Bedouin as "'askar Ibrahim Pasha" ("Ibrahim Pasha's soldiers").[15]

This was a form of socioeconomic symbiosis, whereby the Bedouin made their land available to the fellaheen for cultivation, while the latter undertook to share the yield. For the Bedouin this arrangement was a blessing, as they invested nothing except "their" land, while all the responsibility fell on the fellaheen and their families. The Bedouin competed for the right to "adopt" as many peasants as possible, in order to augment their manpower and land yield, and make it possible to continue their nomadic life-style based on herding. Fellaheen migration to Bedouin areas was not a one-time phenomenon; it lasted from 1841 until the start of the British occupation in 1917.[16] The shift in the function of the land from grazing to agriculture, and the resulting rise in land value, explain why wars over territory increased precisely at the turn of the century.

SEMINOMADIC STAGE AND SETTLEMENT (1858–1917)

An additional factor pushing the Bedouin toward land possession and settlement was the Ottoman Land Law of 1858, especially the clause dealing with *mewat* (dead) lands, which defines the right of landholders in the desert, i.e. the Bedouin. Baer notes that "in the wake of the Ottoman Land Law, instructions were issued in February 1860 to register land, but these were carried out only temporarily and partially."[17] He maintains that the very promulgation of the law served to incite the reprisal wars between one Bedouin tribe and another, and between the Bedouin and the frontier settlements. According to Baer, the tribes throughout the Empire were aroused "to seize as much land as possible," because they felt it was their last opportunity to strike roots. Proof of this claim can be found in Bedouin story and song, most of which are based on events still embedded in tribal memory. Space limitations prevent a detailed listing of these sources.

---

14   Among the numerous sources citing these facts is: Y. Ben-Arieh & Y. Bartal (eds.), *The History of Palestine at the End of the Ottoman Period (1799–1917)*, VIII, Jerusalem 1981, pp. 28–29 (Hebrew).

15   J. Ben-David, "Stages in the Sedentarization of the Negev Bedouin: The Transition from Former Seminomadic to Settled Population," Doctoral dissertation, The Hebrew University, Jerusalem 1982, pp. 35–47 (Hebrew).

16   A classification of the lands that was accepted during the Ottoman regime appears in: A.J. Levi, *Essays on Jurisprudence*, Jerusalem 1969, p. 137 (Hebrew).

17   Baer (note 2, supra), p. 35.

In my opinion, as early as the mid-1800's the Bedouin in the Negev and Sinai deserts adopted an active approach with regard to the possibility of settling on land and becoming fellaheen. It is apparent that the wars were due largely to the desire to gain possession of plots with agricultural potential. It was not by chance that the Bedouin clashes took place within a semiarid geographic region known as the "desert frontier" or the "settlement frontier." Nevertheless, conditions varied from one locality to another, and over time certain tribes leaned more to agriculture than others.

Not only did the Bedouin attempt to settle on the desert frontier, they also sought and found occasional opportunities to move to the settled regions of the country. Thus different parts of the Wahidat branch of the Jubarat tribe settled simultaneously in northern Sinai, Transjordan, the Negev and even in the vicinity of Jerusalem.[18]

El-'Aref, who was the governor of the Beersheba District in the 1930's, notes that the Hanajrah tribe had "the finest lands, in which sesame and all sorts of summer crops will grow well."[19] He adds that Freih Abu-Middin, the Hanajrah's best known sheikh, "became an owner of wealth, sheep, vineyards and land, after having been a persecuted bandit."[20] It is apparent, then, that the Bedouin underwent far-reaching changes when they incorporated agriculture into their economic system.

The struggle to gain control of agricultural land and to settle it escalated at the turn of the century, and the stronger tribes edged out the weaker ones. El-'Aref comments that the Sa'idiyin tribe "which has no agricultural land ... lives in poverty and misery."[21] He states that "the Tarabin received an inadequate share of the land booty" in the Zar'e War of 1875, which indicates that even though the struggle was not geared directly toward agriculture, this dimension was prominent.[22] The war between the Tarabin and 'Azazmah tribes in 1887 was waged to rectify the situation for those who "felt that they had not received their fair share of conquered land."[23]

Apparently, only when the authorities publicized the tribal map in 1906 (see Fig. 2), to complement their resolute police actions and the severe punishments

18   A. El-'Aref, *The History of Beersheba and Its Tribes*, Tel Aviv 1937, p. 16 (Hebrew). This book, originally written in Arabic, is an important and unbiased source, at least with regard to the evidence on the second and third stages, as depicted in Table 1.
19   *Ibid.*
20   *Ibid.*, p. 147.
21   *Ibid.*, p. 133.
22   *Ibid.*, p. 156.
23   *Ibid.*, p. 160.

DISTRIBUTION OF THE BEDOUIN TRIBES IN THE NEGEV
BEFORE 1948

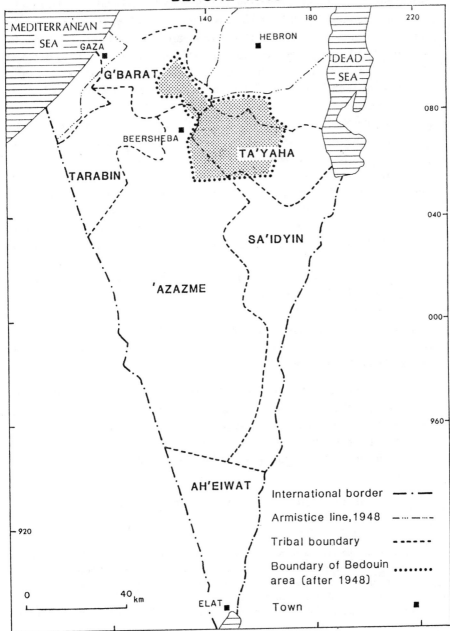

Fig.2

they had been meting out, did they succeed in ending the tribal wars and establishing order and stability. These developments, along with the founding of Beersheba as an administrative center in 1903, spelled the end of nomadism for the Negev Bedouin. With the restoration of order and the removal of age-old threats of conquest, the Bedouin came to regard their land as a solid basis for settlement and agriculture. The moment the land situation stabilized, the need arose to apportion the cultivable areas as private plots. The sheiks and other leaders gained control of most of this land, while marginal tracts fell to the lot of the remainder of the tribe.

Had it not been for the founding of Beersheba, and its indirect and unintended effect on the Bedouin, all of the government's efforts to persuade them to settle down in the Negev would have been in vain.[24] As a place of residence, Beersheba never attracted significant numbers of Bedouin; only a few sheiks and their coteries built homes there, while continuing to live in tents in the desert. Its population consisted chiefly of merchants who had moved from Gaza or Hebron, mainly in order to bring their businesses closer to the Bedouin. Although the town served as the Bedouin's "capital," and could offer them such attractions as a school, a mosque and medical services, they remained indifferent. Their interest was not aroused until they realized that Beersheba could be a boon for their agricultural endeavors. The town was a market for surplus yields, especially barley, and supply could not keep up with demand. The sale of livestock was more limited, because there was competition from Bedouin outside the country's borders. A first-hand account of the situation in 1911 is presented by Izhak Ben-Zvi, who quotes Moshe Elkayam:

> The main trade was in barley.... Jews would come to the desert with camels loaded with goods.... Each Jewish merchant had a Bedouin tribe "of his own," with which he bartered assorted merchandise for barley.... The Jews of Gaza sent one and a half million bags of barley to England each year, each bag weighing 5 rotls [over 14 kilograms, thus giving a total of 22,500 tons].[25]

It transpires that the Bedouin barley was extremely well suited for the English

---

24   It transpires that the head of the 'Azzazmah tribe at the time requested the aid of the authorities in his forceful attempt to end the tribal wars and establish a police stronghold to preserve order. Such a framework was set up in 1896, and was later to become the nucleus of Beersheba, which was founded in 1903 and dedicated in 1906. Not coincidentally, in the latter year a map of the tribes was published. For more on this subject, see: J. Ben-David (note 15, supra), pp. 27–28, and Ben-Arieh & Bartal (eds.) (note 14, supra), pp. 40, 175.

25   Izhak Ben-Zvi, *Expeditions*, Jerusalem 1980, p. 46 (Hebrew).

beer industry. The quantity of barley cited above attests to the fact that from the turn of the century fellaheen agriculture had grown to commercial proportions; at least 250,000 dunams of cultivated land are necessary for a yield of 22,500 tons. This unprecedented boom allowed the Bedouin to become consumers of many goods that they could not produce themselves. Conversely, the taste of a higher standard of living induced them to increase their income by hiring greater numbers of fellaheen land tenants from Egypt and Sinai, in addition to fellow Bedouin from Sinai who wished to earn a salary and purchase grain during the harvest season. There is written testimony that agricultural products sold in Beersheba reached distant areas, such as Transjordan and the Sinai Peninsula. The Bedouin market in the town, which operated one day a week, was called Suk al-Barren (market of the two deserts). Thus Beersheba's founding caused Negev agriculture to flourish.

The symbiotic relationship that developed between the fellaheen land tenants and the Bedouin did not suffice to sustain the social and economic links between the two groups for long. In drought years, especially when consecutive, the Bedouin landowners had to trade on credit, and they were prodigal in their daily affairs and their celebrations.[26]

The Beersheba merchant can be considered the third leg in a symbiotic triangle, as Fig. 3 illustrates:

According to this model, the merchant played three roles; he purchased the Bedouin's agricultural surplus, sold him equipment and merchandise, and offered credit in times of crisis. The Bedouin's attitude and expectations regarding their land changed once their economy came to be based on monetary transactions. A Bedouin who was unable to pay his debts in cash was eventually forced to sell part of his land.[27] Even the tribes that did not engage in agriculture offered the town's merchants some of their lands in order to reach the same consumption level as their "brother farmers." Thus a growing trend of land transactions was set in motion.

The founding of Beersheba, then, initiated a process leading to the Negev Bedouin's permanent settlement on the land. The town's influence was indirect; markets for surplus produce stimulated agricultural pursuits, and later settlement. (See Plate 3)

---

26 As Abu-'Atiya al-'Azzami, one of the elders of the 'Azzazmah tribe, told me in 1987: "The fellaheen worked, the merchants sold candies to the Bedouin, and the Bedouin loafed and celebrated." He did not even rule out the possibility that the exaggerated reputation that the Negev Bedouin had earned as gracious hosts derived primarily from the period of affluence in agriculture and trade.

27 Ben-Zvi (note 25, supra), p. 47.

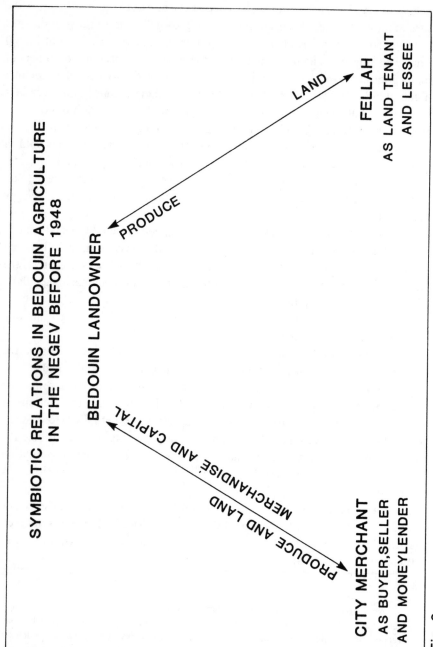

Fig. 3

PERMANENT SETTLEMENT STAGE (1918–1948)

During the British Mandate period the Bedouin went through a seminomadic stage, marked by a broadening of agricultural endeavors.[28] Purely practical considerations played a decisive role in the struggle between nomadism and agriculture; during rainier years, when crops brought in profits, the Bedouin were less mobile, while droughts forced them to seek water and grazing land outside the Negev. Nevertheless, a distinctly new pattern emerged. Firstly, the wandering Bedouin always returned to their permanent Negev bases, which, not coincidentally, were located on their land used for raising field crops. This dry crop competed with livestock, and at times was vital for the animals, as it was used for fodder at the end of the harvest season. Thus the Bedouin have always practiced mixed farming, which they have termed their "traditional source of livelihood." According to various estimates, during the Mandate period the Negev Bedouin cultivated some half a million dunams of land.[29] (See Plates 4, 5 and 6).

The second deviation from the traditional pattern was that the government became an active agent in the Bedouin economy; during droughts it helped them move their flocks to grazing land in other parts of the country, and provided direct aid. As the Bedouin grew accustomed to a money-based economy, some of them sought employment as government workers. Thus a seminomadic pattern, related to agriculture, came into being. The Bedouin's bases served as departure points for nomadic excursions, and eventually became permanent settlements. There were several signs of sedentarization:

1) the *mantara*, which served as a granary, next to which were left all of the belongings which the Bedouin did not take with them during their winter and spring wanderings; the tent was folded up in the summer; (See Plate 7).

2) the *harabah*, a cistern dug out of the chalk rocks; the Bedouin discovered some that had been quarried as early as the Nabatean and Byzantine periods; since these were insufficient for the growing population, individual families adopted the ancient method of quarrying in their cultivated and grazing lands;

3) the *baika*, a structure built of coarse local stone or clay, used mostly in the rainier areas of the western Negev, and a distinctive feature of agricultural settings; the Bedouin built it next to the *mantara*, on the threshing floor square; it was later to serve as the first edifice on the permanent settlement.

28 For a description of this period, see: S. Bar-Zvi & Y. Ben-David, "The Negev Bedouin during the Thirties and Forties of the Twentieth Century: A Seminomadic Society," *Studies in the Geography of Israel*, 10 (1978), pp. 107–136 (Hebrew).

29 Y. Porat & Y. Shavit, *The History of Palestine, the Mandate and the National Home (1917–1947)*, 9, Jerusalem 1981, p. 306 (Hebrew).

One of the basic differences between this period and the preceding one was that the Bedouin themselves performed the physical labor, whereas previously the actual farm work was done mainly by the fellaheen attached to the tribes. It is noteworthy that during the Mandate period twelve shallow wells were dug in the environs of Beersheba, in addition to three that had been on the site before the town was built. On each well was constructed a *sakia*, i.e. a pumping wheel into whose outer rim were fitted containers. It had been imported from Egypt, and was operated at first by animal and later by diesel power.

The wells were often named after their owner, for example: "Sakiat Abu-Yihia," "Sakiat al-Malta'a," or "Sakiat al-A'asam." They were used for growing vegetables and gourds, which were sold in the town's markets. The novelty of this type of cultivation lay in its being intensive, unlike that of the fellaheen, and based on irrigation. It served as a model for Bedouin agriculture in general, which began to use dams to channel runoff water into lowlands where initially summer vegetables and tobacco were grown, and later orchards with a variety of fruit trees were planted.

Both the establishment of a land court in Beersheba in 1921 and the collection of crop tithes furthered the institutionalization of Bedouin agriculture. The former was part of a campaign by the British authorities to regulate land sales by the Bedouin to other parties, or among themselves, and to resolve land conflicts between Bedouin claimants.[30] This does not mean that the Mandatory Government recognized the litigants' ownership rights; rather, it wished to impose legal order upon Bedouin practices. The Bedouin, for their part, felt no need to demonstrate their ownership, for they had long acted as de facto owners, without interference by the authorities. In the 1920's and 1930's there was a surge in Bedouin land transactions. Swindling was not uncommon, such as the sale of a tract to more than one person, the denial that a sale had been transacted, or the extraction of land from a debtor by forcing him to unwittingly sign a bill of sale. Most notorious was Sheik Jad'u al-A'asam, who used his father's seal to conclude sales involving the latter's lands, without his knowledge.

It is evident, then, that the Bedouin no longer regarded their land as a "free commodity," as they had during their nomadic days. Every tract underwent parcellation, except for uncultivable grazing areas. Also hastening the sedentarization process were the agricultural settlements established in the early twentieth century by the first Jews to move to the Negev. The arrival of increasing numbers of Jewish settlers toward the end of the Mandate further accelerated this trend. The year 1948 marked the outset of the fourth and final phase of Bedouin settlement, an inevitable outgrowth of the preceding stages.

30   Levi (note 16, supra), pp. 138–141.

CONCLUSION

Nomadism leads naturally to one of two directions: urbanization and village agriculture. The former represents a more radical change, as it is newer, foreign, and even hostile to the nomadic way of life. The disappearance of nomadism in an urban culture is inevitable.

This becomes clear upon inspection of both the elderly and the children in Bedouin towns today. The elderly man who had formerly been accustomed to a tent culture, with its peregrination and its pastoral qualities, has little in common with the child born in a town with running water, electricity, and even a bathroom within the house. Furthermore, the urban child is quite unlike his peer growing up in a tent some half a kilometer away. Their outlook, concepts, sensibilities and behaviour differ markedly. (See Plate 8)

By contrast, a transition toward the latter alternative is more natural and less problematic, both because Bedouin agriculture has been in existence for over a century, and because it retains nomadic elements, such as livestock, open spaces, tribal and family structures, and in general the Bedouin way of life. Although the negative aspects of a nomadic way of life have induced governments to bring the Bedouin into towns, nothing could be more natural than placing them in agricultural villages, whose environment is familiar to them. For their own part, they will always aspire to realize this wish. As one elderly Bedouin said to me, "You will never understand this, because you are not a Bedouin."

GERMAN ANTECEDENTS OF RURAL SETTLEMENT IN PALESTINE UP TO WORLD WAR I

ZVI SHILONY

INTRODUCTION

The Jewish National Fund (JNF) was established by the Zionist Organization as the body under its auspices responsible for acquiring, nationalizing, apportioning and settling land in Palestine, and afterwards planning and administering rural communities. The idea of setting up such an organ was adopted by the First Zionist Congress in August 1897, and it was officially founded by the Fifth Zionist Congress in December 1901. Two years later, in August 1903, the Sixth Zionist Congress issued final approval for the JNF's activities to get under way in Palestine.[1]

It may be assumed that the planning and execution of a settlement enterprise organized and financed by an official body, such as the JNF, would be influenced by three main elements: the settlement authority, the settlers, and the prevailing conditions in the field. While the latter two factors have already been described in detail,[2] there has been little discussion of the first.[3] This article

---

1   This article is mainly based on the following work by the author: Z. Shilony, "The Jewish National Fund as a Factor in Shaping the Colonized Landscape of Eretz-Israel from the Time of Its Foundation to the Outbreak of World War I (1897–1914)," Ph.D. thesis for the Hebrew University, Jerusalem 1987 (Hebrew). For more information on the development of the Jewish National Fund idea, the establishment of the organization and the granting of approval for it to begin functioning, see pp. 1–2, 13–17, 27–29 of this work.

2   The particular conditions prevailing in Palestine during the period under discussion were described in detail in: A. Granott (Granovsky), *The Land Policy in Palestine*, Tel Aviv 1949 (Hebrew); M. Doukhan, *Land Laws in the State of Israel*, Jerusalem 1953 (Hebrew); L. Doukhan-Landau, *The Zionist Societies for Land Acquisition in Palestine, 1897–1914*, Jerusalem 1980 (Hebrew); N. Gross, *Banker for an Emerging Nation — The History of Bank Leumi Le-Israel*, I, Ramat Gan 1977 (Hebrew). The specific conditions of the various settlement sites have been described in memoranda, articles and studies too numerous to mention.

3   Little material is available on this topic, and most of it can be found in jubilee and memorial books published by the JNF and the other Zionist settlement institutions. Hence it is more propagandistic than scientific. Most of the studies on the original documents have attempted

examines the perceptions and plans of the heads of the Zionist Organization and the JNF with regard to settlement types, the extent to which these ideas suited the conditions prevailing in the land, and the influence of these concepts on the development of the rural settlement landscape in Palestine up to the outbreak of World War I.

THE ZIONIST ORGANIZATION AND JNF LEADERS UP TO WORLD WAR I

Throughout the period from the First Zionist Congress to the outbreak of World War I, the Zionist Organization, including its various settlement institutions, was led by German Jews. Dr. Theodor Herzl presided over it until his death in June 1904, working alongside an Executive composed mainly of Austrian and German Jews. He was succeeded by David Wolffsohn from Cologne, who was also appointed to the Zionist Executive, along with Prof. Otto Warburg from Berlin and Jacobus Kann from The Hague.

Similarly, the JNF's Directorate, which from 1901 until the summer of 1906 functioned in an unofficial capacity, was from the outset composed of German Jews. It was headed by Johann Kremenetzky from Vienna, but was effectively under the control of the president of the Zionist Organization and the Zionist Executive. The Palestine Commission was established in August 1903 by the Sixth Zionist Congress to aid with the planning and execution of the Zionist settlement enterprise. Its members were Prof. Warburg, Dr. Franz Oppenheimer from Berlin, and Dr. Zelig Soskin, a Russian-born German citizen with settlement experience in Palestine.

The Palestine Commission was asked, *inter alia*, to evaluate various settlement proposals, submit its own recommendations, and administer the estates of the JNF until such time as its Directorate could be officially established. In August 1906 the Third Zionist Yearly Conference decided to appoint Dr. Max Bodenheimer from Cologne as chairman of the JNF's Directorate, which, like the other Zionist bodies, had a membership consisting largely of German and Austrian Jews. Bodenheimer's suggestions were accepted with regard to several specific projects and the settlement policy in general. In May 1907 the JNF was

to encompass the entire Zionist settlement enterprise from 1882 until the founding of the State of Israel in 1948, and even afterwards, making it impossible to reconstruct through them the detailed process of planning and executing any of the particular projects. See, for example: A. Bohm, *Die Zionistische Bewegung bis zum ende des Weltkrieges*, Tel Aviv 1935; idem, *Der jüdische Nationalfond*, Jerusalem 1926; A. Bein, *The Return to the Soil: A History of Jewish Settlement in Israel*, Jerusalem 1952; C.Gvati, *A Hundred Years of Settlement*, Jerusalem 1985.

registered as a limited company in London, and its first official Directorate was appointed. The by-laws stipulated that the Directorate would have an independent standing vis-à-vis the president of the Zionist Organization and its Executive, and that it would be subordinate only to the Zionist Congress itself. Bodenheimer was assisted by Kremenetzky, Arthur Hantke from Berlin, Leopold Kessler from London and Yechiel Tschlenow from Moscow. In order to forestall sharp differences of opinion with the Zionist Executive, two prominent members of that body, Wolffsohn and Warburg, were also appointed to the JNF Directorate, as governor directors. The membership of the Directorate remained unchanged up to World War I.

In the summer of 1907, a joint decision was taken by the Zionist Executive, the Palestine Commission and the JNF Directorate to establish the Palestine Office in Jaffa to represent them and other organizations with regard to settlement affairs. Dr. Arthur Ruppin, born in Posen and later resident in Berlin, served as its head, while Dr. Jacob Thon, a Russian Jew who also settled in Berlin, became his assistant. The JNF, which provided most of the Palestine Office's operating budget, designated these two men as its official representatives in Palestine with regard to land acquisition and settlement. Ruppin and Thon, along with Warburg in Berlin, also stood at the head of the Palestine Land Development Company, which had been established in parallel with the Palestine Office, and which cooperated with the JNF on several important land transactions and settlement projects.[4]

As the Zionist leadership was predominantly German and Austrian, it may be assumed that their knowledge and experience in the field of settlement derived mainly from the German settlement endeavors and the German literature and journalism on this subject. Furthermore, several of these people were themselves involved in various German settlement movements and projects. Warburg, for example, was a member of Das Deutche Kolonial Wirtschaftskommittee and the editor of its journal *Der Tropenpflantzer*. He also served as advisor to the Prussian Colonization Committee (PCC), which administered German settlement in the district of Posen, taken from Poland when it was divided between Russia, Austria and Germany. Oppenheimer, one of Europe's foremost economists, advocated nationalization of land, agrarian reform and cooperative settlement in Germany, and actually conducted experiments of this sort near

---

4   For a detailed description of the development and staff of the Zionist Organization's institutions throughout the period under discussion, see: M. Eliav, *David Wolffsohn — The Man and His Time (The Zionist Movement in the Years 1905–1914)*, Jerusalem 1977 (Hebrew). For further details on the development and personal composition of the JNF leadership, see: Shilony (note 1, supra), pp. 13–17, 27–59.

Berlin (see Plate 1).[5] Even the Russian Zionist leaders, the second most powerful group in the Zionist Organization, drew their inspiration from the German experience, primarily in Posen. Most of them acquired their academic training in Germany or Austria, spoke and read German, and frequently passed through the German settlements in Posen and East Prussia while traveling to and from Western Europe. Several key figures in the Zionist establishment, notably Warburg and Ruppin, occasionally declared outright their intention of imitating the German settlement ventures in Posen, in terms of both organization and actual settlement.[6]

THE GERMAN SETTLEMENT MODEL IN POSEN

The German settlement enterprise in Posen and the rest of the Ostmark (Eastern District) constituted a convenient model for Zionism, since it served as a means for the government in Berlin to Germanize mainly rural areas densely populated by Poles, in a peaceful, nonmilitary manner. This would be accomplished by purchasing most of the land, and by encouraging Germans to move to the area until they formed a clear majority of the population. The body in charge of the planning and execution of this project was the PCC. The settlement types were determined by three complementary factors: 1) the policy of acquiring land and preparing it for settlement; 2) the kinds of economic enterprises to be established; and 3) the physical layout for each settlement type. These components will be examined separately:

Land Acquisition and Preparation for Settlement
With the aid of the German Treasury and special banks set up to finance settlement, the PCC purchased as much land as possible from the Poles, mainly from absentee landlords with large estates, and resold it on attractive terms to settlers who had moved from Germany proper. It also took care of any necessary preparation, such as draining swamps, removing rocks, and ensuring a permanent water supply. Some of the land was allotted to PCC subsidiaries that experimented with new crops and trained agricultural workers, but most of it went to private settlers.

In order to prevent the tracts from reverting to Polish ownership, in 1900–1901 the German Reichstag passed a law entitled *Das Gesetz über Rentengutern*, which made the government a 10% partner with regard to the land sold to each

---

5   *Ibid.*

6   S. Reichman, "Geographical Elements in the Zionist Colonization Method in Late Turkish Times," *Eretz-Israel*, 17 (1984), p. 119 and references (Hebrew).

and every farmer. Thus if the farm should fail and be offered for sale, the state had the first option to purchase it. Since the price was to be set by an assessing committee in accordance with predetermined criteria, land speculation was entirely avoided. Any plots acquired in this manner were to be immediately resold to new German settlers. The system was a form of partial nationalization.[7]

Settlement Types

There were two main categories of settlements in Posen: preparatory and permanent. The former included the following types:

a) the agricultural experimental farm (*Versuchstation*), designed to seek ways of improving the already-existing crops, introduce and acclimatize new crops that promised to be profitable, and improve both manual and mechanical farming techniques in all branches;[8]

b) the agricultural training farm (*Lehrefarm*), geared to training the inexperienced immigrants in the various agricultural tasks over a minimum of two years, during which time they worked on the farm in exchange for wages that allowed them to put aside a small sum that they would need upon becoming independent farmers;[9]

c) the preparatory and interim-cultivation farm (*Zwischenwirtschaft*), where land was prepared for a year or two before being occupied by the permanent settlers; although each of the laborers signed a private contract with the PCC, and received a salary commensurate with his output and the type of work he performed, the farm as a whole was run on a contractual basis under the management of an expert agronomist or an experienced worker.

The latter category, the permanent agricultural settlements, included the following:

a) the large estate farm (*Grossbetriebwirtschaft*), of which there were two kinds: one run by wealthy private investors (the JNF, for its part, disallowed this sort of farm on its lands, since its capital came from countless contributors of modest

---

7   For more information on the definition of the German settlement goals and partial land nationalization policy, see: W. Mitscherlich, *Die Ostmark*, Leipzig 1911; W.H. Dawson, *The Evolution of Modern Germany*, London 1919; S. Reichman & S. Hasson, "A Cross-Cultural Diffusion of Colonization," *Annals of the Association of American Geographers*, 74, No. 1 (1984), pp. 57–70; Reichman (note 6, supra), pp. 117–127.

8   A detailed article on the goals, structure and *modus operandi* of agricultural experimental stations throughout the world, including the German colonization in Poland, was published at the time in the Hebrew edition of the Zionist Organization's newspaper *Die Welt*: Y. Levontin, "Settlement Methods — First Article: Experimental Stations," *Ha'olam*, 11–12, April 2, 1909, pp. 6–8, and April 18, 1909, pp. 3–7 (Hebrew).

9   Dawson (note 7, supra), pp. 257, 480.

means), and the other, which operated in places where small stable plots could not be maintained, under the management of the PCC; due to economic considerations the latter type was usually based on cattle or orchards, but where this was impossible it relied on forestation;[10]

b) the smallholders' village (*Kleinbauerndorf*), the most common and important form of German rural settlement in Posen; hundreds of these were established by World War I, and besides the partial nationalization of land discussed above, they were also characterized by the following: 1) small, equal plots, to allow for the maximum number of families per area; these could not be divided among several inheritors, and no farmer was permitted to own more than one plot in any village; 2) intensive, mixed farming, which allowed for self-sufficiency with regard to most foods, spread the work out quite evenly throughout the year, and eliminated the need for hired laborers, mostly Poles, who were willing to work for wages far lower than those received by the Germans; 3) encouragement by the German Government of cooperative frameworks, by making available both credit on convenient terms and legal advice, in order to lower the farmers' expenditures on machinery, raw material, processing, marketing, and establishing public institutions; government-aided cooperative banks with mutual liability were set up in the villages, as well as cooperative purchasing and marketing services, dairies, and associations for agricultural education and the advancement of production; both the egalitarian apportionment of land and the encouragement of cooperative frameworks were carried out simply for the sake of economic and organizational efficiency, and not out of any ideological considerations whatsoever, whether socialist, communist or otherwise; 4) an official minimum of sixty families per smallholders' village, which was considered to be the numerical threshold for community services;[11]

c) the laborers' village (*Arbeiterdorf*), consisting of houses and auxiliary farms set up near cities and sold to German wage earners for low prices as an alternative to the expensive rental housing in the cities, in order to help them compete with the lowly-paid Polish workers, thus keeping the latter out of urban industries and services. Because the owner, with the aid of his family, could cultivate the auxiliary farm after finishing his day's work in the city, and could fall back on it in times of unemployment, he could afford to accept the same wages as the Poles. For the same reasons as those that applied in the smallholders' village, the land was apportioned into small and equal family plots, intensive mixed farming was practiced, cooperative frameworks were encouraged, and a

10   *Ibid.*
11   *Ibid.*, pp. 244–306, 481; Reichman (note 6, supra), p. 120.

minimum of sixty families was required for each village. The only substantive difference between these two types of village was that in the *Arbeiterdorf* the plot made available to each family was intended as an auxiliary farm only, rather than the main source of livelihood, and hence it was far smaller than that in the *Kleinbauerndorf* and ranged from 0.25 to 5 acres, in accordance with the availability and quality of the land, and its proximity to the city. Over 200 of these villages were established in Posen by the start of World War I.[12]

Physical Layout

Preparatory settlements had three standard components: the administration house, living quarters for the workers, and the farmyard, in which were located a granary, storehouses, and sheds for livestock and machinery. Since the manager was supposed to be an educated family-man and a permanent official of the settlement company, he was deemed worthy of housing conditions comparable to those in the city. By contrast, the farm workers and the apprentices, who were young, transient, and almost invariably unmarried, were given modest quarters, with several to a room. In order to underscore the need to treat the manager with respectful detachment, his living quarters were located at a distance from those of the workers, and were markedly superior.

The administration house was nearly always a two-storey stone building of relative elegance. On the top floor was the spacious residence of the manager's family, while the ground floor contained the office, storage rooms, and a small apartment for the assistant manager. The farmyard usually took the form of a square or rectangular inner courtyard that could be closed off by means of gates. The entrances of the buildings and sheds faced inward, toward the courtyard, and the rear walls linked up to form a sort of rampart.

Several minor differences in layout existed between the various settlement types. The agricultural experimental farms hired only a few workers, usually from the adjacent villages, so that it was unnecessary to construct living quarters for them. Since livestock was ordinarily not raised there, and the experimental crops were not expected to reach commercial proportions, these farms contained only the administration house, stables, machinery sheds and a large storehouse, all around a small inner courtyard.

On the agricultural training farms, intensive work under the manager's supervision was stressed, and relations between him and those under his charge were quite informal. As a result, all of the buildings stood next to each other, around a large farmyard, with the livestock sheds and dairy at one end, the

12   Dawson (note 7, supra), pp. 262–306.

administration house at the other, and the workers' quarters and storehouses in the middle.

No permanent structures were built on the *Zwischenwirtschaften*, where settlement was temporary in nature; instead, a number of cabins were erected, which could be easily dismantled and moved. They were used as living quarters, storehouses and stables, and located around a small, central courtyard. There were common showers, toilets, kitchen and dining room.

On the large estate farms, salaried laborers were hired in great numbers, many of them on a seasonal basis only. The authority and standing of the manager were much emphasized; the administration house was completely separate from the farmyard, and at a distance from it, so that the manager and his family would be spared the noise, contagion and odor emanating from the livestock sheds and the farm activity. The workers' quarters were located in the farmyard.

As mentioned above, the settlers in the smallholders' village and the laborers' village had private family farms and worked independently, without the supervision of any company appointee. The *Strassedorf* model was often followed, with houses laid out along both sides of a single long street. At the back of each house were a barn, stables and storehouses for the family farm, while the plots were located even further to the rear. Approximately midway along the street, or at times where a cross street intersected the main one, were located the public buildings: stores, dairy, village office, school, church, etc. This model had long been popular in many areas of Germany, and other places throughout the world where Germans settled. One example is the German colonies founded by the Templers in Palestine from the 1870's, which usually followed the pattern of minimal population, egalitarian apportionment of land, and a tendency toward a measure of cooperativeness in consumption, marketing and public institutions.[13]

SETTLEMENTS ON JNF LAND

The same three aspects we have examined in the case of the German settlement in Posen — method of acquisition and apportionment of the land, settlement types, and physical layout — shall now be reviewed with regard to the settlement that developed on JNF land in Palestine:

---

13   A. Carmel, *German Settlement in Palestine in the Late Ottoman Period — Policy and International Difficulties*, Jerusalem 1973; see also the article by Yossi Ben-Artzi in this volume.

Land Acquisition and Preparation for Settlement

Unlike the situation in Posen, where the Germans held full authority, Palestine was not controlled by the Jews either politically or militarily. Hence from the outset the JNF adopted the principle of complete nationalization of land it acquired as a means of ensuring Jewish control, despite the adverse conditions. This policy made possible unimpeded planning and administration of settlement, guaranteed contiguous cultivation and forestalled land speculation. The Zionist Organization of the early twentieth century decided that no major settlement projects should be attempted until the Sultan and the Sublime Porte granted an official charter for the establishment of Jewish autonomy in Palestine. In the meanwhile, only preparatory settlement was authorized, and permanent settlement did not commence until close to the outbreak of World War I.[14]

Settlement Types

The agricultural experimental farm at Atlit was the first settlement project to which the Zionist Executive committed itself, and the first to be granted the approval of the Sixth Zionist Congress, which in August 1903 resolved that the JNF would make available 500 dunams of land for it. Warburg and the Palestine Commission in Berlin, along with the young agronomist Aaron Aaronsohn in Palestine, were the driving forces behind this endeavor. By the end of that year the Palestine Commission began to purchase the land on behalf of the JNF, near the moshava Atlit at the foot of Mount Carmel, south of Haifa. For various reasons the transaction was not completed until the summer of 1910, at which time construction and research got under way.[15]

The Herzl Forest plantation farms were also approved at an early stage. The Association for Olive Tree Donations (*Oelbaumspende*) was set up by the Zionist Executive to raise capital through contributions, which could be used to generate profits through plantations. In order to minimize advertisement and administration costs, and to avoid fierce competition with groups seeking donations for land acquisition, fund-raising was entrusted to the JNF. In return, the JNF agreed to lease to the Association whatever land it needed for the olive groves. Following Herzl's death, the Seventh Zionist Congress decided in August 1905 to honor his memory by naming the future groves the "Herzl Forest." In 1908 the JNF acquired the first tracts for the project, at Hulda in Judea, and it was decided to run a large estate farm, under the direct supervision and management of an official subordinate to the Association and the JNF. In

14   Shilony (note 1, supra), pp. 7–8, 13–17.
15   *Ibid.*, pp. 91–108.

parallel, the *Oelbaumspende* planted olive groves on the JNF land at Ben Shemen, also in Judea. Since there were abandoned buildings of a former agricultural school on the site, it was deemed unnecessary to construct new buildings.[16]

In early 1908 the Zionist Executive and the JNF Directorate resolved to turn over to the Palestine Land Development Company 6,500 dunams of JNF land south of the Sea of Galilee (Lake Kinneret), for an agricultural training farm. The project was launched in June 1908, and was named after its location: "Kinneret Farm."[17] Two additional training farms were founded by the JNF in the summer of 1910 in Hulda and Ben Shemen, after it transpired that the olive groves had brought heavy financial losses. As farmhouses already existed on both sites, there was no need to erect new buildings.[18]

When it became apparent in October 1909 that Kinneret Farm was unable to cultivate the entire area it possessed, the JNF Directorate and the Palestine Office in Jaffa decided to hand over its southern portion, Umm Juni, to a small group of farm laborers who would work the land on a piecework basis. The JNF provided them with work animals and plowing equipment, and each individual received a regular monthly salary. It was also decided that the group would share with the JNF any profits to accrue, on an equal basis. Six workers were selected ad hoc as members of the group, and at their own expense they hired a woman to cook and do the housework. The group moved onto the land in December 1909, and practiced extensive farming in a single branch, cereals. It dispersed after the harvest season, and was replaced by another piecework group called the "Hadera Commune."[19]

Beginning in December 1910, another piecework community was established on the JNF tract at Fuleh, in the heart of the Jezreel Valley, where they engaged in interim cultivation, and a similar system was instituted as of fall 1913 at Tel 'Adash. In each case the JNF provided work animals and machinery at its own expense, and paid personal salaries, while receiving 50% of any profits.[20]

The smallholders' village was regarded as the ideal permanent settlement type by the Zionist Executive and the JNF Directorate, and they thus made repeated attempts to establish it wherever possible. Among its features were the egalitarian apportionment of lots, intensive mixed farming by each family, an inclination toward cooperativeness in consumption and production, and a minimum of

16   *Ibid.*, pp. 123–142, 349–352, 380–381.
17   *Ibid.*, pp. 59–75, 294–297.
18   *Ibid.*, pp. 369–375, 382–384.
19   *Ibid.*, pp. 311–318.
20   *Ibid.*, pp. 268–269, 276–279, 326–331.

forty families per village, as compared to sixty in the German model. Unfortunately, nearly all the efforts to realize this ideal proved futile, since potential settlers who owned some private capital were unwilling to invest it in real estate on nationalized land leased from the JNF.[21]

The only project of this sort that actually got under way was carried out by a group called Ha'ikar Hatza'ir (The Young Farmer), composed of young Jews from the United States and Palestine who in October 1912 took over, on a rental basis, the JNF land and buildings on the Kinneret Farm, which had been abandoned due to successive financial failures. The members themselves financed the livestock and the machinery, which included the most modern American equipment. That year, however, for all practical purposes the group worked as a piecework community, and they too disbanded due to economic difficulties. Thus, no smallholders' village actually came into being before World War I. With the war's end in 1922, some former members of Ha'ikar Hatza'ir were among the founders of the first moshavim, a settlement type that closely resembled the *Kleinbauerndorf*.[22]

Similar to the bid to have German workers replace Poles in Posen, part of the Zionist settlement effort concentrated on exploiting the Jewish working potential as a means of eliminating the need for Arab labor. Also like in Posen, the primary means of achieving this was through the establishment of laborers' villages (moshvei poalim), near the largest Jewish rural settlements (moshavot), where the Jewish farm workers received living quarters and a small auxiliary farm on most attractive terms. The plots were equal in size, intensive mixed farming was practiced, cooperativeness was encouraged, and a minimum was set of forty families per village. The only full-fledged laborers' village established on JNF land up to World War I was En Ganim, next to Petah Tiqwa. In addition, near several of the veteran moshavot Yemenite neighborhoods were set up, whose goals and planning principles resembled those of the *Arbeiterdorf*, the only major difference being the even smaller size of the auxiliary farm.[23] An original type of independent laborers' village was established on the JNF land in Ben Shemen by a group of Yemenite craftsmen who had trained at the Bezalel school of art in Jerusalem. They worked in a jewelry workshop set up for them in the village, and cultivated small plots adjacent to their homes. This settlement

21   This holds true for all of the permanent settlements proposed for JNF land up to 1910. For
      details on certain examples of this — such as the proposals for settlements in Ben Shemen,
      plans to settle Jews from Caucasia and southern Russia on Kinneret lands, and the attempt to
      establish a settlement for ultra-Orthodox Jews near Jerusalem — see: Shilony (note 1, supra),
      pp. 166–168, 213–214, 287–293, 375–376.

22   *Ibid.*, pp. 306–309.

23   *Ibid.*, pp. 397–400, 408–415.

was disbanded after a short while due to poor management, financial difficulties and its small size — ten families.[24]

When the Zionist Organization first conceived of the settlement type known as the *kooperazia*, it was believed that the new format would play a central role in the settlement enterprise. Oppenheimer proposed that it be initially established as a training farm for people wishing to settle there. In the next stage, those proving suitable would receive land to be cultivated on their own, and if this too proved successful they would be allowed to build homes there in the framework of a smallholders' village. Special stress was to be placed throughout the process on the deep personal acquaintance between all the candidates, training in close quarters over a protracted period, and the high level of cooperativeness in consumption and production. The only actual attempt in Palestine to implement this idea took place on the JNF land in Fuleh, and the settlement was called Merhavya. The first, or training farm stage was carried out and nearly completed when the onset of World War I brought on financial and organizational difficulties that prevented the experiment from reaching more advanced stages.[25]

The kvutza (communal group) was a settlement type indigenous to Palestine. It developed out of the piecework community, adding a communal dimension to the economic and social life of the settlers. Its origins lay in the Hadera Commune, which had assumed the form of a piecework community and adopted the principle of equal pay for male and female members. A year later, when this community decided to settle permanently in Umm Juni, its members began to seek a farm structure and a combination of branches that would "get the women out of the kitchen" and integrate them in the agricultural work. The intensive mixed farm, with barnyard animals and a dairy industry, was found to be most suitable for this purpose. Shortly thereafter it was resolved to forgo personal salaries and channel all incomes into a joint communal fund. Starting in the spring of 1911, the JNF financed the construction of permanent buildings on a small hill near the Sea of Galilee's outlet into the Jordan River, and the settlers selected the name Deganya for the new community.[26]

24   *Ibid.*, pp. 358–369; see also: C.Y. Peles, "Attempt to Establish a Religious Moshava before World War I," M. Eliav (ed.), *Shraga'i Book*, I, Jerusalem 1982, pp. 87–95 (Hebrew), and the article by Michal Oren in this volume.

25   Shilony (note 1, supra), pp. 147–165, 331–333; F. Oppenheimer, *Die Siedlungsgenossenschaft — Versuch einer positiven Überwindung des Kommunismus durch losung des Genossenschafts Problems und der Agrarfrage*, Berlin 1896; idem, *Merchavia — A Jewish Cooperative Settlement in Palestine*, JNF, 1914.

26   Shilony (note 1, supra), pp. 315–321; Y. Baratz, *Deganya A*, Jerusalem 1947 (Hebrew); *The Path of Deganya — Story of Fifty Years of the Kvutza*, Tel Aviv 1961 (Hebrew); H. Nir, "Each Person and His Deganya," *Cathedra*, 29 (September 1983), pp. 63–78 (Hebrew).

Three kvutzot designed to be permanent, Kinneret, Hulda and Gan Shemuel, were later founded on JNF land,[27] and following World War I their members became the founders and mentors of a wide-scale settlement program encompassing many hundreds of kvutzot and kibbutzim.

Physical Layout

Generally speaking, the physical layout of the rural settlements set up on JNF land up to World War I followed the model of German settlement in Posen. At the Atlit agricultural experimental station, an administration building, a large warehouse and an array of sheds were constructed on three sides of a small rectangular yard. The few workers came mainly from the nearby Arab villages, so that it was unnecessary to build living quarters for them.[28]

At the Herzl Forest plantation farm at Hulda, operated in the format of a large estate farm, an attractive administration building (see Fig. 1) and farmyard were built at a distance from each other, with the workers' living quarters being contained within the latter.[29] All the buildings at the Kinneret training farm formed a sort of enclosure around a large rectangular yard. The administration building located at one end and livestock sheds at the other were set off at a great distance from one another, and living quarters for the workers, as well as the storehouses, were located between them (see Fig. 2).[30]

As the training farm at Ben Shemen developed and expanded, it took on a shape resembling that of the German model (see Fig. 3 and Plate 2a),[31] while at Hulda the separation between the administration house and the farmyard was maintained.

The contractual kvutzot that introduced interim cultivation temporarily made do with the simple, nonpermanent adobe buildings that the Arab land tenants had left behind, along with several tents and wooden cabins. All of these

27   Shilony (note 1, supra), pp. 384–387; *Kinneret in Its Jubilee Year — 1914–1964*, Kinneret 1964 (Hebrew).

28   A plan for the buildings of the experimental farm was proposed by Prof. Warburg in June 1907. See: Shilony (note 1, supra), p. 103. Photographs are available of the buildings that were eventually erected. See, for example, the photograph presented in: Z. Vilnay, *Ariel — Palestine Encyclopedia*, Jerusalem 1979, VII, p. 6038 (Hebrew).

29   German aerial photograph no. 369 (May 12, 1918), in the Aerial Photographs Collection of the Department of Geography, Hebrew University, Jerusalem; Vilnay (note 28, supra), III, p. 2228. For a detailed discussion, see: Shilony (note 1, supra), pp. 380–382 and the plan of the administration house in Hulda on p. 380a.

30   *Ibid.*, pp. 297–303 and the plan of the Kinneret farmyard on p. 302a.

31   *Ibid.*, pp. 376–377 and the plan of the Ben Shemen farmyard on p. 376a.

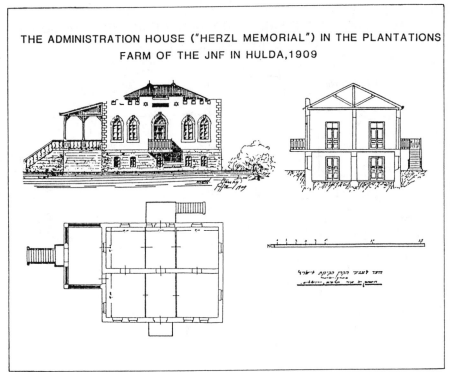

THE ADMINISTRATION HOUSE ("HERZL MEMORIAL") IN THE PLANTATIONS FARM OF THE JNF IN HULDA, 1909

Fig. 1

structures were abandoned once the land was given over to permanent settlement.[32]

The *Strassedorf* model that was selected for the smallholders' villages was not realized by World War I, but a a settlement type inaugurated after the war, the moshav, incorporated many of its elements. The laborers' village at En Ganim, and the Yemenite neighborhoods on moshavot and in Ben Shemen, adhered to *Strassedorf* layout, with public buildings concentrated in the center. Although the contours of the land and other factors occasionally dictated minor changes, this model was followed as closely as possible (see Fig. 4).[33]

The first stage of the *kooperazia* in Merhavya was designed in an agricultural school format, but in a manner allowing for the outward expansion of the

32   *Ibid.*, pp. 227, 313, 316, 327–331.
33   *Ibid.*, pp. 360–361, 400–401, 412–415 and the plans on pp. 412a, 412b, 414a.

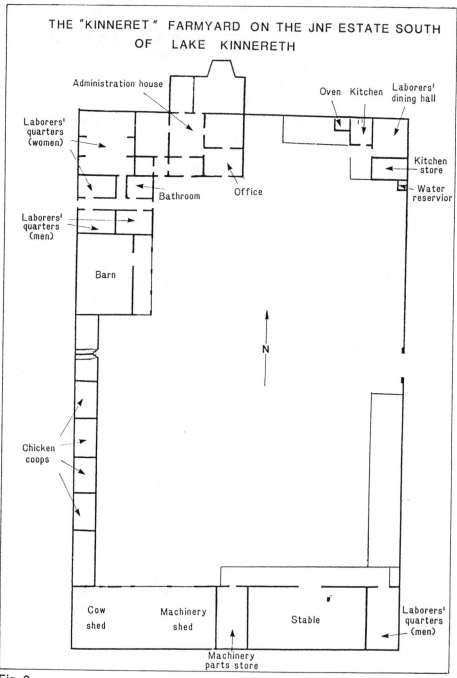

Fig. 2

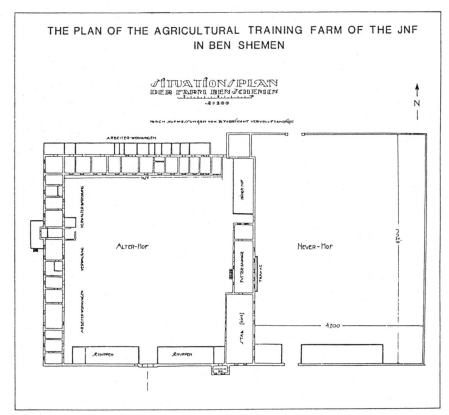

THE PLAN OF THE AGRICULTURAL TRAINING FARM OF THE JNF
IN BEN SHEMEN

Fig. 3

settlement (see Plate 2b).[34] With regard to the communal kvutza in Deganya, whose future and purpose were still unclear, it was decided to construct its permanent buildings in the large estate-farm pattern. The underlying idea was that in any case the members would soon attempt to cultivate their own plots as private farmers, while the remaining land on the estate would be administered by the JNF as an experimental farm on a profit basis. Hence a farmyard and administration house were built as separate units, with the former at first containing the workers' dwellings, and the latter serving as their living quarters

---

34 *Ibid.*, pp. 333–336; "Plan for the Merhavya *Kooperazia*" by the German-Jewish architect Alexander Berwald in spring 1912, Berwald Archives, Elissar Library, Technion, Haifa; German aerial photographs nos. 527, 1250, 1256 (fall 1917), Aerial Photographs Collection (note 29, supra).

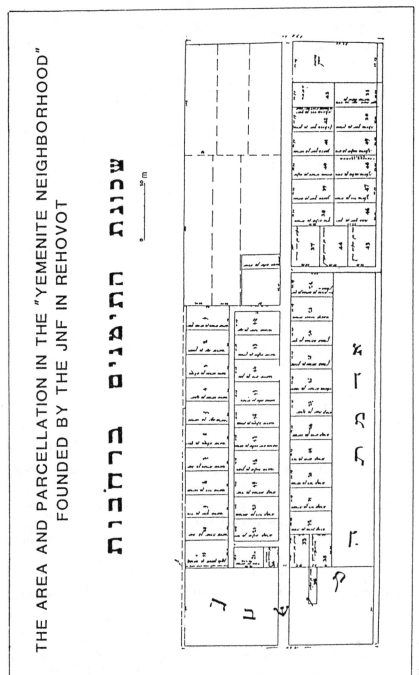

THE AREA AND PARCELLATION IN THE "YEMENITE NEIGHBORHOOD"
FOUNDED BY THE JNF IN REHOVOT

Fig. 4

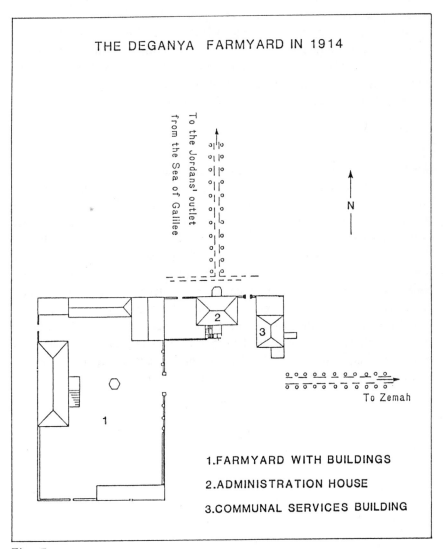

THE DEGANYA FARMYARD IN 1914

N

To the Jordans' outlet
from the Sea of Galilee

To Zemah

1. FARMYARD WITH BUILDINGS

2. ADMINISTRATION HOUSE

3. COMMUNAL SERVICES BUILDING

Fig. 5

later, due to the absence of an official manager. The workers demanded and received another building outside the farmyard, with a common kitchen, dining room, storage room, and shower (see Fig. 5 and Plate 3a),[35] thus possibly laying the foundation for the strict separation between three distinct areas — work, residential and common public services — practiced in all kvutzot and kibbutzim to this day. In the communal kvutza at Hulda, the administration house was from the outset separate from the farmyard, and another building containing all of the public services was added later (see Plate 3b).[36] The kvutzot in Kinneret and Gan Shemuel utilized existing buildings, and did not begin to conform to the typical physical layout until after World War I.

CONCLUSION

We have seen that despite the complex difficulties besetting the settlement enterprise planned by the Zionist Organization, the rural settlement on JNF lands before World War I bore a striking resemblance to the German model in Posen, with regard to nationalization, preparation and apportionment of land, both temporary and permanent settlement types, and physical layout. Even if the Zionist leadership and the JNF Directorate lacked a comprehensive and well-defined settlement plan, which is understandable in light of the prevailing conditions, they did have before them a clear model of a successful settlement enterprise, many of whose elements could be transplanted in Palestine. Furthermore, despite the fact that the Zionist leaders as a rule resided far from the settlement sites, and that they had to deal with complex, rapidly-changing problems unique to Palestine, the settlement undertaking that they led corresponded to a surprising degree with the German model.

35 Shilony (note 1, supra), pp. 318–320 and the plan of Deganya on p. 320a; German aerial photograph no. 178d (1918), Aerial Photographs Collection (note 29, supra).

36 Shilony (note 1, supra), p. 385; German aerial photograph no. 396, Aerial Photographs Collection (note 29, supra).

DEVELOPMENT OF THE MOSHAV OVDIM IDEA

MICHAL OREN

INTRODUCTION

Historical geography has devoted much attention to the evolvement of the various settlement types.[1] Starting from the end of the nineteenth century, Palestine became the target of mass immigration. However, this was not immigration in the ordinary sense, i.e. simply a movement of population from one place to another. Rather, it was interwoven with the notion of the return of the Jewish people to its homeland. This idea was linked to yet another concept — a return to working the land as a means of earning a livelihood, in contrast to the occupations that had been common among Diaspora Jewry. Although the newcomers did not find in Palestine a settlement type completely suited to their aspirations in regard to an agricultural way of life, they had brought with them from abroad new conventions and ideas concerning the ideal mode of settlement, and devised other new concepts after their arrival. Hence from the inception of large-scale Jewish immigration to Palestine in the nineteenth century until the present day, new agricultural formats have continually been created. One of them, which has become very widespread, is the moshav ovdim — the smallholders' cooperative settlement. The first such moshav — Nahalal — was founded in 1921, but its roots extended far back, to the Second Aliya (wave of immigration to Eretz-Israel).

The Second Aliya[2] comprised people who had been induced to move to Palestine in the wake of the anti-Semitic pogroms taking place in Russia from 1903 to the outbreak of World War I in 1914. Some 30,000 to 35,000 immigrants reached Palestine, but only 4,500 remained in the country. A minority among them turned to agriculture, as hired laborers. These were, as a rule, young, educated nonconformists and atheists (although from religious families)

---

1   See the articles by Ran Aaronsohn, Yossi Ben-Arzi, Yossi Katz and Amiram Oren in this volume.

2   For more on the Second Aliya, see: A. Bein, *The Return to the Soil, A History of Jewish Settlement in Israel*, Jerusalem 1952, pp. 26–137.

possessing a high level of political consciousness and holding cosmopolitan, revolutionary views originating in Russia. With such backgrounds, they aspired to create and build up an agricultural proletarian class in Palestine to work as wage earners on the existing moshavot, frameworks which they regarded as representing the capital unavoidable for economic development in Eretz-Israel. They also saw as a Zionist ideal the "conquest of labor," i.e. the proliferation of Jewish workers, who would replace the numerous Arab laborers preferred by the moshavot farmers because they accepted low salaries and because the relationship between these farmers and the new immigrants was strained.

The workers were organized in two political parties and in regional labor unions, and over the years the latter took upon themselves several of the ideological functions of the former. One such function was the devising of settlement types that could offer a solution to the spiritual and material difficulties that the workers had been encountering over the years. The brunt of the development of the moshav ovdim idea took place within the apolitical trade unions.

The moshav ovdim concept is that of a rural settlement composed of working-class people, based on family farms and individual working of the land. Ostensibly this is a copy of many agricultural villages throughout the world, but in fact the moshav ovdim is different. Its principles derive from a combination of elements: the socialistic conceptions that the Second Aliya immigrants brought with them; the worldwide trend at that time to abandon the vestiges of the old feudal land regime in favor of a system based on small landowners; and the existing communities in Palestine. The first principle was that of settlement on national rather than private land. The second principle — which differentiates the moshav from the classical individualistic settlement — is that of self-labor, i.e. work performed by the entire family rather than by wage earners. This was predicated on the idea of Hebrew labor. Settlers of the moshvei ovdim had formed group frameworks prior to their arrival in Palestine, and they held the exclusive right to select new members. These communal nuclei took upon themselves the task of cultivating the land, and responsibility was placed on the individual; there were no managers, administrative functionaries or middlemen. Thus a characteristic component of the moshav ovdim came into being: mutual responsibility and liability.

Various studies have pointed to the connection between the socialistic baggage that the Second Aliya immigrants had brought with them and the unique mode of collective settlement that they established in Palestine.[3] This article explores

---

3   R. Frankel et al., "Discussion: Ideological Motives in the Formation of the Kvutza during the Second Aliya Period," *Cathedra*, 18 (January 1981), pp. 111–129 (Hebrew).

the roots of the moshav ovdim idea, tracing the manner in which it grew out of the forms of communal frameworks that had already developed in the country. However, it shall also be argued here that the principles of the moshav evolved not only from collective settlement types, but also from individualistic ones — i.e. with private homes, no common dining room, etc. — both inside and outside of Palestine. In other words, the moshav ovdim was born out of an attempt to create a new type incorporating the advantages of various earlier ones.

The initiators of this new type came mainly from the working sector for which it was designed, but the personnel of the national Zionist institutions who engaged in the settlement of Palestine joined in with the initiative, and we shall examine the interaction between these two groups, as well as their views and opinions as expressed in conventions, congresses, memoranda, newspaper articles and memoirs.

CRITICISM OF EXISTING SYSTEM AS CATALYST FOR MOSHAV IDEA

The initial idea of individualistic communities of workers stemmed from criticism of the Jewish settlement types already existing in Palestine — moshavot and private holdings — and from a desire to ameliorate the situation of workers who were subject to the will of owners of large holdings, officials, or even managers of the Zionist national farms. In the eyes of the workers, the following were the sorest evils in the moshavot: the privately-owned plots were too large and remained largely untilled, and the farmers preferred exploiting hired laborers — primarily Arabs — to working their own land themselves. These ills were brought on by a lack of knowledge and agricultural training on the part of the Jewish landowners, and insufficient institutional support, which trickled in irregularly. Produce consisted solely of luxury items rather than basic staples, and as a result agriculture was dependent on foreign markets and hired labor, and farming was extensive, providing no incentive for self-labor. These drawbacks were symptomatic not only of individual farms but of the overall situation, on a national level. The number of moshavot in Palestine seemed too small relative to the Zionist goals, the farmers suffered deprivation, and their numbers failed to increase. They were not tied to the land, speculative land sales to the highest bidder flourished, and the workers saw no future in their salaried labor.

The solution that had been practiced at first was, through philanthropy, to turn the outstanding Jewish hired laborers in the moshavot into farmers, often on other moshavot — but the workers of the Second Aliya considered this system as contravening their beliefs. They advocated the development of *private* farms in Palestine, in which each settler would possess certain means, while the salaried workers would constitute a separate class. The national Zionist institutions also saw the future of the land as resting upon private capital, but their outlook differed somewhat from that of the new immigrants. In 1907 Dr. Arthur Ruppin, director of the Palestine Office of the World Zionist Organization,[4] also declared his support for encouraging hired laborers to become farmers, but without resort to philanthropy. He proposed that workers acquire small farms through private means saved up over the years of their salaried labor.

Contrary to the stand taken by the workers' parties and the Palestine Office, other opinions favored the settlement of penurious workers through national means — in other words national rather than private settlement — viewing this as the World Zionist Organization's primary area of activity. Their feeling was that only the workers could redeem the land, and forge a true bond with their plots. This opinion was held by Yitzhak Wilkansky,[5] and as far back as 1908 by Joseph Vitkin[6] and Dr. Hillel Joffe.[7] Despite the fact that their view was not accepted, it represented the dawning of thought on a national-individualistic community of workers on small farms.

THE FIRST STEP — MOSHVEI POALIM

The first step taken by the workers toward a change in their status was their acceptance of the moshvei poalim established by the Hovevei Zion Association.[8] These frameworks were designed to solve the problem of the worker who lacked a stable economic base, by providing him with a small farm to supplement his salaried labor and supply the basic needs of his family. He was supposed to work

---

4   The supreme body coordinating the Zionist movement throughout the world was called the Zionist Organization. Its representative in Palestine was the Palestine Office, founded in 1908 and headed by Dr. Arthur Ruppin.

5   Yitzhak Wilkansky received a degree in agronomy in Germany, moved to Palestine in 1908 and was active in the Palestine Office.

6   Vitkin, who moved to Palestine in 1898, was part of the Second Aliya working class, even though he engaged primarily in teaching. He belonged to one of the workers' parties and was the first of the workers to call for mass immigration to Palestine by young people, and settlement on the land.

7   Hillel Joffe was a Zionist activist, a pioneer and a doctor. He moved to Palestine in 1891, and aided the Jewish settlement movement in various spheres. He was outspoken in his stand regarding settlement-related issues.

8   This society established and supported several of the settlements, from the First Aliya in 1882 onward.

on this farm in the seasons when his services were not required in the moshavot, while the other members of his family could tend the farm the year round.

For convenience sake these moshvei poalim were established in close proximity to the moshavot. From among the four moshavim that can be called moshvei poalim, only one — En Ganim — fulfilled some of the requirements stipulated above, but even this settlement "transgressed" by attempting to make the hired labor of its members secondary and by concentrating on the work on the private plots. The tracts given to the moshavim settlers were too large, and these people had to desist from their work in the moshava in order to cultivate them. Occasionally they even employed workers to assist them on their private plots, while simultaneously serving as hired laborers on the moshavot.

In light of the deviations of the moshvei poalim from the principles that had been outlined for them, the workers leveled severe criticism at the system. Nevertheless, their very consent to move onto the land, and the fact that their constant peregrination was drawing to an end, constituted novel developments. The system was generally considered to be positive, so long as there was no intention of turning the hired laborers into independent farmers. The workers were to continue cultivating the land in the moshavot, while their small plots were to serve merely as a supplementary source of income.

As the years passed the bankruptcy of the "conquest of labor" ideal, along with the dashing of hopes for an influx of foreign capital to redeem the land, induced also the workers to consider the idea of settlement. They edged closer to Ruppin's stand regarding the need to solve their problem through this means. However, unlike Ruppin, they envisioned a type of settlement that was not private and acquired through their own resources, but — more like Vitkin and Wilkansky — on national land. This was the position advocated by leaders of the working sector, who operated mainly in the framework of apolitical, regional labor unions. Opinion generally favored a collective settlement type, and this became the object of the workers' aspirations, since it was regarded as a refreshing novelty in the process of Zionist fulfillment through socialism. In parallel, this idea became the cornerstone for the first kvutza shitufit, or kvutza for short.[9] The founding of Degania in 1909 symbolized the end of the wanderings and the beginning of a permanent, collective framework. The kvutza served as a forerunner for the larger kibbutz.

9   Since the founding of Degania, this settlement type has been known as the kvutza, a term signifying a life-style based on socialistic principles, and involving cooperative activity in work and daily affairs.

Still, there were other leaders such as Eliezer Joffe[10] and Berl Katznelson[11] who in the second decade of the century began to consider individualistic settlement, and the bulk of the working class followed their lead.[12] Opposition to the existing type prompted these leaders to resist the practice then current of turning the moshavot workers into farmers. They suggested as an alternative the establishment of "reformed moshavot," although others felt that the solution lay in amending the path of the farmers, not in devising new formats.

In 1913 the Zionist Organization altered its position. It was resolved that the goal should be the transformation of the hired laborers into small farmers, but the National Fund lacked the capital necessary for a settlement project for the impecunious workers. Ruppin also accepted the idea, and if, in early 1913, he still refused to give his approval for the founding in Kinneret of the moshav ovdim-style community proposed by a group of immigrants called Ha'ikar Hatza'ir, which was headed by Eliezer Joffe and whose members had undergone agricultural training in America — a year later he acceded to Katznelson's proposal to establish a moshav ovdim, and nearly succeeded in implementing it.

The proponents of the moshav reached the conclusion that this settlement type offered not only a preferable way of life for an individual wishing to free himself from bondage to those who possessed capital, but also an effective tool for the redemption of the land, as it would be densely populated, in contrast to the moshavot, with their relatively sparse population. This advantage carried great weight for any immigration movement to Palestine. The true conquest of the land would be carried out by the small farmer, for only he would invest his energy in exploiting its full potential.

Wilkansky greatly developed the small-farm concept.[13] Similar ideas had surfaced previously, but not necessarily of farms run by workers. Wilkansky found that with no hope to some day possess his own plot, the worker loses his

10   Eliezer Joffe was an agricultural laborer and a Zionist thinker. He is regarded as the initiator of the moshav ovdim concept. In 1904 he left Russia for agricultural training in the United States, where he established the Ha'ikar Hatza'ir youth organization, whose goal was to provide agricultural training for those intending to immigrate to Palestine. On the eve of World War I he headed the Galilee Labor Organization.

11   Berl Katznelson was a leader of the Labor Zionist movement in Palestine, a thinker and an *Hapoel Hatza'ir*, 3–4 (December 1, 1911), pp. 6–9 (Hebrew).

12   The main discussions by the workers on the topic of the moshav took place in the 1913 and 1914 conventions. See the journal of the Poalei Zion Party — *Ha'ahdut*, 11 (December 27, 1912), pp. 16–21; *Hapoel Hatza'ir*, 14 (January 16, 1914), pp. 13–16.

13   Wilkansky's opinions were expressed in conventions held by the workers, and published in *Hapoel Hatza'ir*. Some of his articles have been collected in a Hebrew pamphlet entitled *Baderech*, published in Jaffa in 1918.

motivation to work, to invest and to take proper care of the field and the machines. On the other hand the farmer who owns a large farm loses interest in working the land, as he turns into a manager. Often he even appoints a surrogate manager, thereby severing his tie to the land altogether.

The members of Ha'ikar Hatza'ir also planned to establish a moshav of small farmers, although it is difficult to determine whether they had in fact conceived of this idea by themselves, even before their arrival in Palestine, or whether it sprang from their experience with collective life during their stay at Kinneret. At any rate, there is no doubt that this group was instrumental in transforming the idea from theory to practice. After the year of working the land as a collective, they proposed turning Kinneret into a moshav ovdim. Ruppin, who at the time opposed the idea of individualistic settlement by workers, being more inclined toward collective responsibility, advised the group to continue as a collective, promising to expand their territory and earmark new tracts for family holdings so that there would at least be some measure of privacy.

As a follow-up to the small-farm concept, it was necessary to find people who would be, on the one hand, capable of settling in these farms, and on the other hand in need of such a framework. It was felt that the greatest potential lay in experienced, impecunious workers who within a number of years would be capable of standing on their own. These settlers would not be crude and dull-witted like their counterparts anywhere else in the world — the mold that the national Zionist institutions attempted to fashion in Palestine as well — but, quite to the contrary, people who would engage in scholarly, cultural and spiritual pursuits. Only by raising agriculture to new heights could the land be truly conquered.

At the time when the moshav ovdim idea was taking form, there already existed in Palestine, in addition to the moshvei poalim and the moshavot established by the First Aliya immigrants, new settlement types, or more precisely, new attempts at creating such types. Their common denominator was the cooperative principle, which was applied in varying degrees. At the start of the second decade of the 1900's, the Weltanschauung of collectivism was still in its formative stages. Its proponents still deliberated over numerous issues, and the search for a course to follow would continue for many years. The moshav ovdim idea began to crystallize in parallel with the establishment of the cooperative types of settlement, at times negating them, although based on similar ideological principles. However, whereas the tenets of cooperatism were not clearly formulated in advance, but rather grew out of assorted ideologies from abroad that had found fertile soil in Palestine,[14] the development of the

14   For more on the debate over whether cooperative settlement in Palestine was a version of a

moshav ovdim idea was gradual and carefully considered. Each and every fundamental was the subject of protracted debate and clarifications that surfaced in various newspaper articles, committee meetings and conventions. Supporters of the moshav idea proceeded with the utmost caution, as if fearful of establishing yet another settlement type that would not prove itself.

Eliezer Joffe's attitude toward a collective way of life was extremely critical. He berated the fact that family life was impeded by the kvutza, and that personalities were played down. While he was at Kinneret with Ha'ikar Hatza'ir, the group rejected collectivism,[15] except as a transitional stage. His experience with this kvutza unquestionably influenced his ideas, since he explicitly favored collectivism before his immigration to Palestine, as had his movement — which is why Kinneret was established on such a basis. Even following this year Joffe advised the Palestine Office to maintain Kinneret's communal framework. It is evidently not true that the group reached Palestine with a clear desire to live as individualistic smallholders rather than as wage earners or members of a kvutza.

Wilkansky, like Joffe, did not understand how an individual in a kvutza could devote all his love and energy to making the land fertile if he was merely a small cog on a large wheel. In this sense, agriculture and industry are dissimilar. Wilkansky placed the collective farm in the same category as the large holding, in that they both nullified the advantages of the small farm. One of the reasons that he negated communal life was that the work of the woman in the kvutza prevented her from taking care of her own home. Wilkansky, who was among those to chart the course that workers' settlements would follow, dared to assume that collective frameworks would ultimately not be the focus of the Zionist Organization's activity. This view was opposed to the one which had gained wide acceptance once Degania proved to be relatively stable, namely, that the kvutza offered the best way to redeem the land, and that the workers comprising the group could be relied upon to accomplish this goal. Nonetheless, Wilkansky believed that work not offering an avenue for expressing individuality could be done on a collective basis, and that tradesmen and professionals could serve everyone on this basis as well.

Wilkansky's ideas were reinforced several years later in light of the experience of groups of settlers in Italy.[16] Thousands of groups of former salaried laborers

      social idea imported from abroad or whether it was born out of necessity, see Frankel et al. (note 3, supra).

15   Minutes of the Ha'ikar Hatza'ir meeting of April 2, 1913. The members were sounded out as to their opinion regarding plans for the kvutza for the year 1914. Central Zionist Archives, Jerusalem (hereafter: CZA), KKL3/101.

16   Y. Wilkansky, "Settlement Groups in Italy," *Hapoel Hatza'ir*, 13 (January 9, 1914), pp. 13–14 (Hebrew).

organized into collectives for work and settlement, in order to eliminate the middleman fees that labor contractors had exacted until then. These new frameworks were also designed to take land away from the owners of large holdings, and transfer it to workers who would cultivate it as smallholders. Wilkansky, who visited these collectives in 1914, returned to Palestine and enthusiastically noted in lectures and writing the similarity between them and the ones he had envisioned. Evidently a lecture that he delivered captured the attention of the workers. He found the Italian model in which the workers acted as entrepreneurs and leased land together, but apportioned it as private farms, to be superior to communal settlement that squelched private initiative. True, in the Italian model there was collectivism in the grazing land, part of the property rights, the loan bank, the receiving of agronomic advice, etc., but this merely reinforced his claim that such a system was worthwhile in any sphere devoid of possible expression of individuality.

Others too among the advocates of the small-farm idea were willing to accept some form of collectivism, unlike the moshavot then existing, which turned a deaf ear to the persistent coaxing of the proponents of this concept. The latter, however, were unwilling to accept the notion that was gaining acceptance in the wake of the kvutza's popularity among the workers — that the kvutza was preferable from both an economic and a social standpoint, and that it contributed more to the nation. Hence Joffe, for example, in his brochure,[17] allowed for the formation of small collectives within moshvei ovdim. Still, the homes on the moshav should, he felt, be built as private, rather than communal dwellings. Joffe's opinion undoubtedly made an impact, since the workers accepted his proposal for a moshav ovdim, even though, to his displeasure, they resolved to recognize the kvutzot as well as a legitimate settlement type. They recommended that there be an initial, transitional stage in which the moshav would be run as a cooperative.

It can be concluded, then, that those who had originally formulated the moshav idea vociferously opposed the collective course of the kvutza. However, since collectivism was the mode of living with which they were familiar, and perhaps since the moshav idea still remained somewhat nebulous to them, the tendency was to integrate "positive" kvutza principles, such as collective marketing and purchasing, mutual liability, communal living as a transitional stage, and even the formation of small collectives within the moshav itself. With

---

17 This brochure, evidently written in 1915, constituted a summation of his thoughts. Published in 1919, it signalled the beginning of the idea's implementation. See: E. Joffe, *The Foundation of Moshvei Ovdim*, Jaffa 1919 (Hebrew).

the founding of the first moshav in 1921, it would be mainly former kvutza members who would support this development, since after experiencing cooperative life for several years they reached the conclusion that such a system made family life impossible. This outlook might reflect a maturity and sobriety that replaced the somewhat romantic dreams of cooperative life.

THE FIVE PRINCIPLES OF THE MOSHAV OVDIM

The principles of the moshav ovdim, as crystallized in the various writings of the initiators of the idea, appear to be largely a far-reaching development of those that had already been put to the test in existing settlement types. The greatest novelty lay not in the formulation of the principles per se, but in their having gained form gradually in assorted committees, in a process lasting for years and attended by serious thinking, cautious formulations and the granting of approval by the workers. Unlike the kvutza or moshav poalim, whose members began to discern obstacles and attempt to overcome them only after the settlement was founded, here careful forethought was applied to all areas of life. The principles of the moshav ovdim were as follows:

National Land
Unlike the situation on the already-existing moshavot and moshvei poalim — where land was private, the burden of payments fell on settlers unable to attain the necessary funds, and land speculation thrived, thus greatly impeding the achievement of national goals — it was determined that the land of the moshvei ovdim would belong to the National Fund and that the settlers would receive it as a perpetual lease. This idea had already been raised by Vitkin in 1908, when he proposed national settlements for workers, i.e. settlements on national land (unlike people such as Ruppin, who favored private land), in which private means would be unnecessary. Wilkansky ruled out any other form of settlement, stating that there was a worldwide tendency toward nationalization of land and its apportionment to independent workers, while only in Palestine did people mistakenly envision a capitalistic community with large private holdings. Indeed, a 1911 article told of the trend in Holland to wrest large holdings from their owners, and to lease them to the workers under favorable terms, so as to forestall bondage to the owners.[18]

The idea of nationalizing the land gained momentum, until the Zionist

18   Hendrick Shpiekman, "The Question of the Land Worker and Small Farming in Holland," *Hapoel Hatza'ir*, 3–4 (December 1, 1911), pp. 6–9 (Hebrew).

Organization and the workers — who initially had advocated its capitalistic development — concurred that it should be acquired and leased to the appropriate party, the workers. This principle had materialized previously, as in the kvutza, but since it had not struck deep roots, and because the moshav ovdim was seen as an improved version of the moshav poalim, which had been founded on private land, it was necessary to clarify that one was referring to settlement on national land.

The principle of nationalization of the land led to another innovation: for the first time the obligation of the Zionist Organization's National Fund was defined as cultivating the land, rather than merely acquiring it and passing it on untilled to the workers. Like many other ideas, this one too did not belong exclusively to the moshav ovdim. It had been advanced by Hillel Joffe in 1908, and Wilkansky again drew conclusions from the Italian experience in attracting new settlers and preventing migration from the south to the north. The Sicilian Government cultivated land in mountainous areas, which were overlooked by private entrepreneurs.

Self-Labor

This concept signified the non-employment of wage earners, even though there were formulae that made allowances for it in extreme emergencies, on condition, naturally, that this was Hebrew labor. Work was to be done only by family members, and the land was not to be left uncultivated. The entire family unit would work as small a tract as possible, in accordance with the family's ability and needs.

The idea of self-labor had already been put into practice in the kvutza, even though there the work was performed on a group basis rather than a personal basis. It originated in the general precept of not exploiting hired labor and of avoiding bondage to landowners. The principle suited the kvutza and the moshav, and stood in contrast to the "conquest of labor" concept, i.e. the hope that the Jewish immigrants would not engage in the kinds of work performed by their coreligionists abroad. Self-labor was not appropriate for the moshvei poalim, whose main income came from wages for hired labor, or for the moshavot established by the First Aliya immigrants. The principle sprang from the sober awakening that the workers underwent regarding the difficult situation that evolved from advocacy of the conquest of labor policy. Still, it is noteworthy that before the workers themselves reached this conclusion, there were others who expressed the opinion that only self-labor would inspire the worker to invest his energy in tilling the land. The Ha'ikar Hatza'ir kvutza — even more than Degania — carefully maintained the policy of self-labor, thus setting a new course in settlement history.

Wilkansky argued that self-labor performed by the family should take priority over that carried out in collective frameworks, citing the Templer colony as a precedent. He implemented this principle on a personal level by vesting various powers and authority in those who worked for him on the national farms. Self-labor, therefore, was practiced on the moshav ovdim, but not exclusively in this framework. The idea of not employing hired labor was adapted to the principle of running a small farm to supply the family's needs through self-labor.

The precept of self-labor was actually related to another, which the settlers did not categorize separately — perhaps because its existence was self-understood. This is the principle of *self-responsibility*, which also was practiced on the farm run by Wilkansky, and by the kuvtza. When Ha'ikar Hatza'ir took over the management of Kinneret, it assumed full responsibility. This principle was born out of the workers' opposition to the situation in the moshavot, where the farmers were not answerable for their actions since there was an official placed above them, and not even this official was fully in charge; in cases of failure there was no one who could be called to task, so that the entire settlement came to resemble a voluntary venture devoid of accountability. A similar situation prevailed in the national farms, as the laborers worked under the supervision of an agronomist who did not let them take part in decision-making, so that they avoided responsibility and concern for the success of their enterprise.

Mutual Liability

This principle, which is related to self-responsibility, involves the payment of debts by the impecunious settlers, who were plagued by doubt as to their ability to fulfill their fiscal obligations. The Palestine Office agreed to put up a surety for the settlers, on condition that they accepted the principle of mutual liability. The Ha'ikar Hatza'ir kvutza, which was the first to propose the establishment of a moshav ovdim, was aware of the lack of confidence evinced by the Palestine Office with regard to the personal accountability of the settlers. Its members therefore suggested that the responsibility be collective — as was the case in Degania, which had become a recognized and credible model — even though the land was apportioned among the members on a private basis.

The idea of mutual liability marked a major turning point in the history of individualistic settlement. It reflected the ambivalence with regard to collective life. Undoubtedly the principle was formulated especially for a settlement type such as the moshav ovdim, since in the kvutza collective responsibility was built into the system, which is why the Palestine Office backed the kvutza and displayed trust in its society. Nonetheless, in the moshav there was a wariness of entrusting responsibility to each and every member separately, and it was thus necessary to find a way of integrating the collective responsibility of the kvutza into the life-style of the moshav. The manner of doing so did not originate with the formulators of the moshav idea, but had been suggested as early as 1908 in one of several settlement proposals, and in the En Ganim moshav poalim this integration was put into practice. Even Wilkansky received his inspiration from the Italian settlement groups, where agreements between the members were based on mutual liability.

Mutual aid, another function of collective life, was related to the above principle. The concept of aiding a member in times of trouble through financial contributions by the other members had originally been suggested by Eliezer Joffe.

Internal Membership Selection by the Settlers

Like the other principles of the moshav ovdim, this one too had antecedents in other frameworks, whether based on the centrality of land or of work, on piecework or on permanent settlement. All of these frameworks selected their own members. The workers on the moshvei poalim sought to adopt this principle as well, but it was hardly put into practice because the body behind these settlements — Hovevei Zion — demanded for itself the right to select members, which resulted in constant friction over this issue.

The precept of internal selection of members is especially important because the character of the settlers played a central role in the success or failure of the moshav. The settlers had organized themselves as groups prior to actually settling on the land, so that they could appropriate to themselves various rights and set their own policy, unlike moshava members, who were subject to an official representative of the settlement body. Internal selection of members constituted the only means of ensuring that they would adhere to the tenets of the moshav ovdim. This principle represented a novel development vis-à-vis the moshavot, and it was triggered by opposition to the situation in this older settlement type.

Hebrew Labor

This principle also had antecedents in Palestine. The workers of the Second Aliya had waged a protracted struggle on behalf of their exclusive employment on the moshavot. In settlements with working-class members, like the kvutzot, Ha'ikar Hatza'ir, the moshav poalim En Ganim, and to a large degree in the national farms as well, this precept was already adhered to.

OTHER PRINCIPLES THAT GAINED ACCEPTANCE

Credit for Equipment

The workers, as well as Wilkansky, opposed the practice whereby the National Fund of the Zionist Organization supplied the credit, since there was a general consensus that its role was strictly to redeem the land and prepare it for settlement. Hence various companies that had thus far established the settlements had to provide the credit in the form of a loan to be repaid in installments, with the Palestine Office as guarantor. The credit had to be sufficient for the purchase of all essential goods, in order to put the venture on solid footing at the outset. The workers sought to avoid the mistake of the moshvei poalim and the moshavot, where credit was so limited and irregular that the settlers were forced to constantly search for additional sources of financing. Wilkansky described in great detail the Italian system, which was diametrically opposed to that employed on the moshavot and the moshavim. In Italy sizable credit, tax breaks for twenty years, and many other forms of necessary aid were made available, in order to stimulate settlement and forestall migration. In Palestine, by contrast, the settlement companies were interested only in boasting of the number of colonies they had established, while they neglected the settlements themselves and allowed them to degenerate once they were founded.

Farm Structure

The various proposals for the moshvei ovdim explicitly detail the desired farm structure, contours of the field, types of produce, and planting cycle. Since the plot allotted to each settler would be as small as possible, it would require intensive working. As opposed to the moshavot, on the moshvei ovdim the type of crops had to be determined in accordance with the needs of the nation. Hence the most basic and nourishing staples, such as wheat, barley, vegetables and poultry, were the main produce, and were raised on *mixed farms*. The settlers refrained from growing luxury crops geared for export, which were lucrative but uncertain. Furthermore, such crops required hired labor and machinery and methods suitable for large holdings.

There had been earlier attempts to introduce mixed farming, primarily by the Ha'ikar Hatza'ir kvutza, which also initiated modern methods of working the land, apparently transplanted from the training farms the members had worked on in America. This was one of the greatest breakthroughs for the settlement enterprise. The Templer colonies served as a successful model for emulation. Still, the greatest contribution toward the introduction of mixed farming into Jewish settlement was made by Wilkansky, although many others had advocated this system on the moshavot. Therefore it is not surprising that the moshav ovdim concept and the idea of mixed farming germinated in such close proximity. Wilkansky lent his wholehearted support to both of them. He saw the mixed farm as a means of redemption for the nation that — as it struck roots in its land — needed a foundation consisting of all the staples. Furthermore, Wilkansky felt that mixed farming would provide an ideal means of tying the farmer to his land, as it would allow him to settle in places distant from the city, while furnishing most of his needs. More of the land throughout the country could therefore be redeemed.

The Number of Settlers

The moshvei poalim had an average of twenty to thirty families. Various proposals spoke of a number ranging from thirty to one hundred, with the ideal being fifty. At any rate, the idea was that intensive farming would make it possible to reduce the size of each family's plot, so that there would be more room for additional families, and the Jewish settlement could be augmented.

Location of the Moshav

This lends itself to comparison with the siting of the moshvei poalim. In 1913, as the subject of the moshvei ovdim was raised for the first time, it was decided to locate them next to the moshavot. This was an indication that the mooted settlement type had not yet weened itself away from the moshav poalim conception of its primary function as a provider of workers for the moshava. One of the arguments against the moshav poalim was that it contradicted the goal of Zionism in that it was always located next to existing moshavot instead of in new areas.

By 1914 it was agreed that the moshavim would not be established as neighborhoods and suburbs adjacent to the moshavot, but as independent communities set up in new and remote locations. The moshavim would be built first, and followed by the capitalistic moshavot. It was even likely that they would provide manpower for the construction of the new moshavot. In other words, there was still a residue of the traditional role of the Second Aliya workers — work in the moshava. Thus the development of agricultural frameworks in Palestine followed a course opposite to that prevalent elsewhere in the world; while as a rule the industrial city stood in the center, and was surrounded by suburbs that supplied it with fresh produce, in Palestine agriculture played the key role rather than industry, so that the city was located in the middle of rural communities that had already come into existence, in order to provide them with services.

True, it would be possible to establish a moshav beside a moshava, but not as an ancillary farm. Unlike the situation in the moshvei poalim, work on the moshava would provide a side income for the moshav ovdim settlers, to supplement the private farms. In this fashion, it would be possible to establish far more moshvei ovdim, each striving for economic independence, around the moshavot. The settlers would find employment on the moshava only until their farms began to show profits, at which time they would desist from working outside, thereby making room for new hired laborers who, like themselves, would eventually gain economic independence on their own land. This process would accelerate the redemption of the land. Berl Katznelson's practical proposal to the Palestine Office for the establishment of a moshav ovdim contained the recommendation that this type of settlement be located beside a large moshava that would provide work for the settlers in the initial years.[19]

The Status of Women
The moshav ovdim was predicated on complete equality between the sexes. This principle, originally formulated by Joffe, was first implemented in full during the year's operation of the Ha'ikar Hatza'ir kvutza in Kinneret. As this was one of Joffe's cardinal precepts, it is no wonder that it was strictly enforced while he was present at Kinneret. In contrast to the moshava, where women only engaged in domestic tasks, as their value system negated any possibility of work outside; in contrast to the piecework groups, which did not admit women (although there were groups of women who raised vegetables on a piecework basis); and in contrast to the kvutza, which, in a dramatic reversal, compelled the women to work on the collective farm rather than in their homes — here an attempt was made to solve the problem of the working woman's status in a way that was natural for her and her family, while simultaneously allowing her to contribute to the economic security of her family. In the moshav ovdim, as in the moshav poalim, the woman was able to play her traditional role in parallel with her work on the family farm, which largely entailed raising vegetables and poultry, and incorporated the principle of mixed farming. The Templer colonies, where the women engaged in housewifery and in dairy farming as their only outside work, served as a model in this sphere as well.

Other principles were suggested for the moshvei ovdim as well: public institutions would be established by the settlers themselves; internal organization of moshav life would be completely autonomous; payment of dues to the public institutions would be made in accordance with the extent of usage by each family; the public institutions would not be able to force their will, views or

---

19   Berl Katznelson, in the name of the Judea Labor Organization, to the Palestine Office: "Proposal for Establishment of a Moshav Ovdim on JNF Land," CZA, L2/66II.

beliefs on the members; non-farmers whose services were required on the moshav would receive a lot for a house and garden, but not a field, on condition that they accept the moshav's principles; it would be forbidden for both the farmers and the non-farmers to work in their profession outside of the moshav, or in another profession within the moshav; Hebrew would be the only language in all spheres of life on the moshav; the allocation of plots would be determined by lottery; assignments could be made on a group basis in light of social ties or a desire to work the land jointly, but the contract would be drawn up with each settler individually; unmarried persons were entitled to receive plots just as families were, in accordance with their ability to work them; in the event of marriage between moshav members, the parties would have to return one of their plots, of their own choosing, to the moshav.

CONCLUSION

We have seen that most of the basic precepts of the moshav had been aired previously, and part of them had been tried. The novelty in the moshav ovdim concept was the integration of diverse principles that had been mooted or actually implemented in a process of trial and error. These tenets were gleaned from the moshavot, moshvei poalim, piecework groups, and the kvutzot. The ideas were culled partly from the Templer colonies in Palestine, and partly from abroad — from the United States (by Ha'ikar Hatza'ir), from Europe (by Wilkansky and via newspaper articles published in various countries undergoing a transition to small farming), and from Russia (ideas concerning the role of the working class vis-à-vis the capitalistic development of the country).

An assortment of persons was involved in shaping the ideas about individualistic settlement, including the personnel of the Zionist Organization, professionals such as Wilkansky, and the workers themselves, who lived in diverse settlement types. There were some whose contribution toward the moshav concept would be appreciated only years afterwards, while at the time they pressed for their ideas they encountered animosity. A relationship based on cooperation and trust between the workers and the Palestine Office materialized only near the end of the Ottoman period, and it did not reach fruition because of the outbreak of World War I. Still, great progress was made in this area during the war, especially with regard to the stands of the Palestine Office — the result being the "natural" establishment of the moshav ovdim at the end of the war, following so many years of clarifications.

The moshav ovdim was the only settlement type planned to the smallest detail in light of lessons learned from previous settlement ventures. It is not our objective to evaluate the validity of these lessons, but the proponents of the idea regarded it as expressly ripe for experimentation. Following the war, in 1919, the aspirations recorded in Eliezer Joffe's brochure reverberated in the hearts of numerous workers, who by this time were ready and able to absorb the new-old ideas that he had favored. Most of these workers had had experience in collective settlement, but after a few years, having grown soberly realistic, they abandoned the romantic vision of collective life they had once entertained, and embraced ideas that had been formulated many years earlier.

THE *KFAR SHITUFI* — A NEW SETTLEMENT TYPE FOUNDED BY GERMAN MIDDLE-CLASS IMMIGRANTS

AMIRAM OREN

INTRODUCTION

This article is a summary of historical-geographical research on settlement in Palestine by groups of Jewish immigrants from Germany in the years 1933–1939.[1] The study focuses on a unique case of immigration, generated not by the attraction of the new land, but by the repelling forces of the old. This move was forced upon a particular group that had felt secure and rooted in the place where it lived: German Jewry of the early 1930's. With the change of regimes in Germany, this community was suddenly compelled to leave its homeland, thus becoming homeless refugees in search of a place to live. Many of these people sought refuge in the countries of Western Europe and the United States, while others endeavored to reach a different destination, Palestine — an area where development lagged behind that existing in their home country, and where the range of possibilities was limited. Still, during these same years Palestine was being rebuilt by and for a people yearning to return to its homeland.

The ascendancy of the Nazis in the winter of 1933, and the onset of their persecution of the Jews, aroused a debate among the central figures and organizations of world Jewry over the proper means of reacting to the grim situation. However, the Zionist movement and the *yishuv* (Jewish community in Palestine) did not take part in this debate, as they felt that the crisis engulfing German Jewry would serve as an impetus for the Zionist enterprise in Palestine. Indeed, immigration from Germany to Palestine began increasing only several months after the start of the persecutions, and by the outbreak of World War II it reached around 50,000. In the terminology of Zionist settlement history this immigration was in fact *aliya* (ascending), and the immigrants *olim*. The influx

---

1   A. Oren, "The Agricultural Settlement of Middle-Class German Immigrants in the 1930's: Seeds of a New Settlement Type," M.A. thesis submitted to the Geography Department, Hebrew University, Jerusalem 1985 (Hebrew).

of German Jews was called the Fifth Aliya since it represented the fifth wave of Jewish immigration to Palestine.[2]

In comparison with the earlier waves, especially the second, third and fourth, the Fifth Aliya was characterized, *inter alia*, by a low rate of young people lacking professions — relative to older people possessing capital and engaged in white-collar professions. On the average, the immigration from Germany from 1933 to 1939 comprised around a quarter of the total *aliya* during this period. The nadir for German *aliya* was 1935, when it amounted to only an eighth, and the peak was 1938–1939, when it ranged from half to three-quarters of the total. Among the German *olim* the percentage with at least £P1,000 in capital among those receiving A1 entry certificates to Palestine from the Mandatory government was identical to that of manual laborers. Moreover, the percentage of Jews with capital reaching Palestine from Germany during period in question ranged from 68% to 78% of all European immigrants with capital; again, 1935 was the only year with a relatively low figure: 29%.[3]

The Zionist institutions, especially the Jewish Agency and its branches, were faced with a new mission — finding a way to successfully absorb a new breed of immigrants: middle-class, urban white-collar workers and academics who owned property and capital. The majority of these people reached Palestine not of their own volition, but because they were driven out of Germany.

Research on these years indicates that a sizable portion of these immigrants were assisted to a small degree by the established institutions. Three-quarters of them were absorbed in the three largest cities: Tel Aviv, Jerusalem and Haifa. They engaged primarily in commerce, crafts and industry, while a small number turned to academic instruction or medicine. The rest received greater assistance from the institutions, and opted for agricultural settlement. The young among them, mainly those who had been organized in pioneering frameworks while still in Germany, were absorbed on kibbutzim. Of the remainder of this group, numbering around 750 families, some were absorbed in the existing settlements — moshavot and moshvei ovdim — while others set up *kfarim shitufim* (cooperative villages).[4] This article examines the question of whether the frameworks established by these people indeed represented a new settlement

---

2   For the Fifth Aliya and those preceding it, see: A. Bein, *Return to the Soil: A History of Jewish Settlement in Israel,* Jerusalem 1952; and C. Givati, *A Hundred Years of Settlement: The Story of the Jewish Settlement in Eretz-Israel,* Jerusalem 1985.

3   "Jewish Immigration into Palestine from Germany during 1933–1939," Department of Statistics of the Jewish Agency for Palestine, Bulletin No. 3 (February 1939).

4   Y. Gelber, *The Absorption of the Aliya from Germany in Palestine between 1933 and 1939,* Jerusalem (Hebrew; in print).

type, suitable for the middle class in general and the 1930's immigrants from Germany in particular.

GERMAN IMMIGRANTS — AGRICULTURE AND ABSORPTION

The following is a profile of the average middle-class immigrant from Germany: aged 30 or over, married, owner of at least £P1,000, a city dweller before reaching Palestine. Needless to say, these people lacked agricultural training.

These were involuntary immigrar.ts. The repelling force was the dominant one. Until the Nazi rise to power they had not entertained the notion of moving to Palestine, and the idea of engaging in agricultural settlement would have seemed even more far-fetched. A sizable portion of them had not received a Zionist education. Moreover, they were assimilated Jews who regarded Germany as their homeland. It was the Nazi takeover and the persecution of the Jews that prompted them to emigrate to Palestine. Some of them resolved to change their life-style even further, and to make the transition to a rural form of living.

The motives behind this radical decision were varied. Those who had been directly hit by anti-Semitic acts, and forced to uproot themselves from their places of residence and their jobs, concluded that their lives had to be rebuilt in Palestine, on a firmer and more secure basis — namely agriculture. As for the minority who had received a Zionist upbringing, the decision was complemented by a desire to realize the goals they had imbibed in their youth. For others, however, this transition to rural settlement stemmed from more prosaic reasons: white-collar workers, especially doctors and lawyers, had difficulty finding employment in their professions. Yet others, whether because of their lack of knowledge of Hebrew or their advanced age, shrank from the financial uncertainties of city life.

The rural settlement option embodied three basic elements. The first was the immigrants' perception of this settlement type. They were white-collar workers with urban backgrounds, who became involved in agricultural settlement without any social or political ideology. Upon their arrival in Palestine they opted for a change in life-style either out of a desire to take part in the national settlement enterprise or due to a lack of choice. They did not wish to adopt the accepted patterns — and this leads us to the second element, the economic one. As owners of private capital, they could afford to select the settlement type they preferred, without having to adhere to conditions and principles dictated by the national and Histadrut institutions. By drawing upon their own finances, they could acquire land and farms, and build their homes, in accordance with the conditions they had been used to. The third element was culture. The absorption of these immigrants was at first impeded by their lack of knowledge of the Hebrew language, and their inability to adjust to the life-style in Palestine, which differed greatly from the one to which they had been accustomed. Evidently they wished to preserve their previous life-style, and they feared that the existing frameworks would make it difficult for them to maintain their standards with regard to precision, order and discipline.

It should be stressed that their settlement endeavors could not have been realized were it not for the support and assistance they received from the Jewish national institutions. Upon encountering the first wave of aliya arriving from Germany in the summer of 1933, these institutions strove to devise ways of quickly absorbing the immigrants in general, and those belonging to the middle class in particular.[5] Until the end of the 1920's the institutions had no notion of how to successfully absorb immigrants of means in agricultural frameworks. Their support was channeled mainly to young people who lacked means, but had received prior agricultural training. In the early 1930's the national bodies revised their thinking on this issue, and altered their approach accordingly. They began to allot national land to people of means, and to supplement the financial resources of these people.[6]

With the inception of this wave of immigration, the heads of the national institutions realized that the existing infrastructure for immigrant absorption was inappropriate for the newcomers from Germany. They understood that these people, especially the well-to-do among them, had to be handled differently. Consequently, a new institutional framework was established to complement the existing one. A committee was set up — Vereinigten Komitee für die Ansiedlung Deutscher Juden in Palästina, or Vereinigten Komitee, for short; it included representatives from all of the institutions in Palestine. This body appointed five subcommittees, one of which was the Agricultural Subcommittee. After several weeks of deliberations, this subcommittee distributed among German Jews in Palestine and in Germany a pamphlet presenting the gamut of possibilities with regard to agricultural settlement types.[7] These types were classified according to both the nature of the framework and the capital that the immigrants had at their disposal (see Fig. 1).[8] Neither the Vereinigten Komitee

---

5   *Ibid.*, Chapter I.

6   Oren (note 1, supra), pp. 1–12.

7   "Landwirschaftliche Ansiedlung von Deutschen Juden in Palästina," Veringten Komitee für die Ansiedlung Deutscher Juden in Palästina, September 1933, Central Zionist Archives, Jerusalem, S7/45.

8   The transfer of the immigrants' capital was made possible thanks to a number of agreements with the German government, referred to as "Transfer Agreements." For more on this topic, see: Y. Gelber, "Zionist Policy and the Transfer Agreement 1933–1935," *Yalkut Moreshet*, 17

nor its Agricultural Subcommittee survived for long. At the 18th Zionist Congress, which convened in October 1933, it was decided to set up a special department in the framework of the Jewish Agency to deal with the absorption of German immigrants — the Central Bureau for the Settlement of German Jews in Palestine, or the German Department, for short.

This department, being an integral part of the Jewish Agency, could take advantage of the assistance offered by the other national settlement institutions. It enjoyed the further advantage of having budgetary independence, and it engaged in the gamut of activity involving immigrant absorption in general, and the settlement of members of the middle-class in particular. In the process of establishing its first three settlements, the heads of this department reached the conclusion that a separate company should be founded to deal with the middle class, in order to free them of this task. This new entity, called Rassco (Rural and Suburban Settlement Company Ltd.), set as its goal the establishment of settlements before the arrival of the immigrants. Rassco was a public company, and even though a portion of its capital was privately owned, the profit motive was not among the reasons for its founding. Only a minimal profit was sought, and the primary aim was to advance the national settlement efforts.

HISTORY OF SETTLEMENT OF GERMAN IMMIGRANTS, 1933–1939

This same period was rife with events and developments in the history of the *yishuv*. Our study indicates that the period is, in fact, divisible into two phases, with the 19th Zionist Congress in the summer of 1935 serving as a juncture between them. The first phase was one in which modest feelers were sent out in different directions, in the search for a settlement type suited to these immigrants. During the second, the appropriate type was found, and the theory behind it was turned into practice.

Initially the heads of the settlement institutions felt that the inexperienced newcomers could most effectively be integrated into agricultural life through the existing settlements. Hence, from the beginning of this aliya in the second half of 1933 until the end of 1934, half of the immigrants of means were settled on moshavot and on moshvei ovdim.[9]

While this process was unfolding, it became clear that the adjustment of the immigrants in these settlements was proving difficult. This was mainly due to

---

(1974), pp. 97–153; 18 (November 1974), pp. 23–100 (Hebrew). The article contains additional references.

9   L. Pinner, *Ansiedlung von 675 Familien aus Deutschland in Einzelwirtschaften. Eine Enquete des Central Bureau for Palestine und Der Hitachduth Olej Germania*, Jerusalem 1938, pp. 3–7.

Preis RM 0,25

Landwirtschaftliche Ansiedlung von deutschen Juden in Palästina

Bericht über den Stand im Sommer 1933

Zusammengestellt von dem
Vereinigten Komitee für die Ansiedlung deutscher Juden in Palästina
(Waad Mëuchad Lejischuw Jehude Germania b'Erez Jisrael)

September 1933

Herausgegeben vom Palästina-Amt der Jewish Agency for Palestine
Berlin W 15, Meinekestraße 10

Fig. 1

social factors — their language handicap and their failure to integrate with the veteran settlers, who were prone to mock the newcomers' speech, manners and behavior. The main problem was their lack of experience and of agricultural training. They were in need of ongoing personal guidance, which was not always forthcoming. With time, it transpired that there was a small dropout rate among the German immigrants on the agricultural settlements, even though most of them eventually overcame their various difficulties and entrenched themselves in their new environment. This experience lucidly demonstrated that rapid and effective absorption of these immigrants in agricultural settlement could only take place in a unique settlement type that especially catered to their financial means, and that facilitated their efforts to overcome their numerous

disadvantages: lack of agricultural training, relatively advanced age, and inability
— due mainly to the language barrier — to integrate quickly into the society of
the *yishuv*.

Between 1933 and 1935 five new settlements were founded during what might
be called a period of modest exploration in various directions. Three were
established by the German Department, in different regions. One of these was
set up on private land, and the other two on national land. One was founded as
an agricultural suburb of a town, and another in the framework of an overall
settlement plan for an entire region. The settlements differed in size and internal
division. In two of them, the area of the farm units was identical, and in the third
it ranged from two to twenty-five dunams. All were based on mixed farming, as
their founders had planned. This settlement type was not new; it was similar in
nature to the moshvei ovdim (see Figs. 2 & 3).

The main change took place in the two other settlements; these were
established through private initiative, without any assistance from the
establishment. One of them, the first of the five, was founded by a group of
immigrants who had acquired the land on a private basis and divided it into
small units of up to seven dunams each. The settlement was to be based on a
main branch, suited to the middle class: chicken farming (see Fig. 4). The other
settlement was established by a private company that had set as its goal the
preparation of the infrastructure in advance of the settlers' arrival. The company
handled the acquisition and preparation of the land; the design of the overall
layout of the settlement and the detailed layout of the individual farms;
construction of a water tower and the laying of an irrigation system; the paving
of roads and the laying of the groundwork for the farms, which entailed building
chicken coops, ordering the chickens and planting seeds. The company also saw
to the professional training of the settlers (see Fig. 5).

It can be said, by way of summing up the first two years of settlement by
middle-class immigrants, that activities by the national institutions, particularly
the German Department, failed to produce a new settlement type suitable for
people of means. The establishment strove to meet the urgent need to absorb the
new arrivals. These people were settled in communities that essentially bore a
strong resemblance to the moshvei ovdim. By contrast, activity carried out
under private initiative, without support or assistance from the national bodies,
did produce innovative settlement types.

It is premature at this stage to speak of an archetypal form of settlement. Size
varied; some absorbed twenty-five families, and others even twice this number.
It had yet to be determined whether the area of the farm units would be identical,
or would differ, primarily in accordance with the owner's financial means.
Around two years after the founding of these settlemets, no clear regional

Amiram Oren

Fig. 2

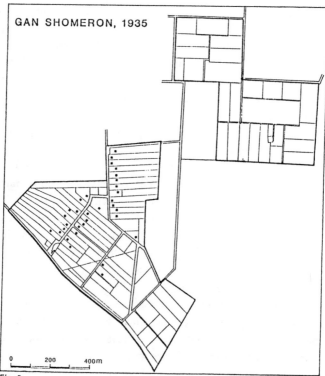

Fig. 3

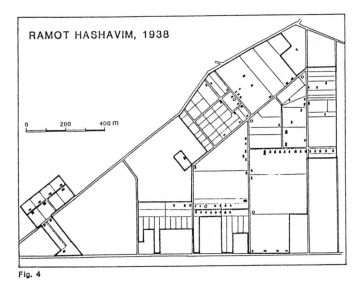

RAMOT HASHAVIM, 1938

0   200   400 m

Fig. 4

preference had emerged. All of them were located on the coastal plain, but each in a different region — from the Galilee coast in the north to the Sharon coast in the south. The tendency was to site the settlements in an area with a Jewish majority, close to central axis roads and cities or large moshavot.

As mentioned, the national institutions mainly supported the settlements that they themselves had established, and they were reluctant to assist those founded independently. Nonetheless, they were willing to alter policy when the need arose. Having concluded that the German Department's handling of the absorption of these immigrants was highly unsatisfactory, they supported the founding of Rassco in the summer of 1934.

In the second phase, from 1935 to 1939, three parallel processes can be discerned: 1) the founding of new settlements; 2) development within those established during the first period; and 3) institutionalization of the supportive organizational network. During this period Rassco became the central body dealing with the settlement of middle-class immigrants. Most of its efforts were concentrated in one region in the center of the country: the Sharon. Its first settlement was not founded until around two years after the company had launched its operations; the delay had been caused by the drawn-out and wearisome process of acquiring land (see Figs. 6 & 7).

This company, having learned from experience what difficulties lay in the way of land acquisition, turned to the national institution specializing in this field — the Jewish National Fund (JNF). Tapping special funds that had been earmarked for this purpose by the German Department, the JNF purchased tracts and

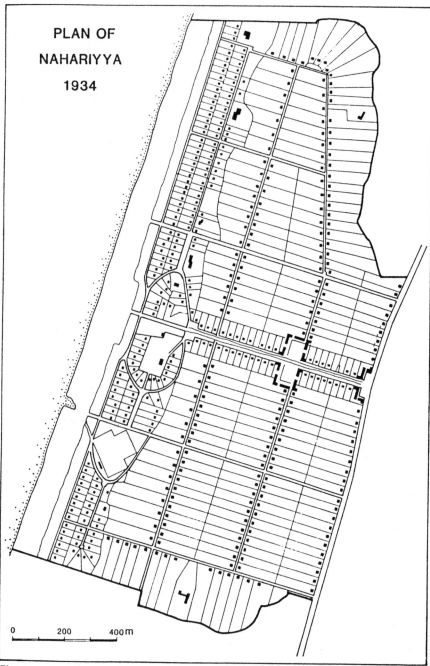

PLAN OF
NAHARIYYA
1934

0   200   400 m

Fig. 5

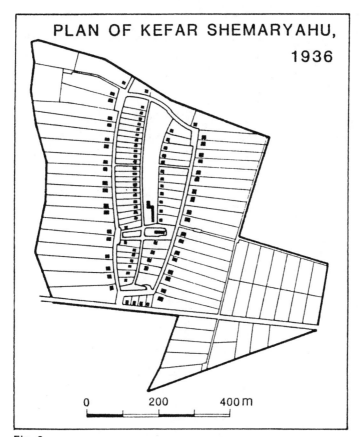

PLAN OF KEFAR SHEMARYAHU, 1936

0   200   400 m

Fig. 6

turned them over to Rassco. Between 1937 and 1940, Rassco erected another five settlements on these lands, where it attempted to apply the lessons it had learned in setting up the five settlements of the first phase. The emphasis was placed on intensive, mixed farming, and preference was given to chicken farming. Each settlement organized a cooperative to deal with economic affairs. The cooperative engaged in the purchase of raw materials, the sale of agricultural produce, water supply and credit arrangements.

During this period the attitude of the national institutions toward settlement by the middle class improved still further. The success of the new settlements induced them to establish within the Jewish Agency a division to handle all of the settlements with middle-class communities — not only those founded by German immigrants. From its inception, until the outbreak of World War II, this division dealt mainly with the granting of loans and credit, while striving to organize the marketing of the settlements' produce.

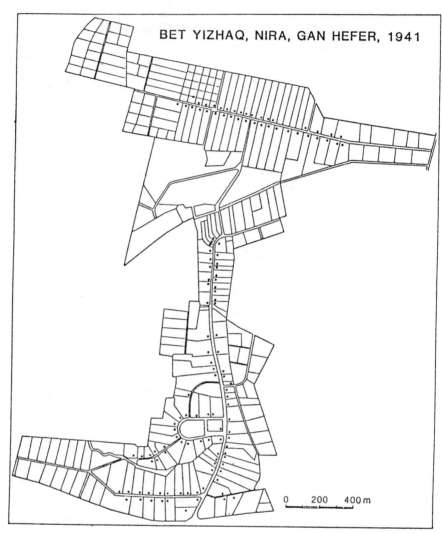

BET YIZHAQ, NIRA, GAN HEFER, 1941

0   200   400 m

Fig. 7

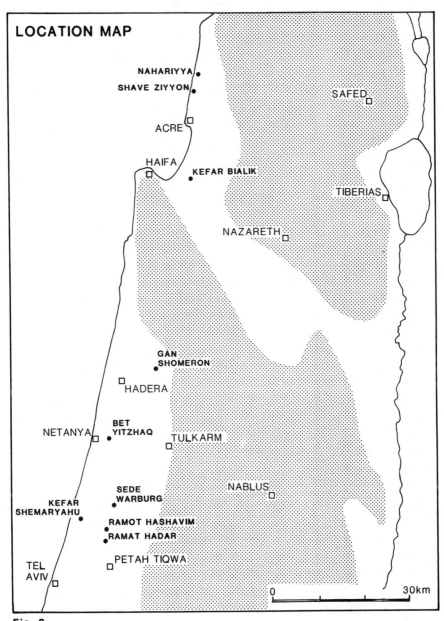

LOCATION MAP

NAHARIYYA
SHAVE ZIYYON
SAFED
ACRE
HAIFA
KEFAR BIALIK
TIBERIAS
NAZARETH
GAN
SHOMERON
HADERA
BET
YITZHAQ
NETANYA
TULKARM
SEDE
WARBURG
NABLUS
KEFAR
SHEMARYAHU
RAMOT HASHAVIM
RAMAT HADAR
TEL
AVIV
PETAH TIQWA
0
30km

Fig. 8

WAS A NEW SETTLEMENT TYPE CREATED?

By the beginning of the Fifth Aliya four settlement types — the moshava, the kvutza, the kibbutz and the moshav ovdim — had crystallized.[10] These types gave expression to various ideologies and social theories, on the part of both capitalists and socialists. Two-thirds of the middle-class German immigrants who tried their hand at agriculture — around six hundred families — preferred the new settlements to those that had already come into being. In order to evaluate their enterprise, one must answer the question of whether or not they in fact created a unique settlement type. These German immigrants were not the first members of the middle class to attempt agricultural settlement; they were preceded by some of the immigrants from the Fourth Aliya. Like the Germans who followed them, for these immigrants of the Fourth Aliya the desire to invest their money in a profitable branch of the economy probably eclipsed any ideological motivation of returning to the land. Most — but not all — of the moshavot founded by them were located in the Sharon, and based on citrus groves. As these settlers did not espouse self-labor, they employed workers — but unlike members of the First Aliya, they preferred "Hebrew labor." By contrast, in settlements founded by German immigrants, the emphasis was on the family farm, based primarily, but not exclusively, on raising chickens. The farm essentially resembled that of the moshav ovdim, i.e. a mixed farm.

Although the settlements of this latter group were not identical, they shared many common traits. Firstly, their population was, in fact, monolithic: middle-class German immigrants, mostly urban, with families and capital, but lacking in agricultural training. This uniformity was a product of the reality of the times, and was not an end in itself. These newcomers, who had arrived in Palestine unenthusiastically, were unsuccessfully absorbed into the local population whose character was so foreign to them. Following the shock that they had sustained in Germany, they elected to change their life-style. They evidently preferred not to assimilate among the existing *yishuv*, but to create something new and different that would preserve the spirit of their land of origin, as well as their social and cultural traits. In other words, they resolved to make the best of an unfortunate situation.

The second common denominator was the initial and primary financing — the private capital that the immigrants had brought with them. Since not all of the members possessed the same amount of capital, each one purchased a farm unit in accordance with his ability and aspirations. This led to the inequality in

---

10   See the articles by Ran Aaronsohn, Yossi Ben-Arzi and Michal Oren in this volume, as well as
     D. Weintraub, M. Lissak & Y. Azmon, *Moshava, Kibbutz and Moshav: Patterns of Jewish Rural Settlement and Development in Palestine*, Ithaca 1969.

the size of the farms. Only in rare cases did the German Department offer loans, and even when these were granted, they constituted but a small proportion of the total investment.

The third shared feature was a settlement type suited to the qualities of the settlers, who were older and inexperienced in agricultural work. Most of the farms were mixed and intensive, with the chief branch being chicken farming. The units were relatively small, ranging from seven to fifteen dunams.

The fourth common factor was location. The settlements were concentrated in areas that were primarily Jewish, and not far from a city or large moshava, as well as axis roads (see Fig. 8).

The fifth joint feature was the organizational structure. In each settlement a cooperative was organized, which dealt mainly with economic matters, and served as a tool for the settlers in areas such as buying and selling, water supply and attaining credit. The organization's basic raison d'être was to represent the settlers vis-à-vis the outside world, and it was not subject to dictates from any external institution. The cooperative belonged to the settlers, and worked on their behalf. It did not intervene in the work plan of the individual farm, and thus a delicate balance existed between the rights of an individual to his own opinions and *modus operandi* on the one hand, and the spirit of teamwork and cooperation with the entire settlement community on the other hand.

The sixth feature — closely related to the fifth — was the separation of the management of economic matters, which was handled by the cooperative, from the administration of communal and social affairs, which was the purview of a settlement committee. This functional division was maintained despite the fact that the cooperative and the committee were as a rule manned by the same people.

The seventh feature these settlements shared was their de-politization. Settlements belonging to the cooperative-labor sector — the kibbutz, the kvutza and the moshav ovdim — had political affiliations. The German immigrants were reluctant to join this political framework and accept its authority, as their entry into the world of agricultural settlement stemmed only from the desire to alter their life-style. They sought to establish a properly-functioning administration, void of political overtones, with regard to both economic and social matters. Their acceptance of collectivism sprang merely from a sober recognition of the reality — where size and effective organization were distinct advantages.

In light of the numerous features that distinguished this form of settlement, one can only conclude that a new type was indeed created. It can be assigned a place somewhere between the moshava and the moshav ovdim, which is to say that it incorporated the essential ideas of both of these types. The principle of inequality was adopted from the moshava; it gained sway because nearly all of the initial investment came from the settlers' own funds. Most of the basic concepts, though, were closer to those of the moshav ovdim. In both the German settlements and the moshav ovdim, each farm unit constitutes an independent economic entity, while the buying and selling are carried out via the cooperative.

Nevertheless, there are a number of substantive differences between these two types, revolving around the practice of self-funding in the German settlement type, and the consequent inequality in farm size. The following characteristics of the German settlements also set them apart from the older types: no political or party affiliation; absence of national land, and lack of equality in size of tracts and means of production; recognition of supplementary farms as productive units with rights equal to those of the other farms; absence of authority on the part of a central, external organization over decisions taken by the cooperative; the possibility of farm units not belonging to the cooperative (in the new settlements, however, this contingency did not materialize); practice of self-labor and mutual aid, although these principles were not compulsory; no mutual liability. In summation, the central characteristic was an acceptance of the authority of the settlement population, which was a voluntary act rather than one enforced by any binding political framework.

CONCLUSION

This study has attempted to elucidate another chapter in the annals of Zionist settlement, through an investigation of an additional layer in the infrastructure of agricultural settlement. The success of the middle-class settlements, and the decision by the national institutions to offer them their support, despite their initially reserved attitude, attest to the fact that these communal frameworks had a rightful place in the modern agricultural settlement of Eretz-Israel. It has also become clear that they cannot proceed spontaneously. The change in framework, on both the local and the institutional level, granted stability to these settlements, and the possibility for future expansion.

We have also called attention to a unique case of "geographical action," the establishment of agricultural settlements by immigrants who were actually refugees forcefully uprooted from their place of residence. In their new land they drastically changed their life-style, and were transformed from urbanites into farmers. Their success was fueled by the capital they had brought with them; it allowed them to select the settlement type they found most desirable. Their accomplishments would not have been achieved were it not for the assistance and guidance provided — albeit belatedly — by the institutions of the Zionist movement engaged in their absorption.

Our study indicates that the German settlements had the makings of an innovative and unique settlement type. The seven traits that characterized them combine to confirm the opinion expressed by the German Department: "The aliya from Germany created a new type of agricultural settlement based on agricultural work, one that will serve as an example for new immigrants."[11] Hence, we are in fact dealing with a new settlement type, which the settlers themselves termed a "collective village." This definition embodies the two central ideas that guided the middle-class immigrants from Germany: firstly, the transition from city to village, in the sense that their livelihood came to be dependent on agriculture; and secondly, acceptance of the principle of collectivism for the sake of economic efficiency, without impinging upon the life of the individual.

It can be said that the success of these settlements hinged on the dedication of the settlers and their adjustment to a harsh new reality that brought them to Palestine and to an agricultural way of life. They aspired to reap quick profits on their financial investments in order to provide for their families. The frameworks they set up functioned properly and efficiently thanks to their "Yekke" personality — a label implying discipline, orderliness, obedience and meticulousness — as well as a feeling of solidarity born of sharing a common fate.

---

11   Report by the German Department of the Jewish Agency to the 22nd Zionist Congress, 1946.

AMERICAN JEWRY AND THE SETTLEMENT OF PALESTINE: ZION COMMONWEALTH, INC.

IRIT AMIT

INTRODUCTION

A number of public bodies took part in the Zionist settlement enterprise, such as the Zionist Organization, with its diversified settlement apparatuses — as well as private circles. The former sought ways to stimulate private initiative in settlement ventures in Palestine. Mifal Ha'achuzot (The Holdings Enterprise), a comprehensive plan to attract the investment of private capital for the acquisition and settlement of land in Palestine, was mooted in 1908.[1] The scheme was based on the purchase of tracts by the owners of private capital, who would postpone the date of their own move to Palestine until such time as the economic stability and profitability of their holdings were guaranteed. In the meanwhile, they would serve in the capacity of absentee landlords.

This plan was not new. Proposals along similar lines had been advanced in the nineteenth and early twentieth centuries, and were adopted by several moshavot in Palestine. Both these programs and the Mifal Ha'achuzot aspired to create a settlement type in which the economic risk undertaken by the private investor would be low, adjustment difficulties encountered by the typical settler in Palestine at the time would be avoided, and Zionist ideology — i.e. an ideology predicated on land in Palestine being acquired and held by Jews — would be fulfilled.

During the period when the Mifal Ha'achuzot scheme was being proposed, moshavot whose main branch was deciduous groves — almonds and olives — developed in Palestine. The man who had originated the idea of Mifal Ha'achuzot — Dr. Arthur Ruppin, head of the Palestine Office — hoped that this agricultural branch would attract private capital to Palestine. His plan called for the establishment of independent Achuza (Holding) companies. These would comprise people who had joined together in a certain city or region to buy a large tract in Palestine. Each such company would work toward the

---

1   See the article by Y. Katz in this volume.

establishment of its own moshava in Palestine. Company representatives would handle the purchasing of the land, and would find residents of Palestine to work it, plant crops and cultivate the soil for the first six to ten years. Once the groves bore fruit, the land would be apportioned into lots upon which the company members would settle.

From the middle of the first decade of the twentieth century to the outbreak of World War I, seventy-six Achuza companies were founded. Seventeen of these were in the United States, fifty-six in Russia and Eastern Europe and three in Western Europe. Only ten succeeded in acquiring land in Palestine, and the number of moshavot actually established by them was small — five. As this program saw minimal success, it was aborted with the outbreak of the world war. The idea was continued in the form of a new company for the acquisition and sale of land — Zion Commonwealth, Inc., founded in the United States in 1914. This company was mainly active following the war.

This article examines the activity of the Zion Commonwealth in Palestine, and seeks to answer the following questions:

1) Was there in fact room for a settlement system of absentee landlords within the framework of a large company, one that attended to purchasing and settling land in Palestine during the British Mandate years?

2) Was the activity of the Zion Commonwealth prompted solely by speculation and a profit motive, as land could be sold for a price higher than the purchase price, or was the dominant motivation ideological, i.e. the desire to acquire land for Jews and to have Jews settle it?

3) What place did a company based on private capital occupy within the overall Jewish settlement enterprise in Palestine in the first decade following World War I (the period in which the Zion Commonwealth operated)?

ESTABLISHMENT OF ZION COMMONWEALTH, INC.

In June 1914 the annual convention of the Federation of American Zionists was held in Rochester, New York. The participants discussed possible solutions to the problem of credit required by the Achuza companies, especially those being organized in the United States and Canada in order to foster settlement in Palestine. It was resolved to establish an umbrella organization called the United Achuzas of America to centralize land acquisition in Palestine through private capital, and to ensure recognition and formal financial credit by American economic circles and by various Jewish circles.

Among those present at the convention was Bernard Rosenblatt,[2] the secretary

2   Bernard Rosenblatt (1886–1969) was born in Berdok, Galicia, immigrated to the United States

of the Federation, an attorney, and a Zionist activist. He called for the establishment of a new company to acquire agricultural land to be used for residence, trade, industry and quarries. The company would promote the redemption of land in Palestine with a high potential for economic profit. Rosenblatt argued that American Jews would be more inclined to invest their capital in land that guaranteed profits than to actually settle on it. The company he envisioned would be called Zion Commonwealth.

Most of the Achuzot representatives were not impressed by Rosenblatt's proposals, except for the Pittsburgh Achuza that had been founded that same year, and that lacked funds to carry out its plans for settlement in Palestine. This Achuza joined Rosenblatt in disseminating among the various Jewish communities and Achuza companies a letter detailing their plans.[3]

Zion Commonwealth, Inc. was founded in August 1914, and legally registered in New York. Its goals were as follows:
1) to promote Jewish immigration from various countries to Asian Turkey (Syria and Palestine);
2) to aid in the settlement of the immigrants by establishing "Jewish colonies" in Asian Turkey;
3) to follow any legal course leading to the development of agricultural and urban enterprises on company-owned lands;
4) to set up company-directed administrative and judicial institutions, in order to handle the rights of possession and utilization of the holdings, for the owners as well as the settlers who would work the land "in accordance with the principles of social justice."

At the end of 1915 the company collected a quarter of a million dollars in the framework of a trust company guaranty. By the end of 1918 the trust company had around five thousand members who had bought land certificates, totaling $3,000,000 in value. Part of this sum was transferred to the company account, and invested in the acquisition of land in Palestine.

---

and became a judge in the state of New York. For more on his life and work, see: B. Sandler, "The Jews of America and the Resettlement of Palestine 1908–1934," Ph.D. thesis for Bar-Ilan University, Kiryat Ono 1978, pp. 34–62 (Hebrew).

3   L. Landau, *The Zionist Companies for Land Purchase in Palestine*, Jerusalem 1980, p. 234 (Hebrew); Official Receiver's Report (hereafter: ORR) on the business affairs and the liquidation process of AMZIC, April 2, 1986, p. 4; In the Central Zionist Archives, file Z/762, there are very detailed plans on ways to raise funds and to maintain the value of the money invested in lands in Palestine. The plans called for 10% of the land purchased to remain in the company's possession, and to be used for industry and commerce. As the settlement developed and the land value rose, it was to receive the land, and thus further its development.

This development was stimulated by a number of factors. One of these was the nature of the contract drawn up between the company and its members. The contract did not contain any clause obligating the members to move to Palestine and to settle on the land purchased. Bearers of land rights could lease the tracts to others. The terms of acquisition were convenient, and the investment risk low.

Furthermore, the outbreak of World War I, which halted all of the settlement endeavors,[4] afforded Zion Commonwealth an opportunity to organize itself financially and administratively before actually implementing its projects.

In order to encourage the investment of capital in Palestine, the company sold stock at five dollars a share, and land certificates for $250 each. The certificates, payment for which was in installments over six years, confirmed that the owners possessed rights to the land. Some of these title deeds specified the area in question, but not the block or lot, while others merely noted the right to land. The money amassed from the sale of stock and certificates was transferred to Palestine and used as payment for tracts promised to the investors (in some cases land was expropriated by the investors before payments were made), or for lands set aside in reserve. (See Fig. 1).

At the end of 1914, with the final drafting of the Zion Commonwealth's articles of association, it was resolved that the company would determine how and at what rate to apportion the plots among the titleholders, to what use it would be put, and how the various tasks would be divided. In the event that the titleholder violated the terms of the agreement, the company could declare the certificate null and void, or, upon the approval of its executive, abrogate the leasing rights and transfer them to someone else.

The articles of association also stipulated that 10% of all the land acquired by the company would remain in its hands, and be used for agriculture, industry, commerce, resort activities — and also as public property. The Zion Commonwealth could lease these holdings in order to gain a steady income. The profits would be earmarked for the improvement of the company's economic state, acquisition of additional tracts and enhancement of the settlements themselves. At a later stage landownership would be transferred to the settlements. A committee elected in each colony would appraise the land, lease it, and even sell it to the Jewish National Fund (JNF) in order to guarantee that Zion Commonwealth land would remain under the ownership of the Jewish people.

4   The war period caused many Achuzot to be reduced or closed. By contrast, Zion Commonwealth expanded, establishing branches in many American cities, an updated list of which, from June 4, 1936, is located in the office of the administrator-general. A considerable number of Achuzot joined the Zion Commonwealth via the Federation of American Zionists.

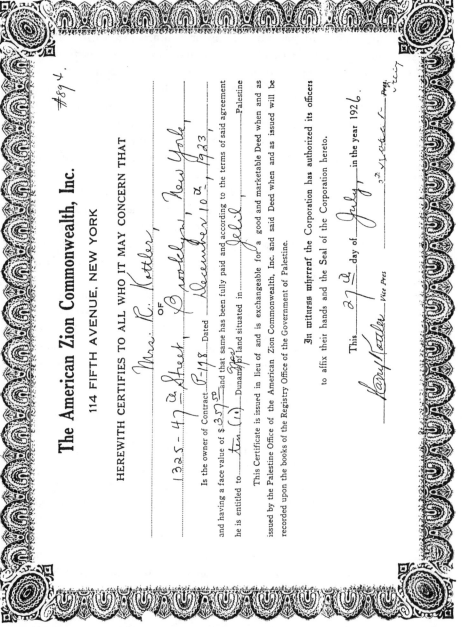

The American Zion Commonwealth, Inc.

114 FIFTH AVENUE, NEW YORK

HEREWITH CERTIFIES TO ALL WHO IT MAY CONCERN THAT

#894.

Mrs. R. Kotler,

OF

1325 - 47ᵈ Street, Brooklyn, New York,

Is the owner of Contract P-198 Dated December 10ᵈ, 1923,

and having a face value of $357⁵⁰ and that same has been fully paid and according to the terms of said agreement

he is entitled to ten (10) Dunam of land situated in Jelil Palestine

This Certificate is issued in lieu of and is exchangeable for a good and marketable Deed when and as issued by the Palestine Office of the American Zion Commonwealth, Inc. and said Deed when and as issued will be recorded upon the books of the Registry Office of the Government of Palestine.

In witness whereof the Corporation has authorized its officers to affix their hands and the Seal of the Corporation hereto.

This 27ᵈ day of July, in the year 1926.

Vice Pres

Pres.

Secy

Fig. 1

THE AMERICAN ZION COMMONWEALTH

The next stage in the development of the company began at the end of World War I. In 1920, in the wake of the Balfour Declaration and the appointment of Judge Louis Brandeis as the honorary president of the company, its name was changed to the American Zion Commonwealth, or AMZIC for short. The stress on the word "American" was designed to attract American Jewish capital. The company account books indicate that land certificates were purchased outside of America as well — in South America, England and even Poland — but that such transactions were of very limited scope. AMZIC now became the agent for the purchase and sale of land in Palestine, with the official support of the Federation of American Zionists, which was entrusted with the decision-making regarding all aspects of company policy and operations.

Starting in 1919 the company owned land in three areas of Palestine: Balfouriyya in the Jezreel Valley; Jelil (Herzliyya) in the central coastal plain, north of Tel Aviv; and Kefar Ata in the northern coastal plain, north of Haifa.

Afterwards AMZIC expanded its holdings, creating three large tracts. At an even later stage it penetrated into urban areas with a Jewish population: Haifa, Tel Aviv and to a smaller extent Jerusalem.

It was the declared intention of the company to refrain from acquiring urban real estate until holdings had been purchased in agricultural areas nearly void of Jewish settlement. Charles Pasmann, AMZIC's representative in Palestine, articulated this policy in January 1925, stating that the goal was "to initially acquire cheap land and afterwards attain expensive land. The profits accruing from the cheap land would bring the urban lands into the company's possession."

Company documents attest to the fact that between 1919 and 1927 AMZIC, along with two of its subsidiaries (Meshek–Palestine Building Company and Haifa Development Corporation),[5] acquired 80,000 dunams from the Palestine

---

5   Meshek was a company founded by Polish Jewry, and AMZIC entered into a partnership with it following a visit by J. Thon, director of the Palestine Land Development Company in Poland. Meshek was founded in 1923, and within a year and a half it sold approximately 8,000 dunams in Afula, 1,000 in Shunam and 1,000 in Kouskous Tivon. The sales were not made directly to individuals, but to large groups which in turn sold them to individuals. For example, in Afula 4,500 dunams out of a total of 8,000 were sold to one group. The company's settlement program maintained that not every member of a group would settle on the land simultaneously. At first representatives would arrive, and they would prepare the land for the rest of the group who would follow. The plan made frequent mention of the Achuzot idea. In November 1924, Rosenblatt proposed that Meshek unite with AMZIC and establish an American farmers' bank. The majority of the stock would be held by AMZIC in light of its financial ability, and this company would sell the stock via its subsidiary, Israel Securities. The bank would provide loans to Meshek settlers on AMZIC land. The essence of the idea was to make possible rapid

Land Development Company (PLDC). At first AMZIC intended to sell these holdings, but only to wealthy American Jews willing to invest in land in Palestine in order to settle there. However, the settlement aspect was not essential, as the company found ways by which the investors could circumvent settling on the land in their possession.

AMZIC offered the certificate holders the option of leasing the land either to relatives, especially East European Jews evincing a desire to settle in Palestine, or to residents of Palestine. Omission of the block and lot from the title deeds made it possible to exchange them for financial securities or to sell them for a profit. There were even instances of land certificates not including the obligation for settlement.

THE FINAL PERIOD: 1925 TO THE PRESENT

In the third period, which began at the end of 1925 with the inception of the economic crisis in Palestine and the rest of the world, and which has continued up to the present, the company has undergone a process of liquidation. The economic crisis impeded the operations of AMZIC, which was dependent on the capital of those purchasing land certificates through it or one of its subsidiaries. These people failed to pay their debts to AMZIC, so that it, in turn, could not meet its obligations regarding the land it had purchased. Hence the company encountered severe liquidity difficulties. It was compelled to take large loans at interest from public settlement bodies. The dependence on their funds augmented their influence on AMZIC and its policy of land purchase and settlement. The process of taking loans and paying debts continued even after the crisis years had ended. Because of AMZIC's inability to extricate itself from its financial problems, along with the fear that its holdings would be lost or would again fall into non-Jewish hands, the administration of the company was transferred to a public settlement body in Palestine — Keren Hayesod (the Jewish Foundation Fund).

settlement on AMZIC lands without involving American Jews, and to forestall competition with Meshek. The unification was effected in January 1926. Letters from C. Pasmann to S. Rosenblatt from December 8, 1925 and January 13, 1926, ORR, BAR 66.

The Haifa Development Corporation was established through the initiative of AMZIC and Meshek, with the purchase of 44,500 dunams in Haifa Bay. The economic crisis in Poland led to a reneging on commitments on the part of the Meshek stock holders. In order to prevent the company from going bankrupt, AMZIC purchased 80% of the Meshek stock — which added to AMZIC's financial burden. See the exchange of telegrams between Pasmann and Louis Lipsky, head of the Federation of American Zionists, from March 1926, ORR, GA/8a.

It is noteworthy that during the two-year transition phase from the second to the third period (1926–1927), the company attempted to conceal its financial plight, and to search for ways to solve its problems with the help of Jewish financiers and various financial intitutions. During these two years the concern lest these circles begin to view it as a company encouraging land speculation and absentee landlordism induced AMZIC to resolve to sell a sizable portion of its holdings to residents of Palestine. This policy was explained in various ways. AMZIC informed the Palestine Zionist institutions whose money it needed that it had come to realize the urgency of settling the land, while potential Jewish investors in the United States were told that settlement and housing construction on the land, coupled with cultivation of the soil, would raise the property value.

Thus Harry Kottler, one of the company directors in New York, stated the following in April 1925:

> The policy of the American Zion Commonwealth directors is to apportion at least half of any large tract of land it acquires to the settlers in Palestine. This policy provides the settlers with land, and money from American Jewry will be invested in the development of the moshava. These facts allow us to sell the land to Palestine residents at cost price, while development costs are disregarded. The land will be sold to the Americans at a much higher price, openly, as their investment will be rewarded by the fact that Jews from Palestine will settle there, thereby enhancing the land value. We are sure that this policy will ultimately prove financially beneficial to American Jewry.[6]

Despite the change in its settlement policy, AMZIC failed to extricate itself from the crisis. Its insurmountable debts were compounded by its inability to meet its obligations to those who had completed their payments, as no land could be turned over to them so long as sums were still owed to sellers or real estate agents. Occasionally those to whom money or land was due initiated legal proceedings against the company. AMZIC began to lose its credibility both in Palestine and in the United States.

The bankruptcy option remained undesirable, not only to the founders of the company, but to Zionist activists in the United States and Palestine as well. A 1927 letter to Rosenblatt, who represented AMZIC in Palestine, from the company's lawyer in New York, Samuel Rosensohn — who also served as legal advisor to the Zionist Executive — poignantly reflects the state of affairs at the time:

6   ORR, GA/8h.

My dear Mr. Rosenblatt:

May we request you to go to Palestine on behalf of the American Zion Commonwealth and arrange to safeguard the interests of the American purchasers of land in Herzlia, Afule, and other places in Palestine.

I need not impress upon the importance of insuring the transfer of title to the American purchasers. Unless that is done, not only will the American Zion Commonwealth be prohibited from continuing its work in America, but all Palestinian activities of every nature whatsoever in America will be stopped. The United Palestine Appeal drives will be seriously interfered with and very little money will be realized from America.

I want also to point out to you that the effect of the failure of the American Zion Commonwealth to give title to the purchasers will be more far-reaching than we expect, since it may seriously interfere with the formation of the Jewish Agency and with the coming in of the non-Zionists like Marshall, Warburg and others into the Zionist work.

From the letters received from Palestine, it is quite apparent to me that they do not realize the critical condition existing in the United States....

We have indeed been fortunate that the American purchasers have not made public their complaint with regard to title, otherwise all the work of Dr. Weizmann in America would have in a great measure gone for nought.[7]

This letter attests to the role played by AMZIC in land acquisition in Palestine at the time, and the extent to which its settlement endeavors influenced Zionist activity in general.

The phase of AMZIC activity which we have referred to as the second period can in fact be subdivided. The first sub-period was from 1919 to August 1924, during which the company did not adopt any clear-cut policy with regard to land acquisition and settlement. Tracts were purchased as opportunity arose, while clarifications were made as to which areas of Palestine were slated for development. As for settlement, AMZIC focused on citrus groves marked for development on the coastal plains, along with almond and olive trees and kitchen gardens in the Jezreel Valley.

The second sub-period began in August 1924, when the company was registered as a nonprofit organization, so that it could operate under the Mandatory laws. When the AMZIC agents in Palestine were asked to present a plan of activity, the company began to crystallize a policy, which was even recorded in writing in various forms.[8]

7   ORR, GA/8i.
8   See ORR, GA/8A. The file deals with the years 1924–1927, and includes the company plans

The three people most active in setting company policy in Palestine were Charles Pasmann, who was in charge of the actual work there, Rosenblatt, who although based in New York traveled frequently back and forth from the U.S. to Palestine during this period, and who advised Pasmann and sounded out the opinions of Jewish leaders and members of the AMZIC executive, and Solomon Weinstein, who replaced Pasmann in the company executive in Palestine.

This article shall not delineate all of the company's acquisitions, settlement methods, and internal debates over each and every case. To exemplify AMZIC's policy lines, two attempts to acquire and settle land shall be examined: Balfouriyya (today a moshav ovdim, two kilometers north of Afula) and Herzliyya (today a town ten kilometers north of Tel Aviv).

Herzliyya and Balfouriyya — Case Studies

Herzliyya

In September 1921 Yehoshua Hankin signed a contract for the purchase of 1,400 dunams in the villages of Jelil and El Harem.[9] The PLDC sought buyers for this land, and Ruppin convinced Rosenblatt that its acquisition was of importance. Rosenblatt informed the AMZIC executive in New York that he hoped to have the title deeds in his hands toward the end of 1924. He added that the company could buy an additional 4,000 dunams adjacent to these villages, and "thereby increase its property with good land for urban development and sizable agricultural ground."[10] In March 1924 AMZIC received 8,760 dunams, and in May 1929 another 5,000 dunams were registered in the company's name. (See Fig. 2).

and discussions during this period. File GA/8D presents plans to foster settlement in Palestine by granting mortgages, and by re-purchasing title deeds from their owners and leasing the land to settlers. File GA/8i deals with the Meshek Company and the Haifa Development Corporation, and discloses more details on AMZIC's policy regarding land acquisition and settlement.

9   See the letter from Y. Zimora to J. Thon from April 14, 1927, Palestine Land Development Company Archives, File 22, Section 3. Zimora informs Thon of how the purchase of lands in Jelil and El Harem had progressed in the years 1924–1927. For further details see: *Herzliyya, the First Fifty Years*, M. Naor, Segal & Herzliyya Municipality (eds.), Herzliyya 1978, pp. 21–27 (Hebrew).

10   The legal problems revolving around the lands adjacent to Jelil and El Harem actually continued until 1934, and were compounded by mortgage payments, and the failure to pay due interest on debts. AMZIC's legal problems connected with the Herzliyya land are detailed in the ORR files, primarily GA/8t, which deals with administrative matters during the years 1932–1942.

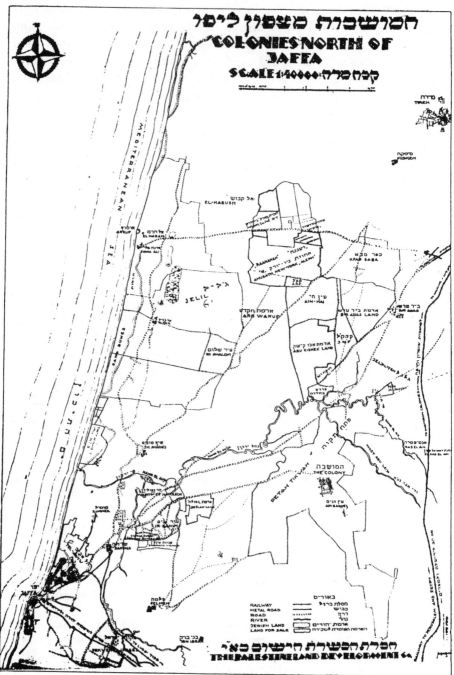

Fig. 2

In the United States bills of sale were distributed without accompanying land certificates specifically detailing the location of the block and lot. The size of each lot was ten dunams. In Palestine, too, bills of sale and land certificates were distributed, and the average size of the plots was 25 dunams.

The bills of sale for lands in Herzliyya were disposed of in the United States extremely rapidly. This success led the company to devise ways to increase the profits. One such method was to sell small tracts and to increase the sale price. Another was to divide the area into districts and to sell them gradually. Areas earmarked for urban development, whether residential or commercial, would be sold at a later stage, after their value had increased due to the development, in the initial stage, of the nearby agricultural lands. The company was supposed to save 25% of the sale revenues, to be invested in projects to improve the holdings. These projects would take the form of public works for the general welfare of the community, as they would provide jobs, benefit the developing settlement and enhance the price of the land, whether settled or unsettled.[11]

The company had been aware of criticism leveled against it for seeking investors abroad in order to increase profits, while tracts were left ownerless for a long time. By proposing that the projects take the form of public works, AMZIC showed that the concerns of Palestine were its own concerns after all, and that it was taking measures to combat unemployment — a problem that plagued the Fourth Aliya.

The land of Herzliyya was divided into four districts. District D was slated for agriculture, and was intended to serve as a catalyst for the rest of the area. In order to accelerate settlement in this district, plots there were sold primarily to residents of Palestine, at lower prices, and long-term mortgages on home construction were promised.[12] (See Fig. 3.)

Between October 1924 and May 1925 around one hundred families settled in the district. Each family had a 25-dunam plot: five dunams for the home and yard, and 20 for irrigated agriculture and groves. District B was designed as a high-class residential district and a garden suburb. The concept of a garden city

11 Settlement in Herzliyya began in District D (see the accompanying map). The land was sold there for $40 per dunam. The district was considered to be less promising economically from the company's viewpoint; it was earmarked for agricultural settlement, and offered to around one hundred middle-class familes residing in Tel Aviv (25 dunams per family). The price of land in District C was $65 per dunam, in District B $75 per dunam, and in District A $80 per dunam.

12 The sum of $1,250 per settler for eighteen years under convenient terms, to be used solely for building a home, barn and chicken coop. See letter from Rosenblatt to Pasmann, April 13, 1924, ORR, Ga/8a.

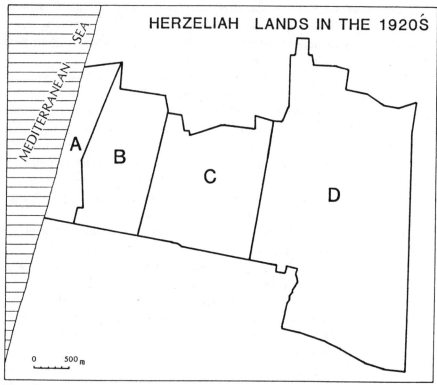

Fig. 3

and a garden suburb surfaced repeatedly in AMZIC's plans. The idea — the most modern trend in urban planning at the time — was proposed by Ebenezer Howard in his book *Garden Cities of Tomorrow* (1902). He offered solutions to the problems that arose in the cities of Europe due to the accelerated urbanization that followed the Industrial Revolution. Howard's plan reflected man's desire to be close to nature while at the same time achieving a social status gauged in accordance with one's domicile in an urban setting. His proposal found expression through the apportionment of urban land, along with open spaces, for private construction, woods, public gardens, wide and well-built streets, a modern urban infrastructure, etc.

District C would become an urban center, and District A, along the coast, a hotel and resort area. Like District D, Districts A, B and C were sold quickly, despite their high price. Inspired by the swift sale of the lands in Herzliyya, AMZIC's executives in New York considered offering the bill-of-sale holders an even "better deal" — to sell their rights to the land back to the company, and have their money refunded along with a 10% profit. Pasmann and Rosenblatt opposed this idea out of concern for the company's image in Palestine. American immigrants began settling District C, which was urban and commercial, in the summer of 1925. Unfortunately, Herzliyya underwent an economic crisis at the time, and as a result the number of immigrants was small and the aid provided by AMZIC quite limited. (See Fig. 4).

Diverse opinions were voiced by members of the AMZIC executive in Palestine and New York with regard to settlement in Herzliyya. On the one hand, there were some who pressed for intensive settlement activity so as to maintain the company's credibility among American Jewry, i.e. among those who had already invested their money, as well as those who might do so in the future. The fear that AMZIC's economic straits would be revealed induced the proponents of intensive development to request financial aid for Herzliyya settlers building their homes and for the creation of the settlement's infrastructure. Despite the company's difficulties regarding liquidity, these people urged it to conduct a search for a way to procure loans from financial institutions in the United States, with pledges given by wealthy Jews. They raised the possibility of distributing various bank securities via the subsidiary Israel Securities, a company founded by Rosenblatt and transferred to AMZIC in May 1924 to enable it to benefit from the profits of the securities company. Among the numerous other proposals advanced by the advocates of intensive development was the issuance of special bonds to finance the construction of small houses in District B, structured as loans for 60% of the land value.

Opposing those searching for ways to salvage the situation in Herzliyya were people who warned against a public sale of the settlement (a sale which took place in 1929 and led to the resolution to liquidate the company). Pasmann, for example, claimed that AMZIC could not support the Herzliyya project any longer. Ultimately AMZIC yielded to despair, and in May 1929 the Keren Hayesod assumed responsibility for the development of Herzliyya.

Balfouriyya
AMZIC began its operations in Palestine with the acquisition of the land of Balfouriyya in 1921.[13] The company's success with the sale of these land

---

13   In Balfourriya (Tel Ada'sh) around 13,000 old Turkish dunams (each measuring 919.3 sq. m., as opposed to the metric dunam which equals 1,000 sq. m.) were purchased, in Shunam next to Merhavya around 10,000 old dunams and in Merhavya 497 old dunams. The purchase of lands in Balfouriyya began in 1919, and the plan was to settle soldiers from the Jewish Legion on 3,500 dunams and to offer the remaining area for sale by issuing title deeds to purchasers in the United States without specifying the location of the lots. For further details on the founding of Balfouriyya (named after James Balfour), see Rosenblatt's summary of the events in Palestine from November 3, 1924 to December 6, 1924, ORR, GA/8A.

Fig. 4

certificates, coupled with the actual attempts at settlement that were carried out, gained initial glory for AMZIC (see Fig. 5). Toward mid-September 1924 the company perceived that the pace of the settlement's development had decelerated. Holders of title deeds did not realize their options, either by settling on the land themselves or by leasing it out so that it could be worked agriculturally. In a meeting of the executive in New York on September 8, 1924, the following proposals were put forward to strengthen the settlement:

a) To build twenty-five homes one mile away from Balfouriyya, on tracts that had recently been acquired — the land of Afula. This would be the inauguration of a new garden city, the construction of homes would generate an increase in the price of the nearby agricultural land, and settlement in Balfouriyya would be spurred.

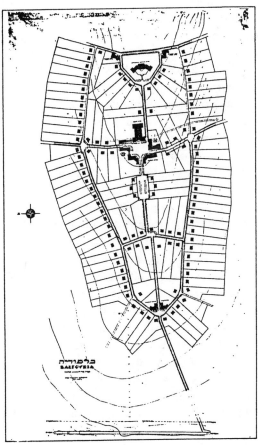

Fig. 5   Balfouriyya

b) To apportion plots officially registered in the land registry to those who had completed their payments on title deeds; holders of these deeds would receive lots dispersed throughout Balfouriyya and its environs — which would stimulate the sale of the other lots.

c) To encourage the holders of title deeds in Balfouriyya who had not completed their payments to exchange the deeds for land. The price per dunam would range from $40 to $60 — a reasonable sum for land in close proximity to a planned garden city.

d) Not to sell 1,000 dunams adjacent to the railroad station. This area would remain in the hands of the company, which would wait until its price rose with the development of both the moshav and the garden city.

A month after the discussion in New York, a detailed proposal was aired with regard to the establishment of a garden city near Balfouriyya (today's town of Afula). The idea was derived from an old plan submitted to the PLDC by the architect Richard Kaufmann. His scheme called for the development of the city around an urban focal point — the railroad station situated at an intersection, and the railroad tracks — around which roads would be laid in a pattern of concentric circles. AMZIC asked the architect to extend the area planned for an urban center, and to earmark 90% of the land for urban agricultural settlement, in accordance with the garden city formula. The size of the lots would not fall below 5 dunams, and their owners could set up auxiliary farms. The proximity to the agricultural settlement of Balfouriyya would stimulate the demand for plots in the garden city of Afula. Confidence in the volume of land sales in the new city was so great that the executive in New York was worried that the supply of lots would quickly be depleted. (See Fig. 6).

In the meantime a difference of opinion emerged between the company's New York and Palestine executives regarding the amount of land that should be sold immediately. The New York branch favored selling a minimum number of lots, just enough to finance AMZIC's land acquisition (the holdings were divided between the Meshek Company and AMZIC). The personnel in Palestine, on the other hand, urged that a maximum number of lots be sold in the new city. Their aim was twofold: firstly, to accelerate the development of both the city and the nearby agricultural settlement, thus forestalling a scattered settlement pattern which would lead to a downswing in property value; and secondly, to avoid the negative image of a company whose sole objective was to earn economic profits. Another argument erupted over the price to be set for a dunam of land sold to the American settlers: the staff in New York wanted to raise it, while their counterparts in Palestine favored lowering it in order to attract as many purchasers as possible.

The debate about the price of land in Balfouriyya and its environs continued

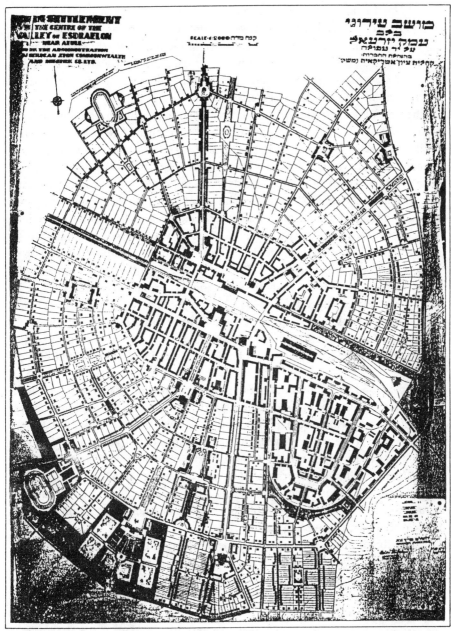

Fig. 6

The garden city of Afula

into 1925. In the meanwhile the rate of sale of land certificates increased, although actual settlement had not yet commenced. Pasmann and Rosenblatt repeatedly warned the New York executive of the image of AMZIC that was evolving in Palestine — of a company encouraging the creation of an absentee landlord class and engaging in land speculation, while seeking only a lucrative investment and easy profits in Palestine.

The New York executive did not relate seriously to the admonitions forwarded from Palestine. Kottler, by now the head of the company's New York branch, replied to his colleagues across the ocean that land settlement cost a great deal of money. AMZIC was a business, and therefore, he argued, it was more important to sell plots to Americans than to residents of Palestine. Kottler contended that the price of land in the Balfouriyya vicinity had to be sufficiently high to allow for additional land purchases both in other urban areas, where small lots could subsequently be sold with ease, and in rural areas, where the sale of as many lots as possible would stimulate the development of the community, even if the settlers did not arrive immediately. It was impossible to offer lots to residents of Palestine or to East Europeans at the same price as the Americans were prepared to pay. Kottler concluded that AMZIC should purchase large tracts, parcel the land as much as possible, make sure the selling price was reasonable, and leave it to the forces of supply and demand to enhance the land value and garner profits for the investors. Settlement would be the concern not of AMZIC but of the purchasers.

Pasmann and Rosenblatt did not oppose the buying of large tracts, but they sought to limit the sales in America to a quarter of the company's holdings. The remaining areas would be earmarked for intensive settlement by Jews from Palestine and those from Eastern Europe reaching Palestine via the Meshek Company. The price of land that was settled and cultivated would increase, and this in turn would raise the price of plots sold in America to a figure four times higher than the selling price in Palestine. The revenues accumulated in the United States would make it possible for residents of Palestine to acquire lots at a low price and on convenient terms.

The deliberations over the apportionment of land and the manner of selling it, both in Balfouriyya and in Herzliyya, revealed the main problem of AMZIC — the disparate approaches adopted by the company's executives in New York and in Palestine. The differences of opinion occasionally led to changes in plans that had already been approved by both sides — which only served to highlight the disunity in setting company policy. An excellent example is the attempt to alter the status of the Herzliyya districts. In April 1925 Rosenblatt suggested that the sale of land in Herzliyya proceed differently from the scheme originally outlined. He proposed that Districts B and C be combined with District D, and that a low price be set for them, one that would make it possible for Palestinian Jews to settle there. Only District A would remain expensive, and be sold to American Jews. He argued:

> If AMZIC intends to sell the brunt of its lands to Jews in America, this will arrest the development of settlement. It will prevent a rise in the price of the land, because the areas will remain unsettled, so that there value for settlement will remain quite low.

A new proposal was aired for Balfouriyya as well. In order to foster agricultural settlement and stimulate sales in the garden city, titleholders — according to the revised plan — should be given the option of selling their deeds, with the revenue being offered as a loan to the settlers to build their homes. Both the capital and the interest to be repaid would redound to the seller of the deed. Such an arrangement would give satisfaction to the titleholders in America, as they would be assisting in the settlement of Palestine, and also free AMZIC of its former commitment to aid in the construction of homes.

Whatever changes were mooted, they did not conceal the fundamental gap between the New York and the Palestine executives — with the former calling for stepped-up acquisition and the latter appealing for concomitant settlement. A letter dated April 6, 1925 from Kottler to Pasmann poignantly reflects this situation:

> You claim that were you simply left alone you would succeed in selling all of the Herzlia lands without difficulty to the residents of Palestine. But this is due only to American money invested in the area and the American buyers who transferred money to Palestine, thus guaranteeing the development of the place. Would the vicinity look the way it does today if the land had remained in the hands of the Arabs, or in the hands of the Palestine Land Development Company? The many Jews who now come to Palestine and are willing to invest in Herzlia would not have been enthusiastic about the land had $750,000 not been invested in it previously, with additional investments to follow in the future....[14]

The Zionist institutions that relied upon public funds and national capital — the Jewish National Fund (JNF), the American-Palestine Bank, the PLDC, and the Palestine Land Office — became embroiled in the debate. When AMZIC was launching its operations, the PLDC had to decide to which body to transfer the lands it had acquired, and it selected the JNF in preference to AMZIC because

14   ORR, Ga/8j.

of uncertainty as to whether the latter organization would actually settle the land, or abandon it. AMZIC itself reached a similar conclusion — that the JNF should take priority over the company in acquiring land in Palestine. It went so far as to declare that its ultimate goal was to transfer its land to the ownership of the Jewish people, i.e. AMZIC would maintain possession until such time as there was a request for the land.

Eventually, as the crisis besetting AMZIC deepened, the various Zionist institutions intervened, and determined the course along which the company was to proceed. This intervention was effected through the granting of loans, rejection of repayments, and ultimately the assumption of control of the actual administration of AMZIC. In an attempt to curb the influence of these institutions, the New York directors set up a network of committees as part of a general reorganization. This situation continued until the executive in New York at long last realized that there was no money to maintain either the New York offices or AMZIC's various agents and clerks, and there was no one left to turn to for additional credit. Only then did the New York branch consent to liquidation.

On April 27, 1929 the Palestine Zionist Executive and the United Jewish Appeal resolved to postpone their demands for loan repayment from AMZIC until that organization succeeded in clearing its debts to other creditors. The administration of the company was gradually transferred to the Keren Hayesod, and in 1949 the latter body officially took charge of AMZIC until its liquidation. This put an end to the sale of land by AMZIC without accompanying settlement. From this juncture the Keren Hayesod has had to find its own ways to induce the titleholders to settle on their land, and to either pay their debts or transfer their holdings to others.

Conclusion

The differences of opinion cited above represent the problematics of AMZIC's operations involving the acquisition and settlement of land in Palestine. They also demonstrate that the company intended to formulate a clear *modus operandi*, but that this goal was thwarted by dissension between its two executives: in New York and in Palestine. The physical distance between Palestine and the United States, and the conceptual gap separating the two factions with regard to the manner of drawing private Jewish capital to Palestine, caused blatant tension throughout the period of AMZIC's operations.

In its early years AMZIC sought to continue the Achuzot enterprise in the format of a single large company providing a financial pledge for investors, and thus enabling them to obtain loans on convenient terms from financial institutions. During these same years it requested members of the company in the United States to pay for the land they were purchasing in installments extending over six years, during which time they undertook either to settle on their land or to lease it to relatives in Palestine or to East European Jews intending to immigrate to that country. If the landowners failed to honor these terms, AMZIC could sell their land rights to others who wished to settle on the land. The new settlers were entitled to loans from the company for the construction of their homes and farms. The settlement conditions would be improved through the division of the land into lots, assignment of tasks, the creation of an infrastructure, etc., leading to a rise in the property value and ensuring profitability for the American investors.

From mid-1925 the gap between the New York and the Palestine executives widened. The company directors in Palestine attempted to alter the course that had originally been set, stressing settlement on the land and not merely its acquisition. They hoped to change AMZIC's image in Palestine as a force working to create a class of absentee landlords.

Their New York counterparts continued to call for land acquisition, without any commitment to settlement. Their primary objective was to attract American Jewish capital to Palestine. They ignored the warnings from Palestine regarding the lack of financial means for land acquisition, imputing this to incorrect policy: instead of selling plots at high prices to American Jews and using the money to purchase additional tracts, the directors in Palestine were handing the land over to Jews for settlement at purchase price, which provided no revenue for further acquisitions.

AMZIC began to lose control over its own operations. This development shows that not only the economic crisis precipitated the failure of the company, but also the absentee landlord system that it adopted, which received no support from any of the other settlement bodies in Palestine. These other bodies claimed that land and settlement in Palestine were inseparable. Eventually AMZIC itself — or at least some of its directors — concurred in this assessment.

PART IV:

THE TWENTIETH CENTURY —
INSTITUTIONAL ACTIVITIES
IN SETTLEMENT

PRIVATE ZIONIST INITIATIVE AND THE SETTLEMENT ENTERPRISE IN ERETZ-ISRAEL IN THE EARLY 1900'S: "NATIONALIST CAPITALISM" OF PRIVATE CAPITAL

YOSSI KATZ

INTRODUCTION

The study of entrepreneurship has long intrigued researchers from various disciplines in the behavioral sciences. It is clear that in most cases the motivation for entrepreneurial initiatives undertaken by the government or any other public body is not the desire to maximize financial profit. Moreover, recent research indicates that in the private sector as well, the incentive need not stem from a wish to gain large profits; often the benefit sought by the private entrepreneur can be defined in terms of values or quality rather than revenue. At the same time, private entrepreneurship is characterized by the desire to minimize financial risk and the reluctance to incur losses.

Arthur H. Cole elaborates on this theme:

> Another element in the definition of entrepreneurship presented above relates to motivation. That business institutions should be concerned with money-making need not be elaborated. But it is important to notice, especially over the past two or three decades, how considerably American corporations have modified any rule of financial maximization that may have existed, so that corporate longevity, community relations or public responsibilities might be taken into account.... Nor is there need any longer to emphasize, at least in the United States, the existence of non-pecuniary incentives among modern business executives.[1]

At a 1954 convention on the history of entrepreneurship, Francis Sutton claimed:

> The observation that businessmen do not work simply to maximize their personal money income is now jejeune and may be taken as the beginning of our problems. If we assume that money income is only one element in a

---

[1]   A.H. Cole, *Business Enterprise in Its Social Setting*, Massachusetts 1959, p. 15.

complex of motivations related to the businessman's role itself and to
other roles that the same individual fills outside his working hours, we
must seek an orderly specification of the various elements in this complex.[2]

Yair Aharoni reaches similar conclusions.[3] Herbert A. Simon, in 1957,[4] and
Wolpert eight years later, suggest that behind such behavior lies the desire for
"maximization of benefit" or "maximization of satisfaction," not maximization
of monetary profit.[5]

Since any settlement activity evolves in accordance with the goals, ideas and
ideologies held by the settlement founders, in addition to environmental
considerations, it might be expected that such activity will reflect the nature of
the motivation involved. Indeed, this article aims to diagnose the motivations
inducing Zionist capital to advance the Jewish settlement enterprise in Palestine
at the turn of the century. We shall attempt to show that the involvement of
private Zionist capital in settlement activity was motivated by factors similar to
those delineated in the theoretical economic literature cited above — specifically,
the aspiration for maximization of value-oriented and national-oriented benefit.
We shall also see that such entrepreneurial initiative in fact led to the creation of
a unique pattern of settlement in Eretz-Israel.

JEWISH SETTLEMENT IN PALESTINE IN THE EARLY TWENTIETH CENTURY

Zionist historiography traditionally cites 1882 as the start of the agricultural
settlement enterprise in Eretz-Israel. From this year to the end of the nineteenth
century, twenty moshavot were founded, with a total population of around five
thousand. Approximately 303,000 dunams of land were under Jewish
ownership.[6] The brunt of the financing and much of the initiative for the
settlement activity came from Baron Edmond de Rothschild, whose support for
these communities was unflagging. Toward the end of the nineteenth century
Rothschild assessed that his system had failed. As the settlements were plagued
by severe social and moral problems, he was induced to place them under the

---

2   "Entrepreneurship and Economic Growth," paper presented at a conference sponsored jointly
    by the Committee on Economic Growth of the Social Science Research Council and the
    Harvard University Research Center in Entrepreneurial History, Cambridge, Mass., November
    12–13, 1954, Section G., pp. 1–2.
3   Y. Aharoni, *The Foreign Investment Decision Process*, Boston 1966, p. 294.
4   H.A. Simon, *Models of Man*, New York 1957, pp. 196–200.
5   J. Wolpert, "The Decision Process in Spatial Context," *Annals of the Association of American
    Geographers*, LIV, No. 1 (1965), pp. 537–538.
6   M. Meirovitz, *A Tour of the Hebrew Moshavot in Eretz-Israel*, Odessa 1900 (Russian).

control of the Jewish Colonization Association (JCA), a non-Zionist organization that had amassed great experience in founding and administering Jewish settlement projects, primarily in South America. The transfer of control took place in January 1900,[7] marking the beginning of a new chapter in the annals of Zionist settlement.[8]

Jewish settlement activity expanded greatly between this year and the outbreak of World War I in 1914. During this period the existing settlements grew and developed, while twenty-seven new agricultural communities, most of them moshavot, were founded. The amount of landed property in Jewish hands increased vastly, as some 184,000 dunams were acquired. The Jewish population on agricultural settlements reached 11,600.

This boom had two different sources. First and foremost were: public settlement bodies such as the JCA, through which Baron de Rothschild continued to channel funds; Hovevei Zion ("Lovers of Zion"), the organization which essentially inaugurated the Zionist movement in Russia in the early 1880's; and the World Zionist Organization (WZO), expecially its Palestine Office and the Palestine Land Development Company (PLDC). A significant role was also played by the private Zionist settlement companies established at the turn of the century in Palestine and abroad.

The private companies operated in three main spheres:
1) acquiring land earmarked for new agricultural settlements and expansion of the existing ones (Geula Company);
2) establishing new settlements (Achuza Company and Tiberias Land and Plantation Company);
3) setting up plantation centers next to existing settlements, which were to sell ready-made plots to new settlers (Agudat Netayim).

In each of these spheres the contribution made by the private companies to the Jewish settlement of Palestine was substantial. They acquired around 50,500 dunams, comprising 27% of the total land that was transferred from Arab to Jewish ownership during this period; established seven new settlements, or 26% of the total number set up in this period; and single-handedly created plantation centers.[9] The broad activity of private Zionist capital stands out as exceptional,

7   E. Y. Ettinger, *Data on the Economic Condition of the Moshavot in Eretz-Israel*, Odessa 1905 (Russian); M. Eliav, *Eretz-Israel and Its Yishuv in the 19th Century*, Jerusalem 1978, pp. 278–314 (Hebrew).

8   A. Ruppin, *The Sociology of the Jews*, II, Tel Aviv 1932, p. 176 (Hebrew).

9   For further information, see: Y. Katz, *Let the Land Be Redeemed*, Jerusalem 1987 (Hebrew); idem, *Private Initiative Regarding Eretz-Israel in the Second Aliya Period*, Bar-Ilan University, in cooperation with Keren Shnitzer (in print; Hebrew).

since private investors ordinarily exert every effort to avoid the possibility of loss, and in this early stage of Jewish settlement the investment risks were legion.

NATIONAL AND ECONOMIC CONSIDERATIONS

It was Zionist ideology, whose goal was the expansion of Jewish settlement in Palestine, that sparked the formation and activity of the private companies. Purely commercial considerations did not play a role, and no profit motive existed per se. In the outlook of these companies, whatever profits accrued would serve merely as a means toward Zionist realization. Although financial risks had to be minimized in order to ensure continued operational success, the private companies did not attempt to maximize profits, and contented themselves with moderate profit margins. Thus Zionist ideology was tempered by limited economic considerations, and the resulting blend of motivations dictated the geographical pattern of land acquisition, the structure of the agricultural sector, and the manpower employed by the private companies.

The integration of ideology and economics finds expression in a 1912 pamphlet distributed by the Russian-based Geula Company, which engaged in land purchase in Palestine:

> Many of those whom we are hereby addressing already know of the existence of the Geula Company. Those well versed in our operations know that the basic capital of the company is ensured at any time, and there is no fear of its diminution since the business affairs in which Geula invests its money are in no danger of loss.... It suffices to carefully regard all that has been said in order to ascertain that investments in Geula stock are as safe as those in other stocks being traded on the financial market....

After reviewing the company's land acquisitions and its great contribution to the settlement enterprise in Palestine, the pamphlet continues:

> From all that has been said the readers of our brochure will ascertain that Geula's role in consolidating and expanding the *yishuv* [Jewish community in Palestine] is enormous, and Geula's income is guaranteed.... We are also addressing those who have thus far stood at a distance from the national movement and the settlement endeavors in Palestine, and are asking them to invest in the Geula Company in order to receive a material reward — a dividend — and a spiritual reward through providing substance for the building of the House of Israel in Palestine.[10]

10   Geula Company 1912 Brochure, Central Zionist Archives, Jerusalem (hereafter: CZA), J85/17.

The entrepreneurs who founded the companies, as well as the members, shareholders and managers, belonged to Zionist circles, and were generally aware that their investment in Eretz-Israel would prove less profitable than would similar investments in other countries, or in other local stocks. Nonetheless, the satisfaction derived from participating in the national rebuilding provided ample compensation. Arthur Ruppin, head of the WZO's Palestine Office and the PLDC, analyzed this phenomenon in 1913:

> What is this private Jewish capital that today flows to Palestine and that must be relied on in the future? It is not huge capital of wealthy financiers, but money that is concerned about Jewish settlement in Palestine. These circles are willing to invest their money in Palestine if the investment is guaranteed, and do not seek the best investment.... They prefer to invest in Palestine rather than anywhere else in the world, even if other investments are more lucrative.... The emotional benefit makes up for the difference.... I would call this form of settlement *capitalistic-nationalistic*, as opposed to pure capitalistic settlement void of emotional value.[11]

Similarly, in 1913 Hovevei Zion called upon those with Zionist capital to foster private settlement in Eretz-Israel of the kind that the Tiberias Land and Plantation Company was developing in Majdal in the Lower Galilee:

> Men of means, or even the extremely wealthy who will never settle permanently in Eretz-Israel and who would not seek to conduct business affairs in Eretz-Israel for the sake of profit alone, but who desire to participate in the redemption of the land and the strengthening of the Jewish community there, can purchase large plots for plantations and mixed crop farms, where groups of Jewish laborers will work.[12]

It seems that in the wake of World War I, policy setters in the Settlement Department of the WZO contended that nationalistic ideology in itself, aside from commercial incentives, would attract a flow of private Jewish capital into Palestine, to be used in private frameworks.[13] Furthermore, they claimed that the Jewish private sector would willingly forego profits for the sake of fulfilling nationalistic goals. Like Ruppin before them, these WZO figures saw ideological and economic motivations as complementary, with the strength of the former compensating for the weakness of the latter.[14]

---

11   *Die Welt*, December 5, 1913, pp. 1655–1656.
12   *Hatzefira*, September 1, 1913, p. 3.
13   *Ha'olam*, December 5, 1919, pp. 1–2. *Jüdische Rundschau*, September 20, 1920, p. 506.
14   J. Metzer, *National Capital for a National Home 1919–1921*, Jerusalem 1979, p. 21 (Hebrew).

NATIONALISTIC CAPITALISM AS EXPRESSED IN SETTLEMENT ACTIVITY

Every phase of the private Zionist companies' settlement operations was influenced by nationalistic capitalism. To start with, the purchase of land was not speculative in nature, but was designed to serve Zionist colonization aims in Eretz-Israel.[15] The Geula Company, for example, did not acquire tracts that had already been redeemed by other Jewish bodies — even if such transactions would have proven lucrative. Nor did it deal with holdings that other Jewish bodies could have negotiated for; instead, its resources were conserved for sites that lay beyond the purview of other Jewish groups. The Geula Company refrained from selling land to Jewish elements that were liable to resell it to Arabs, even if this policy meant foregoing a chance to make a profit or to minimize loss. It kept its urban property to a minimum, and resisted the lure of the Tel Aviv area, even when, starting in 1911, it became apparent that the profitability of real estate in this emerging city far exceeded that of agricultural lands.[16]

While Ruppin's "nationalistic capitalism" continued to serve as the guiding principle, the private companies differed among themselves as to the emphasis they placed on each of its two components: nationalism and capitalism. When the companies founded and centered in North America planned to establish new settlements, they stressed the economic aspects and the potential for personal gain — thereby, it would seem, reflecting the culture in which they were immersed.[17] Consequently their preference was for lands in the vicinity of large civic centers — cities (Tel Aviv, Jaffa), and communal villages (Petah Tiqwa, Rishon leTziyyon) — in the center of the country.[18] Thus when the Achuza Company in Winnipeg, Canada, strove to interest investors in purchasing land in Sheikh-Munis, north of Jaffa, they advertised as follows in a 1914 brochure:

> Our land is located in the middle of the Jewish populace, next to the sea,

---

15 See for example: letters by M. Dizengoff (Geula Company representative in Palestine), October 18, 1908 and May 7, 1909, CZA, J85/284; minutes of the Second General Assembly of Geula Company, January 30, 1909, CZA, J85/284.

16 Letter from Jaffa to Ettinger, December 2, 1911, CZA, J85/27; letter from Ettinger to Dizengoff, November 19, 1909, CZA, J85/11; minutes of the Second General Assembly of Geula Company, January 30, 1909, CZA, J85/284.

17 On the transformation of the Jewish immigrant from Eastern Europe into a materialist and a practical businessman due to the influence of American culture, see: A. Levy, "Amerikanische Palästina Pioniere," *Die Welt*, May 23, 1913, pp. 642–741; *Hapoel Hatzair*, September 15, 1912, p. 5; *Hapoel Hatzair*, October 15, 1913, p. 22.

18 On the attempts by a California company to purchase land, see CZA, L18/251; on those of a Cleveland company, see CZA, L18/256; on those of a New York company, see CZA, L18/252.

not far from the port, only three quarters of an hour ride from Jaffa on the Jaffa–Haifa road, half an hour from the large communal village Petah Tiqwa.... We are situated in the vicinity of Jaffa, the center of education in Eretz-Israel these days; our children can attend the famous local high school and the other excellent schools.

Still, nearly all of the American companies ultimately bought land wherever possible, even if the site originally targeted proved unavailable, and the purchase had to be made somewhere in the Galilee, on Palestine's periphery. This, then, was the acid test of their nationalism.[19]

In contrast to the North American companies, those based in Russia and England did not have any clear priority in terms of location for land purchase in Eretz-Israel, since ideology overshadowed practical considerations. As a result they acquired land wherever the Zionist public bodies responsible for these matters recommended — including the northern Negev. For the European companies, the Zionist bodies held the authority to determine which areas could provide the greatest benefit to the settlement enterprise, and in which areas settlement activity had the greatest chance of succeeding.[20] A striking example of this is She'erit Yisrael, the Achuza Company in Moscow, which turned down an opportunity to acquire lands in the center of the country, in favor of those in Jamama in the northern Negev. This transaction extended the settlement map southward; the site was a nine-hour ride from Jaffa and a four-hour ride from the communal village Be'er Toviyya, heretofore the southernmost point of Jewish settlement.[21]

For nationalistic reasons the private companies made sure that most of the workers on their settlements were Jewish, and not Arab, despite the fact that Jewish laborers were as a rule nearly twice as expensive. By contrast, most of the large moshavot at the time hired mainly Arab workers.[22] The heads of the

---

19 CZA, L18/256. For more information on the attempts by a Winnipeg company to purchase land, see: Y. Katz, "The Plans and Efforts of the Jews of Winnipeg to Purchase Land and to Establish an Agricultural Settlement in Palestine before World War One," *Canadian Jewish Historical Society Journal*, XV, No. 1, pp. 1–16.

20 On the attempts by Achuza Company in St. Louis to purchase land, see CZA, L18/250/1 and L18/255; on those by Achuza Company in Chicago, see CZA, L18/255, L18/258, L18/120/3 and J15/3878.

21 On the attempts by the She'erit Yisrael Company of Moscow to acquire land, see CZA, L18/59/2, L18/259 and L18/257/2.

22 Letter from A. Eisenberg to Y. Tchirmbok of South Africa, October 4, 1914; letter from A. Eisenberg to Yitzhak Epstein, May 26, 1914 — both in CZA, A208/12; Y. Katz, "The Achuza Projects in Eretz-Israel, 1908–1917," *Cathedra*, XXII (January 1982), pp. 119–144 (Hebrew).

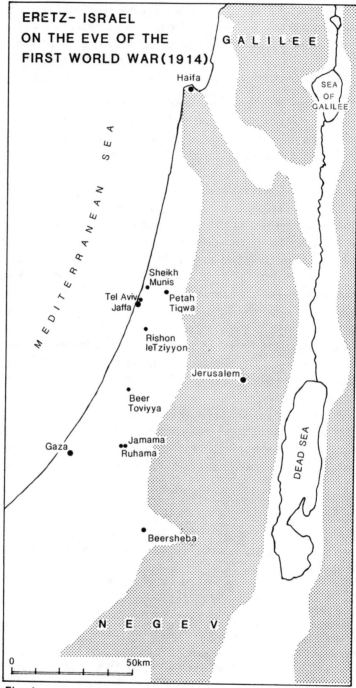

Fig. 1

She'erit Yisrael Company stated their policy in a letter to Ruppin at the end of 1912:

> We would like the workers in Ruhama [the settlement at Jamama set up by the company in Moscow] to be Jews. Hebrew labor is a major principle in all of our work. I greatly fear that if they now begin working on our holdings with the help of Gentile workers, the latter will take over the work for good, and there will be no room for the Hebrew workers. I dread this satan who will corrupt our holdings in Jamama.[23]

As a rule the private companies strove to assist each other and cooperate with the public settlement agencies in all spheres of activity, especially land acquisition.[24] It was maintained at a general meeting of the Geula Company in July 1912 that this sort of cooperation was vital for the achievement of nationalistic settlement goals. The private companies of this period — unlike those to follow them[25] — refrained from entering into competition, even in places where sizable profits were guaranteed.[26] Plans were even formulated for a complete union of the private and public companies. This collaboration gave rise to a de facto geographical division of settlement efforts between the various companies, private and public alike, and made it possible to exploit the relative advantages of each.

The private companies made a concerted effort to learn from experience, and to alter their plans accordingly. Their very existence derived from the failure of the support system practiced by Baron de Rothschild and Hovevei Zion, and from the conclusion that only private capital could provide a solid basis for the development of Eretz-Israel. The form of settlement chosen was one that could attract private capital, and which had proven successful both in Palestine and, with minor variations, in New Zealand, Australia and California. The system was based on the principle of postponing the settlers' move onto the land until after the creation of a suitable infrastructure, and attainment of the stage in which the settlement could support its inhabitants. The various preparatory

23   Letter from She'erit Yisrael Company to Ruppin, November 21, 1912, CZA, L18/257.
24   Katz (note 22, supra).
25   See for example: letter from Jaffa to the management of Geula Company in Odessa, December 26, 1911, CZA, J85/27; letter from Ruppin to the management of the PLDC, May 8, 1913, CZA, L/18/103/2; *Hatzefira*, May 2, 1913, p. 3; *Hapoel Hatzair*, April 10, 1914, pp. 8–10; minutes of the General Assembly of Geula Company in Odessa, July 30, 1912, CZA, J85/284.
26   Y. Katz, "Internal Zionist Competition over Land Acquisition in Palestine: The Establishment and Activities of the 'New Society for the Acquisition and Sale of Land': 1912–1914," *Ha-Tzionut*, XI, pp. 119–158 (Hebrew).

activities were carried out by a manager selected by the company and by local workers. The companies opted for sure and profitable crops, and by using modern equipment, selecting suitable manpower, and exploiting both economy of scale and external economy, made constant efforts to increase the efficiency of the labor, raise production and reduce expenses.[27]

The private companies refrained from financial or any other activity that carried the risk of loss, irrespective of the national importance of such projects. Land purchase, for example, was only carried out where two essential market criteria were met: a) the land was in demand, so that it could be resold quickly and easily; b) the company had full and unassailable right to the land, and the chances of the ownership being contested due to litigation or any other dispute were minimal. Aside from the natural instinct of private capital to avoid losses, the private companies felt that the damage to the settlement enterprise caused by financial loss would surpass any benefit that might accrue from the execution of any particular transaction. Financiers tended to withhold investments from companies that showed losses, and partners in such companies often terminated their involvement for the same reason, thus making it difficult for them to survive. As the private companies believed that investments with ideological significance but substantial risk should be the purview of the public bodies, they often requested that these bodies undertake financial ventures of this sort.[28]

It appears that "national capitalism" led to the private companies' stressing settlement realities over settlement ideology, and preferring the former when the two clashed. Ideology could surface only after significant progress had been made in the field. Thus the Geula Company sought to separate the immediate need of Jewish settlement in Palestine for private capital from the goal of both the Jewish National Fund and the Palestine Labor Movement to nationalize the land — a goal which could be fulfilled sometime in the unforeseeable future.

---

27 Letter from Eisenberg to S. A. Levin, October 25, 1903, CZA, A208/1; letter from Sokolovski to Ussishkin, September 17, 1905, CZA, A24/49; M. Ussishkin, *Our Zionist Program*, Warsaw 1905, p. 28 (Hebrew); *Ha'olam*, October 31, 1907, pp. 529–530 (Hebrew); A.R. Burns, *Comparative Economic Organization*, N.Y. 1955, pp. 76–82; J.S. Marais, *The Colonization of New England*, Oxford 1927, pp. 222–225; *Die Welt*, June 23, 1899, pp. 4–5; *Palestina*, V/VI, 1902, pp. 186–188; *Palestina*, I/II, 1903/1904, p. 93; *Ha'olam*, October 31, 1907, pp. 529–530 (Hebrew); *Razviet*, June 20, 1914, pp. 25–26; *Razviet*, March 16, 1912, p. 11 (Russian); Katz (note 22, supra).

28 See, for example: minutes of Geula Committee meeting in Palestine, November 25, 1909, CZA, J85/120. On the attempts by the Achuza Company from Cleveland to purchase land, see CZA, L18/256; letter from Ettinger to Dizengoff, January 19, 1909, CZA, J85/11; letter from Dizengoff to Geula Company in Odessa, December 16, 1909, CZA, J85/27.

This company viewed blind and immediate adherence to the idea of nationalization as detrimental to the settlement movement.[29]

With a similar penchant for pragmatism, Agudat Netayim planned for a mass immigration of East-European Jews to the vicinity of Constantinople and Anatolia in Turkey, where the newcomers would implement settlement projects. The arguments advanced by the organization for operating outside the borders of Eretz-Israel were primarily political, since there had been reliable reports that if Zionist settlement efforts were concentrated solely in Palestine rather than spread out throughout the Ottoman Empire, the Turks would forbid any further Jewish settlement activity there. Agudat Netayim rejected the view held by many Zionist circles that any Jewish settlement activity outside of Eretz-Israel — albeit provisional, as it had envisioned — was an unthinkable violation of Zionist creed.[30]

A third example of the private companies foregoing ideology for the sake of practicality was their rejection of the Labor Movement's demand to hire only Jewish workers in their settlements ("pure Hebrew labor"). These companies contended that compliance with this demand under the prevailing circumstances would stir up political problems, and, even more important, would precipitate certain financial losses due to the high cost of Hebrew labor. If such losses were incurred, private initiative in the settlement endeavor would be squelched, thus damaging settlement efforts in the field.[31]

CONCLUSION

The settlement activity carried out in Eretz-Israel by the private Zionist organizations during the years 1900–1914 proceeded on the basis of "nationalistic capitalism." It was marked by unique characteristics, distinguishable from parallel efforts by public bodies on the one hand, and by the ordinary functioning of private capital on the other hand.

It appears that the *modus operandi* employed by these private companies was the only form of activity that allowed for the involvement of private capital in land purchase during these years. The economic and political conditions prevailing in Palestine during most of this period acted as a deterrent to private investments, which instinctively seek out low risk, high availability of natural

---

29 Ussishkin (note 27, supra), pp. 22–23.

30 Y. Katz, "Paths of Zionist Political Action in Turkey, 1882–1914: The Plan for Jewish Settlement in Turkey in the Young Turks Era," *The International Journal of Turkish Studies* (in print).

31 Letter from Eisenberg to Kaplan in Pittsburg, June 26, 1914, CZA, A208/12.

resources, and high returns. No government existed that could remove at least some of the obstacles and pave the way to the investment of normal private capital in the settlement enterprise. Only near the end of the period, when there was a measurable improvement in the country's economic and political conditions, did normal private capital begin to flow into settlement projects.

The unique way in which private companies investing in settlement operated was an amalgam of the deeply rooted Zionist ideology held by the founders and members of these companies, and their capitalist background. In all probability, the fact that their investments in Eretz-Israel comprised only a limited portion of their total economic investments, and that their income did not depend on profits from this source, facilitated their adoption of a "nationalist capitalism" course of action.

SOCIAL ARCHITECTURE IN PALESTINE: CONCEPTIONS IN WORKING-CLASS HOUSING, 1920–1938

IRIS GRAICER

INTRODUCTION

World War I marked the end of an era in Europe. Old regimes vanished, to be replaced by new ones attended by new ideals. Democracy, equality, social and cultural betterment, urban planning, and working-class housing became major, interwoven themes for most Western societies. Both during and after the Russian Revolution, socialistic movements sprang up in Palestine and elsewhere, intending to give cultural, social and physical expression to the working class as part of the new, democratic society that was crystallizing. A free, "new man" was being created.[1]

The difficulties that the weaker classes encountered in obtaining living quarters, and the inhuman housing conditions prevalent in urban centers, had begun to engage the attention of many countries even before World War I. Following the war housing became one of the prime concerns of most European nations. Because the war had essentially paralyzed construction, the situation had deteriorated markedly. The social and political arousal of the working class in the wake of the Russian Revolution necessitated urgent spatial planning solutions that blended in with the latest social ideologies, while varying in nature and degree from one country to another. In those countries not possessing a socialistic regime the housing solutions were mainly linked with universalistic conceptions of quality of life, whereas the socialistic regimes pondered hesitantly over the issue of a workers' environment and all that it signified, as well as the connection between spatial planning and the creation of a cultural community implementing through its life-style the ideals of a socialistic society.[2]

In every case, whether the issue on the agenda was council housing in Great

---

1   For a comprehensive survey of the housing processes following World War I, see: C. Bauer, *Modern Housing*, Boston-New York 1934, pp. 119–141. For more on the "new man" concept, originating in Austro–Marxist ideology, see: J. Weidenhalzer, "Red Vienna: A New Atlantis?," A. Rabinbach (ed.), *The Austrian Socialist Experiment — Social Democracy and Austro-Marxism 1918–1934*, Boulder-London 1985, pp. 195–199.

2   M. Tafuri & F. Dal Co, *Modern Architecture*, I, London 1986, pp. 153–174.

Britain, the *Siedlung* (residential estate) in Germany, "social housing" in Vienna or "ten-thousand-inhabitant neighborhoods" in Holland, an attempt was made to physically mold, by means of urban planning, residential environments that would meet the needs of the working man. In Palestine as well, despite the fact that the Jewish population did not enjoy political freedom, there was a similar wrestling with the issue of the urban worker. The planning of residential environments for the urban working class and the solutions that were implemented proved similar, and in fact organically related, to parallel developments in Europe, since many of the immigrants and the professional planning staffs in Palestine during the 1920's and 1930's came from the Continent. In Palestine the planning of workers' neighborhoods was referred to as "social architecture."[3] This term signified the shaping of a physical environment expressing a working-class life-style and facilitating a communal life for the workers in the city.

This article traces the sources of social architecture in Palestine and explores its bond with the movement for working-class housing in West European countries between the two world wars. The similarities are striking, and the messages of the socialistic movements underlying this enterprise identical. Nevertheless, the working-class housing in Palestine was unique, due to its particular cultural-political milieu.

WORKING-CLASS HOUSING AFTER WORLD WAR I

The movement to provide living quarters for the working class in postwar Europe had a number of characteristics that must be examined in order for one to gain an understanding of its counterpart in Palestine. In Europe such activities were intimately connected with the creation of powerful political frameworks among the working class — frameworks that, in the wake of democratization and expanded suffrage, could wield organized pressure, primarily electoral pressure, on governmental systems, whether on the national or the local level.[4] In Vienna the workers succeeded in forming a majority and taking over the municipal government. In Berlin and other cities as well the workers became the major political force and managed to introduce extensive reforms benefiting the working class.

The efforts in Europe to provide the workers with living quarters would have

---

3   This term, with all that it implied, was first used by David Remez in a meeting of the Histadrut housing personnel in the Borochov neighborhood in November 1942. Archives of the Labor Movement, 333/4 (Hebrew).

4   Bauer (note 1, supra), p. 122.

been unthinkable without ramified legislation. In Great Britain the government took an interest in such projects as a means of quelling social unrest that was liable to result in a sociopolitical revolution.[5] The handling of this activity was assigned to the local authorities, which, via special legislation, gained substantial government subsidies to finance construction. In Vienna working-class housing was given vital momentum by a change in the rental regulations and the urban tax laws; an increase in the tax burden of the upper classes made it possible to finance the housing of those lacking in means. Vienna became a model of municipal socialism for all of Europe.[6] In Germany too, municipal legislation enabled expansion of the areas owned by the local authorities, thereby lowering construction prices for the weaker classes. Similar ordinances were enacted in most other European countries.[7]

The new social climate in postwar Europe gave rise to a wide range of new expressions in the field of urban planning and construction. Novel approaches and schools of thought emerged, and academic institutions dealing with this field trained professional manpower to incorporate architectural design, and art in general, into the structures used in every walk of daily life. In parallel with the crystallization of municipal planning as a profession, designers and architects began to deepen their involvement in politics, and attained positions of power, primarily in the municipalities. The various perceptions of urban planners in the large cities of Europe exerted a long-term influence: Peter Behrens in Vienna, Cornelis Van Easteren in Amsterdam, J.J. Oud in Rotterdam, Ernst May in Frankfurt, Martin Wagner in Berlin, Bruno Taut in Magdeburg, Fritz Schumacher in Hamburg, and Raymond Unwin in Great Britain. This list is only partial, as there were many others who were influential. Prominent schools, such as the Bauhaus in Germany, the Ecole des Beaux Art in Paris, and the Akademie der Kunste in Berlin, and groups like De Ring in Germany, De Stijl in Holland and the Art and Craft Movement in Great Britain, by exchanging and publicizing new ideas and techniques, cumulatively affected the design of the Western city from the Soviet Union to North America.[8]

---

5   M. Swenarton, *Homes Fit for Heroes: The Politics and Architecture of Early State Housing in Britain*, London 1981, pp. 65–87.

6   C.A. Gulick, *Austria from Habsburg to Hitler*, I, Berkeley 1948, pp. 391–400.

7   L. Benevolo, *History of Modern Architecture*, II, London 1971, pp. 507–539; N. Bullock & J. Read, *The Movement for Housing Reform in Germany and France 1940–1914*, Cambridge 1985, pp. 182–183; R. Wiedenhoeft, *Berlin's Housing Revolution: German Reform in the 1920's*, Ann Arbor 1985, pp. 8–10; H. Searing, "With Red Flags Flying: Housing in Amsterdam, 1915–1923," H.A. Millan & L. Nachlin (eds.), *Art and Architecture in the Service of Politics*, Boston 1978, pp. 230–269.

8   Tafuri & Dal Co (note 2, supra), pp. 105–174.

It is only natural that many of the planners and architects who flourished in the postwar era — and who identified with the workers' parties politically — were linked to construction for low-income classes and to cooperative housing projects for workers in most of the European cities, especially in Germany, Holland and Austria.[9]

Palestine of the 1920's and 1930's was, from the cultural standpoint, an extension of Europe. However, unlike the processes taking place throughout the Continent, where, in compliance with social pressure wielded by the workers' movements, national and municipal governments took an active role in the building of hundreds of thousands of housing units, by enacting appropriate legislation and providing assistance to planners and architects — the situation in Palestine was different.

The strength of the working class in Palestine grew in the rural areas. The settlement bodies sought to create a new society in Palestine founded on agricultural rather than urban settlement. Although the urban proletariat comprised the majority of the country's working class, they did not receive any ideological, moral or material support from the labor leaders, at least until the mid-1920's.[10] Moreover, the city in Palestine was the bastion of private capital and of bourgeois political movements that, with the aid of undemocratic election laws and the backing of the local British authorities, barred the working-class public from exercising the elementary right of suffrage. In Tel Aviv, the city with the largest Jewish population, the fact that the right to vote and to run for office was granted only to property owners turned the issue of housing for low-income groups into a potential political tool for the workers' parties. In contrast to most of the cities in Europe, the municipality of Tel Aviv shirked its responsibility and elected not to involve itself in working-class housing in order to avoid increasing the electoral strength of the proletariat and thus endangering private capital's control in the city.[11]

The housing situation of the urban workers in Palestine was not much better than that of the low-income groups in postwar Europe. As in Europe, they wielded political pressure, but for want of a proper target in the municipalities or in the Mandatory Government, this pressure was directed at the labor movement leadership and the Histadrut institutions. These circles, fearing a credibility

9   *Ibid.*
10 For more on the problem of the urban workers and the institutions of their movement, see: I. Graicer, "Workers' Estates: Socio-Ideological Experimentations in Shaping the Urban Scene in Palestine during the British Mandate," Ph.D thesis, the Hebrew University, Jerusalem 1982, pp. 41–116 (Hebrew).
11 *Report of the Council of Jaffa's Workers*, Histadrut, Tel Aviv 1927, pp. 193–265 (Hebrew).

crisis within the movement, were compelled to take upon themselves the working-class housing projects in Palestine.[12] The fact that the institutions of the workers' movement themselves operated as an independent housing body, with nearly total autonomy within the municipal system, had far-reaching repercussions for neighborhood design, the planning system, and the land policy accompanying urban housing activities.

THE PLANNING NETWORK AND THE "ARCHITECTS' CIRCLE"

The planning system dealing with housing for workers in Palestine had very strong ties to the European planning frameworks. In contrast to the architects who practiced the eclectic style that had typified urban construction in Palestine up to the late 1920's, those of the 1930's had been trained in modernist schools of design and had acquired professional experience while working alongside the foremost architects of Europe. In response to the social reforms sweeping the Continent, the novel architectural approaches stressed humanistic and popular housing, and offered architectonic solutions to social problems. These solutions gave rise to a new "international style,"[13] characterized in every aspect by a reliance upon rational and functional theories of design that found expression in an outwardly ascetic simplicity of construction: flat roofs, smooth and unadorned walls, porches, windows, and extensive use of glass and pillars. The change from the past was most notable in the inner spaces, the living rooms, kitchens and bathrooms, where there was great stress on the microclimate with respect to light, sun and ventilation. The layout of the neighborhood was based on low density, broad green areas and a network of services that could provide adequate quality of life.

The "Architects' Circle," which heralded social architecture in Palestine, was founded in 1935 by three newcomers to the country: Arie Sharon, a graduate of the Bauhaus school who had worked with Hannes Meyer in Berlin, acquiring from him a sense of strong affinity between the social and the architectural worlds; Zeev Rechter, who had studied at architectural schools in Italy and Paris, and had absorbed the planning perceptions of Le Corbusier; and Yosef Neufeld, who had studied in Vienna and Rome, and served as assistant to Erich Mendelsohn in Berlin and as right-hand man to Bruno Taut in Berlin and Moscow. They were joined by others, graduates of art and design academies in Ghent, Paris, Vienna and the United States, as well as the Technion in Haifa.[14]

---

12 Graicer (note 10, supra), pp. 116–121, 214–225.
13 Tafuri & Dal Co (note 2, supra), pp. 219–254.
14 A. Sharon, *Kibbutz Bauhaus, an Architect's Way in a New Land,* Stuttgart 1976, p. 47.

The "Architects Circle" became the central forum in the realm of planning in Palestine. It held discussions on problems of construction and planning in the land. Through its journals *Habinyan Bamizrah Hakarov* ("The Building in the Near East") and *Habinyan* ("The Building"), it strove to create a new architectonic climate, which it hoped would penetrate into the relevant bodies: the Union of Engineers and Architects, the municipalities and the Mandatory Government. Social architecture was viewed as signifying not only by incorporating social values into their work, but also the issuing of public tenders, sanctioning free competition, opening the door to new architects, bringing the future residents into the process from the outset, appointing architects to serve as advisors on municipal planning and construction committees, and creating a permanent framework for planning the city of Tel Aviv, in which architects, social scientists and economists would participate so as to arrest what they saw as the ongoing destruction of the city at the hands of city officials lacking any architectonic education.

The "Architects' Circle" demanded, *inter alia*, that the Tel Aviv municipality terminate real-estate profiteering by instituting a communal land policy that would neutralize the influence of private capital on the development of Tel Aviv. The Circle also urged that the slums be razed through a comprehensive operation involving popular housing and extensive communal construction. In light of the identical ideologies held by the Circle and Histadrut bodies with regard to working-class housing in Palestine, it was only natural for the Circle's members to form a tie with these organizations — notably the Center for Workers' Neighborhoods, founded in 1927 to coordinate urban construction for workers, and later the Shikun ("Housing") Company, founded in 1934. Sharon claimed that the architects of Palestine fit the social values of the workers' movement "like a hand in a glove." Other architects set up offices and resided in the communal, cooperative housing they themselves had designed.[15]

CONCEPTIONS FOR WORKING-CLASS HOUSING DESIGNS

The establishment of working-class neighborhoods should be viewed from two perspectives: social and political. From the social standpoint such neighborhoods were supposed to allow for a life-style suitable to this class, within a quasi-bourgeois social environment, and also to place the living conditions of the

---

15 *Ibid.*, pp. 48–49; Z. Rechter, "Town Planning Order 1935," *Habinyan Bamizrah Hakarov* (November 1935), p. 8 (Hebrew); I. Dicker, "Housing the Low-Incomes," *Habinyan Bamizrah Hakarov* (November 1935), pp. 6–7 (Hebrew).

urban worker on a par with those of the agricultural worker, in order to forestall a split in the working class in Palestine. The idea of a working-class life-style implied maintaining a community whose cultural values were predicated on equality, the negation of private ownership of land and property, education toward the values held by the proletariat, and the fostering of a working-class culture. It was desirable for such a community to provide itself with as many services as possible on a cooperative basis, such as schools, nurseries, health services, food supply, eateries and laundries, in order to be as independent as possible of the surrounding municipal network.

From the planning standpoint, housing for the urban working class had to give expression to the political and ideological struggle and to the polarity between the social outlook of the labor movement and that of the bourgeoisie. Unlike Great Britain, for example, where the authorities elected to equalize the living conditions of the workers with those of the middle class as a means of defusing political agitation on the part of the former,[16] in Palestine — as in Vienna, Berlin and Frankfurt — the goal was the reverse: heightening class consciousness and pride. In all instances in Palestine the tendency was to highlight the political strength of the workers through unique urban construction that would serve as a model to be emulated in terms of quality of life, and a symbol to identify with.[17]

In Tel Aviv the housing enterprise had an additional, unique objective; in the mid-twenties an attempt was made by the workers' party, with the support of the small parties ideologically close to it, to control the municipal government for three years. This endeavor to democratize the municipal election regulations, which had enfranchised only those possessing capital and property, evoked the opposition of the Tel Aviv property owners, who appealed on this issue to the Supreme Court. After a brief deliberation Judge Highcroft abrogated the recent changes in the regulations, arguing that they violated the spirit of the Orders of the British Military Administration of January 14, 1919.[18] This ruling facilitated the victory of the propertied class in the elections of 1928, as a result of which the workers' movement in Tel Aviv was again placed on the defensive. This movement felt it necessary, on the one hand, to provide the urban worker with

16 Swenarton (note 5, supra), pp. 81–87.
17 A. Rabinbach, "Red Vienna: Symbol and Strategy," Rabinbach (note 1, supra), pp. 187–194; P. Marcuse, "The Housing Policy of Social Democracy: Determinants and Consequences," Rabinbach (note 1, supra), pp. 201–221; J.R. Mullin, "Ideology, Planning Theory and the German City in the Inter–war Years," *Town Planning Review*, 53 (April 1982), pp. 115–130.
18 See *Yediot Tel Aviv*, 20 (1926) (Hebrew). The entire issue is devoted to "Tel Aviv's courtcase in the Supreme Court."

an environment where he could find moral support and maintain his life-style, and on the other hand to continue demonstrating its strength; it was being deprived of rights not because of insufficient electoral clout but because of discriminatory municipal regulations. Thus the housing issue became a double-edged political tool. The Tel Aviv Municipality refrained from establishing neighborhoods for workers in order to prevent the number of voters for the labor parties from growing, while the Histadrut, in order to augment its electoral strength, sought to turn the urban proletariat into property owners. The unique shaping of the landscape highlighted even further the determination of the workers' party to remain a political factor to be reckoned with in Tel Aviv.

The search for alternative urban forms, different from those prior to the 1920's, was not restricted to Palestine. In Berlin and Frankfurt the *Seidlung* was already regarded as the nucleus of the alternative city that would sprout around semi-urban, semi-rural suburban neighborhoods composed mainly of family homes with gardens — ideas that had already been attempted in Great Britain in the framework of the garden city on the eve of World War I.[19]

In Palestine the Histadrut came out in 1925 with the *shekhunat ha'ovdim* (workers' estate) idea as a new model for a suburban neighborhood of one thousand families, patterned after the *Seidlung* but combining a community structure, cooperative and individualistic, with supplementary farms to augment their income, which was mainly earned in the city. Moving the workers to areas outside of the city — a policy implemented in Amsterdam, Berlin, and Frankfurt, and even in the framework of Great Britain's council housing — was unsuitable as a solution in Palestine, primarily because the Jewish National Fund, which had to purchase the tracts intended for working-class neighborhoods because of the principle of national ownership of the land, was unwilling to invest in highly priced real estate in the suburbs of the large cities.[20] With the exception of Kiryat Haim, founded in the early 1930's in the Haifa Bay area, no working-class neighborhoods outside the city were established until the Arab riots of 1936. Hence the true planning challenge remained within the city limits.

In 1930 the first attempt was made in Tel Aviv to erect apartments on a cooperative basis — an endeavor that spread to all the large cities in Palestine. During the 1930's the enterprise known as *me'onot ovdim* (workers' cooperative housing) became the crowning achievement of socialistic housing in Palestine. It was here that the Histadrut planning institutions, whose members included

19   Tafuri & Dal Co (note 2, supra), pp. 156–161; Swenarton (note 5, supra), pp. 5–26.
20   I. Graicer, "The J.N.F.'s Urban Land Policy and Its Influence on Urban Development in Palestine during the Mandate," *Karka* (July 1983), pp. 70–86 (Hebrew).

architects belonging to the "Architects' Circle," concentrated their activity. In Tel Aviv, where most of the construction took place, twenty cooperative apartment blocks were erected during the 1930's, providing accommodation for a total of four hundred families. In Haifa eighty-four families moved into workers' cooperative housing, and in Jerusalem another ninety-five families did the same.[21]

The architects involved in these projects were faced with three demands, relating to three levels of planning. On the overall city level they were required — as mentioned — to express the unique sociopolitical perception of the workers. On the neighborhood level they had to stress a "return to basics" — i.e. simplicity and functionality of construction, and financial savings — while maintaining equality among the residents through maximum uniformity of living conditions. On the living unit level they were charged with effective internal planning and with providing hygienic and salubrious living conditions that suited the life-style of the working family.

On the city level one of the main problems in Tel Aviv was inherent in the municipal parcellation. The Scottish city planner Patrick Geddes was commissioned to design Tel Aviv northward, up to the Yarqon River. His plan, which was approved in the latter half of the 1920's, apportioned the city into small building blocks that allowed for construction of relatively small four-to-six-family houses, with high building density. In order to mold a city landscape more suitable to the ideology behind working-class housing, it was necessary to nullify the existing parcellation and relocate the apartment houses in larger complexes, while enlarging the open spaces between them. In the new planning the building facades were redesigned to face inner courtyards, while large green areas were created between one building and the next. This neighborhood model had typified the working-class suburbs of Holland and Germany since the 1920's (see Fig. 1). In reality, though, only the first housing complex of the *me'onot ovdim* project, on Ma'ase Street in Tel Aviv, was built similar to the neighborhoods in these countries. The later ones adopted as a model the Viennese *Hof*, with a large yard enclosed on all sides by multi-storeyed residential buildings (see Fig. 2).

Sharon, the chief architect of workers' cooperative housing, explained that the large, enclosed yard placed less emphasis on private ownership and more on the spirit of collectivism, expressed through cooperation in the gardening work and spending leisure hours together. Hence, he asserted, this form of housing

---

21 Graicer (note 10, supra), pp. 291–292.

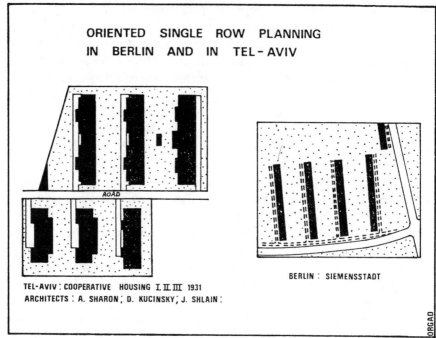

ORIENTED SINGLE ROW PLANNING IN BERLIN AND IN TEL-AVIV

TEL-AVIV : COOPERATIVE HOUSING I, II, III 1931
ARCHITECTS : A. SHARON; D. KUCINSKY; J. SHLAIN :

BERLIN : SIEMENSSTADT

Fig. 1

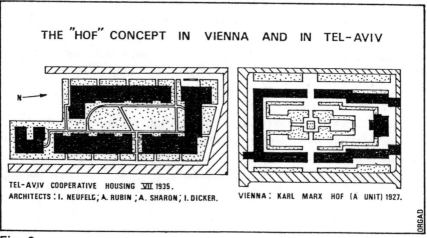

THE "HOF" CONCEPT IN VIENNA AND IN TEL-AVIV

TEL-AVIV COOPERATIVE HOUSING VII 1935.
ARCHITECTS : I. NEUFELG; A. RUBIN ; A. SHARON; I. DICKER.

VIENNA : KARL MARX HOF (A UNIT) 1927.

Fig. 2

highly suited the ideology of the working-class neighborhoods in Palestine.[22] This ideology regarded the common yard as the most important aspect of the urban worker's life-style. The bond between the working man and the land would steer him away from the frivolous, time-wasting activities so prevalent in the city, and bring him closer to family and community.[23]

The combination of reparcellation, relocation of homes, and the addition of large, variegated green areas became the trademark of the *me'onot ovdim* in all the large cities. In the second housing complex of this enterprise in Tel Aviv, on Frishman Street, Le Corbusier's idea of building on pillars was incorporated into the Histadrut housing. The pillars in the facade of the buildings formed a sort of monumental entrance leading into the inner yard and garden. An identical design was used in the third Tel Aviv complex, on Ben-Gurion Boulevard, and in the fourth one, on Nordau Boulevard. In a discussion conducted to evaluate Sharon's plan for workers' cooperative housing on Nordau Boulevard, it was explicitly noted that "the facade should be given a monumental shape and that the nature of the housing project made it necessary for it to be closed in the direction facing the streets."[24] There was a demand for the porches and rooms of the apartments to face the yard rather than the street, but the municipal ordinances prohibiting the construction of toilets facing the street somewhat obstructed the implementation of these ideological-architectural concepts.[25]

The Jerusalem architects who built the *me'onot ovdim* in the city, in the Rehavia neighborhood, saw as a negative example the *batei haluka* "charity homes" whose name derived from the fact that their ultra-Orthodox residents lived on charity. Although the buildings had certain positive features, such as common yards, the traditional design limited family privacy. Hence the planners sought to create a new model of joint apartments for the city's workers, in which the cooperative elements, such as the common, enclosed yard, would be preserved, but which would grant maximum privacy to each family (see Fig. 3).

22   Sharon (note 14, supra), pp. 47–49; Z. Mach & A. Mach, "Suggestions for Improving Workers' Co-op Flats," *Twenty Years of Building* (hereafter: *Twenty Years*), Histadrut Engineers', Architects' & Surveyors' Union, Tel Aviv 1940, pp. 97–99 (Hebrew); A. Sharon, "Housing and Dwellings from the Architectural Viewpoint," *Organized Housing*, Histadrut Engineers', Architects' and Surveyors' Union, Tel Aviv 1944, pp. 86–91 (Hebrew).

23   J. Korner, "Workers' Co-op Flats and Individual Detached Houses," *Twenty Years*, pp. 94–96 (Hebrew).

24   Minutes of the executive meeting of Shikun Ovdim Company, July 2, 1935, Archives of the Labor Movement, Shikun Section (Hebrew).

25   A. Sharon, "Workers' Cooperative Flats IV, V, VI," *Habinyan* (August 1937), pp. 8–11 (Hebrew).

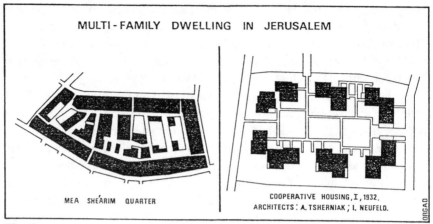

Fig. 3

Unlike the situation in Tel Aviv, the two workers' cooperative housing complexes in Rehavia were only two storeys high. In accordance with a request made by the residents in one of them, on Gaza Street, the entrances faced the inner yard, rather than the street. In addition, separate, private, external staircases were built for those living on the top floor, and these were located at a distance from one another in order to achieve maximum individuality and to differentiate these apartments as much possible from the model of the *batei haluka* yard that included common porches and entrance hallways — so typical of Jerusalem's old neighborhoods.[26]

It is difficult not to discern the marked similarity in the planning of the workers' cooperative housing in Palestine and in Vienna. In both cases an attempt was made to plan working-class neighborhoods not only on a basis of universal values such as quality of life, but also with the goal of creating a framework allowing for a working-class life-style.[27] In Vienna, between 1923 and 1933, around sixty thousand housing units were built within complexes, the smallest of which contained dozens of units, while the largest ones, the superblocks, had up to 1,600. In parallel with the construction of these apartments, a network of services was established, which made the complexes

26   A. Cherniak, "Multi-Family Dwellings of the Haluka in Jerusalem, a Chapter from History," *Habinyan* (August 1937), pp. 6–7 (Hebrew).

27   S. Ingberman, "Normative and Evolutionary Housing Prototypes in Germany and Austria: The Viennese Superblocks 1919–1934," *Oppositions*, 13 (1978), pp. 84–87.

self-sufficient in all aspects of daily urban life. Within the large yards there were nurseries, schools, day-care centers, assorted clinics, pharmacies, libraries, clubhouses, grocery stores, youth movement branches, night schools for working youth, adult education centers, laundry rooms, showers, and workshops — all on a cooperative and communal basis.

In Vienna and other cities of Europe, such as Frankfurt and Amsterdam, the municipal authorities owned a large percentage of the land, thus making it possible to erect huge housing complexes with an array of services. In Tel Aviv, by contrast, for a variety of reasons — including general unavailability of land and the high price of whatever was available — working-class housing projects of diverse dimensions were scattered throughout the city. Consequently, the size of some communities fell below the minimum "threshold" for establishing community services, and the same services could not be provided in each neighborhood. In order to overcome the spatial diffusion of the neighborhoods, the planning institutions of the Histadrut adopted a policy geared to restricting the acquisition of land earmarked for Tel Aviv complexes to four areas, and providing a network of cooperative-communal services on a regional rather than a neighborhood basis.[28] Because the working-class population in Tel Aviv was much smaller than that in Vienna, not as wide an array of community services could be established. Nevertheless, cooperative grocery stores, nurseries and schools teaching in the spirit of the workers' movement, laundries, kitchens and clubhouses were set up in the workers' housing in the city. Since only a minority of the working-class families in Tel Aviv were privileged to move into this housing, services funded by the upper salary thresholds, such as hospitals, clinics, mother-and-child stations, and night schools were furnished on a city-wide rather than neighborhood basis. Services on a city-wide basis were also provided to working-class families in Jerusalem and Haifa.

The planning of both the workers' estates in Vienna and the *me'onot ovdim* in Palestine stressed spatial seclusion. In Vienna the workers' estates were supposed to create a "new man," educated and culturally refined, who would propagate the Austro-Marxist ideology among the other classes and draw them into the socialistic revolution by means of social reform. For this purpose, it was necessary to plan a residential environment that would instill the tenants with pride and promote cooperative, communal life. The enclosed yard in and around which community life was conducted was seen as the most appropriate model. Even though the workers comprised a decisive majority in Vienna, this was not the case in Austria as a whole, and planners had to take into account the

---

28 Graicer (note 10, supra), pp. 137–151.

possibility that it would be necessary to bear arms in defense of democratic-socialistic values — which in fact transpired in the battles against fascism in February 1934, when the enclosed architecture of the neighborhoods provided a favorable defensive position and turned the _Höfe_ into workers' fortresses.[29]

In contrast to the monumental architecture of the workers' _Hof_ in Vienna, with its skyscrapers, turrets, huge openings connecting the inner yards with the outside, swinging, lockable iron gates, integration of classical and modern elements, and enormous statues bearing ideological messages — "a combination of palatial monumentality and practicality bold and impressive"[30] — the architecture of the cooperative housing in Palestine was far more modest. As opposed to the heavy Wagnerian style of construction in Vienna, the working-class housing in Tel Aviv was built in the international style, expressly modern, innovative, and modest in its architectural contours. In both places the designers, working during the exact same period, felt a need to physically make the working-class neighborhoods stand out on the local municipal landscape — and hence the difference in architectural styles of the two cities. Vienna, capital of a former empire, had historically been characterized by large-scale architecture and impressive public buildings. Because the working-class neighborhoods had to find a style that would stand out and convey social messages against this grandiose background, the result was even heavier and more impressive architectural design. In the small city of Tel Aviv, in order to create a unique landscape it sufficed to follow the basic model of the Viennese _Hof_, with joint apartment buildings and long facades facing the street (see Fig. 4). Although the international style, with its functional contours, was initially a symbol of workers' cooperative housing in Tel Aviv — primarily due to the concentration of such structures in the large housing complexes — in the 1930's and 1940's it became the accepted style in the city as a whole, including its private construction.

In Great Britain, working-class housing founded by philanthropists in the mid-1800's had stressed sunlight and ventilation. Not until the postwar period, however, did climate become one of the cardinal factors in the planning of residential neighborhoods throughout Europe. Buildings were situated far enough apart to eliminate shadowing from one to the next, and to allow for a free flow of air and sunlight even to the bottom floors. Corners were determined in accordance with the wind direction and the sun's orbit, with special attention

---

29   M. Tafuri, _Vienna Rossa, La Politica Residenziale nella Vienna Socialista 1919–1933_, Milano 1980, pp. 139–140; A. Rabinbach, _The Crisis of Austrian Socialism from Red Vienna to the Civil War 1927–1934_, London 1983, pp. 61–61; _Davar_ (February 12–18, 1934), editorial (Hebrew).

30   Rabinbach (note 29, supra), pp. 61–62.

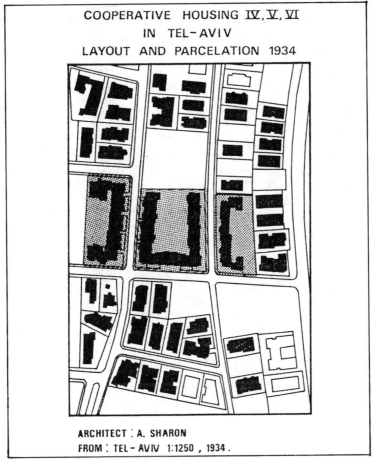

Fig. 4

to sunrise and sunset. Apartments in Tel Aviv were designed with the living and dining rooms facing the west, the direction with the best ventilation in the afternoon and evening, while the bedrooms faced east, the direction with the best ventilation late at night and in the morning (see Fig. 5).

The apartment design was the crowning achievement of the international style. The stress on functionality and efficiency precipitated changes in the standard apartment size. The living room was enlarged at the expense of the bedrooms. The cooking area, which for lower- and middle-class families before World War I was most often a mere corner within the living room, was replaced by the Frankfurter kitchen, first appearing in the planning of Ernst May in Frankfurt: a separate room, fulfilling the additional function of an eating area.

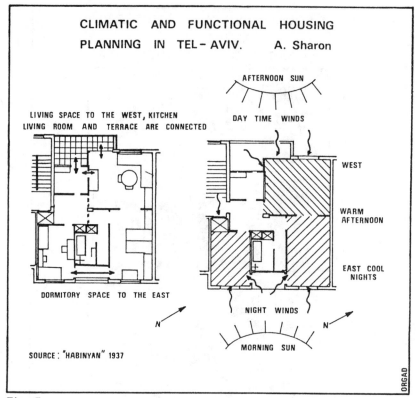

CLIMATIC AND FUNCTIONAL HOUSING
PLANNING IN TEL – AVIV.   A. Sharon

AFTERNOON SUN

LIVING SPACE TO THE WEST, KITCHEN
LIVING ROOM AND TERRACE ARE CONNECTED

DAY TIME WINDS

WEST

WARM
AFTERNOON

EAST COOL
NIGHTS

DORMITORY SPACE TO THE EAST

N

NIGHT WINDS

N

MORNING SUN

SOURCE : "HABINYAN" 1937

ORGAD

Fig. 5

In Palestine more than in colder countries, the porch played a vital role in family life; it was here that the family gathered after working hours and spent the evening hours, and the western porch, which was part of the apartment structure, became an essential element in the design. The physical link between the living room, kitchen and family porch — first emphasized in the planning in Germany of Alexander Klein (who later moved to Palestine and served as a teacher in the Technion in Haifa and as a city planner)[31] — became the cardinal design component (see Fig. 5), in Palestine as well as elsewhere. The shorter the walking distance between these three living spaces, the better was considered the quality of design, in the mind of the planners.[32] Not only was the "Architects' Circle,"

---

31 Bauer (note 1, supra), p. 203.
32 *Researches, Findings of the Building and Technics Research Institute*, I, Histadrut Engineers', Architects' and Surveyors' Union, Tel Aviv 1943, pp. 47–86 (Hebrew); A. Sharon, "Planning

especially Sharon, instrumental in the implementation of the principles of international architecture in the framework of working-class housing, but the planning bodies of the Histadrut were the first to consent to the demands raised by the Circle with regard to the overall planning process.

Part of the design conception — constituting a novel development in its own right — was the participation of residents in the planning. Sharon told of meetings he had with the residents, and his attempt to convince them of the advantages of the unconventional construction of the cooperative buildings and of the long facades that had characterized the initial *me'onot ovdim*.

Plans were discussed with the future residents; contractors aided in the selection of building materials; work details and proposed changes were decided in coordination with trained professionals — all of which resulted in dwellings that made best use of the technical possibilities and suited the needs of the population. In most cases the planners managed to convince the residents that the proposed designs offered optimal advantages. Occasionally the planners were compelled, even against their better judgment, to alter their designs in accordance with the demands put forth by the residents — or at least to adapt them to the means, capabilities and inclinations of the dwellers.[33]

Another novel development in the planning process of the Histadrut housing institutions was open competition. Starting in 1922 this had become an accepted procedure in the planning of schools throughout the world, especially in the United States.[34] Among the judges and advisors charged with selecting the architects were representatives of the residents, whose criteria in evaluating the plans included cultural quality, economic savings, and the uniformity and equality in living conditions. Even then the residents' approval for each detail of the apartment was required, including the women's assent to the kitchen design. Many architects participated in the competition, and the Center for Workers' Neighborhoods and the Shikun Company used to convene the planners, architects and future residents for joint discussions on housing issues.

of Cooperative Houses," *Habinyan* (August 1937), pp. 1–3 (Hebrew); idem, "Houses and Dwellings," *Organized Housing*, pp. 86–91; L. Cohen, "The Apartment and Its Use," *ibid.*, pp. 91–98.

33 Sharon (note 14, supra), pp. 47–49; A. Tsherniak & Z. Neufeld, "Workers' Cooperative Apartments, I," *Habinyan* (August 1937), p. 21 (Hebrew).

34 The first competition of this sort took place in Chicago, with the design of the Chicago Tribune building. Architects from all over the world participated, and since then the idea has become accepted for architectural projects. See: Benevolo (note 7, supra), p. 486.

PLANNING DECISION: CLASS UNITY OR CLASS CLEAVAGE?

The working-class housing in Palestine was built partly before the collapse of the socialistic regime in Vienna, and partly afterwards. In the jargon produced by the struggle for power in that city, working-class housing was depicted in terms of "workers' bastions," "fortresses," "property of the workers' movement," and "territory of the workers."[35] These expressions reached Palestine as well, and were used to describe the working-class housing there. The question is to what extent did this enterprise in Palestine retain its popular, folk, working-class quality.

In contrast to the working-class neighborhoods in Europe, which were entirely financed by the municipal authorities and by public bodies, and which were largely built outside of the cities, on cheap land, thus affording equal opportunity to all those in need of housing — and in contrast to the Viennese model, where the rent was set no higher than the maintenance costs — the housing complexes in Tel Aviv demanded a substantial sum from the residents. Because of the principle that a worker could not be a landowner in Palestine, along with the unwillingness on the part of the Jewish National Fund to purchase expensive land in the city for housing purposes, the brunt of the financing for housing fell on the labor unions.

Despite the fact that cooperative, joint ownership of the land and of the built-up property kept the workers' estates free of land speculation — unlike the working-class neighborhoods consisting of single homes and small lots — and despite the sizable financial aid that the Histadrut offered through loans and mortgages, the sum that the urban worker had to invest was substantial. As a result, only someone who had a permanent job and a reasonably high income could acquire an apartment in the city, so that the urban housing that had been created in theory for the entire working class became available to only its upper strata.

Against this background, it is understandable why the design of the workers' houses became increasingly less standardized. In most of them, especially those built after the peak years in the mid-1930's, three- and four-room apartments of 120 sq. m. each were planned — greatly exceeding the limits of housing geared to the average urban worker.

The criteria for the size of popular housing were debated in many of the housing projects in Europe, and the solutions varied. In Great Britain the desire

35   Graicer (note 10, supra), p. 134; H. Froumkin, "For Action," *Working-Class Neighborhoods*,
      I, Tel Aviv 1927, p. 9 (Hebrew); L. Kaufman, "Urban Workers' Housing," *Hameshek Hashitufi*,
      A (January 31, 1933), p. 42 (Hebrew).

to put the living conditions of the urban worker on a par with those of the middle class led to the development of the ideal model of a two-storey home with living room, kitchen and toilet facilities on the first floor, and three bedrooms on the second floor.[36] The designs drawn up in Frankfurt and Berlin were for houses of varying dimensions, suited to any family size and to any budget.[37] Vienna, by contrast, was characterized by an austere style, with most of the apartments having one to one-and-a-half rooms, without a washroom. Only a small portion had two or three rooms.

The design of the workers' houses in Tel Aviv was closer in spirit to that in Great Britain than to that in Vienna, even though the buildings in the latter city were constructed on a cooperative basis, as they were in Tel Aviv. In Vienna, the argument in favor of small apartments was that the family spent most of the day in the clubhouses, laundry room, washroom, and playgrounds, and that the home mainly served as sleeping quarters. Furthermore, reduction in the size of the units made it possible to include a greater number of them in each building and to lower the housing costs. In Tel Aviv, by contrast, the large size of the homes can only be explained by the fact that the residents had a solid financial basis.

From the standpoint of the workers' parties and the Histadrut, the construction of several hundred housing units certainly did not offer any solution to the housing crisis besetting the urban working class in Palestine. Indeed, already by the latter half of the 1930's, as a result of internal pressure and criticism of the class split deriving from planning policies, which was exacerbated by a rise in land prices within the cities, the emphasis was shifted to working-class housing outside of the large cities. The new trend was toward cooperative working-class small towns, which eventually turned into urban communities in their own right — such as Giv'atayim, Holon, and Qiryat Amal. The Viennese model of the *Hof* was not transferred to these places because there was no social or political tension that compelled spatial seclusion from the surroundings. It was possible to plan more rational housing models. Nevertheless, the high level of planning and execution achieved by the urban working-class housing of the 1930's merits respect and appreciation. It is considered to be the best housing of this sort ever constructed in Israel.

---

36 A. Sayle, *The Houses of the Workers*, London 1924, pp. 97–100; Swenarton (note 5, supra), pp. 88–111.

37 Wiedenhoeft (note 7, supra), pp. 33–52.

Conclusion

The construction of working-class housing in Palestine between the two world wars was part of a social process that was sweeping nearly all of the Western countries in the world, including North America, where, as a result of the ideological upheaval stemming from the Russian Revolution, workers organized on individual, institutional and municipal bases in order to ameliorate their economic situation.

The weaker classes' consciousness of their problems spread not only among politicians, but also within schools of design, of architecture and of art, which trained planners and architects to offer new, modern solutions, in the spirit of the times, to the housing dilemma of the workers. In Palestine too, the *me'onot ovdim* constructed by the Histadrut reflected the enormous advancement in urban planning in the land. The great development of the workers' institutions in Palestine turned the Histadrut housing into a laboratory for experimentation with new currents and schools of thought in modern architecture, which, being based on functionality and rationalism, appeared most suitable for the urban, egalitarian society that the workers' movement sought to create in Palestine.

There were numerous similarities between working-class housing in Palestine and that in Western and East European countries, which revolve around two essential points:

1) organization of the operations on a class basis, either as part of the housing policy of the local authorities, as in Vienna or Frankfurt, or as part of that of the workers themselves, as in Palestine and in a number of similar projects in the United States:[38]

2) architectonics conveying social messages and the conversion of working-class housing into a hotbed of architectural ideas aimed at socially molding the community of workers from the inside, and conveying the messages to the society outside.

Apart from these similarities, there were also several aspects that exclusively characterized the projects in Palestine:

a) absence of a perception of the housing problems of low-income groups as an issue demanding a solution on the urban-municipal plane, and disregard by the local authorities in Palestine, in comparison with many European cities, of the need to provide housing to workers;

b) disregard by the Mandatory Government of housing problems in Palestine; in

---

38   *Thirty Years of Amalgamated Cooperative Housing 1927–1957*, Amalgamated Housing
      Corporation, New York 1958.

contrast to the situation in Great Britain, where housing for the lower classes was provided between the two world wars, the British regime in Palestine did not cooperate at all with the local institutions, or facilitate the housing process by apportioning land for working-class apartment blocks in the city, or by rendering financial aid;[39]

c) social cleavage inherent in the housing solutions, stemming from a lack of support by the local authorities, which caused the housing enterprise to restrict itself to to the upper strata of workers — along with a rejection of popular housing solutions for the post-statehood period.

In most European cities, especially in Holland and Germany, the neighborhoods built in the 1920's and 1930's have become a model of improved quality of life up to the present day. Even the apartments of the Viennese *Höfe* were redesigned, and once their area was enlarged and washrooms and elevators were added to the buildings, they became — and remain today — a symbol of high quality within the city. In most of the Israeli neighborhoods built on a cooperative basis, this framework has survived. The workers' houses of Tel Aviv, like those of Haifa and Jerusalem, have preserved cooperative associations, fiscal relics of a vanished life-style, until this day.

Thanks to the cooperative basis of the working-class housing projects, designed to reinforce the actual and the electoral strength of the urban workers' movement, they have remained unique on the housing landscape of the land. Thanks to the cooperative element, the singular design of the working-class neighborhoods, where social and architectural values were grafted onto the fabric of the city, has also been preserved. This same element has also made an important contribution to preservation of historical-architectonic values of the city in Israel, as expressed in the urban landscape of the large urban areas, especially Tel Aviv.

39   Graicer (note 10, supra), pp. 77–78; A. Granot, *Agrarian Changes in Israel and the World*, Tel Aviv 1956, pp. 66–67 (Hebrew); I. Ben–Zvi, "Our Demands from the Labour Government in England," *Kuntress*, 165 (March, 1925) (Hebrew).

AERIAL PERSPECTIVE OF PAST LANDSCAPES

DOV GAVISH

INTRODUCTION

Israel is one of the few countries in the world blessed with aerial photographs of its land taken over a span of more than seventy years — in fact, from the dawn of aerial photography. This rich inventory has survived both in archives and in private hands, and proves to be a veritable treasure chest of visual records providing direct documentation of the appearance of the land.

This article aims to elucidate the research value of the aerial photographs as visual documentation and as a source of historical-geographic information, and to present the inventory of aerial photos available to researchers of Eretz-Israel.

WHY AERIAL PHOTOGRAPHS?

Through the aerial photograph, the landscape revealed to the camera lens is translated into visual language. The visual message is universal, direct, immediate, easily understood, always available for reexamination, and independent of secondary sources. The photograph captures scenes and events that have vanished with time, and the testimony it embodies is unassailable. Still, the aerial photograph has both advantages and disadvantages relative to all other forms of documentation or records, including those in the same visual category, such as an ordinary photograph or a map. The aerial photograph, like a conventional photograph, can be exploited for detection and discovery, reconstruction of landscapes, verification of impressions and corroboration of facts. However, it differs in that it is taken from an external, distant, and ostensibly neutral observation point, and subjective factors such as selection of the photographer's position and camera angle do not affect the result. Ordinarily, wide areas are taken in, and there is no "dead ground" in between. Although a map also has its own clear and legible visual language, explained and improved by the cartographer, the aerial photograph differs from the map in that it includes no topical selection, unbalanced intervention by man, silencing, or erased and empty areas. Nor does it resort to graphical abstractions, iconic symbols or alien signs.

AERIAL PHOTOGRAPHS AND HISTORICAL GEOGRAPHY

An aerial photograph is an essential instrument for a geographer exploring the past. While it is difficult to perceive the present, with the aid of a camera we can grasp the past. Filled with expectancy, we search for traces of the past on the surface, our assumption being that each event leaves some signs and testimony. Nevertheless, inspection of an aerial photograph, like that of the landscape in general, cannot be undertaken without a specific goal in mind; one must have a clear idea of what might be found in the picture, in order to establish a position with regard to phenomena, and to understand and "debate" with the landscape. In a single photograph are recorded the physical situation, historical facts and evidence, and legal proof of what did and did not exist in the landscape at the time it was taken. Nonetheless, even if we have succeeded in historical-geographical research in producing photographed evidence of a site or event, our accomplishment is incomplete. The popular saying "a picture is worth a thousand words" is true only within certain limits; it has validity with regard to the physical event per se, but a photograph on its own freezes the situation, and without words — perhaps somewhat fewer than a thousand — not even a superb picture is sufficient. As Andrew Brookes asserted in his book on the history of aerial photography, "The camera cannot lie but neither can it tell the whole truth."[1]

Author and critic Susan Sontag found intellectual stimulus in photographs, since "the aerial photographs, which cannot themselves explain anything, are inexhaustible invitations to deduction, speculation, and fantasy."[2] Thus the photograph should not be regarded as a self-explanatory historical document, but as corroborative evidence and a springboard for additional questions. The scene that appears in a single photograph is a link in the chain of the landscape's ever-changing and ever-evolving history; there is a story that preceded it, and another one that followed it. Undoubtedly there exist other documents and forms of evidence either explaining and supporting the photograph, or providing contradictory information that alters the direction of the research — but in all cases expanding the canvas. It does not suffice to exclaim that "the photograph showed" — the triumphant opening words of the fascinating book entitled *Evidence in Camera*, written by Constance Babington Smith, one of Britain's foremost photo interpreters during World War II.[3] The intelligence stored in a photographic document is not revealed on direct and immediate examination —

---

1   A.J. Brookes, *Photo Reconnaissance*, London 1975.
2   S. Sontag, *On Photography*, New York 1978, p. 23.
3   C. Babington Smith, *Evidence in Camera*, Newton Abbot-London-Vancouver 1974.

a fact which the British photo interpreters discovered only in the midst of the war, and which gave rise to three phases of interpretation. In the third phase, the least urgent, the interpreters could afford to devote time to a deep and comparative analysis. A document issued by a photo interpretation unit near the end of the war suggested a clear-cut distinction between "photographic research interpretation" and "direct interpretation."[4]

The single photograph depicts a temporary situation. A series of aerial photographs taken at different times creates a chronological sequence revealing the situations "before" and "after," and allows for a comparison and measurement of the changes. "During the First World War," Smith writes, "it had come to be accepted as axiomatic that the value of evidence from a sequence of covers far transcends the evidence of a single sortie." The aforementioned British war document states that "the more that is known from past photographs — the more that will be known from the next photographs." The assemblage of solitary events into a historical sequence imparts to the series an independent quality, and offers invaluable accessibility to points of time in history. Nevertheless, even in a chronological sequence there are hiatuses and blank areas between one photograph and another, which must be filled in with information, if not speculation, so that the gaps can be closed.

THE AERIAL PHOTOGRAPH IN PALESTINE

To the best of my knowledge, Palestine was first photographed from the air in December 1913, with the arrival of two French airplanes the first ever to land in the country. Unfortunately, my efforts to locate these photographs have been unsuccessful. The earliest photographs in our possession were taken in 1916, during the war, by French and British seaplanes. Because the land was still under Turkish rule at the time, the British did not have landing grounds in the area. Due to the short flight range of these planes, they were carried close to the target in the hold of cargo vessels sailing out of Port Said, Egypt. After being lowered from the ships into the water near the coast of Palestine, the planes took off on reconnaissance missions, and upon their return they landed in the water. In the course of these flights photographic intelligence was collected on the battle-readiness of the Turks.

On the western front and in the Middle East, this was the first modern war in which operational flying units took part alongside the traditional mounted and

---

4   "The Organisation of Photographic Reconnaissance for Strategic Purposes in the European Theatre," p. 6, Sect. 36, 106GR/50/2/AIR, October 30, 1944, Public Record Office [hereafter: PRO], AIR2/7846.

artillery units. The main assignments of the flying squadrons at the start of the war were reconnaissance, observation, and placement and direction of artillery. However, once the vast potential of aerial photographs for intelligence and mapping purposes became apparent, all of the squadrons were equipped with cameras, and many thousands of pictures were taken in the course of the war. German flying squadrons operated in Palestine alongside the Turks, and were opposed by the British squadrons and one Australian flying corps.[5] A sizable portion of the photographs produced have been preserved up to the present, but it is known that numerous others have been lost. The surviving photos are presently located in archives in Munich, Canberra, Jerusalem, and, in smaller numbers, in London and in private hands.

At least one photographic project was carried out in Palestine for scientific-historical purposes during the war — by the German archaeologist Theodor Wiegand, who appreciated the scientific value of aerial photographs for the documentation and preservation of ancient sites.[6] After conducting excavations in Asia Minor, he prevailed upon the German High Command to permit him to establish and head the *Denkmalschutz-Kommandos*, a special mission for the preservation of ancient monuments. Its chief goal was to prevent the continued destruction of the Byzantine cities in the Negev, whose building stones were being removed by the Bedouins and used in the construction of the southern towns Beersheba, Auja el-Hafir and Quseima. In September and October of 1916 Wiegand conducted an archaeological survey and mapping of the ancient cities with the aid of aerial photographs taken especially for him by a German squadron that had reached the Palestine front in order to take part in the Ottoman campaign at the Suez Canal.

With the war's end in late 1918 the squadrons left Palestine, and aerial photography waned. A British military administration was installed in Palestine, to be replaced in July 1920 by a civil government headed by a British high commissioner. Among the figures who attained senior positions in the new regime were those who during the war had become cognizant of the potential benefits of aerial photography, and who therefore pressed for its continuance — this time for the purposes of engineering, urban planning, land settlement and archaeological surveying. Their steady persuasion bore fruit, and several photographic sorties were carried out for a variety of purposes. Nevertheless, aerial photography was used only in exceptional cases, so that in the postwar years the land was photographed sporadically and unsystematically by both

---

5   D. Gavish, "Air-Photographs by First World War Pilots in Eretz-Israel," *Cathedra*, 7 (1978), pp. 119–150 (Hebrew).

6   T. Wiegand, *Sinai*, Berlin-Leipzig 1920.

civilians and military personnel. At the request of the authorities, every so often military photographers took pictures — especially of sites of particular interest — for the sake of mapping or planning.

One of the most tendentious and critical photography and interpretation operations took place in 1930 at the behest of Sir John Hope Simpson, who had been appointed by the British government to investigate the land problem, immigration and plans for development, in the wake of the 1929 Arab disturbances against the Jewish population.[7] The investigation, which focused on Palestine's economic capacity, was based on selective aerial photography of the land. This formed the basis for Hope Simpson's provocative recommendation to prohibit additional Jewish immigration, as there was, he opined, no room for more immigrants.

Among the civilian photographers who were impressed by the rapid rate of development in Palestine — as witnessed from an aerial view — were curious journalists and both amateur and professional photographers, who took pictures for commercial purposes as well as for propaganda, surveys and newspaper illustrations. The passengers of the German zeppelin that flew over the area in 1929 and in 1931 also took aerial shots. It is worth noting that all of these sorties together did not provide a complete photographic picture of the entire territory of Palestine.

In World War II the "photographic barrier" was broken, and trained units photographed broad tracts of land within Palestine as part of their wide-ranging aerial photography missions throughout the Middle East. Still, only toward the end of the war, in December 1944, when political considerations reinforced military arguments, did the British consent for the first time to conduct complete, systematic and orderly aerial photography, thanks to which we have aerial coverage of the entire area of Palestine. This series, photographed over a five-month period, became the standard which we use daily when comparing photographs from various periods. In 1947–1948, when it became apparent that the British Mandate was drawing to a close and that an armed struggle would break out between the Arabs and the Jews, the underground representing the organized Jewish community began to take aerial shots of Arab villages and military targets.

Thus a sizable and historically valuable inventory of aerial photographs has been amassed over the years. It serves investigators in many fields, as well as those who are merely curious.

7   J. Hope Simpson, *Report on Immigration, Land Settlement and Development*, London 1930 (CMD 3686).

USE OF AERIAL PHOTOGRAPHS IN HISTORICAL-GEOGRAPHICAL RESEARCH IN ISRAEL

The study of the historical geography of Eretz-Israel throughout the ages is aided by aerial photographs. Assuming that up to the end of the nineteenth century the landscape did not undergo major changes, it is possible to see the remnants of the distant past captured forever in photographs. Nevertheless, it is natural that the photographs mainly serve those studying the modern period. Geographical-historical research of Eretz-Israel in the modern period primarily concentrates on explaining the processes and changes taking place on the surface as a result of the accelerated development ushered in by the massive immigration, land purchase, settlement, and economic investments, as well as the social upheaval generated by the ongoing conflict between Jews, Arabs and the British rulers up to 1948. This research is aided by aerial photographs in its endeavor to define a particular temporal and spatial situation in comparison with others, and to analyze the dynamics of the change. Still, every so often, whether deliberately or accidentally, the ceaseless perusal of photographs leads to the discovery of topics that no one had known about or thought of, or to which proper attention had not been devoted.

I have selected two surveys as examples of research that relies upon aerial photographs as a source of information and as a historical-geographical document. In the first, the aerial photograph is one of the tools — in fact the best one — in the service of the systematic, chronological, developmental approach, as it concretizes and describes the settlement-related changes taking place in the landscape. In the second study the aerial photograph is itself a unique historical document in which an accidental and surprising revelation exposes and captures an event of geographical, historical and military significance.

FIRST EXAMPLE: PHOTOGRAPHS TRACING THE CHRONOLOGICAL SEQUENCE OF RURAL-SETTLEMENT CHANGES

Qastina, a small Arab village in the south of the country, formerly in the Gaza district, had a population of 406 in 1922. The residents gained their livelihood from dry farming in an area with an annual rainfall of 450 mm. The village was photographed on December 1, 1917 by the German air force, about one week before the capture of Jerusalem by General Allenby (see Plate 1). In the photograph there appears an unpaved road surrounding the village — what is today the main road connecting the northern part of the country with Beersheba. The homes in the village are built of adobe. The land appears scorched during the first month of the winter rains. Some of the plots adjacent to the village are enclosed by stone fences that stand out prominently in sharp contrast to the exposed land. These plots were evidently owned privately by the village notables, while the rest of the land was owned jointly by the villagers.

In order to understand the change which the village landscape underwent, it is important to become familiar with the landholding system that was widespread at the time. In this village, like many others, the *musha'* system of communal land ownership was practiced, in which the village lands were temporarily partitioned and redistributed periodically, every two or three years, among the residents, who were expected to till the soil for a livelihood. The continual re-division of the lands was designed to compensate those who had received relatively poor plots and were eager to exchange them, hoping to improve their fortunes. Unfortunately, this system led to the impoverishment and neglect of the land, since the penurious farmers refrained from investing in and improving their tracts, which they knew would soon pass into the hands of others. Similarly, the Ottoman system of taxation on produce — the tithe — served as a negative incentive vis-à-vis the effort to strengthen the economy and enhance the standard of living. These conditions led to a deterioration of the farm economy and a deepening of the material poverty of the villagers.

The negative results of this system of agriculture are evident from the appearance of the photographed land of Qastina, which is uncared for and lacks any visible division according to ownership. The difference between the land at this time and that appearing in a 1945 photograph is striking (see Plate 2).

In the British Mandate period the Arab village in Palestine underwent a number of changes, which perhaps did not alter the traditional life-style but found expression in the methods of farming and land ownership practiced. The Mandatory government abolished the tax system that had been applied to crops, and set the tax rates on land in accordance with its agricultural value, following a fiscal survey of rural property encompassing the entire Mandate territory from Beersheba northwards and ending in 1934. A cadastral survey was begun in 1928, for the sake of a legal land settlement. In the framework of this settlement the village lands were partitioned and divided among the fellaheen, and title deeds were issued in the villagers' names. These changes made their mark on the appearance of the village of Qastina, as can be seen in a photograph from January 27, 1945 (see Plate 2). The village population nearly doubled and the built-up area increased, while maintaining its inward and agglomerated character in two concentrations. The village area totaled 12,500 dunams, and the tilled land extended to the edge of the fields belonging to the neighboring villages. The division of plots in accordance with the governmental land settlement is clearly visible on the surface, mainly thanks to the narrow and elongated type of parcellation that was practiced for the sake of topographical adaptation, simplicity and the technological limitations of tilling the soil with livestock. It is possible, though, that this type of division also reflects mutations resulting from the fact that the land was bequeathed to children, and then to their offspring, etc. As for the road — in World War II British army camps were set up near the village, and the heavy traffic made it necessary to convert the neglected path of 1917 into a major highway leading from the north of the country to the south.

With the outbreak of Israel's War of Independence in 1948, several battles took place in the vicinity of Qastina between the Jews and the invading Egyptian forces, and the village was abandoned. The site of the village is visible in a 1987 photograph (See Plate 3), in a wood planted at the curve of the road, which adheres to its original contours. Following the war Jewish immigrants settled in the area, and from this juncture completely different settlement patterns were imprinted on the landscape. The immigrants set up moshvei ovdim, workers settlements of smallholders with independent but cooperatively worked farm units. The spatial organization of the moshavim is completely different from that of the Arab village. They are designed in a variety of open geometric shapes, the construction is planned, beside each home is a supplementary farm, and behind the home stretches a private plot of land irrigated by means of pipes, and therefore not dependent on the rainfall. Near the village a town and an industrial district have been established, with the former providing services to the moshavim.

The Arab village in Palestine developed somewhat during the Mandate period, relative to its state during the Ottoman period, but it was the establishment of the state, with the accompanying sweeping change in social structure and ideology, as well as the allocation of government resources, that precipitated a complete revolution in the perception of the land. The three aforementioned photographs, taken in 1917, 1945 and 1987, vividly demonstrate the extent of the change that took place in the landscape, and the value of the information that bridges the time gap between the pictures. It is obvious that in the absence of historical information the photographed facts would hold almost no significance, other than for purposes of propaganda and illustration.

Second Example: the Photograph as a Historical Document
The "Renovation" of Jaffa Captured on Film

The historical event that changed the face of the old city of Jaffa in 1936 was exposed thanks to the discovery of two aerial photographs.[8] Only after these

---

8   D. Gavish, "The Old City of Jaffa 1936 — a Colonial Urban Renewal Project," *Eretz-Israel*, 17 (1984), pp. 66–73 (Hebrew).

photographs (see Plates 4 & 5) were examined was a scholarly investigation launched, and consequently an unknown story uncovered. In retrospect it transpires that the incident had been recorded in a few sources, most of them military and classified; its dimensions were unknown, and it was lost in the flux of events at the time, and forgotten.

On April 19, 1936, an Arab uprising broke out in Palestine. The Arab leadership declared a general strike and paralyzed the economy in order to coerce the British government into halting Jewish immigration. The strike began in the port of Jaffa, which had become a symbol of Arab resistance, and was attended by a great deal of violence, which spread throughout the country. The rule of law and order was disrupted, and the limited British military forces found it difficult to maintain internal security. Consequently military reinforcements were rushed in from Malta and Egypt, armed guards were assigned to sensitive installations, and mobile units patrolled the roads and escorted convoys. The nucleus of the revolt lay in the ancient city of Jaffa, where the rioters enjoyed countless advantages. The city rises above a hill bordering on the sea on one side, thus allowing for control of the port. On the other side the city overlooked, and dominated, the police station and district government offices. The maze of agglomerated houses and sinuous alleyways in the old city and the intricate underground sewer system served as ideal escape routes for rioters fleeing from the army. The old city was barricaded, and access roads were covered with glass fragments, nails and assorted scrap. Shells and sniper fire rained from the area.

In May 1936 the municipal services to the old city were cut off, streets were filled with dung and garbage, and no policeman or official dared enter. The old city became a "citadel," to quote British documents. The High Commissioner was determined to assert his authority over the city and to suppress the uprising. After nonmilitary efforts to influence the Arab leadership failed, he asked the army to devise a plan for striking at the heart of the revolt. The army proposed a number of solutions, and in the end the British opted for a plan that did not carry too heavy a risk for either side — a multi-force operation involving the security arms of the army and the police, as well as ground, naval and air forces. The operation was to be carried out in four stages: 1) barraging the city every night so as to silence the fire emanating from within; 2) forcing the local residents to clear away the barricades; 3) clearing a path through the old city from east to west by blowing up houses along the way; 4) in similar fashion, clearing a path from north to south, following the outline of curving topographic features — thereby gaining a position overlooking the port. The plan's success, therefore, hinged on clearing wide swaths by blowing up homes, in order to allow the army to move securely on foot or by vehicle in the heart of the Kasbah.

The plan was approved, and immediately acted upon. The first stage began on

May 28, 1936, and the second shortly thereafter. On June 16 the third stage got under way. The residents of Jaffa were awakened at dawn by a siren. A light bomber dropped 72 boxes containing thousands of leaflets in Arabic requesting the inhabitants to evacuate their homes that very same day "for the improvement of the old city." The government contrived an alibi for its actions, claiming that its policy was motivated by humanitarian considerations — namely the desire to enhance life in Jaffa's Kasbah. On the evening of June 17, 1936, around 1,500 soldiers and six tanks entered Jaffa, a British warship sealed off the city from the sea in order to prevent the rioters from escaping, and a reconnaissance plane circled above to find out whether any Arab resistance to the operation was in the offing. Search and detonation squads broke through to the Kasbah at 4:00 a.m. and found it deserted. About an hour later the British Royal Engineers began to blow up the homes in the ancient quarter in a row from east to west, as according to plan. The explosions reverberated far and wide throughout the day, building fragments soared into the air, and a cloud of dust wafted upward and covered the city.

At 6:00 p.m. the mission was completed, and the force withdrew, leaving behind an open strip 10 to 30 meters wide that had been cut through the heart of the city from end to end. At no point during the day was it necessary to call in the backup forces. Evidently the brash insurgents had been cowed by the determination of the authorities, and reconciled to a British victory. The pilots circling above the city all day did not contribute to the demolition of the homes, and contented themselves with photographing the event. On June 29 the security forces returned to the city and implemented the fourth stage of the plan, carving a swath along the arch-like topographical features from north to south.

Two photographs (see Plates 4 & 5) found by accident in 1967 revealed the true dimensions of the operation. They show the Jaffa citadel before (May 30, 1936) and after (July 2, 1936) the campaign. The photographs created a shock, and triggered an investigation in archives in Israel and London. As a result, voluminous material was uncovered about the event. Numerous aerial photographs taken at the moment of the bombing were also found, showing the dust of the building ruins wafting upward over the city (see Plate 6). This incident had public and legal ramifications due to the "city-planning" alibi that the government had fabricated. Despite the fact that a British court in Palestine later ruled that the government had misled the public and had concealed its security motives, the authorities persisted in couching the operation in urban planning terms, and the government adviser on urban planning designed a sketch which officials nicknamed the "Anchor Plan," after the shape of the streets on which homes had been razed (see Fig. 1). The Anchor Plan was never implemented.

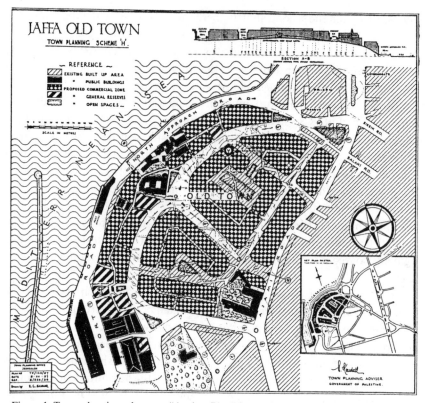

Figure 1. Town-planning scheme or "Anchor Plan" for the improvement of Jaffa's old city.

The "Jaffa Operation" was in fact a punitive action carried out in accordance with special emergency regulations, as no other way was found to subdue the rebel leaders. The government evidently attempted to minimize publicity about the method they had selected for a "face-lifting" of Jaffa's old city. The operation did damage to an Arab city and an Arab populace, and it is reasonable to suppose that if the campaign had been directed against the Jews, it would not have been silenced, and effaced from the national memory. Had the event not been photographed from the air, it would not have become known to posterity, and had the photographs not been discovered, the affair would not have been investigated. Furthermore, even if the Jaffa affair had been uncovered and investigated, but without the photographs, it would certainly have been difficult to concretize what actually took place in the city.

In an internal military document on the Jaffa operation, entitled *Military Lessons of the Arab Rebellion*,[9] the campaign is described as "a fair sample of

---

9   "Military Lessons of the Arab Rebellion in Palestine 1936," PRO, AIR 5/1244, p. 156.

the methods adopted for subduing an urban area," and it is said to "provide a good illustration of a means of reducing a recalcitrant urban area by the most human means."[10]

CONCLUSION

The aerial photograph is one of the means available to us for gathering data for historical-geographical research. In Eretz-Israel, where there has been such extreme and dynamic development in the modern period, visual documentation is an interminable source of vital and credible information that makes it possible to verify written records and memoirs. Furthermore, the aerial photograph cannot be surpassed as a means of graphically demonstrating and chronologically tracing phenomena that have put their stamp on the area. The two studies presented above are merely samples of the voluminous research in which aerial photographs comprise scientific, and not just illustrative, raw material whose importance is incontestable.

10   *Ibid.*, p. 159.

PARTITION AND TRANSFER: CRYSTALLIZATION OF THE SETTLEMENT MAP OF ISRAEL FOLLOWING THE WAR OF INDEPENDENCE, 1948–1950

SHALOM REICHMAN

INTRODUCTION*

The 1948 War of Independence brought about significant and lasting changes in the settlement map of Eretz-Israel. The area of the Jewish state was enlarged by 37%, from the 14,900 sq. km. allotted by the U.N. Partition Plan of 1947, to 20,500 sq. km. under the effective control of the Israeli Army at the war's end in 1949.[1] Moreover, at the instigation of their own leaders, a large exodus of Arabs took place. These people left behind vacant lands and villages, while seeking refuge in other parts of Palestine and in adjacent countries. This evacuation created a new and unforeseen situation, and eventually led to a reformulation of Israel's settlement policy, later referred to as "post-factum transfer."[2]

This article deals with two interrelated subjects. The first is the "settlement strategy," with its attending institutions and instruments, designed by the Zionist national bodies to foster the planning and establishment of new settlements in Palestine from the time of the first partition plan in 1937 up to the actual division of the country in 1948.[3] The considerations that entered into this strategy included not only the suitability and agricultural resources of the land in question, but also its potential integration into the Jewish state, and contribution to country's territorial goals. It shall be demonstrated how elements of the settlement strategy influenced the final shaping of the U.N. Partition Plan.

Secondly, the reactions of the Jewish establishment to the unexpected exodus of Arabs from Palestine during the course of the 1948 war are described, along with the adoption and implementation of the "post-factum transfer" policy, and its implication for the settlement map of Eretz-Israel.

* The assistance of Ms. Vered Shatzman is gratefully acknowledged.

1 A. Granott, *Agrarian Reforms and the Record of Israel*, London 1956, pp. 85–112.
2 Central Zionist Archives, Jerusalem (hereafter: CZA), Joseph Weitz Files.
3 E. Orren, *Settlement Amid Struggles: The Pre-State Strategy of Settlement*, Jerusalem 1978 (Hebrew).

SETTLEMENT STRATEGY AND ITS IMPLEMENTATION

The latter part of the British Mandatory period in Palestine, from 1937 onwards, was marked by proposals put forward by various commissions, with the aim of dividing western Palestine into two states: Jewish and Arab. Probably the most notable of these plans was the one recommended by the Royal Commission headed by Lord Peel in July 1937, whose operating principles had a lasting influence in shaping subsequent developments.[4]

The first of these may be termed "the future-growth principle,"[5] and stressed the territorial units' development potential. Potential-growth areas were singled out in the northern and southern extremities of Palestine, with the Galilee initially assigned to the future Jewish state, and the arid Negev to the Arab state. However, the Jews set up eleven settlements in a single day in October 1946, a feat that formed the basis for a Jewish claim to the Negev. Indeed, the U.N. Partition Resolution included the Negev in the Jewish state, while dividing the Galilee into two separate areas: Jewish and Arab.

The second, which had a significant impact on future settlements, may be called the "allocation" or "segregation principle," whereby territory was to be awarded to one side in the dispute on the basis of past history, especially with regard to land ownership. This guideline was mainly applied when there were clusters of settlements in the area in question.

The third and final element may be termed the "aggregate control principle," according to which political control would be maintained by the majority population in a territory as a whole. A natural corollary of this was the possibility of population and/or territorial exchange, later referred to as the transfer option, aimed at minimizing minority problems. The only action taken on this recommendation was the establishment by the Jewish Agency of a Transfer Committee, which was active from November 1937 to June 1938.[6] It was headed by Jacob Thon who, in an effort to familiarize himself with a precedent, visited the Greek and Turkish territories where a transfer had been effected in 1923.

---

4   Palestine Royal Commission, H.M.S.O., Cmd. 5479, London 1937.

5   These principles were laid down throughout Chapter XII of the Peel Report. For example we find that "the natural principle for the partition of Palestine is to separate the areas in which Jews have acquired land and settled them from those which are wholly or mainly occupied by Arabs..." (paragraph 17, p. 282). Elsewhere we find allusion to the other principles: "Allowance is made within the boundary of the Jewish State for the growth of population and colonization" (paragraph 18, p. 283); the precedent for a population transfer is referred to on p. 289, paragraph 35.

6   Y. Katz, "Deliberations of the Transfer Committee of the Jewish Agency, 1937–1938," *Zion*, 53, No. 2 (1988), pp. 167–189 (Hebrew).

A gradual process of change took place with regard to the implementation of the principles formulated in the Peel Commission Report. An additional commission of inquiry was dispatched to Palestine by the British Government to explore the feasibility of the partition plan, and its findings were negative.[7] Nevertheless, the questionable standing of the partition idea notwithstanding, the Jewish national bodies adopted the allocation principle advocated by the Peel Commission, and applied it to their subsequent settlement-location policy.

This principle was first implemented in the "Stockade and Tower" settlement process taking place in the Bet She'an Valley in late 1937. A large number of settlements were established in that region due to its proximity to the proposed boundary of the Jewish state. The innovative method that was employed, based on meticulous preplanning and occupation of the site within twenty-four hours, met with considerable success.

A similar approach was adopted in the western Galilee near the Lebanese frontier, but it proved less successful in territorial terms due to the limited areas of agricultural land offered for sale to the Jewish settlers. Settlements were planned in May 1939 as part of the "Northern Project" in the upper Hula Valley, also near the Lebanese border, and in 1942 in the framework of the "Southern" or "Dov Hoz Memorial" Project in the northern Negev.

Out of the experience gathered during these many "operations" grew a definite *modus operandi*, shared by the three main bodies involved in the settlement enterprise:

1) the political bodies of the Jewish Agency, particularly the Zionist Executive and the Political Department, under the leadership of David Ben-Gurion and Moshe Shertok (Sharett) respectively, who were responsible for the location and timing of the new settlements;

2) the settlement movements, which contributed the manpower for the new communities, working under the Agricultural Center of the Histadrut, headed by Abraham Harzfeld; although the Center was ordinarily not involved in nonagricultural settlements, it made certain exceptions, as when it helped to set up the private company Afikim Banegev, which participated in building a new urban center in Beersheba between 1946 and 1948;[8]

3) the "national" institutions in charge of funding the settlement enterprise, especially the Jewish National Fund (JNF) responsible for land acquisition, and the Keren Hayesod (Foundation Fund) dealing with settlement expenditures,

---

7   Palestine Partition Commission, H.M.S.O., Cmd. 5854, London 1938.

8   H. Tal-Krispin, *Land of the Negev*, I, Tel Aviv 1980 (Hebrew); idem, "Plans for Establishment of a Hebrew Urban Center next to Arab Beersheba," Y. Gradus & E. Stern (eds.), *Beersheba*, Jerusalem 1979, pp. 111–118 (Hebrew).

except for land; the head of the Land Department of the JNF was Joseph Weitz.

A further step in the collaboration of these bodies was the formation of ad-hoc territorial agencies, particularly in regions where settlement was known to be difficult, such as the Mountain Farmsteads in 1943 and the Negev Commission in 1947, both headed by Weitz.[9] The establishment of the Negev Commission marked a process of convergence between settlement strategy based mainly on the allocation principle, and that based on the other two, particularly the future-growth principle. One of the main tasks of this body was to supervise the construction and operation of a regional water pipeline extending from artesian wells in one corner of the Negev to the settlements in another corner, linking the latter to a common network.[10] As protagonists of the various settlement strategies began to work together near the end of the Mandatory period, they set their sights on a wide-scale, regional scheme, and envisioned the linkage of the potential-growth areas in the Galilee and the Negev through a national water carrier, a "TVA [Tennessee Valley Authority] on the Jordan," as suggested by W.A. Lowdermilk. The project was intended to form the spinal cord of the new Jewish state.

"POST-FACTUM TRANSFER": CAUSES

The 1948 War of Independence, during which the State of Israel was established, may be divided, from the standpoint of settlement, into three distinct stages. The first, from December 1947 to May 1948, was marked by local hostilities between the Arab and Jewish inhabitants, while the country was still under British rule and free of significant military intervention from outside. Very few Jewish settlements were founded at this time, even though land was being vacated due to a large-scale and mostly spontaneous exodus of an estimated 335,000 Arabs.[11]

The second period, from May to July 1948, started with the invasion of the newly-created State of Israel by the regular armies of five neighboring Arab states: Egypt, Transjordan, Iraq, Syria and Lebanon. It was characterized by fierce battles throughout the country, as the Jewish army successfully strove to contain the invading forces.[12] Few settlements were founded, although many urban neighborhoods previously vacated by Arabs were settled by incoming

---

9   S. Reichman, "The Attempts to Establish Regional Frameworks for Advancing Jewish Settlement at the End of the British Mandate," *Horizons, Studies in Geography*, 23–24 (1988), pp. 29–34 (Hebrew).

10   M. Naor, *Emergence of a Leader, Pinhas Sapir, 1930–1949*, Tel Aviv 1987 (Hebrew).

11   CZA, Joseph Weitz Files.

12   T.E. Griess (ed.), *Atlas of the Arab-Israeli Wars, The Chinese Civil War and the Korean War* (hereafter: *Atlas*), West Point Military History Series, 1986, especially Map 2.

Jewish immigrants. Many Arab villages were destroyed in the fighting, and approximately another 100,000 Arabs fled.

The final stage ended with the signing of the various armistice agreements, between February and July of 1949. It was marked by successive counteroffensives of the Israeli army, which forced the Arab troops to retreat. These operations particularly affected villages in the southern part of the country, which had been occupied by the Egyptian army, as well as some in the Galilee, although most of the northern towns and villages, such as Nazareth, surrendered to Israel and were left unmolested. Some 200,000 Arabs abandoned the war zones. Altogether, the number of Arabs who left Palestine during the War of Independence is estimated at between 630,000 and 650,000 (see Fig. 1).[13] There was a slight increase in the number of new settlements relative to the previous period, established mainly in the western Galilee and the Judean foothills.

This division into stages requires a methodological clarification: the War of Independence is poorly researched as yet, and only recently have records in state archives in London and Jerusalem been released for public perusal. Other sources are not accessible, particularly the documentary material in Arab states. Hence researchers must often rely on secondary sources, so that caution should be the rule. While it may be possible to piece together the overt behavior of the parties concerned, as reflected in the abandonment of real estate, their motivations are more difficult to ascertain.

For instance, one explanation for the mass exodus of the Arabs is that because they lived within or near the battle zones they feared reprisals by Jews. A diametrically opposed theory is that, moved by self-confidence, especially in the early phases of the conflict, many Arabs moved out so as to clear the way for the impending liberation, in which they themselves would take part. To these two interpretations should be added the influence of the hortatory broadcasts of Arab leaders, who repeatedly called upon the local Arab population to leave Palestine, pending the forthcoming thrust from the neighboring countries. The size of the combined Arab armies that invaded Israel is estimated at thirty thousand men.[14]

However, in geographical terms this disruption of an entire settlement system, including both its rural and its urban components, deserves other explanations. One of these focuses on the nature of the regions where the exodus occurred in March and April of 1948. The key area was the citrus belt along the coast between Jaffa and Netanya, known as the Sharon Plain. Most of the Arab

13   Granott (note 1, supra); R. Bachi, *The Population of Israel*, Jerusalem 1978, especially Appendix 6.10.
14   *Atlas* (note 12, supra).

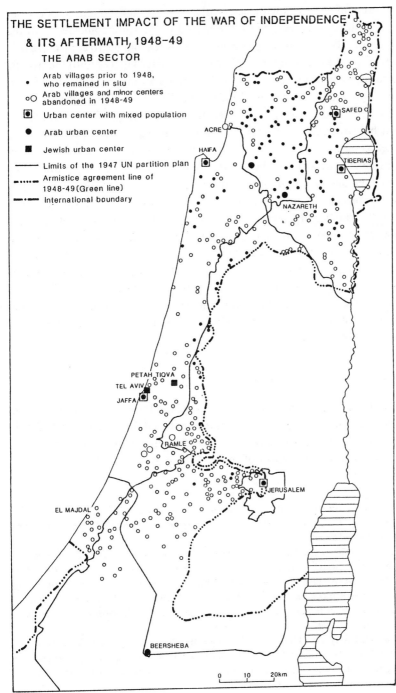

THE SETTLEMENT IMPACT OF THE WAR OF INDEPENDENCE
& ITS AFTERMATH, 1948–49
THE ARAB SECTOR

- • Arab villages prior to 1948, who remained in situ
- ∘O Arab villages and minor centers abandoned in 1948-49
- ▣ Urban center with mixed population
- ● Arab urban center
- ■ Jewish urban center
- —— Limits of the 1947 UN partition plan
- ▪▪▪▪▪ Armistice agreement line of 1948-49 (Green line)
- —▪—▪— International boundary

SAFED
ACRE
HAIFA
TIBERIAS
NAZARETH
PETAH TIQVA
TEL AVIV
JAFFA
RAMLE
JERUSALEM
EL MAJDAL
BEERSHEBA

0   10   20km

FIG. 1

villages there had close ties with sister villages some eight to ten miles further inland, on hilltops or slopes. Since the period in question coincided with the termination of the citrus-picking season, it seems reasonable to conjecture that the Arabs along the coast sought shelter in these sister villages until the trouble should subside, in a "transhumance" process. Large urban centers were affected as well, such as Tiberias, although located at a distance from the coastal plain, and Haifa. The exodus was spontaneous and not coercive, and Jewish notables tried their best to convince their Arab friends and neighbors not to leave.[15]

Another geographical explanation stems from a branch of mathematical geography called catastrophe theory. It examines an entire system rather than just a single village or community. Although a settlement system might offer security of habitat from one generation to the next, a variable such as a military threat might endanger that security. The theory maintains that a point in time is reached when the clash between the two opposing forces causes a dramatic break or shift in behavior patterns, which could then be translated into a virtual exodus and abandonment of the secure habitat. This phenomenon is referred to as a "cusp catastrophe," named after the shape of the mathematical functions employed.[16] One of the merits of this theory is that it explains why some manifestations of the exodus became evident at a later date, rather than in the course of the 1948 conflict.

ISRAELI REACTION

Unlike the above discussion on Arab motives behind the evacuation, an analysis of the Israeli reaction to the population movement, and the process by which this reaction turned into deliberate policy,[17] can rely on primary source material, including personal reminiscences of some of the participants.[18]

---

15   E. Danin, *Unconditional Zionist*, I, Jerusalem 1987, pp. 217–218, 297–317 (Hebrew).

16   E.C. Zeeman, "Catastrophe Theory," *Scientific American* (April 1976), pp. 65–83; B.H. Massam, *Spatial Search*, Oxford 1980, pp. 16–21.

17   J. Weitz, *My Diary and Letters to the Children*, III: *Watching the Walls, 1945–1948*, Ramat Gan 1965 (Hebrew); G. Yogev, *Political and Diplomatic Documents, December 1947–May 1948*, Israel State Archives, Jerusalem 1979 (Hebrew); G. Rivlin & E. Orren (eds.), *The War of Independence, Ben-Gurion's Diary*, I, Tel Aviv 1982 (Hebrew); a historical, although not spatial, overview of the question is presented in: B. Morris, *The Birth of the Palestinian Refugee Problem, 1947–1949*, Cambridge 1987.

18   In his detailed diary (note 17, supra) Weitz frequently refers to the "post-factum transfer" (pp. 257, 291, 297 and elsewhere). Danin (note 15, supra, pp. 297–317) cites a large portion of the ad-hoc committee's report. Rivlin, editor of Ben-Gurion's war diary (note 17, supra), clarifies certain of the author's comments.

The subject of the Arab exodus was first brought to the attention of Shertok, foreign minister of Israel, by Weitz of the JNF, who in late May 1948 requested the formation of an ad-hoc committee to prepare recommendations and directives pertaining to the unexpected situation.[19] Such a committee was indeed set up, and Weitz himself served on it, along with Ezra Danin and Eliyahu Sasson. The Cabinet devoted a full-scale debate to this issue in mid-June, and although no details are available on the opinions expressed, it endorsed the ad-hoc committee's proposal to treat the situation as a "post-factum transfer." This term, which served as the title of a document that Weitz and his colleagues had prepared, implied an association between the Arab exodus and the population transfers that frequently occur in times of war. Three operational measures were approved: 1) not to allow the return of persons who had fled; despite pressure from many quarters, the Government adhered to this policy; 2) to actively seek a solution, such as resettlement of the refugees in alternative sites; the numerous efforts by various emissaries to settle them in Arab countries met with failure;[20] 3) to launch without delay a large-scale Jewish settlement program within Israel, intended to fill the territorial vacuum left by the Arabs; the risks involved in leaving this land unattended imparted a sense of urgency to this task.

The Government formed another committee, again composed of Weitz (chairman), Danin and a third civil servant, who this time was surveyor and land assessor Zalman Lipschitz,[21] to appraise the situation within ninety days. Its report of October 31, 1948, entitled "Memorandum on a Possible Arrangement for Arab Refugees," examined the feasibility of various resettlement schemes in Arab countries, with funding expected to come from three main sources: compensation by Israel for properties abandoned, grants from Arab states, and financial assistance from the U.N. and other nongovernmental agencies.[22]

The Government's efforts were mainly directed toward the implementation of a comprehensive settlement program, a project that continued through the end of 1950. The greatest achievement of the "post-factum transfer" policy was the establishment of 177 new settlements by the end of 1949 (see Fig. 2). While no documentary evidence is available as yet on the considerations that guided the

19   Israel State Archives, Foreign Ministry Files, 2562/20.

20   Danin (note 15, supra).

21   Zalman Lipschitz, whose official title was "advisor to the Government on land and boundaries," was involved in all the deliberations on the boundaries mooted in the various partition plans, from the Peel Commission Plan to the U.N. Partition Plan. In fact, he served as the untitled "geographer" of the Jewish Agency.

22   Danin (note 15, supra).

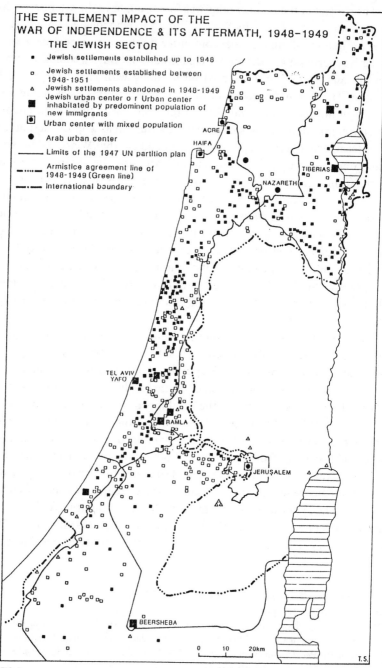

THE SETTLEMENT IMPACT OF THE
WAR OF INDEPENDENCE & ITS AFTERMATH, 1948–1949
THE JEWISH SECTOR

- Jewish settlements established up to 1948
- Jewish settlements established between 1948–1951
- Jewish settlements abandoned in 1948–1949
- Jewish urban center or Urban center inhabitated by predominent population of new immigrants
- Urban center with mixed population
- Arab urban center
- Limits of the 1947 UN partition plan
- Armistice agreement line of 1948–1949 (Green line)
- International boundary

ACRE
HAIFA
TIBERIAS
NAZARETH
TEL AVIV YAFO
RAMLA
JERUSALEM
BEERSHEBA

0   10   20km

T. S.

FIG. 2

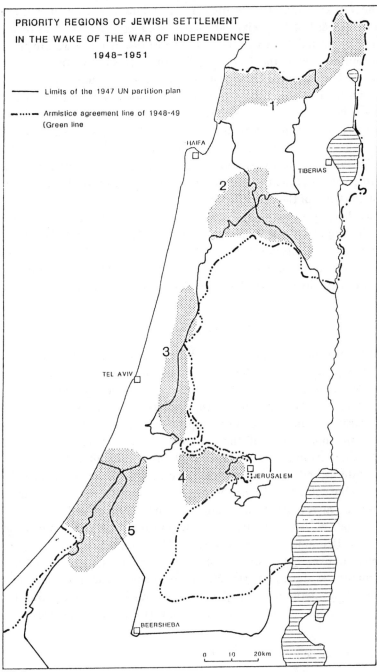

PRIORITY REGIONS OF JEWISH SETTLEMENT
IN THE WAKE OF THE WAR OF INDEPENDENCE
1948–1951

——— Limits of the 1947 UN partition plan

—·····— Armistice agreement line of 1948-49
(Green line

HAIFA

TIBERIAS

1

2

3

TEL AVIV

4   JERUSALEM

5

BEERSHEBA

0   10   20km

FIG. 3

national bodies' selection of the settlement locations, it is evident that five regions stand out as being especially attractive (see Figs. 2 and 3): 1) the region bordering Lebanon and Syria in the Galilee, where the settlements were to play a significant buffer role; 2) the Jezreel Valley, on both sides of the partition boundaries, which ensured both latitudinal and longitudinal territorial continuity, particularly important for the future national water carrier; 3) land that widened the narrow coastal plain (the "slim waist" of the country); 4) the corridor to Jerusalem, which ensured accessibility to the capital; 5) a territorial link to the Negev, through which the national water carrier could supply water from the Jordan River to the southern part of the country. This effort was designed to create a de facto situation on the ground that would ensure the permanent existence of the Jewish state.

A detailed land survey carried out by the Ministry of Agriculture in 1950 estimated the size of the abandoned land at 4,200,000 dunams.[23] Finally, an Administration of Absentee Property, later incorporated into the Development Authority in the Ministry of Finance, was established to handle the legal aspects, but not before virtually all of the lands involved were nationalized.[24]

CONCLUSION

The Peel Commission proposal in 1937 and the U.N. resolution a decade later, both advocating partition of Palestine, thrust the issue of the territorial boundaries of a Jewish state into the forefront of the dramatic events taking place in the region at the time. The Jewish representative bodies formulated a settlement strategy, and judiciously applied the allocation principle in determining the boundaries of the proposed Jewish state. The War of Independence and Arab exodus of 1948–1949 brought about a change in the settlement patterns; settlement strategy incorporated the notion of population transfer with what could have been viewed as merely widespread transhumance. This attests to a degree of perspicacity not found in the attitude and behavior of Arab representatives, who persistently negated the partition plan and invaded the territory of Palestine in defiance of the U.N. resolution. By contrast, the Jewish representatives, having drawn conclusions from the territorial conflicts involving minorities during World War II, overcame their misgivings and consistantly accepted the concept of partition, with its underlying transfer principle, as a solution to the territorial conflict between the two peoples.[25]

23   Granott (note 1, supra).
24   *Ibid.*
25   T. Lie, *In the Cause of Peace*, London 1954, pp. 195–196.

CONTRIBUTING AUTHORS

Ran Aaronsohn   Lecturer, Department of Geography
                       The Hebrew University of Jerusalem

Irit Amit   Ph.D. Student, Department of Geography
                       The Hebrew University of Jerusalem

Yehoshua Ben-Arieh   Professor of Geography
                       The Hebrew University of Jerusalem

Yossi Ben-Artzi   Lecturer, Department of Eretz-Israel Studies
                       Haifa University

Joseph Ben-David   Lecturer, Department of Geography
                       Ben-Gurion University

Gideon Biger   Senior Lecturer, Department of Geography
                       Tel Aviv University

Moshe Brawer   Professor of Geography
                       Tel Aviv University

Dov Gavish   Ph.D., Aerial Photographic Section, Department
                       of Geography, The Hebrew University of Jerusalem

Joseph Glass   Ph.D. Student, Department of Geography
                       The Hebrew University of Jerusalem

Iris Graicer   Lecturer, Department of Geography
                       Tel Aviv University

Ruth Kark   Associate Professor, Department of Geography
                       The Hebrew University of Jerusalem

331

Yossi Katz   Senior Lecturer, Department of Geography
                        Bar-Ilan University

Idit Luzia   M.A. Student, Department of Geography
                        The Hebrew University of Jerusalem

Amiram Oren   Ph.D. Student, Department of Geography
                        Tel Aviv University

Michal Oren   M.A. Student, Department of Geography
                        The Hebrew University of Jerusalem

Shalom Reichman   Professor of Geography
                        The Hebrew University of Jerusalem

Rehav Rubin   Lecturer, Department of Geography
                        The Hebrew University of Jerusalem

Shaul Sapir   Ph.D. Student, Department of Geography
                        The Hebrew University of Jerusalem

Zvi Shilony   Lecturer, Department of Geography
                        Tel Aviv University

Naftali Thalmann   Ph.D. Student, Department of Geography
                        The Hebrew University of Jerusalem

PLATES

Plate 1. Christ church, view of entrance prior to enlargement [*JI* (April 1888), p. 61]

Plate 2. St. Paul's Church (Hechler, *The Jerusalem Bishoprie documents*, p. 75)

Plate 3. St. George's College Church, view of east end
[*BL*, 34 (October 1907), p. 18]

Plate 4. New Anglican Hospital [*JMI* (January 1898), pp. 8–9]

Plate 5. Gobat's Diocesan Boys' School
(Hechler, *The Jerusalem Bishoprie documents*, p. 78)

Plate 6. St. George's College, view from west [*BL*, 55 (January 1913), p. 94]

Plate 1. Aerial view of Bahji during the early development. (Source: Ruhe, 1983)

Plate 2. Shrine of the Bäb, 1973. (Source: Ruhe, 1983)

Idit Luzia

Plate 3. The international Baha'i Archives building, 1957. (Source: Ruhe, 1983)

Plate 4. Aerial photograph of the Seat of The Universal House of Justice, 1981.
(Source: Ruhe, 1983)

Plate 1. Side by side: a typical pattern of a traditional Arab village–Katra, near the Jewish Moshava–Gedera (1917)

Plate 2. A German Colony–Layout (Wilhelma, 1902)

Plate 3. A German Family by a Typical German Dwelling (Haifa)

Plate 4. Later Pattern of a German House (Bethlehem)

Plate 5. A Jewish "Moshava" (Rosh Pinna, 1894)

Plate 6. A General View of a Jewish "Moshava" (Rehovot, 1905)

Plate 7. A Typical Jewish Dwelling (Metula)

Plate 8. A Jewish Family by their House (Yesod ha–Maàla)

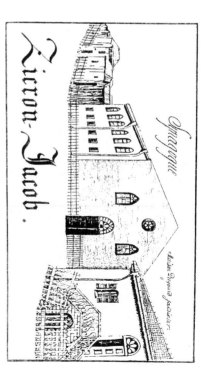

Plate 1. Public buildings in Zikhron Ya'aqov: the Baron's Administration building, synagogue,
hospital, 1890's [A. Scheid, "Memoires sur les Colonies Juives 1883–1899," MS, Paris 1900,
pp. 64–81, 109 (Hebrew edition: Jerusalem 1983)]

Ran Aaronsohn

Plate 2. Salaried workers in the Rosh Pinna spinning mill, 1895 [E. Schiller, *The First Photographs of the Holy Land*, Jerusalem 1979, p. 44 (Hebrew)]

Plate 3. The Settlers' Band, Rishon leTziyyon 1898 [I. Raffalovich & M.E. Sachs, *Ansichten von Palästina und den Judischen Colonien*, Jerusalem-Berlin 1899, p. 5 (photographed edition: Jerusalem 1979, p. 24)]

Plate 4. The Library Committee in The Rishon leTziyyon Community Center, 1897?
[D. Yudelevitch, *Rishon leTziyyon 1882–1941*, Rishon leTziyyon 1941, p. 316 (Hebrew)]

Plate 5. The school in Rishon leTziyyon — gym class, 1897
[Yudelevitch (see Plate 4, supra), p. 197]

Plate 6. Inaugural meeting of the "Federation of Teachers," Zikhron Ya'aqov 1903
(*The First Aliya*, I, p. 175)

Joseph Ben-David

Plate 1. Expanded Bedouin family during spring migration

Plate 2. The Bedouin and his best
friend, on a background of the desert
landscape

Plate 3. Sedentarized Bedouin camp site

Plate 4. Harvesting the barley by hand

Plate 5. Threshing with the help of donkeys, on a background of fallah fields and a grove

Plate 6. Winnowing of grain seeds by a
Bedouin family of farmers

Joseph Ben-David

Plate 7. Pit for grain storage, typical of Bedouin agriculture in the Negev.

Plate 8. Several generations in a traditional Bedouin camp site

Plate 1. Dura, a large village on the southern fringes of the settled areas in the Judean highlands; the old, nucleated part of the village is situated on a hilltop overlooking the terraced and cultivated slopes and valleys

Plate 2. Dura, a close-up of the old, extremely clustered, part; expansion to adjacent stony hills separated from the old nucleus by cultivated valleys

Plate 3. Kafr Jimal, a small, nucleated village in western Samaria, with clustered *écart* of adjacent hills and initial expansion downhill into neighboring valley

Plate 4. Qibya, a village in the western foothills of the central highlands, in initial stages of dispersion; the large buildings are schools located in most villages well outside the densely built-up areas

Plate 5. Ya'bad, a large village in the northwestern central highlands; the old, nucleated part is seen in the center, extensive expansion and dispersion, mainly along the roads leading into the village

Plate 6. Musheirifa, a small isolated village on the fringes of the Esdaerelon Valley (Emek Yizrael); old clustered part on stony hilltop, new dispersed part on slope and in an adjoining valley

Zvi Shilony

Plate 1. Leaders of the Zionist Organization and the JNF before World War I

a: Dr. Theodor Herzl (Vienna) — founder of the Zionist Organization and its first president

b: David Wolffsohn (Koln) — second president of the Zionist Organization and governor-director of the JNF

c: Prof. Otto Warburg (Berlin) — third president of the Zionist Organization, governor-director of the JNF and chairman of the Palestine Commission

d: Dr. Max Bodenheimer (Koln) — chairman of Directorate of the JNF

e: Dr. Franz Oppenheimer (Berlin) — ideologist of land nationalization and the "kooperazia," and member of the Palestine Commission

f: Dr. Arthur Ruppin (Berlin) — head of the Palestine Office in Jaffa and representative of the JNF in Palestine

Plate 2. Rural Settlement Types in Palestine Before World War I

a: Buildings of JNF's training farm for agricultural laborers
in Ben-Shemen, 1918. (detail from German aerial
photograph No. 159, Department of Geography, the
Hebrew University, Jerusalem)

b: The "kooperazia" settlement of
Merhavia (Stage I), 1918, designed
as a training farm with the option to
develop into a cooperative
smallholders' village (detail from
German aerial photograph No. 527,
Department of Geography, the
Hebrew University, Jerusalem)

Zvi Shilony

Plate 3 Rural Settlement Types in Palestine Before World War I (cont.)

a: Components of Degania, 1918, which was designed to become the Center of a large JNF farm: farmyard (1), administration house (2) and the communal services building (3), added for the kvutza group

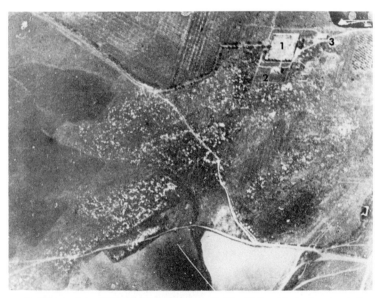

b: Buildings of the JNF's Plantation farm in Hulda, 1918, with the farmyard (1), administration house (2), and a communal services building (3) that was added later, (detail from German aerial photograph No. 396, Department of Geography, the Hebrew University, Jerusalem)

Dov Gavish

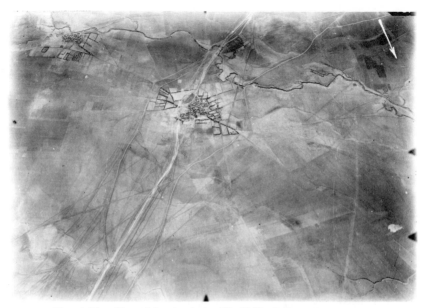

Plate 1. The village of Qastina during World War I, December 1, 1917
(photograph: The Bavarian Fliegerabteilung No. 304)

Plate 2. Qastina during World War II, January 27, 1945
(photograph: No. 680 Squadron, RAF)

Dov Gavish

Plate 3. Qastina 1987 (photograph:
Pantomap Ltd., No. 87/8931)

Plate 4. Old City of Jaffa on May 30, 1936 (aerial photograph taken in preparation
for the operation). Visible are the old city of Jaffa and the port at its feet

Plate 5. Aerial view of the old city of Jaffa on July 2, 1936, following the destruction in the shape of an "anchor"

Plate 6. Smoke wafting upward over Jaffa following the explosion, June 18, 1936, 15:40 hours